Limitations of religions
by privileged state religions (ecclesiae)
particularly in authoritarian states
but also in democracies

Religion – Staat – Gesellschaft

Zeitschrift für Glaubensformen und Weltanschauungen/
Journal for the Study of Beliefs and Worldviews

herausgegeben von/edited by

Gerhard Besier

in Zusammenarbeit mit/in cooperation with
Eileen Barker, Massimo Introvigne,
James T. Richardson, Richard Singelenberg,
Hermann Weber

20. Jahrgang (2019) Heft 1 – 2

LIT

Limitations of religious freedom by privileged state religions (ecclesiae) – particularly in authoritarian states but also in democracies

LIT

Sigmund-Neumann-Institut
für Freiheits- und Demokratieforschung e. V.
Schlehenbogen 8
24944 Flensburg
Tel. +49 (0)3 51-87 34 25 46
Fax +49 (0)3 51-87 34 25 45
E-Mail: gbesier@aol.com
Internet: http://www.r-s-g.info

Erscheint zweimal jährlich,
Abonnementpreis jährlich 52,00 Euro;
für Studenten jährlich 41,60 Euro;
Einzelheft 29,90 Euro
zzgl. Versandkosten.

Bibliographic information published by the Deutsche Nationalbibliothek
The Deutsche Nationalbibliothek lists this publication in the Deutsche
Nationalbibliografie; detailed bibliographic data are available in the Internet at
http://dnb.dnb.de.

ISBN 978-3-643-99729-6 (pb.)
IBBN 978-3-643-99229-1 (PDF)
ISSN 1438-955X

A catalogue record for this book is available from the British Library.

© LIT VERLAG GmbH & Co. KG Wien,
Zweigniederlassung Zürich 2020
Flössergasse 10
CH-8001 Zürich
Tel. +41 (0) 76-632 84 35
E-Mail: zuerich@lit-verlag.ch   http://www.lit-verlag.ch
Distribution:
In the UK: Global Book Marketing, e-mail: mo@centralbooks.com
In North America: Independent Publishers Group, e-mail: orders@ipgbook.com
In Germany: LIT Verlag Fresnostr. 2, D-48159 Münster
Tel. +49 (0) 2 51-620 32 22, Fax +49 (0) 2 51-922 60 99, e-mail: vertrieb@lit-verlag.de

Inhalt

Preface by Birte Wassenberg 9

Introduction by Gerhard Besier 13

Treatises and Essays/Aufsätze und Essays

James T. Richardson and Barbara McGraw
Congressional Efforts to Defend and Extend Religious Freedom and the Law of Unintended Consequences 33

Derek H. Davis
Backdoor Efforts to Advance Christianity in America During the Administration of Donald J. Trump 49

Willy Fautré
The Rise of Nationalisms in Bulgaria and their Impact on Religious Freedom – Some reflections about the interactions between national identity, nationalism, state and society, with minority religions or beliefs 63

Jukka Korpela
Russia's Religious Empire, non-Rational Power and Pussy Riot 77

Wolfram Slupina
"Every Day It Just Gets Worse" – Jehovah's Witnesses Under Ban in Russia Facing Criminal Charges 93

Régis Dericquebourg
The Invention of the French Notion of "sectarian therapeutic drifts" *(dérives sectaires thérapeutiques)* 117

Gerhard Besier
Religion – What Does This Mean Today? 123

Anders Jarlert
The Religious Scene After the End of the Swedish State Church Since 2000 – Non-transparency and Confusion 135

Eileen Barker
We're Happy to Talk, But Dialogue …? Courteous Discrimination
in Establishment Parlance 143

Patricia Duval
Participation of State Privileged Religions in the Fight Against
Religious Minorities 169

Tim B. Müller
"Your Human Rights, Your Fundamental Freedoms Are in Danger".
Crusade Against Christianity, Jehovah's Witnesses, and the Fight for
Religious Freedom 191

Jolene Chu
The Practice and Consequences of Apolitical Christianity by Rwandan
Jehovah's Witness Community Before and During the Genocide 223

Rückschau/Review 255

Contributor

Eileen Barker, Department of Sociology, London School of Economics, 29A Crawford Ave, Wembley, HA0 2HY, UK
(e.barker@lse.ac.uk)

Gerhard Besier, Sigmund-Neumann-Institut für Freiheits- und Demokratieforschung, Bachstraße 4, 10555 Berlin, Germany
(besier.gerhard@gmail.com)

Jolene Chu, 1 Kings Drive, Tuxedo Park, NY 10987 USA
(jochu@bethel.jw.org)

Régis Dericquebourg, 3 rue Saint Philippe, 06000 Nice. France
(redericq@netcourrier.com)

Patricia Duval, Avocat à la Cour, 6 avenue du Coq, 75009 Paris, France
(duval.patricia@gmail.com)

Willy Fautré, Human Rights without Frontiers, Brussels, Belgium
(w.fautre@hrwf.net)

Jukka Korpela, University of Eastern Finland, Joensuu, Finland
(jukka.korpela@uef.fi)

Anders Jarlert, Lund University, Department of Theology and Religious Studies, LUX, Helgonavägen 3, Box 192, SE-221 00 Lund, Sweden
(anders.jarlert@ctr.lu.se)

Barbara McGraw, Center for Engaged Religious Pluralism, Saint Mary's College of California, 1928 Saint Mary's Rd., Moraga, CA 94556, USA
(bmcgraw@stmarys-ca.edu)

Tim B. Müller, Verband Deutscher Sinti und Roma, Landesverband Baden-Württemberg, B 7, 16, 68159 Mannheim, Germany
(tm@sinti-roma.com)

James T. Richardson, Mail Stop 311, University of Nevada, Reno, NV 89557, USA
(jtr@unr.edu)

Wolfram Slupina, Am Steinfels 1, 65618 Selters, Germany
(wslupina@jw.org)

Birte Wassenberg, Professeur en Histoire contemporaine Institut
d'études politiques (IEP) Université de Strasbourg, Klausmattstraße 57,
77694 Kehl, Germany
(birte.wassenberg@unistra.fr)

THE COUNCIL OF EUROPE'S EFFORTS FOR THE PROTECTION OF RELIGIOUS FREEDOM AND INTERRELIGIOUS DIALOGUE

There could not be a better choice than the City of Strasbourg for the organization of a Conference on religious freedom. As the seat of the Council of Europe and the European Court of Human Rights (ECR), Strasbourg has indeed been established as a center for the protection of human rights and individual freedoms, including the freedom of religion.

It was at the Congress of The Hague in May 1948, where 740 Europeanists from 18 European countries were gathered under the honorary presidency of Winston Churchill, when the idea was born to create a European Organization with the aim to "unify the European people". This Organization was to be built on the basis of three principle values – democracy, rule of law and respect for human rights. They are indeed inscribed in the Statute of the Council of Europe, signed on 5 May 1949 in London by ten Member States,[1] the headquarters of which were to be installed in Strasbourg at the Franco-German border, as a symbol for the European reconciliation process.

The final declaration adopted at the Hague Congress in May 1948 had already envisaged a specific convention on the protection of human rights, with an independent European court to enforce it. It is therefore not surprising that one of the first legal instruments which the Foreign Ministers of the Council of Europe adopted on 4 November 1950 was the Convention for the Protection of Human Rights and Fundamental Freedoms, usually known as the European Convention on Human Rights (ECHR)[2]. The Convention's political philosophy was set out in the Preamble: one way of achieving greater unity among the Council's Member States was "the maintenance and further realization of human rights and fundamental freedoms", and the chief aim was to provide for "collective enforcement" of those rights and freedoms. Section 1 of the Convention listed 18 rights and freedoms among which the freedom of thought, conscience and religion (Art. 9).

The most important element of the ECHR was however not so much the list of human rights and individual freedoms which it protected, as this did not largely differ from the UN's Universal Declaration on Human Rights of 1948; it was rather the mechanism of control foreseen to ensure effectively the respect of these

---

[1] Belgium, Denmark, France, Ireland, Italy, Luxemburg, the Netherlands, Norway, Sweden, United Kingdom.

[2] Council of Europe, European Treaty Series N° 5.

rights and freedoms, especially the provision for the creation of a European Court of Human Rights, which the European people could seize individually. This supposed the acceptance by the Council of Europe's Member States of the supranational authority of the Court, on the one hand, and of the right of individual petition on the other. The ECR was therefore only set up in 1959, when 10 Member States had ratified the ECHR including these two elements. From this moment onwards, the Court has watched over the right to hold religious beliefs, people's rights to practice their religion and the right of organizations to operate without government interference. Numerous cases have been ruled by the Court which did not hesitate to condemn Member States of the Council of Europe if it estimated that the freedom of religion was not respected by them.

But beyond the abundant case-law of the ECR, the right to freedom of religion also has to be considered in the much wider context of protecting the principle values promoted by the Council of Europe. Thus, according to the Guide on Art. 9 of the Council of Europe (2020), the respect of this right has to be regarded as corollary of the guarantee of European democratic society:

> "Freedom of thought, conscience and religion as enshrined in Art. 9 of the Convention represents one of the foundations of a "democratic society" within the meaning of the Convention. It is, in its religious dimension, one of the most vital elements that go to make up the identity of believers and their conception of life, but it is also a precious asset for atheists, agnostics, sceptics and the unconcerned. The pluralism in-dissociable from a democratic society, which has been dearly won over the centuries, depends on it. That freedom entails, inter alia, freedom to hold or not to hold religious beliefs and to practice or not to practice a religion."

Freedom of religion, as much as other fundamental freedoms protected by the ECHR, therefore form an indispensable condition for the democratic functioning of the Member States reunited in the Council of Europe.

Despite this essential role and the efforts undertaken by the Council of Europe to protect the right of freedom of religion, there has been an increase in the 2000s of intolerance, xenophobia and hate-speech throughout Europe. The Islamist terrorist attacks on the United States on 11 September 2001 and the European terrorist crisis of 2015 has created a general mistrust against the Muslim religion threatening the protection of free religious beliefs for everybody on an equal level. The trend towards intolerance and violence against the "Other" has led the Council of Europe to engage in the promotion of intercultural communication, an activity, which has already been a priority for a long time in the Youth sector, since the creation of the Strasbourg Youth Center of the Council of Europe in 1971. To generalize this intercultural work, the Council of Europe published in 2008 the "White Paper on Intercultural Dialogue – Living together as equals with dignity" in order to give advice not only to Youth organizations, but also to decision makers in politics, administration and education, as well as to representatives of the media, Non-Governmental Organizations (NGOs) and to religious communities on how to engage in intercultural dialogue.

Within this framework, the Council of Europe also decided to organize an "Exchange" on the religious dimension of intercultural dialogue. This event has taken place for the first time in 2008, and since then the "Exchanges" are organized annually in order to foster mutual respect and awareness, tolerance and mutual understanding within the European society. The Exchanges associate representatives of religions traditionally present in Europe, but also representatives of non-religious convictions and other actors of the civil society. They have tackled such issues as religious education in state schools, the relationship between freedom of expression and freedom of religion, inclusive societies, and the prevention of religious radicalization.

The Council of Europe in Strasbourg has therefore proven a major investment since its creation in 1949 in order to protect the freedom of religious beliefs and practice. Not only is the right to freedom of religion enshrined as a guaranteed fundamental right into Art. 9 of the ECHR, but it is also controlled by the ECR. The Court has established throughout the years by its case-law a whole jurisprudence of protection of religious freedom and has already condemned many Member States of the Council of Europe, who had to adapt their legislation in function and provide compensation to the plaintiffs. Just as important, in order to foster the legal protection of religious freedom, the Council of Europe has also launched political activities with a regular interreligious dialogue in order to prevent infringes free expression and practice of religious beliefs.

Birte Wassenberg

Introduction

Limitations of religious freedom by privileged state religions (ecclesiae) – particularly in authoritarian states, but also in democracies

Gerhard Besier

The situation regarding religious freedom worsened across many parts of the world in 2018/19. This is the finding in the 2018 annual report of the United States Commission on International Religious Freedom. The intention of the report is to make the US State Department aware of the "CPC – countries of particular concern". Unlike the previous year's report, the list has not changed. According to the report, the most serious violations of religious freedom occur in 16 states: China, Eritrea, Iran, Myanmar, North Korea, Saudi-Arabia, Sudan, Turkmenistan, Tadzhikistan, Uzbekistan, the Central African Republic, Nigeria, Pakistan, Russia, Syria and Vietnam. Violations of religious freedom are serious in a further twelve countries, but not so severe that they require listing on the CPC list – specifically in Afghanistan, Azerbaijan, Egypt, Bahrain, Cuba, India, Indonesia, Kazakhstan, Laos, Malaysia, Iraq and in Turkey. In addition, the Commission once again classified the terrorist organisations "Islamic State" (Syria, Iraq), Taliban (Afghanistan) and al-Shabaab (Somalia) as "EPC – entities of particular concern". This year, they also added to this list the Shiite Houthi Movement (Yemen) and the radical Islamic militant group Hay'at Tahrir al-Sham (Syria), which is closely aligned to the terror network Al-Quaeda.

In 2018, the imprisonment of Christians increased significantly in **Iran**. While 2017 saw the arrest of 16 Christians, the number rose to 171 in 2018. Generally speaking, the Iranian government treats imprisoned Christians as enemies of the state. Even their lawyers are at risk of being placed under arrest. Officially, Iran recognises Christians, Jews and Zoroastrians as minority religions in their country and permits them to exercise their faith "within the legal framework". According to the Commission, however, private church services in so-called home churches, private celebrations of Christmas, and international travel to attend Christian conferences are punishable with imprisonment. Protestant congregations, in particular, face persecution, as they hold their services of worship in Persian and seek to convert people of different faiths to Christianity. Pastors of home churches are frequently accused of committing crimes against national security and encouraging others to change their religion.

According to the report, **Russia** further consolidated its "repressive attitude" towards religious communities. Anti-terror laws that came into force in 2016 were officially enacted to combat extremism. However, their rather vague wording makes it possible for the state to prosecute religious activities. Among Christian congregations, the Jehovah's Witnesses have been hit particularly hard by this ruling to date. In 2017, they were the first religious community in Russia to be banned on the basis of the anti-terror laws. As a consequence of the law, authorities confiscated church property to the value of over 80 million Euro in 2018. By the end of 2018, some 23 Jehovah's Witnesses had been imprisoned and 27 had been placed under house arrest. A further 41 had been banned from leaving their city, and preliminary proceedings had been initiated against 121 Jehovah's Witnesses. With the government granting preferential treatment to the Russian Orthodox Church at the end of the Soviet Union, the hostile attitude towards other Christian communities increased. This has only increased under President Vladimir Putin. Likewise, in the Russian occupied territories of the Crimea and in Eastern Ukraine, Christian congregations have been systematically intimidated and church buildings have been expropriated.

In the primarily Muslim country of **Indonesia**, which has been known for its religious tolerance in the past, attacks instigated by government bodies on religious minorities have decreased significantly, according to the report. Moreover, there have been increasing numbers of attacks by radical Islamic groups. In total, an increasing rate of radicalisation has been noted in Indonesia. In 2018, the government enacted a number of laws and legal guidelines that substantially limit freedom of religion. Furthermore, there are little or no attempts to oppose or counter radical groups and individuals that discriminate against and carry out violent attacks on members of particular faiths. At the end of 2018, the government initiated the development of a law that would determine how schools and religious institutions should teach religion, in order to counteract radicalisation in this area. According to a study, some 60 percent of Muslim teachers of religion held negative views regarding other religious communities. Some had even banned their students from having any contact with minorities such as Christians and Jews. Religious minorities are very apprehensive that the proposed law is likely to make it very difficult in future to gain permission to conduct activities such as Sunday schools and Bible studies.

Problems do not only occur in Africa, Asia and Near East. The conference, held in Strasbourg in November 2019, and documented in this issue, primarily dealt with the topic **Religious Freedom in Europe and North America,** although not exclusively.

James T. Richardson (Reno) and **Barbara McGraw** (Moraga, Cal.) explore the origins of how religious freedom is understood in the United States in their religious-legal article *Congressional Efforts to Defend and Extend Religious Freedom* *and the Law of Unintended Consequences*, and describe the defence and expansion of freedom of religion. The original Protestant hegemony over the comprehension of religious freedom changed over the course of the 20th century, evolving from a process of incorporation of religious minorities implemented by means of Supreme Court judgement to a broad acceptance in support of the freedom of all religions. Up until 1990, the Supreme Court ruled in favour of small religions and permitted exemptions for these if laws or regulations affected their practices of religious freedom. Nevertheless, the 1990 case of *Employment Division vs. Smith*, ruling on a member of the Native American Church who had been dismissed after consuming peyote, changed the Supreme Court's preceding position in that its ruling on the case did not come down in favour of the church's practises of religious freedom. Under President Bill Clinton, it was intended that the 1993 *Religious Freedom Restoration Act* (RFRA) would reinstate the original legal practice of religion. However in 1997, when a Catholic Church congregation in San Antonio (Texas) – with reference to the RFRA – wanted to expand its buildings in a protected historical quarter of the city, the Supreme Court ultimately declared the RFRA to be unconstitutional. In 2000, the *Religious Land Use and Institutionalized Persons Act* (RLUIPA) was adopted by both houses of Congress – with the goal of restoring freedom of religion in all its original extent and breadth. In 2005, on the basis of this law, the Supreme Court ruled in favour of religious freedom for five prisoners who worshipped new-age religious cults, even before the Supreme Court had definitively confirmed the constitutionality of the RLUIPA. And yet this did not end the conflict over the protection of religious freedom. Influential groups within American society continued to oppose the RLUIPA; it was their belief that religion was becoming too powerful in American society and was significantly undermining other social values. The impact of the RLUIPA can be seen in a powerful expansion of the definition of "exercise religious rights", primarily to the benefit of followers of minority religions serving jail sentences, as well as soldiers serving in the USA Army. In the course of subsequent rulings, courts did limit, however, individual expressions of sincerely held beliefs, for example for a soldier, if these severely limited their military readiness. At the same time, conversely, there were also further restrictions to the rights to exercise religion in order to protect other fundamental rights. "Cases such as Masterpiece Cakeshop vs. Colorado Cicil Rights Commission (2018) have made it clear that, not only could religious exercise rights prevail over rights to contraception and abortion, but individuals who, due to their religious beliefs, did not want to provide services to homosexuals may sometimes prevail in the courts."

In his article *Backdoor Efforts to Advance Christianity in America* during the Administration of Donald J. Trump, **Derek H. Davis** (Dallas) shows how the 2016 elected President is seeking to break down the rule of separation of State and Church, the Establishment Clause and religious pluralism in the USA that is based on these. He seeks to achieve this goal by offering the Christian Evangelical Right, his political supporters, unilateral support and privilege while discriminating against other religions.

Since 2011, Trump has consistently polemicized against Muslims, culminating in his declaration in early December 2015 that the USA should prevent all Muslims from entering the country. At the end of June 2018, the Supreme Court endorsed Trump's travel ban towards Muslims from Iran, Libya, Somalia, Syria and Yemen – also affecting citizens of North Korea and Venezuela. According to statements in defence of the measure, the ban was not directed necessarily solely against Muslims, but against citizens of those states that finance terrorism, thereby also explaining why North Korea and Venezuela, two non-Muslim states, were also included in the ban. Davis maintains that this decision is contrary to the American constitution, which states that all religions should be treated equally and no religion is permitted be treated with favouritism.

At the end of the 1990s, the USA government adopted a series of measures that allowed the State to subsidise religious organisations' social services and welfare institutions, so long as these pursued secular aid programs with their work. In this way, policies from the 1980s were fundamentally changed – policies that deemed it impossible for religions to separate the secular aspects of their activities from the religious components. In addition to the traditional argument that religious groups and communities prosper best when they are self-supporting rather than financed by the state, the new state-based subsidisation of religious organisations faced the further challenge that there should be no preferential treatment for any single religious community or group. In the George W. Bush era (2000–2008), however, this principle was clearly breached as 98.6 percent of state subsidies were directed towards Christian organisations. Even though the office granting state subsidies was renamed and rebranded during the Obama era and there was greater awareness of the problem of the de facto privileged treatment of Christian denominations, the status quo ultimately remained largely the same as during the Bush administration. Barely in office, the Trump administration created a new office that, in turn, had the primary task of channelling state funds to faith-based organisations that were actively involved in social programs.

Civil rights organisations expressed very real concerns that people whose lifestyles did not correspond to conservative Christian values – such as homosexuals – would face discrimination and were quickly able to give concrete examples.

Two prominent ministers in the Trump administration, Secretary of State Mike Pompeo and Attorney General William Barr, describe themselves as "Christian leaders", exercising their offices according to God's will and the Bible's Commandments. Barr argued that traditional Christian morality is being forced on to the defensive by the forces of militant secularism. He endorsed the expectations of the mostly white, conservative Protestants, and he does not stand for freedom of religion for all Americans in the USA. Likewise, with regard to the nomination of judges for the Federal Courts, Trump undoubtedly favours Evangelical Christians.

According to the 1954 Johnson Amendment, the U.S. Tax Code prohibits all Not-for-Profit organisations from endorsing or opposing any political candidate. Otherwise, they would lose their tax exemption status. At the beginning of May 2017, Trump sought to repeal the Johnson Amendment with an executive order to "vigorously enforce Federal law's robust protections for religious freedom", in order to allow religious organisations to support their preferred political candidate and their party. Ultimately, he failed in the attempt and according to a survey, 66 percent of Americans in the USA were not in favour of religious support for political candidates.

Even though Trump's lifestyle, just like his pronouncements and various comments, clearly earmarks him as not being a Christian, and he has also patently not concerned himself with the content of the Bible, critical Evangelicals have nevertheless identified a narrative that enables them to support this Republican who represents and reflects their values. They see him as a "modern Cyrus" who – as an instrument of God – will transform God's plans into reality.

Davis sees Trump as a serious threat to America's traditional values. The President is committed to tearing down the twin towers of American freedom: "Religious liberty and the separation of church and state".

It is not only in the USA but also in the European Union that developments can be identified that represent a serious threat to freedom of religion. **Willy Fautré** (Brussels) offers an example of this reality in his essay *The Rise of Nationalisms in Bulgaria and their Impact on Religious Freedom*, exploring the situation in a country on the south-eastern border of the EU. In Bulgaria, a form of nationalism prevails in the amalgamation of extreme right-wing political parties and within the Bulgarian Orthodox Church that is leading to a situation where the majority Orthodox Church exerts significant influence on the course of politics and religious minorities are being marginalised across the country. According to the Bulgarian constitution, freedom of religion and belief is guaranteed; however, the Bulgarian Orthodox Church occupies a privileged position as the traditional church of Bulgaria. While all other 156 religious communities are required to be registered, this is not the case for the Orthodox Church, and the country's far-right political parties are continuously attempting to repress and force away the non-Orthodox churches. On October 11, 2018, the right-wing conservative powers wanted to curb the rights of religious minorities, in particular Muslim groups, with draft legislation. The intention was to ban the flow of money to these religious communities from sources in other countries and to prevent foreign clerics from shaping religious life in Bulgaria. Theology schools, training institutions for priests, missionary activities and unrestricted preaching outside of places of worship were to be restricted. Religious groups with membership numbers below one percent of the total population should be excluded from government funding. In order to lodge official registration of a group as a religious community, 3,000 members would now be required, rather than the current 300 members. The draft legislation met with widespread protests, not only from institutions such as the OSCE, the USA and the EU, but also from Church associations and affected religious minorities themselves in Bulgaria.

Following heated debate, the Bulgarian National Assembly adopted a modified form of the legislation on December 21, 2018. Subsequently, the Bulgaria Orthodox Church, with 4 million believers, was granted government subsidies amounting to 7.5 million Euro, while Muslim communities with 600,000 members received 3 million Euro. In future, all religious communities and denominations will be required to submit an annual list of their places of worships to the religious authorities. The extreme right-wing party United Patriots, which supports the Bulgarian government, was not happy about the de facto strengthening of the Muslim communities, the more so as the proposal to ban foreign subsidies was also not adopted. However, the United Patriots were pleased about the imposition of a ban preventing mosques from using loudspeakers to call the faithful to prayer.

Even though the draft legislation had been inherently weakened thanks to the international protests, societal discrimination continued and continues today against Muslims and small religious communities across Bulgaria. Bulgarian executive authorities make no attempt to prevent attacks on Mosques instigated by far-right organisations – events that the European Court of Human Rights in Strasbourg unequivocally condemned. Local authorities seek to prevent Jehovah's Witnesses from undertaking missionary activities in public spaces, while campaigns have been initiated in the media against this religious community. Jehovah's Witnesses have at least generally been able to defend their rights before Bulgarian courts but this did not bring an end to the societal discrimination directed towards the religious community and the attacks on individual members and entire groups.

Developments to the east of the EU borders are developing to an even more serious level than events in Bulgaria, where human rights organisations and the European Court of Human Rights are mostly simply ignored.

In his article about *Russia's Religious Empire, non-Rational Power and Pussy Riot*, **Jukka Korpela** (Joensuu) uses the example of the harsh judgement against the Pussy Riot feminist punk rock group to demonstrate how close the symbiotic relationship between the State and the Orthodox Church in Russia actually is. Furthermore, he shows how this interdependence is founded on a centuries old tradition. Since the 14th century, Russia has considered itself a Holy Empire that incorporates patriotism, nationalism and religious missionary zeal. The Soviet Union – just as Putin's Russia – would assimilate this self-conception. In this respect, it makes no difference whether Russian citizens are devout or not. Orthodox language and its symbols have always been so inherently a part of Russian society and their State, assimilated by the Church, that the sense of being Russian and of being Orthodox cannot really be separated. They are simply part and parcel of the Russian citizen's identity. Through systematic religious-political actions, such as erecting a statue to St Vladimir in the immediate vicinity of the Kremlin in 2016, Putin symbolically accomplished the subjugation of Kiev and the Ukraine under Moscow. More than any constitution, religion legitimises the ruler and identifies him as the God-given shepherd of his people. However, not only Byzantine traditions have flowed into this self-perception, but also Muslim traditions. In both of these traditions, divine wisdom, embedded in a holistic philosophy that manifests itself in mystical allegories, plays a greater role than jurisprudence in the sense of natural law, which simply does not exist in Russia. Likewise, the West's rational enlightened tradition is unable to harm this irrational mysticism. This is why is its simply misleading to want to analyse Russian relationships based on western forms of categorisation. Putin does not need "soft power". All along, it has not been individuality, but symphonic collectivism, that has characterised the concept of being Russian, the Russian disposition to conform to this collective togetherness – while also avoiding acts of violence against itself. To the present day, collectivism characterises the Russian-Eurasian ideology, while the Orthodox Church is the trustee of these state values. To this extent, Putin represents an exemplary model of the political and religious-ideological ruler; in 2012, Patriarch Kirill of Moscow described him as "a miracle of God".

This background helps explain why minorities occupy a very vulnerable position in the Russian Empire. Not only do they have convictions contrary to the accepted norm, but they also implicitly contradict the wise ruler as the guarantor of the law, of truth, justice and peace. In this way, they are the hostile force and represent the presence of evil. According to Orthodox canon law, the mistaken or erring party can only return to their rightful place in the community by demonstrating repentance, a turnaround of position and commitment to symphonic agreement with society. Therefore, there simply cannot be legitimate opposition to the Russian ruler, society and the Church. Foreign pluralism, as is customary in the heretic western civil societies, as well as pluralism within religions, poses a serious threat for Russia and must be stamped out. NGOs with contacts to other countries are considered to be foreign agents, which smuggle ideas into the country that are very different from the longstanding, traditional truth. Human rights are not seen as individual rights, but as the right to live in compliance with church doctrine, while the ruler is the guarantor of these human rights. Thus, the sovereign entitlement of "Holy Russia" extends beyond just the territory of the state to pursue the "concept of the near abroad" or, in other words, is intended for all Russian-Orthodox people in the entire world.

The rock-band Pussy Riot attacked the legitimization of power and the symphonic concord of state and church – the centrepiece of Russian ideology. Furthermore, the band demonstrated no remorse and, therefore, had to be punished so harshly. Their pivotal offence was to challenge the source of power and to strive to destroy the prevailing unanimity in Russia.

The potential ramifications of this symphonic collectivism thinking for "those considered different" is described by **Wolfram Slupina** (Selters) in his article *"Every Day It Just Gets Worse" – Jehovah's Witnesses Under Ban in Russia Facing Criminal Charges*. Following the collapse of the USSR, this religious community that has existed for the last 125 years in Russia, despite consistent bouts of persecution, hoped for a new beginning under democratic and constitutional auspices. Initially, the constitution did meet the Jehovah's Witnesses' exceptions, together with the laws created on the basis of the constitution. However, the 1997 Law on Freedom of Conscience and Religious Associations and the 2002 Federal Law on Counteracting Extremist Activity enabled Russian courts to perpetuate discrimination against small religious communities. 2017 saw an escalation of the situation when the Supreme Court of the Russian Federation criminalised Jehovah's Witnesses and outlawed their religious activities. In the preliminary stages, it was not only the Russian Orthodox Church that pursued this legislation and its ramifications; Anti-Cult movements in the West also came out in support of the laws (see below, Patricia Duval).

The Russian legislation alone and its execution on a regional level enabled local authorities and courts to restrict religious minorities and to discriminate against them. A further legislative change in July 2016 outlawed missionary activities for religious minorities if these took place without state approval, implicitly strengthening opponents' attacks on these religious communities. As a consequence of the 2002 Federal Law on Counteracting Extremist Activity, the Ministry of Justice has maintained a register of "extremist materials" since 2007. This included numerous editions of the religious magazines *Watchtower* and *Awake*, and even the *New World Translation of the Holy Scriptures*. Using this classification of the Jehovah's Witnesses' literature, Russian regional courts were able to confiscate these print media.

In a number of sessions at a series of conferences, in particular at a conference in St. Petersburg in mid-May 2009, the anti-cult organisation FECRIS, primarily financed by Russia and the French government, declared the Jehovah's Witnesses to be a totalitarian sect – a label that undoubtedly played into the hands of the Russian authorities and the Russian Orthodox Church.

Two Russian NGOs, devoted to the protection of children and families, perpetuated the sinister reputation about Jehovah's Witnesses, which had been initiated on an international basis. Various Russian provinces passed legislation to contain their missionary intentions and to regulate their activities. The Bishops' Council of the Russian Orthodox Church expressed its conviction that Jehovah's Witnesses, "threaten the integrity of our national consciousness and our cultural identity". In spite of various attacks, especially on the part of the Moscow District Court, The Russian Ministry of Justice granted Jehovah's Witnesses recognition as a Christian religion across all of Russia in the Spring of 1999. Nevertheless, local courts continued their harassment, culminating in the Moscow District Court declaring a ban against the Jehovah's Witnesses and ordering the dissolution of the local congregation. An appeal from the Witnesses was rejected. The Russian Orthodox Church, the Jewish community and the press welcomed the ban because the Jehovah's Witnesses were deemed to be a "dangerous sect". From this point onwards, attacks on the Jehovah's Witnesses and their Kingdom Halls steadily increased, frequently tacitly sanctioned by the authorities. They were spied upon, their literature was confiscated and destroyed, further registrations were frustrated and they were precluded from buying any buildings. Since 2010, the Jehovah's Witnesses have brought some forty complaints before the European Court of Justice, resulting in considerable success. These have ensured some temporary easing of the pressure and financial compensation for the material damage incurred. And yet, in December 2015, Putin signed a draft bill that exempted the Constitutional Court of the Russian Federation from necessarily accepting decisions from the European Court of Justice. On April 20, 2017, the Supreme Court ruled to validate the application from the Ministry of Justice to prohibit Jehovah's Witnesses in Russia. Jehovah's Witnesses' worship services and missionary activities were banned, and the religious community's property was confiscated to the value of around 51 million Euro. Around 170,000 believers lost their institutional religious basis, their bank balances were frozen, and systematic house searches were ordered, as well as Jehovah's Witnesses' children experiencing pressure and discrimination at school. In addition, many believers were retrenched. If young Jehovah's Witnesses refused to undertake military service, they were sentenced to terms of imprisonment. Hundreds of accusations of extremism and terrorism are still pending against Jehovah's Witnesses – following the judgement about independent institutes for religious research's consistently fabricated proceedings based on "fake news" of rival religious groups and former Jehovah's Witnesses. In the meantime, a number of Jehovah's Witnesses have been sentenced to draconian terms of imprisonment. Ultimately, the only accusation against them was that of belonging to the religious community of the Jehovah's Witnesses. In order to obtain confessions and discover the names of other Witnesses, there is ample evidence in numerous well-documented cases of the use of torture.

Against the background of this report, it is reasonable to assume that the guarantees documented in constitutions in support of freedom of religion would not violate, or would only marginally violate rights in Western and Northern Europe. It goes without saying that believers in smaller religious communities in these European regions are not subject to torture. However, on closer inspection, it is still not difficult to identify serious limitations of religious freedom, even in these countries.

Ever since the 1970s, conservative Christian powers, as well as secular socialist groups in Western and Central Europe, have been fighting against religious movements outside of the established mainstream churches. These anti-cult movements, which have mostly originated as a result of their founder's personal experiences, prevail across France and in Germany. In his article, *The invention of the French notion of "sectarian therapeutic drifts"*, **Régis Dericquebourg** (Lille) highlights a particular aspect of the anti-cult rhetoric in France. These concepts work on the assumption that small religious communities bring about a psychological destabilisation of their victims through the use of illegal therapeutic interventions, which the psychiatrist Philippe-Jean Parquet described as a form of mental control, designating ten characteristics of these. Some highly different groups can be counted among the around 172 "sectarian therapeutic drifts" listed by the responsible government authority (Inter-ministerial Mission for Vigilance and Combating Sectarian Aberrations). These are frequently not directly of a religious nature, and incorporate various psychological practices, self-improvement strategies and alternative medicines in their program. Dericquebourg offers two examples of doctors who were indicted because there were suspicions that they were not solely guided by medical principles in their therapies, but had been influenced by the doctrine of their "dangerous" religious communities (Movement of the Graal and Notre Dame de la Lumière). In both cases, the doctors were acquitted of all charges, but their reputations had nevertheless suffered serious damage.

Gerhard Besier (Dresden) presents how freedom of religion is not only at risk under authoritarian regimes and their relentless insistence on the conservative state church in his essay *Religion – what does this mean today?* Using primarily the example of Germany, Besier explores an enlightened, leftist-centrist-Green social mainstream, which is not willing to tolerate evangelical-Biblicist positioning within the horizon of universal human rights. There is no obligation for Christian believers from all denominations to consider a rational, historical-critical consideration of their basic faith principles. Evangelically oriented Christians trace the wording of Holy Scripture back to God himself. They are not concerned with the consistently liberal standpoint of any of the mainstream Protestant churches, which are bound to Public Theology and always ready to enter into dialogue, always willing to compromise. Nor do they care about the respective changes in the law and legislation.

Because – according to the "unscientific" wording of the Bible, taken entirely out of context – for example, Holy Scripture forbids homosexuality, some evangelical pastors are not prepared to bless same-sex marriages. Increasingly, they and their followers are sanctioned for assuming this stance – to the point of losing their appointed position – if they publicly preach and push for their position of belief. Evangelists, such as Franklin Graham, are unable to hire rooms or halls and are accused of engaging in hate speech. Those who do not satisfy modern acceptance-standards are not accepted in open society; they need to accept they will face social discrimination. A restriction of freedom of religion can also be seen in this situation.

Anders Jarlert (Lund) establishes in his essay *The Religious Scene after the End of the Swedish State Church since 2000: Non-transparency and Confusion*, that when the Church of Sweden ceased to be a state church in 2000, the relationship between Church and State became even more opaque and unclear than ever before. While the General Law on Faith Communities pertains to all other religious communities, the former state church was granted a law of its own. In this legislation, Parliament defined the denominational character of the Church of Sweden as "Evangelical-Lutheran", pushing back the medieval-episcopal traits of this Lutheran church in favour of a more liberal understanding. Furthermore, the legislation described the Church of Sweden as an "open people's church". In reality, this openness only relates to a church member's free choice regarding which services of worship they would like to attend. Church taxes, however, flow exclusively to the local church congregation where a church member lives. Likewise, the prescribed cooperation between a democratic organisation and the Office for Church Affairs makes it impossible for the Bishop of a diocese to transfer or replace a pastor or priest within the diocese should problems arise. While the law requires the Church of Sweden to develop its activities nationwide, this is increasingly not the case, especially in the south of Sweden, as a result of structural changes – a reduction in the number of pastors and a restructuring towards a congregational type of church. In the cathedral chapters, which also function as church courts, there is no separation between a prosecutor and a judge. However, since 2000, Cathedral chapters perceive themselves less as church courts than as institutions for supervision. In this new church order, bishops find themselves in a dubious double role, lacking transparency – acting in the first instance as pastoral worker, but also as judge on occasions. In addition, there are no general provisions within the church order, so that the various cathedral chapters deal with cases brought before them in quite different ways.

Ultimately, the overt secularisation of the state is causing city councils to see specific church buildings as secular real estate, increasingly becoming like museums. From the state perspective, the Church of Sweden is considered Sweden's most significant institution of cultural heritage; the Church acts like a state authority by reporting about conditions and undertaking restoration activities for the preservation of antiquities. With very few exceptions, the Church of Sweden continues to assume responsibility for the country's public cemeteries – including those for Muslims. Every Swedish citizen is required to pay a form of cemetery tax, which nonetheless does not cover the costs for a funeral or burial.

When considering each of the developments since 2000, Jarlert summarises, it is not a case of actual separation of Church and State, but a restructuring of their cooperation, whereby the Church is, in part, supervised and also exploited.

Eileen Barker (London) offers a lucid overview of religious developments in the United Kingdom since the 16th century in her contribution, *We're Happy to Talk, But Dialogue...? Courteous Discrimination in Establishment Parlance*. She reports how – with the support of the Church of England and the Home Office – she established the network INFORM in 1988, with the objective of throwing light on and correcting fantasy stories disseminated by Anti-Cultists by means of research findings and empirical foundations about "new religious movements".

The United Kingdom is now a multi-faith society, an ethnic and religious extremely colourful mix. The "established church", the Church of England, has been steadily losing members; in 2018, the church could count as its members only 12 percent of the 52 percent of the overall population who professed and practised a form of religion. Against this backdrop, the question needs to be raised all the more urgently as to why the Church of England should occupy such a privileged position in society – with subsidies for their schools and seats in the House of Lords – even though it no longer represents the majority of believers. At the same time, many British citizens argue that the Church of England does assume an important role in society – with public prayers by their priests and the coronation of the monarch by the Archbishop of Canterbury. The Church of England itself is certainly not considering giving up its position as the primary Christian partner among equivalent Christian denominations; however, the concept of equivalence among Christian churches only includes those that do not disseminate heretical teachings. Therefore, those who do not acknowledge the Trinity remain excluded from Holy Communion in the Church of England. In this way, the Church of England indicates the boundaries in its willingness to engage in dialogue, even though the Church participates in numerous ecumenical dialogues with Christian and non-Christian religions. The Church of England is open to talk with almost everyone but The Church will only conduct a dialogue on a common platform, which implicitly provides the dialogue partner with legitimacy, with those who can demonstrate they do not have a "proven record of internally abusive or corrupt behaviour", as formulated by the Archbishop of Canterbury, Rowan Williams, in 2012. Where exactly the borderline runs – whether it is according to the respective individual and societal assessment of the actors – is extremely blurred.

Some of the religious communities that are variously described as "cults", "Sects" or "New Religious Movements" (NRM) are not in the least interested in dialogue with those that they consider "unbelieving others", choosing instead to remain to one side. Others have established a series of associations in order to start conversations with one another. The origins of the oldest Interfaith Organisation, the World Congress of Faiths (WCF), reach back to 1893; WCF members are not sourced from religious organisations but consist of individual people. Spin-offs from the respective denominational families have not been welcome in the network. After the application for admission from the Druid Network was rejected in 2012, this association initiated, together with other groups, a protest campaign in the House of Lords, with the objective of the defence of religion. The Druids' law firm accused the IFN of religious discrimination on grounds of belief and called on the government to discontinue the Network's subsidisation. On the strength of this, the IFN modified its admission policy and accepted the Druids, together with other small religious communities.

In 2009, the Church of England had made a clear distinction between its relationship to world religions and that with NRMs. Criteria for the differentiation related to the age (at least 200 years old) as well as the consolidated teachings and theology of the established religious communities. The Church of England does not seek to enter into formal dialogue or worshipping community with the NRMs, but it does listen to the communities and encourages informal local interactions with pastoral assistance, should these be desired. The Church of England explicitly undertakes no action that might be considered an attempt to suppress these communities; it also does not support any anti-cult groups.

The Church of England has since revised its position and, since 2017, no longer makes a clear distinction on its website between the traditional faith communities and NRMs.

Nevertheless, it does warn about problems in relation to some NRMs and offers counselling and advice. The Church, however, does name core principles when dealing with NRMs, including "honesty, knowledge, respect, empathy and vigilance". Eileen Barker concludes with the observation, "Finally, it could be argued with good reason that were a minority religion to want to be accepted by society [...] contemporary England (together, perhaps, with parts of northern Europe) could be one of the least unwelcoming countries in which to settle. Not only is the law of the land open to law-abiding citizens of all faiths and none, but the Established Church, if not enthusiastically welcoming, tends towards courteous toleration and, in some of its manifestations, it will even celebrate the religious kaleidoscope that is part of the make-up of England in the twenty-first century."

In her article, *Participation of State privileged religions in the fight against religious minorities*, **Patricia Duval** (Paris) covers the discrepancy between the legal basis of freedom of religion and its violations. On the one hand, she explores the European Convention on Human Rights and Fundamental Freedoms, in particular, and the International Covenant on Civil and Political Rights – and, on the other hand, their violation by privileged state churches and their charities. Established churches' resistance to small religious communities becomes particularly inflamed when faced with missionary zeal and individuals' indisputable right to change their religion or religious community and allegiance. Time and again, UN reporters have expressly warned against the criminalisation of non-violent forms of missionary activities, with reference to freedom of religion and forms of belief. In June, 2010, in the legal proceedings of Jehovah's Witnesses of Moscow vs. Russia, the European Court of Human Rights expressly endorsed the right of adults to convert religion.

The European Court of Human Rights found that the Russian prosecutors' allegation that the Jehovah's Witnesses exerted psychological pressure and mind control could not be validated. Not one single converted individual could be summoned to give evidence that their freedom of conscience had been violated through the Witnesses' missionary activities. On the contrary, converted individuals confirmed that their decision to change religion was entirely voluntarily, and of their own free will.

With regard to the Russian Federal Law on Counteracting Extremist Activity, it would need to be demonstrated that the Jehovah's Witnesses' literature provokes religious hatred and intolerance; otherwise, every religious community remains free to persuade people about their teachings.

The European Court of Human Rights emphasised the obligation of governments to ensure neutrality towards religions practised in their respective countries. Certainly, a state is free to offer traditional mainstream religions clear privilege, but not in a form that leads to discrimination against smaller religious communities.

Likewise, in 1999, the Organization for Security and Co-operation in Europe (OSCE) distinguished between a state's fundamental right to treat all religions equally, while also granting a particular religion certain privileges, assuming that this does not equate to discrimination towards the other religious communities. Austria, which differentiates between the basis-status of a religious community and the higher status of a full religion, was caused to recognise in the proceedings of the Jehovah's Witnesses religious community and others vs Austria (1998) that such a differentiation needed to have clear criteria and the opportunity to achieve the higher level of status on application.

There are states – Patricia Duval names Germany and Russia as examples here – that have not only granted privileges to their traditional churches, but which have also supported and sustained these in the battle against religious minorities.

Both mainstream churches have not only received considerable subsidies from the state, but have also used their income to instigate actions against small religious communities by means of appropriate sub-organisations and "sect-commissioners". According to Duval, if a church receives public money, then they are consequently bound to make use of the means in a neutral manner similar to that implemented by the state, and not to use it to lead ideological arguments against competitors. Otherwise, international human rights' norms will be infringed. For this reason, in the spring of 1992, the Federal Constitutional Court placed a ban on Germany granting financial support to the Anti-Cult-Organisation Action for Mental and Psychological Freedom (AGPF).

In order to prevent the "infiltration" of the business world by Scientology, some states implemented so-called "sect-filters", starting with Hamburg in 1995, with what was called a "Scientology protection declaration". Applicants and companies were required to fill out a declaration indicating if they had ever adopted or circulated the technologies of L. Ron Hubbard, and they needed to guarantee that they would also not do so in the future. In one action, this explicit discrimination infringed on both the protected right to freedom of religion and to freedom of conscience. Accordingly, the city of Hamburg was condemned in a series of court judgements for violating the freedom of religion and of conscience for individual scientologists. In mid-December, the Federal Constitutional Court handed down the decision that the "sect-filter" violated Article 14 of the German constitution. Even so, German states continued to employ the "sect-filter". In this way, the state of Bavaria underwrote a program to encourage the use of E-Bikes in 2018; all potential participants could apply for a state subsidy of 500 Euros. However, anybody who adhered to the "Technology of L. Ron Hubbard" was expressly excluded.

In 1997, at the instigation of the then Bavarian Minister of the Interior, Günther Beckstein, who was also a member of the Lutheran Synod, state ministers resolved that the Church of Scientology should be monitored by the Office for the Protection of the Constitution. Even so, the Office for the Protection of the Constitution found nothing that was able to justify the surveillance order.

After Russia adopted the Law on Freedom of Worship in October 1990, a diversification of the religious landscape began to emerge, which generated a sense of threat to the Russian Orthodox Church. The Church initiated a strict anti-cult movement, aimed at preserving Russia's "spiritual security" and traditional values. In 1996, the Orthodox Bishop Kirill, who was appointed Patriarch of Moscow and all Russia in 2009, complained that "hordes of missionaries" were invading Russia, agitating against the "people's national and religious sentiments" and seeking to destroy the "spiritual unity of the people and the Orthodox faith". He claimed that Russia was losing its "cultural identity as an Orthodox nation". A new Russian law, the Law on Freedom of Conscience and Religious Associations, was passed in September 1997, which differentiated between traditional and non-traditional religious communities. The law also denied re-registration to a series of non-established religions. In the summer of 2002, a further Anti-Extremism Law offered the state the tool to classify the activities of certain religious communities and their literature as "extremist". The European Court of Justice and the Commission for Democracy through Law (Venice Commission) considered the vague legal phrasing to be unsuited for identifying if a relevant group and its literature did actually propagate violence or hate. It is in the nature of monotheistic religions to consider themselves superior, or of a higher importance, than others. As a religious community, they want to have the right to win over potential members, to persuade them to convert, in order to protect them. The Supreme Court of Russia did not follow the objections raised, choosing instead to resume its repressive policies against non-traditional religious communities in order to strengthen the position of the Russian Orthodox Church. In April, the Supreme Court of Russia decided that the administrative centre of the Jehovah's Witnesses and 395 of their local centres were extremist. Shortly after followed mass persecutions, convictions and public discrimination against Jehovah's Witnesses (see above, article by Wolfram Slupina).

In July 2016, the Yarovaya Law amended and supplemented the already restrictive legislation, placing considerable further restrictions on the possibilities for missionary activity among non-traditional religious groups.

Aleksander Dvorkin is one of the most important organisers of Anti-Sect-Activities, in his role as Vice President of the Anti-Cult-Organisation, European Federation of Centres of Research and Information on Sectarianism (FECRIS). He is the Head of the Russian anti-cult organisation Saint Ireneus of Lyons Centre for Religious Studies and is a member of the Missionary Department of the St. Tikhon's Orthodox University in Moscow. He has been proactive in the fight against "cults" or "sects" for 20 years, implicating them in criminal activities and spreading prejudices that lead to the repression of and bans on small religious communities. Furthermore, he works to destroy their reputation, which only encourages some to perpetrate threats, acts of physical violence and vandalism against these religious groups. According to the beliefs of the Russian anti-cult propagandists, if anyone has a relative or friend who subscribes or professes to one of these religious communities of dubious repute, then that person has a responsibility to bring the misguided individual to one of the "rehabilitation centres". Once at the centre, any psychological dependence on the cult would be broken and, afterwards, a catechist of the Russian-Orthodox Church would teach the individual about the true faith. This process of "rehabilitation" occurs with the endorsement of the Russian authorities.

In his article *"Your Human Rights, Your Fundamental Freedoms Are in Danger". Crusade Against Christianity, Jehovah's Witnesses, and the Fight for Religious Freedom*, **Tim B. Müller** (Mannheim) reflects on the Jehovah's Witnesses' unique intellectual contribution with regard to freedom of religion since the 1920s, set against the backdrop of the historical conflicts faced by this religious community.

The treatment of Jehovah's Witnesses in the respective countries has been more than just a test case for the right to freedom of religion and other freedoms in force in those countries. In reality, Jehovah's Witnesses have also contributed significantly, albeit often inadvertently, to the development and shaping of human rights in many countries with their adherence to their principles and the defence of these in courts of law. In any case, "a working partnership" has been forged on occasions between the Jehovah's Witnesses, their lawyers and various human rights organisations with the European Court of Human Rights.

During the Third Reich Nazi regime, Jehovah's Witnesses consistently offered silent, but sustained, resistance to totalitarianism, extreme nationalism, racism, violence and war. At the same time, the majority of the German population, the Church and even a large part of the resistance movement had endorsed the war in the first instance. Jehovah's Witnesses were not seeking to overthrow the Nazi regime, but the regime would have collapsed very rapidly had a majority of the population assumed a similar approach to the Jehovah's Witnesses. As Klaus von Dohnanyi and others have established, the Jehovah's Witnesses' ethical principles were not strictly speaking "political". Nevertheless, in all likelihood, they could have had great significance for social coexistence. The Witnesses' subjective neutrality leads to objective political resistance if the rule of law, fundamental human rights and concepts of liberal democracy are violated.

During the Weimar Republic, Jehovah's Witnesses were generally able to wage a successful fight before German courts against the manifold attempts by special interest groups and the mainstream churches to curtail their right to freedom of religion. Likewise, in the early years of the Nazi dictatorship, Jehovah's Witnesses attempted to use legal means to defend themselves against Nazi oppression. Müller holds the firm belief that the book "Crusade against Christianity" [*Kreuzzug gegen das Christentum*] (1938) occupies a central position in the anti-totalitarian battle to maintain human rights, as the book documents the brutal persecution of Jehovah's Witnesses in Germany. If one considers the linguistic context in this book, it quickly becomes apparent that Jehovah's Witnesses – in keeping with their social ethics – defended human rights, especially the right to freedom of conscience and belief. This was also understood by their contemporaries. Here, like in other writings by the Jehovah's Witnesses, there was a cautious vote for democracy, because political social and legal equality for all people is in accordance with the Will of God – even if a genuine and true democracy could only be built after God's Kingdom is established. "Democracy" is used as an umbrella term for a non-totalitarian order or system, where the Jehovah's Witnesses' opponents are also portrayed as opponents of democracy. "Crusade against Christianity" analyses how the Nazi regime misappropriates the instruments of the rule of law in order to create an illegitimate or unjust state. It also demonstrates a pluralist understanding of modern societies with its understanding of religious freedom and human rights. The concept of a racially homogenous national community is explicitly condemned. Based on religious grounds, the Jehovah's Witnesses welcomed and approved of a multicultural, multi-religious and pluralist society, which – in contrast to totalitarian regimes – guaranteed human rights and freedom of religion within democracies. In all of this, Jehovah's Witnesses aimed to defend the Judeo-Christian tradition, and condemned the Nazis' policy of anti-Semitism. The anti-Judaism that is endemic in German Protestantism remained substantially unheard-of for Jehovah's Witnesses. A Jehovah's Witnesses' series of articles from 1938 also specifically names all the other groups that were to suffer under the Nazi regime's persecution. Even members of the Protestant mainstream churches, including Karl Barth and Ernst Staehelin, were included in this spirit of solidarity, so long as they were opposed to and sought to resist the Nazi regime. With respect to Catholicism, there was clear suspicion of cooperation with fascist regimes, which was confirmed, to a certain degree, through the position assumed by the Austrian episcopate in 1938. The book "Crusade against Christianity" undoubtedly deserves a position in the chorus of the early protest literature expressing clear defence of freedom of religion, the rights of minorities and human rights. Under different circumstances, these facts and this issue could easily have been overlooked.

Jolene Chu (Warwick) presents a continuation of the disputes over reasonable religious attitude in ethnic conflicts in her essay *The Practice and Consequences of Apolitical Christianity by Rwandan Jehovah's Witness Community Before and During the Genocide.*

With the exception of the religious community of Jehovah's Witnesses, numbering some 2,500 members, all Christian churches were involved – directly or indirectly – in the genocide of 1994. If it is necessary to establish an important reason why the Christian churches were involved in the genocide, one need not look further than the all too close relations between State and Church, especially the Catholic Church. By contrast, the Jehovah's Witnesses had not been involved in wars, civil wars or even genocides, not in Rwanda nor in previous conflicts. In Rwanda, they had assumed "a position of apolitical nonviolence", which led to Jehovah's Witnesses having to face hostilities from both religious and from political authorities.

State-Church collaboration was first instituted in Rwanda during the period of colonisation of the country. Initially, missionaries played an integral role in helping the Tutsi monarch and his small elite to consolidate power over other groups and establish a 'divide and rule' system. The missionaries' top-down-strategy faltered as a consequence of Tutsi-King Musinga's resistance to joining to the Catholic Church. Therefore, in 1931, the Belgian Governor ensured that Musinga's son, Mutara, who had been brought up as a Catholic, would seize power. The racist theory of the inherent superiority of the now overwhelmingly Catholic Tutsi over the Hutus was also corroborated and strengthened on the part of the Church by reference to the Hamitic myth, claiming that the Tutsi were descendants of Noah's son Ham. At the end of World War II, King Mutra sought to channel both the nationalist movement and the emancipation of the Hutu, by bringing an end to discriminatory practices. He wanted to break the Catholic Church's education monopoly by establishing an independent school system. The Catholic Church opposed this plan vehemently. In 1956, the Catholic Archbishop of Kabgayi modified his church policy in favour of social-justice issues, causing the Hutus to rise up against the small Tutsi –elite. The Hutu rebels took up the Hamitic myth and described the Tutsi as a separate race that had oppressed the Hutus. The Church increasingly redirected its sympathy and support towards the Hutu emancipation movement. In this way, and in spite of the country's independence in 1962, the Catholic Church was able to maintain its influence over the government, which was now dominated by Hutus and, thus, continue the State-Church collaboration.

In contrast, the Jehovah's Witnesses assumed a strict policy of political neutrality from the beginning, specifically from 1975 – in spite of considerable pressure on the state's part – and held on to this approach, even during the civil war in 1990 and the genocide in 1994. In October 1979, the government published a list of religions that it officially recognised. Jehovah's Witnesses did not feature on the list, even though their membership numbers were constantly on the rise. Requests for recognition lodged in 1980 and 1982 remained unanswered. Shortly thereafter, Jehovah's Witnesses were banned, leading members were arrested and sentenced to terms of imprisonment. Their Kingdom Hall was closed down.

When the government decreed in 1985 that every citizen on reaching the age of 18 would automatically become a member of the State party, and would need to pay a membership fee, Jehovah's Witnesses refused to pay what was effectively a political tax or levy. Consequently, they were arrested, tortured, removed from their workplaces and sentenced to long years in prison. Jehovah's Witnesses also refused to follow the example of the Catholic Archbishop and wear a badge bearing the portrait of the President; they would not sing the national hymn and would also not differentiate between the Hutus and Tutsis. Among Jehovah's Witnesses, marriages between the two tribes were customary and Hutus would help disadvantaged Tutsi to find jobs. In the year 1992, Jehovah's Witnesses finally gained official recognition as a religious community in Rwanda, even though they would not take an active part in the religious-nationalistic rhetoric in support of the regime and its discrimination against the Tutsi minority – in contrast to the mainstream churches. Following the crash of the President's plane in April 1994, the genocide began. Around 400 Jehovah's Witnesses were also murdered – in part because of their ethnic background but also because they adhered to their apolitical, non-violent Christian ethic and did not consider themselves as belonging to either or any political party.

A clear separation of State and Church, we learn from these articles, prevents privileged religions, as well as evangelical movements supported by state interests, from becoming power-political factors that seek to mould a society according to their own values and to their benefit. To this end, restraint is essential on the part of both the State and the Church. All too often, politicians are happy to accept ideological support on behalf of a religious community or a religious grouping, and then seek to further the interests and to promote these groups. Even though the two countries demonstrate fundamental difference with respect to their constitutional foundation, we are very aware of such constellations in both the USA and in Russia.

Congressional Efforts to Defend and Extend Religious Freedom and the Law of Unintended Consequences

James T. Richardson and Barbara McGraw

1. Introduction

The United States approach to religious freedom was unique at the time of the promulgation of the First Amendment to its Constitution in 1791, two years after the Constitution came into force. The now famous and much copied (at least in part)[1] First Amendment guaranteed a number of freedoms important to establishing a tradition of religious freedom. The First Amendment reads as follows:

> **Congress shall make no law respecting an establishment of religion, or prohibiting the free exercise thereof**; or abridging the freedom of speech, or of the press; or the right of the people peaceably to assemble, and to petition the Government for a redress of grievances.

The two religion provisions were the result of a political compromise based on the fact that none of the religious groups present in various parts of the new nation had the political power or will to assert and maintain a claim to become the established religion for the country. Thus the "lively experiment" (Mead 1963) began. Since that auspicious beginning, religious freedom has experienced many vicissitudes within the American experience (Waldman 2019), including some recent ones which will be described herein.

2. The United States Form of Government

In order to grasp the meaning of recent machinations concerning religious freedom in the United States, it is necessary to first understand how the government of the nation was constructed over 200 years ago, and how it functions today. The

---

[1] Note that wording similar to the free exercise clause now appears in nearly all constitutions of nations around the world, even if honored sometimes in the breach. However, the clause prohibiting establishment of a state religion appears less frequently, as many nations have either a formalized or traditional accepted state established religion (or sometimes more than one).

Constitution laid out a plan for "separation of powers" that theoretically granted equal power to three branches of the federal government: the executive branch, the legislative branch (Congress), and the federal court system. The Executive branch includes the President and the officers and agencies that operate the government following laws approved by Congress.

The legislative branch, comprised of a 100-member Senate (two senators from each state) and a 435 member House of Representatives (distributed to individual states according to population), passes legislation that governs the nation. However, for a federal law to be enacted, the President must sign all legislation (unless a presidential veto is over-ridden by a two-thirds vote in each house of Congress), and all legislation passed by Congress and signed by the President is subject to review by the federal courts, which determine the legislation's constitutionality.

The federal court system is headed by the Supreme Court, a nine-member court whose members are nominated by the President and must be approved by a majority vote of the Senate. The court system below the Supreme Court is comprised of 13 appellate courts and 94 district courts distributed across the country. The federal courts may consider, if asked by a plaintiff with adequate standing, the constitutionality of any legislation passed by Congress (and signed by the President), as well as any Executive Order promulgated by the President or any rules established by a federal agency as it attempts to implement laws passed by Congress and signed by the President.

3. Major Legal Developments Concerning Religious Freedom in the United States

3.1. Application of First Amendment Protections to States

For over a hundred years after the establishment of the United States of America, the management of religion was left to local and state governments, as the federal constitution with its Bill of Rights[2] was assumed not to apply at those levels of government. However, in the 20th century the U.S. Supreme Court began a process of "incorporation" whereby over time various provisions of the Bill of Rights were deemed applicable to local and state governments. The process of incorporation was accomplished gradually and selectively by applying the due process clause of the post-Civil War Fourteenth Amendment to the state and local governments as

---

[2] The Bill of Rights was a series of 10 amendments added to the Constitution after much controversy arose because the original draft constitution contained few protections for individual freedoms and from actions of the new federal government. The First Amendment cited above is the focus of this treatment, but see Legal Information Institute (https://www.law.cornell.edu/wex/incorporation_doctrine, accessed January 2020) for details on other Bill of Rights amendments and their history of incorporation.

cases arose clearly demonstrating that personal freedoms were being infringed upon by some local and state actions. Section 1 of the Fourteenth Amendment reads as follows:

> All persons born or naturalized in the United States, and subject to the jurisdiction thereof, are citizens of the United States and of the state wherein they reside. No state shall make or enforce any law which shall abridge the privileges or immunities of citizens of the United States; *nor shall any state deprive any person of life, liberty, or property, without due process of law*; nor deny to any person within its jurisdiction the equal protection of the laws. (Emphasis added)

The incorporation process using the due process clause included the religion clauses of the First Amendment. Incorporation started a gradual process toward transforming the nation from one with a Protestant hegemony, which had existed for most of the young nation's history, to one more accepting of religious diversity (McGraw 2016; Davis 2016). The Supreme Court began as early as 1940 to rule in favor of some plaintiffs from minority faiths of different persuasions and also disallowed some overt efforts to maintain the Protestant hegemony.

In 1940 the Supreme Court, in *Cantwell v. Connecticut*, ruled in favor of a Jehovah's Witness who had been prosecuted for proselytizing in a predominantly Catholic neighborhood in Connecticut.[3] The Court ruled that the free exercise clause applied to states by virtue of being incorporated through the Fourteenth Amendment's due process clause. In 1947 in *Everson v. Board of Education*, a case involving aid to parochial schools, the Court ruled that the Establishment clause of the First Amendment also was applicable to the state governments.

In 1963 in *Sherbert v. Verner* the Court again held that the free exercise clause obligated states to allow the exercise of religious freedom rights. The *Sherbert* case involved a Seventh Day Adventist who had been denied unemployment benefits after being fired from her job for refusing to work on Saturdays, the Adventists' Sabbath. And, in 1972 in *Yoder v. Wisconsin,* the Court ruled that the free exercise clause takes precedent over a state law requiring school age children to attend public schools past the eighth grade.

These two cases taken together established the need for a "compelling governmental interest" to be demonstrated before religious freedom could be limited by state law, and that a government must in such situations apply the "least restrictive means" to accomplish its goals. Thus, these two famous cases established what is known as the "strict scrutiny" test, which applied in situations where application of an otherwise neutral law resulted in a substantial burden on religious freedom, thus requiring a religious liberty "accommodation."

---

[3] The Jehovah's Witnesses have been regular and successful "repeat players" in the forum of the Supreme Court, with over 50 cases won since the late 1930s. See Cote and Richardson 2001 for a discussion of the approach taken by the Witnesses to litigation, and Richardson 2015, 2017 for updates on how successful this group has been in various judicial forums in the western world.

Despite the seeming promise for religious minorities of the *Sherbert-Yoder* strict scrutiny test, religious minorities' exemptions from laws that burdened their religion in actuality were rarely successful (Wybraniec and Finke 2004; McGraw and Richardson 2020b, 15). Further, in its 1987 ruling in *Turner v. Safley*, the Supreme Court ruled that the *Sherbert-Yoder* analysis was inapplicable to incarcerated persons, substituting a different analysis which deferred to correctional institution authorities in determining religious liberty exemptions, i. e., accommodations. Thereafter, correctional institutions' "penological interests" nearly always prevailed over inmates' requests for religious liberty exemptions from general policies that burdened their religion. The Court's deference to prison authorities had the effect of burdening even some religious practices of inmate adherents of recognized Protestant Christianity sects and Catholicism. However, adherents of minority religions felt the impact much more severely because permitted religious practices were based on normative assumptions about legitimate religion that were based on those mainstream religions. These developments concerning religious freedom in corrections and incarceration have proved to be salient for eventual developments in the law, as discussed below.

3.2. Dramatic Shift by Supreme Court Religious Freedom Jurisprudence

Application of the strict scrutiny test to situations raised by various religious groups and practitioners led sometimes to seemingly inconsistent decisions by the courts as they tried to determine when a compelling governmental interest existed and what the "least restrictive means" really meant in practice. The Supreme Court attempted to resolve the issue in 1990 in quite dramatic fashion when it ruled in *Employment Division v. Smith* that exemptions from otherwise facially neutral laws would not be granted, unless a law specifically targeted a religious group or practice.[4] Thus the strict scrutiny test was abandoned and a "neutrality principle" was henceforth to be applied in such cases. This case involved two practitioners of the Native American Church in Oregon who were fired from their jobs as drug counselors because they were using peyote in their religious practices. They were denied unemployment benefits by the state and sought redress in the courts. They won their case in Oregon courts, but the Attorney General of Oregon sought review within the federal court system, and eventually won a dramatic decision that tossed out decades of accepted (even if difficult to apply) law in this area.

---

[4] In *Church of the Lukumi Babalu Aye v. City of Hialeah* 1993, the Supreme Court made clear that a law designed to target a specific religious group, in that case the Santería, is unconstitutional even if the law is written to appear neutral.

3.3. Swift Reaction to Smith Decision by Congress

The response to the *Smith* decision was swift and strong. Many who valued religious freedom were incensed that the Court had so casually dismissed claims that religious freedom could be and was being compromised by governmental actions around the nation. An impressive coalition of various groups and individuals, some of whom were normally at odds on various issues, was formed and lobbied for Congress to take action to overturn the effects of *Smith* (McGraw and Richardson 2020a). *Smith* even became an issue in the presidential race when then candidate Bill Clinton pledged to sign legislation that overturned the effects of the decision if he was elected.

Congress did act, and in 1993 passed the Religious Freedom Restoration Act (RFRA) overwhelmingly (only three Senators voted against it and no members of the House of Representatives did so), and President Clinton signed the Act with considerable fanfare. RFRA reinstituted the strict scrutiny test, requiring that any rule of general applicability could not substantially burden religious activities unless there was a compelling governmental interest, and even under that circumstance the remedy must be narrowly drawn. The Act was to cover federal agencies and also state and local governmental entities, and thus reinstitute the way the First Amendment's free exercise provision was being applied if *Smith* had not reversed it.[5]

3.4. The Supreme Court Exerts Its Authority Once Again

The euphoria over passage of RFRA was, however, to be somewhat short-lived. In 1997 in a case from Texas, *City of Boerne v. Flores*, the Court ruled that RFRA lacked an adequate constitutional basis for application to state and local governments. The case involved a Catholic Church in a suburb of San Antonio, Texas, which wanted to renovate and expand its facilities to better serve its growing constituencies. However, the Church was in a historical district with restrictions on what could be done to buildings therein. Local officials denied the request from the Church, and the Church sued (in the name of Archbishop Flores) in federal court on the basis of RFRA. The Church lost at the District Court level, with that Court declaring RFRA unconstitutional as applied to local governments. On ap-

---

[5] Also about half the 50 states in America passed "mini-RFRAs" to make sure that religious freedom was protected at the state level whatever happened at the federal level and some state court decisions have provided RFRA-like analyses. (See list of state-RFRAs at https://en.wikipedia.org/wiki/State_Religious_Freedom_Restoration_Acts). Those mini-RFRA laws varied in their specific language and intent, but did demonstrate the importance of this value to many in American society. Some enacted later, however, seemed specifically designed to grant primacy to religious beliefs over equality rights, in particular LGBT access to various services; such statutes were quite controversial. See, e.g., the debates about the Indiana Religious Freedom Restoration Act (https://www.americanbar.org/groups/litigation/committees/minority-trial-lawyer/practice/2015/indianas-religious-freedom-restoration-act-sparks-controversy/).

peal, the Fifth Circuit Court ruled in favor of the Church's claim and stated that RFRA was constitutional. However, the case then was appealed to the Supreme Court which ruled against the Church and declared RFRA unconstitutional as pertaining to state and local governments.

RFRA was, however, still applicable to the many agencies of the federal government. This was made very clear in a manner that offered solace for those concerned about religious freedom for minority faiths in the United States. The constitutionality of RFRA as applied to the federal government was confirmed in 2006 when the Supreme Court ruled unanimously against the federal Drug Enforcement Agency (DEA) in *Gonzales v. O Centro Espirita Beneficente Uniao do Vegetal*. The case involved the use of an otherwise illegal substance in a religious ceremony of a small religious group in New Mexico which was derived from a Brazilian-based religion (Richardson and Shoemaker 2014).[6]

3.5. Congress Tries Again, and Again

After the Supreme Court ruled that RFRA was unconstitutional as it pertained to state and local governments, many assumed that the battles over the *Smith* decision might be over. However, Congress was not to be denied in its efforts to demonstrate strong support for religious freedom, and continued attempts were made to pass legislation that might nullify or limit effects of the *Smith* decision. Initial efforts involved attempting passage of the Religious Liberty Protection Act (RLPA) which contained most of the provisions of RFRA, but with a different legal basis that was thought to overcome the Court's basis for the *Boerne* decision. However, this effort foundered mainly because of growing opposition among some of the initial supporters of RFRA over concerns that religious claims might override other important considerations.

When RLPA failed to gain support, this was again viewed by some as the end of efforts to overcome *Smith*. However, a more narrow coalition of groups involved in ministering to prisoners, along with the American Civil Liberties Union (ACLU), developed a bill more limited in scope, but with major implications for the manner in which religion would be managed in American society. The Religious Land Use and Institutionalized Persons Act (RLUIPA) addressed only two specific but very broad areas of regulation, land use and institutionalized persons (including prison inmates).[7] These two areas had heretofore been left to states and

---

[6] The Court stated that the federal government must show a compelling governmental interest in restricting religious conduct, and it indicated that since exceptions had been made for the use of peyote, the same could be done for the "sacred tea" used by the New Mexico group. In 2009 this case was determinative precedent for a similar small religious group in Oregon. Both groups had to agree to some strict rules for usage of the substance in their rituals, but they were allowed to use it henceforth.

[7] "Institutionalized persons" has come to mean, through legislation and case law, any person living in some sort of publicly supported facility on a long-term basis. Included are prisons, jails, men-

local governments to manage, with correctional institutions subject only to the limited First Amendment review of *Turner v. Safley*'s "penological interest" analysis, referenced earlier. Passage of RLUIPA would mean a dramatic shift in power and control to the federal government. But RLUIPA went even further with its explicit language that religious beliefs and practices did not need to be mandated or central to a religion in order to gain protection. RLUIPA stated: "religious exercise" includes "…any exercise of religion, whether or not compelled by, or central to, a system of belief." (42 USC §2000cc-5(7) (A); McGraw and Richardson 2020b).

RLUIPA passed both houses of Congress by voice vote on July 7, 2000, an indication of the strong support for religious freedom in Congress. The strong support was perhaps also an expression of the frustration members of Congress felt toward the Supreme Court's efforts to limit such protections. But criticisms of the passage of such a far-reaching law were also quick to arise, based on concerns about the broad expansion of federal power over two areas traditionally left to states and local governments, and also over concern that the new law would empower prisoners to an extent that managing prisons would be much more difficult. Also, there were concerns expressed about the rapid manner of passage of RLUIPA that, in the view of some, did not allow a full airing of concerns about the impact of such legislation (Hamilton 2003).

3.6. The Supreme Court Considers RLUIPA

Thus, the issue of how to protect religious freedom was again back within the purview of the Supreme Court, as it was just a matter of time before cases testing the constitutionality of RLUIPA would work their way to the Court for final adjudication. Predictably, the first test case accepted by the Court dealt with religious rights of prisoners. *Cutter v. Wilkinson*, decided in 2005, resulted in a unanimous verdict in favor of five prisoners who claimed that their religious rights under RLUIPA were being violated. The five included two members of Asatru, a minister of a Christianity-based White supremacist organization, a Satanist, and a Wiccan. The five plaintiffs won at the District Court level, overcoming the State of Ohio argument that to allow their religious freedom rights would violate the establishment clause of the Constitution. But that decision was overturned by the Sixth Circuit Court of Appeals, leading to an appeal to the Supreme Court. The Court's ruling made clear that at least the institutionalized persons part of the Act was indeed constitutional.

To date, the Court has not ruled explicitly on the constitutionality of the land use provisions of RLUIPA, but that part of the Act has been implemented and has had profound effects nonetheless. As described in McGraw and Richardson

---

tal hospitals, nursing homes, and institutions for persons who have some sort of mental or physical handicap. Thus, RLUIPA is quite broad in its coverage.

(2020a) various agencies of the federal government have been active in enforcing those provisions, and minority faiths have benefited. Particularly Islamic groups have had success in building mosques and acquiring places to worship in areas where they were unpopular, but other groups have been able to overcome zoning regulations and other efforts to limit their activities as well.

Thus, the Supreme Court chose to accede to Congressional pressures to make clearer that religious freedom rights are to be respected, at least in certain substantive areas (Gill and Jelen 2016). However, as will be shown below, the battles are far from over. Significant efforts are being made to undermine the effects of both RFRA and RLUIPA by opponents, some of whom think religion has become too powerful in American society, and are concerned about religious claims undermining other important societal values.

4. Aftermath of the Battles between Congress and the Supreme Court: Unintended (or Unexpected) Consequences

Not recognized at first for its historic expansion of religious liberty protections, RLUIPA's broad definition of "religious exercise" began to have a profound effect as the courts interpreted the reach of the new law. This was no less so because when that definition was adopted for RLUIPA, it also was applied to RFRA. While limited to federal actions, RFRA was not limited in its subject-matter scope, as was RLUIPA (institutionalized persons and land use). As we shall see below, that definition has led to, for many, unintended or at least unexpected consequences.

At first the impact of the new definition at the federal and state levels was felt most strongly in prisons. There, inmate adherents of previously recognized religions began to request additional religious liberty rights "accommodations" of their practices, as they were no longer limited to practices that were central to or mandated by their beliefs. In addition, minority religion adherents, who previously had been accommodated in very limited ways – or not at all, increased their accommodation requests. Many of their supporters recognized that the new definition would provide more positive results in the cases they filed than had been provided under the previous "penological interests" standard of the First Amendment under the Court's *Turner v. Safley* ruling.

The lower state and federal courts at first tended to analyze the prison cases through the *Safley* deference-to-prison-authorities lens, regardless of the new laws' strict scrutiny standard and expanded definition of religion. However, after a few federal appellate court rulings where the application of RLUIPA's and RFRA's strict scrutiny analysis in the prison context was clarified, it was evident that a wide variety of religious practices would have to be accommodated, as never before.[8] The court analyses resulted in unanticipated outcomes and implications for the future of religious liberty in two significant respects.

On the one hand, as the cases wended their way through the courts, it became abundantly clear that prison institutions had been unfairly privileging certain religions and their basic practices over other religions without a valid basis for doing so. The courts and correctional agencies previously supported those restrictive results under *Safley's* deference to prison authorities. That deference had resulted in denials of religious accommodations for various seemingly important reasons, but which made no sense when viewed from a wider, more fair perspective. For example, without considering the wider context, a prison authority denied a Hindu access to prayer beads. The beads were perceived to be a potential threat to safety as they could be used to strangle or hit another prison inmate or prison staff. However, Catholics had been permitted rosaries for decades, and they were a greater threat as the beads were often made of glass and, of course, they included a metal cross (McGraw 2018). Clearly, the historical (and institutionally entrenched) religious programs reflected preexisting policy, which was not challenged, while new requests were often denied.

Application of the RFRA/RLUIPA strict scrutiny analysis, together with the expanded definition of "religious exercise," required the courts and correctional agencies to consider accommodating "any" practice. Moreover, if a requested accommodation was similar to or the same as one that had been permitted previously for traditionally accommodated religions, the argument that there was a compelling governmental interest not to allow the requested item or practice fell apart. Slowly, correctional institutions have been changing their policies to accommodate more and more diverse religious practices, which is in effect a "quiet revolution" that gradually has been dislodging the Protestant privilege that had had a hegemonic hold on prison policy. A similar development has been occurring in other governmental agencies, for example in the military (McGraw 2016).

On the other hand, it eventually became evident that the broad definition of "religious exercise" may, in fact, have no bounds. Clearly, the "exercise" component of the definition had been greatly expanded. However, the boundlessness appears to apply to the "religion" component of the definition, as well. The statute itself states that the scope of religious exercise must "be construed in favor of a broad protection of religious exercise, to the maximum extent permitted" (§2000cc-3(g)). Further, it is widely accepted in the United States that courts cannot define religion for the purposes of religious liberty protections, as doing so would itself amount to an establishment of a particular view of religion.[9] Due to the Supreme Court's guidance in such cases as *United States v. Ballard*, involving

---

[8] See, e.g., *Warsoldier v. Woodford* 9th Cir. 2005; *Greene v. Solano County Jail* 2008.

[9] Usman 2007, 146, citing Weiss 1964, 604. See Usman 2007 generally for an extensive discussion of the issues involved in defining "religion" for the purposes of the law.

"I AM," a minority Christian sect, and *United States v. Seeger*, involving a conscientious objector, the courts have turned to a case-by-case analysis of whether a particular claimant's belief (and the practices based on that belief) are "sincerely held" rather than whether those beliefs and practices amount to "religion" per se.[10] In effect, "sincerely held belief" has become a stand-in for a definition of "religion."[11] What counts as worthy of protections has become, therefore, individualized. For example, the Department of Defense has instructed: "The military departments will accommodate individual expressions of sincerely held beliefs (conscience, moral principles, or religious beliefs) of service members" unless there are compelling reasons not to, such as military readiness (Department of Defense Instruction 2014, 4.b.; see DeVuono 2014). Further, it is worth noting that at least one appellate court has ruled that atheism is a religion for the purposes of free exercise of religion rights.[12] Further, the experience in correctional institutions, where religious liberty requests and their accommodations have increased under RLIPIA, is reflected in cases well beyond prisons.

The Supreme Court could have in its post-RFRA/RLUIPA rulings provided some guidance about the extents and limits of "religious exercise" when it agreed to hear RFRA and RLUIPA religious liberty cases. However, in 2014 the Court's reasoning in *Burwell v. Hobby Lobby*, a RFRA case, made clear that the Court was going to interpret the law as expansively as Congress had written it. Even doing business is an "exercise" of religion, the Court reasoned. The Court granted religious liberty rights, under RFRA, to a closely held corporation owned by committed Christians whose "sincere belief" included conducting their businesses according to the precepts of their religion as they understood them to be. Noting that "Congress went far beyond what this Court has held is constitutionally required," the Supreme Court reasoned that religious exercise includes physical acts that are "engaged in for religious reasons," including doing business in the form of a closely-held corporation. Arguably, therefore, since *Hobby Lobby any* physical act that is based on a sincerely held belief may be deemed by the courts to prevail over the benefits and rights of others. If doing business counts, it is difficult to imagine what would not.[13]

---

[10] See, e. g., *Torcaso v. Watkins* 1961; *United States v. Seeger* 1965; *Welsh v. United States* 1970; *Wisconsin v. Yoder* 1972; *Fleischfresser v. Directors of School District 200* 7th Cir. 1994, 688 n. 5. See also Usman 2007, 168–187.

[11] Courts and governmental agencies have been attempting to address whether even the Church of the Flying Spaghetti Monster (or Pastafarians) is a religion deserving of religious liberty rights. However, at least one district (trial) court has ruled that this church and its practices will not be recognized for the purposes of accommodation in prisons, as it is a "parody religion" (*Cavanaugh v. Bartelt* 2016).

[12] See *Kaufman v. McCaughtry* 7th Cir. 2005 and *Kaufman v. Pugh*, 7th Cir. 2013.

[13] *Hobby Lobby* was followed in 2015 by *Holt v. Hobbs*, a prisoner case in which the Supreme Court even more strongly applied RLUIPA's strict scrutiny analysis. The Court ruled in favor of a Muslim

At stake in *Hobby Lobby* was women's access to contraception, which had been provided as a benefit under the Patient Protection and Affordable Care Act (Obamacare) in 2010. However, religious liberty rights have come into conflict with other rights in additional unanticipated ways. Some original supporters of RFRA and RLUIPA did not consider that the two acts might be used to undercut recently achieved LGBT rights. But cases such as *Masterpiece Cakeshop v. Colorado Civil Rights Commission* (2018) have made it clear that, not only could religious exercise rights prevail over rights to contraception and abortion, but individuals who, due to their religious beliefs, did not want to provide services to homosexuals may sometimes prevail in the courts.

In addition, the Supreme Court has adopted an expansive approach to "substantial burden." In *Zubik v. Burwell*, the Court ruled that even a requirement that Catholic organizations submit a form to be *exempt* from providing contraception was a significant enough burden to require an accommodation. Thus, such organizations are not be required to take any action to further the provision of contraception by the government, not even submitting an exemption form.[14]

Such cases are part of a "rights revolution" that seeks promote the idea that religious rights should prevail over virtually all other rights within the public area (Lewis 2017). In the face of such efforts, some who had originally supported the passage of RFRA and RLUIPA have reconsidered their position, and have found common cause with others who had opposed such an expansion of "religious exercise" from the beginning.[15]

5. Conclusions and Implications of Recent Developments Concerning Religious Freedom

The broader definition of what is protected under RFRA and RLUIPA has had immense ramifications for religious liberty jurisprudence. It has in effect shifted the focus to regulations limiting religious expression rather than on the legitimacy of a given religion or its practices. Thus, the questions asked and the manner in which the courts respond has changed in significant ways. This shift seems to

---

man whose religious commitments included wearing a beard. In *Holt*, the Court was clear that religious accommodation rights would prevail over prison authorities' institutional concerns.

[14] The Supreme Court remanded the case to the lower court, instructing it to find an accommodation that would not require such action on the part of the Catholic organizations. Subsequently the Trump administration issued an Executive Order exempting such organizations from compliance with those contested provisions of the Act.

[15] University of Pennsylvania law professor Marci Hamilton had successfully argued the *Boerne* case before the Supreme Court. Her subsequent writings have made it clear that she is strongly opposed to the intent of RFRA and RLUIPA (Hamilton 2003, 2005) and thinks they are violative of the establishment clause.

mean in practice that practitioners in minority faiths are afforded more protections than was the case both pre- and post-*Smith*. Thus, from one perspective RFRA and RLUIPA have had a positive impact, contributing to the expansion of religious freedom for minority faiths in America.

However, the changes wrought by RFRA and RLUIPA have not all been positive from the perspective of the courts. The courts must assess a wide assortment of claims based on a religious belief or conviction, which has been made more difficult given the much broader scope of religious acts that are to be protected and given the Supreme Court's recent expansive application of the RLUIPA/RFRA definition of "religious exercise", as well as the Court's broader interpretation of "substantial burden." Courts must also continue to consider whether a compelling interest asserted by a governmental entity is valid. If a court determines that a compelling interest is valid, the courts must then assess whether the governmental entity has used the least intrusive means in resolving the dispute—a requirement that courts now often find has not been met unless an accommodation has been made.[16]

There are also longer-term implications of the implementation of RFRA and RLUIPA. The Protestant hegemony extant at the American founding had been in a process of gradual disestablishment over the course of the nineteenth and twentieth centuries (Green 2010 and 2019). Yet due to the "quiet revolution" referenced above (McGraw 2016), it seems clear that if RFRA and RLUIPA continue to function as they are now, the effect will be that the Protestant hegemony's remaining hold on American institutions and law will be diminished precipitately. As more minority faiths gain protections and are allowed to function openly in the United States, and as recognition of their beliefs and practices in governmental institutions require policy changes, the law and governmental policies will be uprooted from their origins in Protestant assumptions. Hence, not only will those assumptions no longer inform determinations of what constitutes legitimate religion, but also what constitutes legitimate laws may be called into question. For many this is a welcome development, resulting in the realization of the American trajectory toward a greater and greater inclusive America that embraces religious diversity. For others, this development is deeply concerning because they believe that the very foundations of the nation arise out of a Protestant Christian tradition that made the ideal of human rights possible: all are created equal because they are made in the image of God. And for yet others, the proliferation of religious exemptions to laws of general applicability are viewed as having the potential to make every person a law unto herself. These conflicting perspectives have been in play for decades (McGraw 2003), but they are even more exacerbated now due to and after the promulgation of RFRA and RLUIPA.

---

[16] This was the situation in *Zubrick v. Burwell* 2016.

Yet whether RFRA and RLUIPA continue to be the law of the land is an open question. The use of those laws in ways described above, which has allowed religious claims to prevail over equality concerns such as with the LGBT community, to excuse unpopular behaviors, or to limit access to contraception remedies, has soured many former supporters of those statutes. Further, application of the broad definition of "religious exercise" is increasingly being seen by some as unworkable. Such a definition may swallow whole nearly everything, making religious exemptions to government policy and law more and more commonplace, and thus policy and law only partially enforceable. There have been calls for the repeal of RFRA and RLUIPA. Indeed, the Supreme Court may be called upon to take actions that would limit the effect of those laws even if they remain (McGraw and Richardson 2020b).

What will happen to religious freedom over the coming decades in the United States is very much an open question. We await further efforts by Congress, the Executive branch, and the federal judicial system to grapple with the complex issues involved. Their future actions will determine how religious freedom will be defined and implemented in the future in the United States of America.

References

Cote, P. and J. T. Richardson (2001): Disciplined Litigation and "Deformation": Dramatic Organizational Change in the Jehovah's Witnesses. Journal for the Scientific Study of Religion 40, 11–25.

Davis, D. (2016). Completing the Constitution: Religion, Rights, and the Fourteenth Amendment, in: B. A. McGraw (ed.), The Wiley Blackwell Companion to Religion and Politics in the U.S., First Edition. New York: John Wiley & Sons, 213–234.

Department of Defense (2014): Instruction: Accommodation of Religious Practices Within the Military Services. Modifying Number 1300 17 February 2009. https://www.esd.whs.mil/Portals/54/Documents/DD/issuances/dodi/130017p.pdf Accessed January 12, 2020.

DeVuono, E. (2014): Accommodating Religious Liberties of Military Personnel: The Religious Liberty Amendments to the National Defense Authorization Act for Fiscal Year 2014. University of Louisville Law Review 53 (2): 327–350.

Gill, R. D. and Jelen T. G. The Religion Clauses in the Twenty-First Century: The Supreme Court Loosens its Grip, in: B. A. McGraw (ed.), The Wiley Blackwell Companion to Religion and Politics in the U.S., First Edition. New York: John Wiley & Sons, 401–415.

Green, S. K. (2010): The Second Disestablishment: Church and State in Nineteenth-Century America. New York: Oxford University Press.

Green, S. K. (2019): The Third Disestablishment: Church, State, and American Culture 1940–1975. New York: Oxford University Press.

Hamilton, M. (2003): Federalism and the Public Good: The True Story behind the Religious Land Use and Institutionalized Persons Act. Indiana Law Journal 78 (1), 311–361.

Hamilton, M. (2005): God versus the Gavel: Religion and the Rule of Law. Cambridge: Cambridge University Press.

Lewis, A. (2017): The Rights Turn in Conservative Christian Politics. Cambridge: Cambridge University Press.

McGraw, B. A. (2003): Rediscovering America's Sacred Ground: Public Religion and Pursuit of the Good in a Pluralistic America, Albany, NY: State University of New York Press.

McGraw, B. A. (2016): Religious Pluralism at the Crossroads, in: B. McGraw (ed.), The Wiley Blackwell Companion to Religion and Politics in the U.S., First Edition. New York: John Wiley & Sons.

McGraw, B. A. (2018): From Prison Religion to Interfaith Leadership for Institutional Change, in: Eboo Patel, Jennifer Howe Peace, and Noah Silverman (eds.), Interreligious/Interfaith Studies: Defining a New Field. Boston: Beacon Press, 181–193.

McGraw, B. A., and J. T. Richardson. 2020a. Religious Regulation in the United States in: P. Djupe, M. Rozell, and T. Jelen (eds.), Oxford Encyclopedia of Politics & Religion. New York: Oxford University Press, 1443–1467.

McGraw, B. A. and J. T. Richardson (2020b): Tolerance and Intolerance in the History and Implementation of RFRA(s) and RLUIPA, in: V. Karpov and M. Svensson (eds.), Tolerance and Intolerance in the History of Religious Liberty Jurisprudence in the United States and the Implementation of RFRA and RLUIPA. New York: Palgrave.

Mead, S. (1963): The Lively Experiment: The Shaping of Christianity in America New York: Harper and Row.

Richardson, J. T. (2017): Update on Jehovah's Witness Cases before the European Court of Human Rights. Religion, State & Society 45 (3–4), 232–248.

Richardson, J. T. (2014): In Defense of Religious Rights: Jehovah's Witness Legal Cases around the World, in: S. Hunt (ed.), Handbook of Global Contemporary Christianity. Boston: Brill, 285–307.

Richardson, J. T. and J. Shoemaker (2014): The Resurrection of Religion in the U.S.? "Sacred Tea" Cases, the Religious Freedom Restoration Act, and the War on Drugs, in: J. T. Richardson and F. Bellanger (eds.), Legal Cases, New Religious Movements, and Minority Faiths. Burlington, VT: Ashgate.

Usman, Jeffrey Omar (2007): Defining Religion: The Struggle to Define Religion Under the First Amendment and the Contributions and Insights of Other Disciplines of Study Including Theology, Psychology, Sociology, the Arts, and Anthropology. North Dakota Law Review 83 (1): 123–223.

Waldman, S. (2019): Sacred Liberty: America's Long, Bloody, and ongoing Struggle for Religious Freedom. New York: HarperOne.

Weiss, Jonathan (2019): Privilege, Posture and Protection "Religion" in the Law. Yale Law Journal 73: 593–623.

Wybraniec, J. and R. Finke (2004). Religious Regulation and the Courts: The Judiciary's Changing Role in Protecting Minority Religions from Majoritarian Rule, in: J. T. Richardson (ed.), Regulating Religion: Case Studies from around the Globe. New York: Kluwer, 535–553.

Cases cited

Burwell v. Hobby Lobby, 573 U.S. 682 (2014)
Cantwell v. Connecticut, 320 U.S. 296 (1940)
Cavanaugh v. Bartelt, 178 F.Supp. 3rd 819 (2016).
City of Boerne v. Flores 521 U.S. 507 (1997)
Church of the Lukumi Babalu Aye v. City of Hialeah, 508 U.S. 520 (1993)
Cutter v. Wilkinson, 544 U.S. 709 (2005)
Employment Division v. Smith, 494 U.S. 872 (1990)
Everson v. Board of Education, 330 U.S. 1 (1947)
Fleischfresser v. Directors of School District 200, 15 F.3d 680 (7th Cir. 1994)
Gonzales v. O Centro Espirita Beneficente Uniao do Vegetal, 546 U.S. 418 (2006)
Greene v. Solano County Jail, 513 F.3d 982 (2008)
Holt v. Hobbs, 574 U.S. 352 (2015)
Kaufman v. McCaughtry, 419 F.3d 678 (7th Cir. 2005).
Kaufman v. Pugh, 733 F.3d 692 (7th Cir. 2013).
Masterpiece Cakeshop v. Colorado Civil Rights Commission 584 U.S. (2018).
Sherbert v. Verner, 374 U.S. 398 (1963)
Torcaso v. Watkins, 367 U.S. 488 (1961)
Turner v. Safley, 482 U.S. 78 (1987)
United States v. Ballard, 322 U.S. 78 (1944)
United States v. Seeger, 380 U.S. 163 (1965).
Warsoldier v. Woodford, 417 F.3d 989 (9th Cir. 2005).
Wisconsin v. Yoder, 406 U.S. 205 (1972)
Zubik v. Burwell, 578 U.S. ___ (2016)

Statutes cited

Religious Freedom Restoration Act of 1993 (RFRA), 42 U.S.C. §2000bb
Religious Land Use and Institutionalized Persons Act (RLUIPA), 42 U.S.C. §2000cc

Abstract

The 1990 *Smith* decision of the United States Supreme Court altered long-standing case precedents offering protections for minority faiths. *Smith* made otherwise neutral laws applicable to religious practices even if they impinge on those practices. Congress responded in 1993 with the Religious Freedom Restoration Act (RFRA), reestablishing the right of exemption from neutral laws unless a compelling reason was justified and the least restrictive means was used to enforce said law. The Supreme Court then ruled that the Act could not be applied to state and local governments, but left RFRA intact for federal agencies. Congress then passed the Religious Land Use and Institutionalized Persons Act (RLUIPA) in 2000 which extended rights of religious freedom to land use (zoning) and "institutionalized persons", two areas heretofore left to state and local governments. RLUIPA's more expansive definition of "religious exercise" (also applicable to RFRA) has benefitted religious groups and even "closely held" corporations under RFRA. However, some backlash has developed against expanded religious freedom rights. How this controversy will play out in American society remains to be seen.

Backdoor Efforts to Advance Christianity in America during the Administration of Donald J. Trump

Derek H. Davis

While the United States of America was profoundly Christian at its founding, the eighteenth-century American Founding Fathers sought not to follow the historic assumption that successful nation-building depends upon the enshrinement of a common religion. Rejecting this fundamental principle, practiced in most societies for millennia, the American founders' sought to construct the relationship between the American order and religion on deeper principles of unity, order, and equality, all of which would be achieved, at least in part, by separating church and state.

As the founders pondered the place of religion in the American experiment, they deemed the past persecution, torture, and slaughter of human beings because of religious differences to be largely a product of government having too much power to dictate conformity to one particular religion. They sought a way to promote freedom of religion so that government might not infringe the religious consciences of its citizens. Freedom of religion meant allowing religion to go its own way, to refrain from cracking down on "heretical" beliefs – in short, to allow religious pluralism to flourish. Perhaps this kind of freedom might unify the American people rather than divide them; maybe they would learn to respect each other's freedom and unify under the banner of freedom. Moreover, Americans would perhaps appreciate being treated equally with respect to their assorted religious beliefs and this would further embed in the American order a strong and shared sense of unity. Separating church and state became the legal/structural tool to achieve these ends but the ultimate goals were unity, equality and a respectable culture of order that permeated both the public and private sectors.

Serious about embracing religious pluralism, the nation gradually became a haven for all kinds of religious groups that immigrated to America in unimaginable numbers. The tensions created by this commitment to religious pluralism were many. These tensions were real and persist to this day. Perhaps half of American society today still does not accept the notion that the Founding Fathers really sought to separate church and state–at least not in the way that the U.S. Supreme

Court sometimes claims. The emergence of the Christian Right in the latter part of the twentieth century, a powerful political movement that remains strong in the current era, is directly attributable to a deepening sense that America is turning away from its Christian roots and needs the power and influence of government to restore those roots before it is too late.

Since the inauguration of President Donald Trump in 2016, his Administration has embraced the notion that Christianity is the backbone of American culture and needs to be elevated to a higher position and role in American political life. Indeed much of Trump's so-called "base" is comprised of the Christian Right who see Christianity slowly losing its place of prominence in American life and much of his prospects for re-election in 2020 depend upon the support he garners from the Christian Right. Consequently, Trump has been active in advancing the goals of the Christian Right in his presidency. Few astute observers really believe that Donald Trump is motivated by anything approaching deep religious fervor in bonding with the Christian Right. Indeed, *New York Times*' Paul Krugman might be correct in observing that Trump must be the "least godly man ever to occupy the White House."[1] His ignorance of the Bible became clear when during his campaign run when he emerged as perhaps the only human being ever to quote from "Two" Corinthians, not the standard "Second" Corinthians. This is hardly what we should expect from one who, while applauding himself for finally being the president who would take on China in a trade war, looked to the heavens and declared himself to be "the Chosen One." But despite such pompous observations about himself (he also retweeted one follower's view that he was the "King of Israel"[2]), and no matter the depth of his religious beliefs, Trump is clearly an opportunist, and he operates shrewdly in aligning himself with a movement that encompasses perhaps as much as one-fourth of the entire American voting public.

We take a look now at some of the more brazen efforts by the Trump Administration to do an end run around the Establishment Clause, thus attempting to violate the Constitution's prohibition against advancing religion, in this case Evangelical Christianity, not always openly through the front door, but often craftily through the backdoor.

1. Trump's Anti-Muslim Stance

It is no secret that Trump has little regard for Muslims. As early as 2011, Trump asserted that President Barack Obama was secretly Muslim. In September 2015,

---

[1] Quoted in Steve Benin, "Facing Crises, Team Trump Takes Aim at the Church-State Line," *MSNBC Online*, October 15, 2019, www.msnbc.com.
[2] Toi Staff, "Trump Declares Himself to be 'The Chosen One,'" *The Times of Israel*, August 22, 2019, www.timesofIsrael.com.

at a campaign rally, a supporter claimed "We have a problem in this country; it's called Muslims," and asked, "When can we get rid of them?" In response, Trump stated: "We're going to be looking at a lot of different things,"[3] implying that he too thought Muslims were a problem and that he would act definitively to deal with the problem.

In November 2015, a year before he was elected to be president, on the MSNBC television program "Morning Joe," Trump said that America needs to "watch and study the mosques." Four days later, he stated that he would implement a database to track Muslims in the United States. Two days after that, he falsely claimed that "thousands and thousands" of Muslims cheered in New Jersey when the World Trade Center collapsed on September 11, 2001. These statements were followed incredibly by his December 7, 2015 declaration that America should ban all Muslims from entering the United States.[4]

On June 25, 2018, the U.S Supreme Court approved Trump's ban on the entry into the United States persons from five Muslim-majority nations: Iran, Libya, Somalia, Syria, and Yemen, as well as North Korea and Venezuela. The High Court, overruling earlier lower court decisions that struck down the ban, found that the Administration's concerns about state-sponsored terrorism in these countries did not violate U.S. Immigration law, that the ban was not necessarily aimed at Muslims, and that anti-Muslim rhetoric from Trump and others within his Administration did not violate the Establishment Clause ban on preferring some religions over others. This ban seems certain to remain in place for the duration of Trump's presidency.[5] He has spoken often of the need to expand the number of countries to which the ban applies.

Despite the Court's ruling, the Trump initiative *really is* a ban on Muslims entering the United States. Since the ban went into effect early in the Trump presidency, 98% of people from affected countries who applied for a visa were rejected, and the other 2% received a waiver, meaning they underwent a close vetting and were granted temporary entry. However, as one writer reports,

> "State Department information does not indicate how many of those 2 percent have received a visa for entry into the United States to date, and there have been lawsuits from potential immigrants who say they have been under waiver for at least 16 months without any resolution. … By contrast, North Korea and Venezuela did not experience a drop in visas issued – contradicting any notion that the travel ban wasn't a 'Muslim ban' because it included two non-Muslim countries."[6]

---

[3] Much of this section draws from an excellent article by Brian Klaas, "A Short History of Trump's Anti-Muslim Bigotry," March 15, 2019, www. https://www.washingtonpost.com.

[4] Ibid.

[5] "Trump Travel Ban: Supreme Court Allows Enforcement as Appeals Proceed," *The Guardian*, June 26, 2017, www.theguardian.com.

[6] Vahid Naiyesh, "Trump's Travel Ban Really was a Muslim Ban, Data suggests," *The Washington Post*, September 26, 2019, www.washingtonpost.com.

The Muslim travel ban is a backdoor establishment of Christianity because the Trump Administration has gotten away with discriminating against Muslims, contrary to what the Establishment Clause permits, by arguing that the countries to which the ban applies are "terrorist" countries. Yet everyone knows Trump wishes for America to be free of Muslims, and favorable to Christianity, which contradicts the Constitution's requirement that all religions be treated equally.

2. Charitable Choice

In the late 1990s, the U.S. government passed a set of measures that attempted to provide government funding of churches and other religious institutions that were willing to administer social service programs – soup kitchens, drug and alcohol rehabilitation programs, clothing pantries, homeless shelters, youth anti-crime programs, and the like. Theoretically, these programs advance secular ends, thus passing constitutional scrutiny. But they are a bold challenge to traditional, pre-1980 constitutional doctrine which held that churches, temples, mosques, and other houses of worship are "pervasively sectarian," which means that their mission and purpose is so pervaded by religion that it is virtually impossible for them to ferret out "secular" aspects of their activity.[7] This legislation, initially dubbed "Charitable Choice" because program beneficiaries under the legislation in which it was first adopted, the Welfare Reform Act of 1996, could choose either a government-funded religious or secular provider, challenged traditional "separationist" judicial interpretations of the Establishment Clause. Proponents of Charitable Choice advance the ancient fear that without government aid, religion will suffer, potential recipients of assistance will be ignored, and society will experience moral decline. Opponents counter with the argument that religion thrives best when it relies on private rather than government resources, and that morality is best fostered in a climate of self-sustaining voluntarism rather than government-sustaining inducements.[8] These are the same arguments that fueled the debate over "separation" ideals in the founding generation, but this time they were spurred by a new constitutional doctrine of "evenhanded neutrality."[9]

During the Administration of President George W. Bush (2000–08), an administrative office was created exclusively to further the Charitable Choice concept. The Office of Faith-Based and Community Initiatives was created by executive or-

---

[7] After *Mitchell v. Helms*. 530 U.S. 793 (2000), the "pervasively sectarian" principle has a precarious status in U.S. Supreme Court jurisprudence.

[8] On Charitable Choice legislation generally, see Derek Davis and Barry Hankins, eds., *Welfare Reform and Faith-based Organizations* (Waco, TX: J.M. Dawson Institute of Church-State Studies, 1999); and Sheila Suess Kennedy and Wolfgang Bielefeld, *Charitable Choice at Work: Evaluation Faith-Based Job Programs in the States* (Washington D.C.: Georgetown University Press, 2006).

[9] See Derek H. Davis, "A Commentary on the Supreme Court's 'Equal Treatment' Doctrine as the New Constitutional Paradigm for Protecting Religious Liberty," *Journal of Church and State* 46 (Autumn 2004): 717–737.

der and paid for out of general appropriations, thus skirting Congressional oversight. The office created satellite offices in twelve government departments which funded various faith-based projects around the country. While, according to one study, only 7.1 % of American congregations received any funding pursuant to the initiative,[10] the program awarded contracts to faith-based institutions averaging more than two billion dollars annually during the Bush years.[11] Nevertheless, one study showed that 98.6 % of funding went to Christian organizations, hardly the kind of nondiscriminatory treatment of religion contemplated by the Establishment Clause, indeed a funding program that can readily be labeled a "backdoor" Christian establishment.[12] One scholar opined that the program only placed social services in the hands of entities – churches and other faith-based organizations – that had borne the weight of providing social services in the nineteenth century. But he neglected to explain that those services were financed largely by the private sector, not by government.[13]

In the first month of his presidency that began in 2009, Barack Obama renamed the office: Office of Faith-Based Initiatives and Neighborhood Partnerships. He promised to make changes that would not entangle church and state, but no significant changes were made. On the campaign trail, Obama had pushed the idea that he would ban discriminatory hiring in faith-based programs, i. e., participating organizations would be unable to hire only its own in administering government-funded programs. But once he became president concerns arose that this would create chaos in some of the faith-based organizations, and many churches and other houses of worship would decline to participate.[14] Consequently, the rules that were in place during the Bush Administration years remained mostly in place during the Obama years.

On May 5, 2017, barely three months into his presidency, President Donald Trump signed an executive order to establish a new office at the White House called the Faith and Opportunity Initiative. Like the two similarly-named offices that preceded it, the office was created to empower faith-based organizations to actively engage in social programs that help the needy, albeit with government funds. The office was renewed a year later under a new executive order.[15]

---

[10] Ann Farris and Claire Hughes, Roundtable on Religion and Social Welfare Policy, "Durability of Bush Administration's Faith-Based Effort at Issue in 2008," January 8, 2008, www.religionandsocial policy.org/news/article_print.cfm?id=7551.

[11] Amy E. Black, Douglas L. Koopman, and David K. Ryden, *Of Little Faith: The Politics of George W. Bush's Faith-Based Initiatives* (Washington D. C.: Georgetown University Press, 2004).

[12] Davis, "A Commentary," 732.

[13] Marvin Olasky, *Compassionate Conservatism: What It Is, What It Does, and How It Can Transform America* (Glenove, Illinois: Free Press, 2000).

[14] No author, "President Obama's Faith-Based Initiative," Institutional Religious Freedom Alliance, www.irfalliance.org.

[15] Julie Moreau, "Civil Rights Groups Wary of Trump's Latest Faith-based Initiative," May 7, 2018, *NBC News,* www.nbcnews.com.

"The faith initiative will help design new policies that recognize the vital role of faith in our families, our communities and our great country," Trump said. "This office will also help ensure that faith-based organizations have equal access to government funding and the equal right to exercise their deeply held beliefs."[16]

But there were concerns. Some civil rights advocates feared it would result in discrimination against lesbian, gay, bisexual and transgender Americans. "This administration has continually promoted the troubling notion that religious freedom is a blank check to discriminate and harm others," Daniel Mach, director of the ACLU Program on Freedom of Religion and Belief, said. "This new initiative creates a bureaucratic regime and adopts policy preferences that will worsen that disturbing trend, he added." Mach cited "concerns about the new order's revocation of protections granted in prior executive orders that required service providers receiving government funds to refer beneficiaries to alternative service providers if the initial provider refused to perform certain services for religious reasons."[17]

Camilla B. Taylor, director of constitutional litigation at Lambda Legal, an LGBTQ advocacy group, noted that "even if a faith-based service provider is open to referring someone to an alternative provider, it can be difficult if the initial provider is the only one in the area. This was the case for a lesbian couple in Texas, who were denied the opportunity to foster a refugee child because they did not 'mirror the holy family.' Taylor added, "There is no other agency in that state that performs those services for refugee children." Lambda Legal is currently suing the Health Department on behalf of the couple. Taylor called Trump's executive order "worrying" and described it as "just the latest assault in a long-term battle that this administration is waging on the members of the LGBTQ community and women in need of reproductive health." She said the order constitutes an "invitation" for faith-based groups to apply for public funding, when they have no intention of serving all members of the public. It is an "unmistakable signal to religious organizations who take government money that they can discriminate without any repercussions whatsoever. It's open season," she added.[18]

While no figures are available, which is hardly surprising given the Trump Administration's tendency to hide any facts that do not support its agenda, there is every indication that the current Administration is continuing the pattern established by the Bush Administration to fund primarily, and perhaps almost exclusively, Christian groups. Arguably this is, once again, a "backdoor" establishment of Christianity.

---

[16] Ibid.
[17] Ibid.
[18] Ibid.

3. U.S. Government Agencies as Christian Advocate

On October 14, 2019, the U.S. State Department's website featured a photograph of Secretary of State Mike Pompeo alongside a headline, "Being a Christian Leader." It was removed the next day, presumably from complaints, but it does indicate the manner in which Pompeo sees his job: he seems to be saying he works for Christ, moreso than he works for the State Department or the American people. The website also promoted a recent speech delivered by Pompeo titled "Being a Christian Leader." He had delivered the speech days earlier to the American Association of Christian Counselors in Nashville, Tennessee. The speech trumpeted Pompeo's commitment as a Christian to handling his office in keeping with God's will and Biblical precepts. "I keep a Bible open on my desk, and I try every morning to try and get in a little bit of time with the Book," Pompeo proudly stated while describing his decision-making process. "We should all remember that we are imperfect servants serving a perfect God who constantly forgives us each and every day," he said.[19]

Not to be outdone by Pompeo, on October 19, 2019, another U.S. Agency head, Attorney General William Barr, who oversees the U.S. Justice Department, gave a notable speech at the University of Notre Dame in which he portrayed his fellow believers as a persecuted and beleaguered minority in America. He spoke critically of "the force, fervor, and comprehensiveness of the assault on religion we are experiencing today. This is not decay; this is organized destruction."[20] He added, "The campaign to destroy the traditional moral order has coincided and I believe has brought with it immense suffering and misery. And yet the forces of secularism, ignoring these tragic results, press on with even greater militancy."[21]

Barr's speech is part of an aggressive effort by the Justice Department to defend religious schools and businesses with their claims to religious liberty. But his program to defend religious liberty is heavily slanted toward preserving the so-called "right" of Christian individuals and groups. For example, in August 2019 the Labor Department took the position in a U.S. Supreme Court case that it is legal for employers to fire transgender employees based on the employer's religious beliefs. In March 2019 the Department of Health and Human Services issued a waiver to a foster care agency in South Carolina to deny services to same-sex and Non-Christian families. Positions like these help Christians overlook more unsavory aspects of the Trump presidency.[22] Rachel Laser, president of Americans United for Sep-

---

[19] Andrew Whalen, "State Department's Promotion of 'Being a Christian Leader' On Website Criticized for Potential Violation of Constitution," *Newsweek*, October 14, 2019, www.newsweek.com.

[20] Jeffrey Toobin, "William Barr's Wild Misreading of the First Amendment," *RSN* (Online), October 18, 2109, www.readersupportednews.com.

[21] Quoted in David Shortell, "Barr Slams Attacks on Moral Values, Says 'Moral Upheaval' Leading to Societal Ills," *CNN*, October 12, 2019, www.cnn.com.

[22] David Crary, "Trump Steadily Fulfills Goals on Religious Right Wish List," *AP News*, August 20, 2019, www.APNews.com.

aration of Church and State, expressed her concern: "It can't be religious liberty just for white evangelical Christians – it has to be religious liberty for all of us. We are witnessing divisiveness as Trump and his cronies and religious extremists all over the country continue to chip away at church-state separation."[23]

President Trump has also been very active in nominating judges to the federal courts. By early 2020, he had already nominated at least 150 judges, which is roughly on par with what past presidents have done in four-year terms, but he has appointed two Supreme Court judges, which exceeds what most past presidents have been able to accomplish, but rather remarkably, he has appointed about two times the number (43 total) of appellate judges appointed by most past presidents.[24] According to Lathan Watts, director of legal communications for First Liberty Institute, "the Supreme Court really only hears about one percent of the appeals that are filed in a year, and that means those circuit court of appeals' decisions end up typically being the final word on a case, so his nominees and then their confirmation to the circuit court of appeals don't always get the same sort of attention that maybe a Supreme Court pick does. But they are extremely important because, in most cases, their opinion ends up being the final opinion."[25] Many of these judges are evangelical Christians bent on stemming what to them appears to be the advance of progressive ideas and secularism under the guise of advancing religious liberty. This is Trump's way, not the American way. The American way powerfully advances the causes of pluralism and religious freedom for adherents of all religions, not just one.

4. Donald Trump and the Johnson Amendment

The Johnson Amendment, named after then-Senator Lyndon B. Johnson, who introduced the legislation in 1954, is a provision in the U.S. tax code that prohibits all 501(c)(3) non-profit organizations from endorsing or opposing political candidates. Section 501(c)(3) organizations are the most common type of nonprofit organization in the United States, ranging from charitable foundations to universities and churches.

Many conservative organizations and politicians, including President Donald Trump, have sought to repeal the provision, arguing that it restricts the free speech rights of churches and other religious groups. These efforts have been criticized because overturning the Johnson Amendment would effectively make political contributions tax-deductible. On May 4, 2017, Trump signed an executive

---

[23] Quoted in ibid.
[24] Caleb Parke, "Trump has Nominated over 125 Judges, Solidifying his Judicial Legacy," *Fox News,* July 15, 2019, www.foxnews.com.
[25] Quoted in ibid.

order "to defend the freedom of religion and speech" for the purpose of easing the Johnson Amendment's restrictions. The Johnson Amendment applies to any 501(c)(3) organization, not just religious 501(c)(3) organizations.

Contrary to Trump's assertions, repealing or modifying the Johnson Amendment is not about restoring free speech but is about permitting churches to donate (without losing their tax exemptions) to their favorite politicians in exchange for backing the churches' favorite political causes. Donations by individual citizens to politicians are generally nondeductible, but if the Johnson Amendment were repealed, donations would undoubtedly begin to pour into churches which could then use the money to support the churches' choices of political candidates or causes. This hardly promotes unity and order, but rather is a way to divide churches. Just imagine, for example, a pastor endorsing a particular candidate and only half of that church's members endorse that candidate. Can you imagine the divisiveness that would follow in churches whose greatest mission historically has been a spiritual message, not a political one? All of this was a concern to Congress in 1954 when it passed the Johnson Amendment because without it, churches would increasingly becoming political activists, thus mixing politics and religion in a way that is not consistent with America's tradition of separating church and state. But upholding one of America's greatest traditions is of no concern to Donald Trump. As First Baptist Church of Dallas pastor and presidential advisor Robert Jeffress said, "Thank God Trump understands there is no such thing as separation of church and state."[26]

President Trump frequently states falsely that he "got rid of" the Amendment, but despite his efforts and the aggressive lobbying to gut the Amendment, it remains on the books. Interestingly enough, one poll found that 66% of the American public expressed opposition to church endorsements of political candidates, thus endorsing the Johnson Amendment.[27] For now, the Johnson Amendment looks safe.

5. Donald Trump:
Does It Take a Christian to Mold a Christian State?

It is clear that Donald Trump strongly aligns himself and his political mission with the Christian Right. He claims to be a faithful Christian Presbyterian, a churchgoer. "I think people are shocked when they find out that I am Christian, that I am a religious person," Trump writes in *Great Again*[28], a book published

---

[26] Sky Palma, "Christian Evangelist James Robison: Trump is Ushering in 'the Greatest Spiritual Awakening in History,'" *Dead State*, September 17, 2019, www.deadstate.org.

[27] Gregory A. Smith, "Most Americans Oppose Churches Choosing Sides in Elections," *FactTank News in the Numbers*, sponsored by the PEW research Center, February 3, 2017, www.pewresearch.org.

[28] Donald J. Trump, *Great Again: How to Fix Our Crippled America* (New York: Simon And Schuster, 2016).

during his presidential campaign. "They see me with all the surroundings of wealth, so they sometimes don't associate that with being religious. That's not accurate."[29] But do the facts, his lifestyle, his rhetoric, not call this into question? Can a Christian be divorced three times; be accused of sexual abuse by at least twenty women; brag about being able to do anything you want with women, such as grabbing a woman's genitals, when you are a "star;" call every political opponent by his own, made-up, derogatory nickname (e. g., Crooked Hillary, Fake Pocahontas [Elizabeth Warren], Lyin' Ted [Senator Cruz], Slimeball James Comey, and Fat Jerry [Congressman Nadler]); be accused of more than 12,000 lies by the *Washington Post* over a 3-year period; and be seemingly totally biblically illiterate? Can his claim to follow Christ be taken seriously, or is it all just part of his political game?

United Methodist minister Martin Thielen, in an American newspaper, Herald Citizen, forcefully asks why so many members of the Christian Right support Trump, despite any evidence that would suggest any commitment by him to traditional Christian values: "A president who brags about sexually assaulting women and is credibly accused of doing so? It doesn't matter. A president who incites racism and white nationalism? It doesn't matter. A president who daily lies to the American people? It doesn't matter. A president who is a serial adulterer? It doesn't matter. A president who pays off porn stars? It doesn't matter. A president who uses fear and hatred to divide people rather than trying to unite them? It doesn't matter. A president who tears little children from their mother's arms? It doesn't matter. A president who is damaging America's reputation and relationships all over the world? It doesn't matter. A president who regularly curses in public, including taking the Lord's name in vain? It doesn't matter. A president who ravages the environment, destroying God's creation? It doesn't matter. A president who uses his charitable foundation for personal gain? It doesn't matter. A president who regularly mocks people, including unattractive women, a disabled reporter, and a teenage girl with Asperger's syndrome? It doesn't matter. A president who gives tax breaks to the rich and reduces help for the poor? It doesn't matter. A president who mistreats and maligns immigrants? It doesn't matter. A president who encourages foreign interference in our democratic elections? It doesn't matter. A president who admires ruthless, murderous dictators? It doesn't matter. A president who violates every value that Jesus taught and lived? It doesn't matter. Ever."[30] Given this laundry list of Trump's sins, it is indeed surprising that he has so much Christian support. Clearly, he is no model Christian.

---

[29] Daniel Burke, "The Guilt-Free Gospel of Donald Trump," *CNN Politics*, October 24, 2016, www.cnn.com.

[30] "Evangelicals and Trump," February 11, 2020, http://herald-citizen.com/stories/evangelicals-and-trump,40316?.

But not all Christians support him. Many, in fact, declare him not to be a Christian at all. *Christianity Today,* the flagship magazine for evangelicals, called Trump "an idolater" and "the very embodiment of what the Bible calls a fool." A Christian columnist said Trump's "obsession" with wealth and power "embodies a Nietzschean morality rather than a Christian one." The pope himself said that anyone who talks about building walls instead of bridges "is not Christian."[31] There are many, however, who believe him to be a real Christian, no matter how immature or backslidden. For example, "With Trump," says noted evangelical preacher James Robison, whom he calls a "devout Christian," "I think we can witness the greatest spiritual awakening in history, and one of the least likely people, many of you would say, will be used by God to accomplish God's will for the blessing and benefit of this nation."[32] My own sense is that most Christians are a bit unsure of what to think about Trump and his religious beliefs. But because he is a Republican and seems to stand for policy positions (e. g., anti-abortion and anti-homosexuality) they support, they stand behind him.

Many Christians have adopted the view that God Himself has chosen Trump to be president. This is the position of Focus on the Family's James Dobson. It is also the position of Christian thinker Lance Wallnau: Trump is a "modern-day Cyrus," an ancient Persian king chosen by God to "navigate in chaos."[33] As Tara Burton notes, "The comparison comes up frequently in the evangelical world. Many evangelical speakers and media outlets compare Trump to Cyrus, a historical Persian king who, in the sixth century BCE, conquered Babylon and ended the Babylonian captivity, a period during which Israelites had been forcibly resettled in exile. This allowed Jews to return to the area now known as Israel and build a temple in Jerusalem. Cyrus is referenced most prominently in the Old Testament book of Isaiah, in which he appears as a figure of deliverance."[34]

Even high-profile figures link Trump and Cyrus. During a visit to Washington, DC, Israeli Prime Minister Netanyahu heavily implied Trump was Cyrus's spiritual heir. Thanking Trump for moving the American embassy to Jerusalem, Netanyahu said, "We remember the proclamation of the great King Cyrus the Great – Persian King. Twenty-five hundred years ago, he proclaimed that the Jewish exiles in Babylon can come back and rebuild our temple in Jerusalem … And we remember how a few weeks ago, President Donald J. Trump recognized Jerusalem as Israel's capital. Mr. President, this will be remembered by our people throughout the ages."[35]

---

[31] Quotes are from ibid.
[32] Palma, "Christian Evangelist."
[33] Tara Isabella Burton, "The Biblical Story the Christian Right Uses to Defend Trump: Why Evangelicals are Calling Trump a 'Modern-Day Cyrus,'" *Vox,* March 5, 2018, www.vox.com.
[34] Ibid.
[35] Ibid.

While Cyrus was not Jewish and did not worship the God of Israel, he was "nevertheless portrayed in Isaiah as an instrument of God – an unwitting conduit through which God accomplishes his divine plan for history. Cyrus is, therefore, the archetype of the unlikely 'vessel': someone God has chosen for an important historical purpose, despite not looking like – or having the religious character of – an obvious man of God."[36] For Christians who subscribe to this narrative, Cyrus is an ideal historical antecedent to explain Trump's presidency: a sinning, nonbeliever who nevertheless served as a vessel to advance God's plans.

Burton adds: "This framing allows for the creation of Trump as a viable evangelical candidate regardless of his personal beliefs or actions. It allows evangelical leaders, and to a lesser extent, ordinary evangelicals, to provide a compelling narrative for their support for him that transcends the mere pragmatic fact that he is a Republican. Instead of having to justify their views of Trump's controversial past, including reports of sexual misconduct and adultery, the evangelical establishment can say Trump's presidency was arranged by God, and thus legitimize their support for him – a support that has begun to divide ordinary evangelicals and create a kind of 'schism.'"[37]

Burton summarizes thusly: "The Cyrus narrative allows evangelicals to thread a difficult rhetorical needle. It allows them to see Trump as 'their' candidate – a candidate who will effect God's will that America become a truly Christian nation – without requiring Trump himself to manifest any Christian virtues. He is, like Cyrus, anointed by God and thus has divine legitimacy (Trump's spiritual advisers, including evangelical figures Robert Jeffress and Paula White, have repeatedly hammered this point), but he has no obligation to live out Christian principles in his personal life."[38]

6. Conclusion

The classical idea of the separation of church and state resulted from the religious pluralism that was an outgrowth of the Reformation and the accompanying recognition that religion is perhaps more a matter of private conscience than public concern. The atrocities of the Middle Ages and the Reformation in which hundreds of thousands died in inquisitions, witch-hunts, and religious wars were thought to be the result of government having too much authority in matters of religion. The evolution of individual rights which began in earnest in the fourteenth century led human government, in the West at least, to abandon its previ-

---

[36] Ibid.
[37] Ibid.
[38] Ibid.

ous role of causing all people to conform to a common faith in favor of a new role of protecting individual rights, including the free exercise of religion.

America was the first nation to construct a constitutional framework that officially sanctioned the separation of church and state. It was a noble experiment in the founding era and remains so today. The experiment was undertaken by the framers in the hope it would enable America to escape the persecutions and religious wars that had characterized the Christian West since the emperor Theodosius made Christianity the Roman Empire's official religion in 380 A. D. The First Amendment's religion clauses have proved to be, in the words of John Courtney Murray, the celebrated Catholic theologian, John Courtney Murray, "Articles of Peace."[39]

For most of American history, religion of all persuasions has been accorded a greater respect in the United States than in any other civilized society. From America's earliest days, many religious leaders have strongly advocated the separation of church and state – for the protection of religion, for the protection of human conscience in religious matters, and for the efficient operation of civil government. The result has been a formal national commitment to the twin pillars of freedom: religious liberty and the separation of church and state. Donald Trump, however, more completely abuses the separation doctrine than any president in American history. Choosing to advance Christian ideals by all political means, some overt attempts, but more often attempts achieved by means of the "backdoor," Donald Trump is a danger to the sacred American ideals of freedom and democracy for all.

Abstract

Pursuant to the U.S. Constitution, the United States prides itself in separating church and state. But while the application of this basic principle is intended, at least in part, to free religious institutions from government regulation, the nation nevertheless regulates religion in multiple ways. Regulation, however, runs counter to Americans' abiding penchant for freedom. This essay explores ways, sometimes controversially, that the United States regulates churches and other religious institutions, despite the ever-present tensions that regulation presents in the face of a strong national commitment to religious autonomy.

---

[39] John Courtney Murray, *We Hold These Truths: Catholic Reflections on the American Proposition* (New York: Sheed and Ward, 1960), 45.

The Rise of Nationalisms in Bulgaria and their Impact on Religious Freedom

Some reflections about the interactions between national identity, nationalism, state and society, with minority religions or beliefs

Willy Fautré

1. Introduction

Nationalism is a concept that scholars have expressed divergent and even conflicting opinions on, resulting in a failure to reach a consensus on its definition. Nationalism often has a negative connotation when it is related to conflicts and various forms of social hostility, but it can also be a constructive tool in a collective identity-building process in other contexts.

Nationalism is a complex phenomenon and is often closely linked to national, ethnic or religious identity. Many scholars argue that there is more than one type of nationalism and that the word should be used in the plural instead of the singular as each form of nationalism is different, has its own ingredients and manifests itself in different ways.

When a state disregards diversity, otherness and inclusiveness without advocating for or using violence against specific religious groups or their members but does marginalize them, we have to do with some form of "soft nationalism". However, after a certain threshold of rejection of otherness, the intensity of the national identity professed by the State can lead to "aggressive nationalism".

Nevertheless, in both contexts there can be nationalist, political, cultural and social movements at work which lead to intolerance, hostility and acts of violence against persons and communal institutions or buildings.

In Bulgaria, nationalism is prevalent in extreme-right political parties and Orthodox movements which permeates other political parties and the whole society. This has led to the politicization of religion and an inflation in influence of the majority religion on politics. The rhetoric of the Bulgarian Orthodox Church is supported by a majority of the population which often leads to political activism and action. This then reinforces the church's position and societal values while simultaneously disregarding the specific needs of religious minorities.

My reflections will focus on the current negative impact of nationalism and nationalist movements on the lives of members of religious communities that are not mainstream in Bulgaria. They will cover the following issues:
- Nationalist and aggressive political forces behind the hostility towards non-Orthodox communities
- Religious freedom in Bulgaria: Constitutional and legislative framework
- The fight against discriminatory amendments to the Religious Denominations Act
- Social hostility against two religious communities: Muslims and Jehovah's Witnesses.

2. Nationalist and aggressive forces responsible for the hostility towards non-Orthodox communities

The UNITED PATRIOTS is a nationalist electoral alliance[1] that was formed in August 2014 by three political parties: the Bulgarian National Party (VMRO), the National Front for the Salvation of Bulgaria (NFSB) and ATTAKA. This coalition is part of the current government in Bulgaria. On 9 May 2018, they submitted a draft law designed to restrict the rights of non-Orthodox religions.

VMRO (Internal Macedonian Revolutionary Organisation) was a revolutionary national liberation movement in the Ottoman territories in Europe, that operated in the late 19th and early 20th centuries. Its founding theology is anti-Ottoman and so anti-Muslim. It was banned under Communism but was re-established as a right-wing political party in the 1990s.[2]

NFSB (National Front for the Salvation of Bulgaria) is a nationalist party that was established on 17 May 2011 in Burgas.[3] The party was a member of the Europe of Freedom and Democracy (EFD) group during the 7th European Parliament legislature.

ATTAKA asserts that it is "neither left nor right, but Bulgarian". It is considered ultranationalist, racist, anti-Semitic, anti-Roma, anti-Muslim and anti-Turkish.[4] It is closely tied with the Bulgarian Orthodox Church.

These are the main nationalist forces which threaten non-Orthodox minorities.

---

[1] Far right political party "United Patriots" worrying role in Bulgaria's EU Council presidency, ARDI, 13 October 2017 (accessed 20 September 2019) https://www.ardi-ep.eu/far-right-political-party-united-patriots-worrying-role-in-bulgarias-eu-council-presidency/.

[2] Internal Macedonian Revolutionary Organization, Encyclopedia Britannica, 1 October 2019 (accessed 21 October 2019) https://www.britannica.com/topic/Internal-Macedonian-Revolutionary-Organization.

[3] National Front fort he Salvation of Bulgaria, Revolvy (accessed 20 September 2019) https://www.revolvy.com/page/National-Front-for-the-Salvation-of-Bulgaria.

[4] Bulgaria's Ataka Party: An unlikely blend of lef tand right, Foreign Policy in Focus, 15 August 2013 (accessed 20 September 2019) https://fpif.org/bulgarias-ataka-party-an-unlikely-blend-of-left-and-right-2/.

3. Religious freedom in Bulgaria: The constitutional and legal framework

The constitution of Bulgaria[5] upholds freedom of religion or belief in Articles 13 and 37, which establish protections for all religions, recognise Eastern Orthodox Christianity as the "traditional religion" of the country and bans the use of religion for violent or political ends.

The main law regulating freedom of religion or belief is the Religious Denominations Act (2002), which provides measures for the legal recognition of religious denominations and communities. Registration is required for all groups if they want to engage in public worship. However, the Bulgarian Orthodox Church is exempt from the registration requirement due to its status as the traditional Church of Bulgaria.[6] There are currently 156 registered religious groups.[7]

In the last few years, there have been attempts by far-right nationalist political parties to reduce the rights of non-Orthodox communities and their members.

4. The fight against discriminatory amendments to the Religious Denominations Act

In May 2018, the three largest political parties in Bulgaria filed a proposed law that could have been used to hinder the religious activity of religious minorities.

On 11 October 2018, lawmakers approved on first reading changes to the Religious Denominations Act. In large part, the amendments to the law began as an attempt, among other things, to stem any influence from preachers of radical Islam in Bulgaria. The initial version of the law thus provided for several restrictions regarding funding of religious groups from abroad and participation of foreign clergy in religious rituals in Bulgaria. However, the amendments also significantly restrained the rights of minority faith groups by hampering theological schools, clergy training, missionary activity and free worship outside of designated buildings. One of the highly contentious clauses insisted on a denomination having at least 300 members to apply for official registration. Later on, the

---

[5] Bulgaria's Constitution of 1991 with Amendments through 2007, Constituteproject.org, 12 August 2019 (accessed 19 August 2019) https://www.constituteproject.org/constitution/Bulgaria_2007.pdf?lang=en.

[6] Religious Denominations Act', Legirel, Centre national de la recherche scientifique, Durzhaven vestnik n.120/29.12.2002 (accessed 9 September 2019) http://www.legirel.cnrs.fr/spip.php?article540&lang=fr.

[7] Bureau of Democracy, Human Rights and Labor, 'Bulgaria', International Religious Freedom Report for 2016, U.S. State Department (accessed 9 September 2019) https://www.state.gov/j/drl/rls/irf/religiousfreedom/index.htm#wrapper.

required membership number for official registration as a religious group was increased to 3,000![8]

This legislation would effectively limit the right to open religious schools and to train denominational ministers, as well as exclude religious communities consisting of less than 1% of the total population from State subsidies. Such a restriction would have discriminated against the Catholic Church (0.7%), the Protestant denominations (0.9% combined) and the Jewish community (only 700 members only). In fact, only the Orthodox Christian and Muslim communities have more than 1% of believers with 60% and 8% respectively.[9]

Paradoxically, the bill's proclaimed intent was to fight radical Islam,[10] but its first draft would have given more rights to this religion than to Catholics, Protestants and Jews.

It could be argued that the objective was to destroy non-Orthodox movements through law.

OSCE, US and EU institutions expressed serious concerns about the draft law.

4.1. National and international protests

Because these restrictions would be applied generally, this led to objections by other faith groups that would have been affected. Several faith groups also underlined that it was not appropriate to address a national security issue by rewriting the Religious Denominations Act.

Under this extreme threat, non-Orthodox believers of various faiths in Bulgaria united. Since the initial proposed bill was tabled, they have organized peaceful marches and protests with Bulgarian flags in front of the Parliament in Sofia and in many towns around the country.[11]

Statements of disagreement with the new legislation were also published by the World Evangelical Alliance (WEA), the European Evangelical Alliance (EEA), the World Methodist Council (WMC), the European Methodist Council (EMC), the Pentecostal European Fellowship (PEF), the Baptist World Alliance (BWA),

---

[8] 3,000 members required for a Bulgarian faith group to obtain judicial entity, Evangelical Focus, 22 November 2018 (accessed 10 September 2019) http://evangelicalfocus.com/europe/4017/Bulgaria_religion_law_3000_members_required_for_faith_group_to_obtain_judicial_entity.

[9] Great victory for religious freedom in Bulgaria, ACLJ, January 2019 (accessed 10 September 2019) https://aclj.org/persecuted-church/great-victory-for-religious-freedom-in-bulgaria?utm_source=Twitter&utm_medium=Informational&utm_content=Persecuted%20Church&sf96860237=1.

[10] Parliament criminalizes propagation of radical Islam on first reading, BTA Bulgarian News Agency, 6 December 2017 (accessed 20 September 2019) http://www.bta.bg/en/c/DF/id/1704807.

[11] Bulgarian Christians continue protests, Baptist Standard, 27 November 2018 (accessed 20 September 2019) https://www.baptiststandard.com/news/world/bulgarian-christians-continue-protests/.

the European Baptist Federation (EBF), and the Conference of European Churches (CEC).

4.2. The parliamentary debates[12]

On 21 December 2018, Bulgaria's National Assembly approved the second and final reading of amendments to the Religious Denominations Act that had been the subject of controversy since the first reading on 11 October 2018.

The version approved by Bulgaria's Parliament on 21 December designates state subsidies for denominations of more than 1% of the population according to the most recent census.

This means that state subsidies for the Bulgarian Orthodox Church and for Bulgaria's Muslims are guaranteed by the law approved on 21 December. However, subsidies may be voted on for other faiths at the discretion of the government and Parliament.

The amendments stipulate that where a state subsidy is used to pay clergy and employees of religious institutions, their salaries may not exceed the average monthly salary of a teacher.

Informal calculations showed that the Bulgarian Orthodox Church, which has four million believers, would receive 15 million leva (about 7.5 million Euro), while the Muslim community of 600,000 members would get 6 million leva (about 3 million Euro).

The law also requires faith groups to submit to the Cabinet's Directorate of Religious Denominations a list of houses of worship used for services annually, which the directorate will compile in a public register.

4.3. Rejected amendments of the far-right nationalist parties and their reactions

The United Patriots, which formed the minority partner in government, were displeased with the amendments to the Religious Denominations Act, especially regarding the rejection of their stricter proposals about state funding and property, as well as other provisions such as the ban on foreign funding.

Iskren Vesselinov said to reporters "Now we are giving millions, and at the same time taking from Turkey, to whom these people will be loyal."[13] This state-

---

[12] Bulgaria's Parliament approves second reading of Religious Denominations Act amendments, The Sofia Globe, 21 December 2018 (accessed 20 September 2019) https://sofiaglobe.com/2018/12/21/bulgarias-parliament-approves-second-reading-of-religious-denominations-act-amendments/.
[13] Ibid., xii.

ment refers to the country's Muslim minority, many of whom are of Turkish descent.

Yulian Angelov, a MP for the VMRO, said that the adopted funding formula within the law was an "insult" to the Church and was "subversive and anti-Bulgarian."[14]

Furthermore, their proposal to set a minimum requirement of having 300 Bulgarian citizens as members to allow formal registration of a religious denomination was voted down. A proposal placing the number at 3,000 was similarly rejected.

Another proposal compelling all religious denominations to fly the Bulgarian national flag outside their houses of worship was also rejected.

One minor victory for the extreme-right parties in Bulgaria was that the Parliament banned the use of loudspeakers and other sound devices by mosques to call their believers to prayer, except for major religious holidays and celebrations.

4.4. Conclusions

Thanks to the mobilization of national and international faith communities and human rights institutions, the main provisions violating freedom of religion were removed from the draft law voted on by the National Assembly of Bulgaria on 21 December 2018. This was a great victory for religious freedom in a member state of the European Union and a lesson for the future.[15]

5. Social hostility towards Muslims: Karaahmed v. Bulgaria at the European Court in Strasbourg[16]

A case filed with the European Court in Strasbourg clearly illustrates the role played by a far-right nationalist political party in the attack on a mosque in Sofia as well as the passivity of the police and the judiciary.

In March 2015, the European Court of Human Rights ruled that Bulgaria violated the right to religious freedom for Muslims by failing to properly investigate a clash between supporters of a far-right party and Muslim worshippers at a mosque in Sofia.

---

[14] Ibid.
[15] Ibid., ix.
[16] Case of Karaamed v. Bulgaria (Application no 30587/13), European Court of Human Rights, 24 May 2015 (accessed 27 August 2019) https://hudoc.echr.coe.int/eng#{"fulltext":["Karaahmed%20 v.%20Bulgaria"],"itemid":["001-152382"]}.

The European Court of Human Rights ruled in the case Karaahmed v. Bulgaria that the attack on this mosque in 2011, which authorities failed to prevent, resulted in a violation of Article 9 (freedom of thought, conscience and religion).

The court held the State responsible for its failure to protect the applicant, Veli Karaahmed, and other worshippers from stones and metal pipes thrown by demonstrators. It also criticized authorities' inadequate – and incomplete – investigation into the attack.

5.1. *The attack*

ATTAKA, a nationalist party in Bulgaria, began a campaign in 2006 against what it called the "howling" emanating from the loudspeakers of the Banya Bashi Mosque in Sofia. In May 2011, party supporters mounted loudspeakers on a car and circled close to the mosque, playing recordings of church bells and Christian chants during the regular Friday prayer that was taking place at the time.

During the next Friday prayer, ATTAKA organized a protest next to the mosque, which had been authorized by the mayor. Around 150 ATTAKA members and supporters, including party leader Volen Siderov and other high-ranking officials, gathered directly in front of the mosque near many worshippers.

Waving flags and banners with nationalist slogans, protesters shouted racist insults, including "filthy terrorists," "scum" and "Turkish stooges." One of the participants slowly cut a Turkish fez with a pocketknife while saying, "Can you hear me? We shall now show you what will happen to each one of you!"

The police allowed the demonstration to continue after protesters began hurling stones, wooden flagpoles and metal piping at the worshippers, and even setting fire to prayer rugs. Only after this violence was underway did officers intervene. Five Muslims, five policemen and one ATTAKA MP were injured in the clash, which was widely reported on and filmed by numerous media outlets.

5.2. *The ruling of the European Court of Human Rights*

The European Court of Human Rights ruled that the applicant and his fellow worshippers were victims of an infringement of their freedom to practice their religion as a result of ATTAKA demonstrators' actions, which the authorities failed to prevent.

In the court's view, given the racist views of ATTAKA on Islam and Muslims, it should have been clear to the domestic authorities what kind of demonstration would coincide with Friday prayers at the mosque. However, no concrete preventive steps to manage the situation were taken until after the demonstration had begun.

It could be argued that the objective of this demonstration was not only about the loudspeaker volume of the Friday call to prayer. The demonstrators voiced slogans that made plain their views of both ethnic Turks and Muslims living in Bulgaria. ATTAKA'S actions were not designed solely to express discontent at noise levels or even to express opposition to Islam but appear to be calculated to cause disruption to worshippers and provoke violence.

The inadequacy of the authorities' actions continued after the attack. The investigation into alleged preaching of religious hatred, opened on 25 May 2011, was still inconclusive nearly four years after the event. No progress had been made in identifying and charging those responsible for throwing objects and setting fire to prayers rugs, even though these individuals can be clearly seen on video recordings.

Finally, with the exception of one ATTAKA official, none of the individuals who took a leading role in the demonstration that day had been interviewed. Therefore, the investigation was an ineffective response to what happened.

The European Court awarded the applicant 3,000 euros for non-pecuniary damages.

5.3. Conclusion

This decision by the European Court was a strong warning for the Bulgarian law enforcement forces and the judiciary.

6. Abuses and restrictions of Jehovah's Witnesses' freedom of religion[17]

Several municipal authorities in Bulgaria have enacted and enforced unconstitutional local ordinances restricting the right to share one's beliefs in public spaces. Such abuses are regularly challenged in courts.

In March 2019, the Bulgarian Supreme Court of Cassation[18] (SCC) issued three separate decisions in favor of Jehovah's Witnesses. These rulings protected their civil rights and freedom of worship. However, this religious community continues experiencing difficulties from officials and private citizens when publicly sharing their faith in some cities.

---

[17] Source: Bulgaria, Religious Freedom Issues, Statement by the European Association of Jehovah's Witnesses at the OSCE/ ODIHR HDIM in Warsaw in September 2019, 20 May 2019 (accessed 29 September 2019): https://www.osce.org/odihr/hdim_2019.

[18] Supreme Court victories protect religious freedom for Jehovah's Witnesses in Bulgaria, JW.ORG, 20 May 2019 (accessed 20 September 2019) https://www.jw.org/en/news/jw/region/bulgaria/Supreme-Court-Victories-Protect-Religious-Freedom-for-Jehovahs-Witnesses-in-Bulgaria/.

Moreover, there are a few media outlets that continue to make slanderous comments about Witnesses, which harms their reputation.

6.1. Violations of the right to publicly share one's religious beliefs in 2019

a) On 5 January 2019, two municipal security officers in Kyustendil approached three Witnesses talking to others about their faith while using a portable literature cart. The officers asked them to show their official permit for the cart, even though a permit is not required by law. As the Witnesses did not have such a permit, the officers seized the cart.

The same Witnesses returned later in the day with another literature cart. Another municipality security officer arrived accompanied by an unidentified man who insulted them about their religious beliefs. The Witnesses called the police, but they allowed the municipal security officer to seize the second cart with its contents. The Witnesses filed a complaint with the prosecutor's office, which found that they had not violated the law and ordered that both carts and all of their literature be returned to them.

b) On 5 April 2019, three municipality clerks and a police officer in Targovishte approached three female Witnesses who were sharing their faith with others. The officials showed the women a municipal ordinance forbidding "advertising" of any religious organization. The three women were issued a notice for violating the administrative code and were then warned that they would be fined if the municipality received future complaints about them.

c) On 27 April 2019, a man shouted at two female Witnesses while they were sharing their faith with others in Targovishte. He called the police and when the officers arrived the Witnesses explained the purpose of their activity. The officers issued a written warning for violating the public order. They also threatened one of the Witnesses that if they received another complaint against her, she would be arrested.

d) On 10 May 2019, the Head of Department of Inspection No. 272 in Targovishte approached two Witnesses who were using a portable literature cart while talking to others about their faith. The official ordered the Witnesses to remove their cart, claiming that they were breaking the law, and requested that they pay a tax.

6.2. Legal battles against city councils' ordinances

In the first half of this decade, councils of more than 40 cities passed ordinances restricting the right to share one's beliefs.[19] Jehovah's Witnesses challenged many of them in local courts. Incidents of violence and administrative penalties esca-

---

[19] Bulgaria: Religious freedom concerns, Office of General Counsel at World Headquarters of Jehovah's Witnesses, Religious freedom concerns: Statement by the European Association of Jehovah's

lated the most in Burgas, likely because it is the city where the nationalist party National Front for the Salvation of Bulgaria (NFSB) was established in 2011.

On 4 June 2016, in Burgas, Nikolai Stoyanov was standing by a small literature display on a public street and offering religious publications to passersby. Police charged him with violating the municipal ordinance and fined him.[20] Similar incidents had taken place in previous months with the same result. The Witnesses challenged the constitutionality of this ordinance and won their cases at the Regional Court of Burgas.

In 2013, NFSB proposed amendments to the ordinance, alleging that some members of the community were disturbed by Witnesses' religious activity in public spaces. The district governor reviewed the amendments and concluded that they were discriminatory. They then issued an order declaring them unconstitutional. However, the next district governor revoked that order, and the city council passed those amendments. The Burgas Ombudsman warned the city council that the new regulations were unlawful, but they remained in effect until the Burgas Regional Court invalidated them in 2016.

Similar incidents occurred in Kyustendil, and the Administrative Court there overturned six criminal rulings and fines imposed on Witnesses for allegedly illegal religious activities. On 24 June 2016, the same court declared the amendments made to the ordinance to be unconstitutional.

Since then, the prosecution of Jehovah's Witnesses has diminished but has not disappeared. In some cities, Witnesses are still threatened and intimidated when publicly sharing their faith with others.

7. Social hostility towards Jehovah's Witnesses[21]

The main drivers behind aggressions targeting Jehovah's Witnesses in Bulgaria are: political and social hostility, stigmatizing media campaigns and police passivity. A few incidents are outlined below:

7.1. Violent incidents and legal battles against the far-right VMRO

On 1 July 2018, in Nova Zagora, two Jehovah's Witnesses, Tatyana Borisova Aleksandrova and Maria Isabel de la Mata Palomino de Lopez, were walking down

---

Christian Witnesses, Organization for Security and Cooperation in Europe, 13 September 2017 (accessed 29 September 2019) https://www.osce.org/odihr/340956?download=true.

[20] Will Bulgarian courts uphold religious freedom? JW.ORG, 14 February 2017 (accessed 28 September 2019) https://www.jw.org/en/news/legal/by-region/bulgaria/will-bulgarian-courts-uphold-religious-freedom/.

[21] Ibid., xx.

the street when a young man punched them. Both of the women were bruised and distressed after the assault. Two days later, they filed a complaint with the police that included the address of the attacker as it was not his first aggression. The authorities did not prosecute him.

On 23 December 2017, in Vratsa, three Witnesses, Tasho Tashev, Krasa Tasheva and Yuha Hyvenen, were at a cart displaying their publications in Macedonia Square in the city centre. Two men associated with the extreme-right nationalist movement Internal Macedonian Revolutionary Organisation (VMRO), Momchil Yankov and Martin Ivanov, began mocking them. One of the Witnesses filmed the escalating situation on her phone and informed the men that they were being recorded. The men shouted threats of violence, used abusive language and made false allegations against the Witnesses. The Witnesses lodged a complaint against these two members of the VMRO.

In 2019, the Supreme Court ruled in favor of Witnesses against VMRO in a case of violence which occurred eight years earlier. On 17 April 2011, Jehovah's Witnesses gathered to commemorate the Memorial of Jesus' death. An aggressive mob of 60 people, organized by the leader of the VMRO Georgi Drakaliev, brutally attacked the Witnesses. The mob inflicted some injuries, and the victims brought this incident to the courts. The case eventually came before the Supreme Court which, on 20 March 2019, ruled against Drakaliev. He must now compensate the Witnesses.

7.2. Stigmatization by the media

Online media has continued to stigmatize Jehovah's Witnesses and publish libelous articles against them.

On 23 May 2019, *Uniconbg* published an article with photographs of Witnesses sharing their beliefs, accusing them of illegally occupying the area where they were carrying out their religious activity.

On 1 April 2019, an online newspaper called *Provaton* called Jehovah's Witnesses a "sect" and claimed that they had deprived local children of the opportunity to practice sports. In reality, the Witnesses had rented the local sports hall for a religious meeting.

On 22 March 2019, *Paragraf 22* posted an online article presenting a negative image of Jehovah's Witnesses.

On 18 May 2018, Petya Petrova posted a stigmatizing article on the website of *Struma* (https://www.struma.com/) and publicized the address of where the Witnesses met. Soon after, vandals smashed the windows of the building, causing the owner to cancel his rental contract with the Witnesses. A follow-up article in the same online paper claimed that the owner had evicted the Witnesses.

7.3. Legal battles against hate speech

In March 2019, the SCC, the highest court of the country, issued favorable rulings in three cases involving Jehovah's Witnesses.[22] Two of the cases involved slander from media outlets.

In 2014, *SKAT TV* began broadcasting news reports and television programs slandering Witnesses. On 9 February 2015, Witnesses filed a complaint with the District Court of Burgas, claiming moral damages from *SKAT TV* and its journalists for inciting religious hatred. On 18 March 2019, the SCC ruled in favor of the Witnesses, stating that *SKAT TV*'s statements were defamatory and went beyond the right of freedom of expression. It ordered *SKAT TV* to pay material and moral damages as well as all court costs.

In 2012, the newspaper Vseki Den published a libelous article against Witnesses. They filed a civil lawsuit with the Sofia Regional Court but lost their case in all lower level courts. They then appealed to the SCC. On 26 March 2019, basing its decision on its previous ruling in the *SKAT TV* case, the SCC ruled in favor of the Witnesses and awarded non-pecuniary damages.

8. Conclusions

Far-right nationalist movements are a constant threat to non-Orthodox religions, especially Muslims and Jehovah's Witnesses. These targeted religious minorities are at the forefront of the legal fight against the intolerance, hate speech and human rights violations perpetrated by vicious political parties. Fortunately, Bulgarian courts are increasingly demonstrating their independence and distancing themselves from these racist and xenophobic organizations. The future of democracy and the rule of law in Bulgaria is in their hands.

Abstract

Since the collapse of Communism in Bulgaria, freedom of religion of belief and non-discrimination, which implies equality of rights for ALL, has always been a battlefield for nationalist forces.

In Bulgaria, nationalism is prevalent in anti-Muslim extreme-right political parties and some Orthodox movements but it also permeates other political parties and the whole society. This has led to the politicization of religion and the increased intrusion of the Orthodox Church in politics. Its aggressive rhetoric targeting religious minorities of foreign origin fuels social and political hostility as well as discrimination.

---

[22] Ibid., xviii.

This paper focuses on the current negative impact of nationalism and nationalist movements on the lives of members of religious communities that are not mainstream in Bulgaria. It addresses four major topics:
- The identification of nationalist and aggressive political forces behind the hostility towards non-Orthodox communities
- Religious freedom in Bulgaria: Constitutional and legislative framework
- The fight against discriminatory amendments to the Religious Denominations Act
- Social hostility against two religious communities: Muslims and Jehovah's Witnesses.

Russia's Religious Empire, non-Rational Power and Pussy Riot

Jukka Korpela

1. The Insult of Pussy Riot

The female collective of artists *Pussi Rayot* (Pussy Riot) made a prayer (*moleben*) performance, *Bogoroditsa, Putina progoni* (Virgin Mary, Put Putin Away), in Moscow's Christ Cathedral on 21 February 2012 and prayed to the Mother of God for her protection of the country against Putin.[1]

The artists were arrested for hooliganism (Russian Criminal Code, Art. 213). Three members were sentenced to two years in prison for the violation of religion (blasphemy). The decision was very harsh.[2] Scholars argue that popular support for the severe punishment reflects the crystallisation of a new Russian normative system characterised by the symbiosis of state and church. Popular analyses have stressed Putin's personal offence at the attack.[3] I seek to analyse the proceedings in the light of the long historical tradition of the Muscovite state power.

The debate has ranged from gender issues, theological details to totalitarianism, political protests and dissident tradition.[4] The case is still alive. *The New York*

---

[1] http://www.youtube.com/watch?v=VtYw-d1CSxQ, http://pussy-riot.livejournal.com/12442.html. Translation into English: http://freepussyriot.org/content/lyrics-songs-pussy-riot. Cf. *Rachel L. Schroeder / Vyacheslav Karpov*, The Crimes and Punishments of the "Enemies of the Church" and the Nature of Russia's Desecularising Regime, in: Religion, State & Society, 41:3: 2013, 292.

[2] http://www.russian-criminal-code.com/PartII/SectionIX/Chapter24.html, *Volha Kananovich*, "Execute Not Pardon": The Pussy Riot Case, Political Speech, and Blasphemy in Russia Law, in: Communication Law and Policy 2015, vol. 20:4, 343–422.

[3] *Schroeder / Karpov*, The Crimes (note 1), 284–311.

[4] Ibid., 293–294, 296–297, *Anna-Marie Korte / Helen Zorgdrager / Katya Tolstaya*, Introduction to the Special Issue of Pussy Riot's Punk Prayer, in: Religion & Gender, 4:2, 2014, 93–99, *Katharina Wiedlack / Masha Neufeld*, Lost in Translation? Pussy Riot Solidarity Activism and the Danger of Perpetuating North/Western Hegemonies, in: Religion & Gender, vol. 4:2, 2014, 151–162, *Kananovich*, Execute (note 2), 347–351, 377–383, 422, *Vera Shevzov*, Women on the Fault Lines of Faith: Pussy Riot and the Insider/Outsider Challenge to Post-Soviet Orthodoxy, in: Religion & Gender 2014, vol. 4:2, 121–144, 131–135, *Cécile Vaissie*, "Black Robe, Golden Epaulettes": From the Russian Dissidents to Pussy Riot, in: Religion & Gender 2014, vol. 4:2, 166–183, *Anna Agaltsova*, Collective Female Identities in Discussions about Pussy Riot's Performance, in: Religion & Gender 2014, vol. 4:2, 185–193, 197, *Nicholas Denysen-*

Times interviewed one of the participants, who explained the case as a warning against Donald Trump's presidency.[5]

The Moscow Church of Christ the Saviour is the official site of state cult. Its wall paintings declare the Thousand-Year-Old union between Russian rulers and church starting from the ancient Kievan Rurikids. The relics of St. Vladimir, the Baptist of Russia, were displayed in the church in 2010.[6]

The act took place on the *soleas*. The artists had their backs to the iconostasis. Perhaps the actors should have been standing on the other side of the Holy Doors and facing the icon of the Virgin Mary, but otherwise the performance was a correct *moleben*. Only as an adaptation of a song sung by the assembly the only minor mistake is the lay person on the *soleas*. Symbolically it is important that sermons are spoken and the gospel read on the *soleas*. The author is aware of Orthodox theological language, and uses adaptations from church texts.[7]

The date of the performance was 21 February (the eighth in the Julian Calendar). This day is the end of the Feast of the Presentation of the Lord (*Stretenie Gospodne*), which belongs to the period of preparation for (Great) Lent. In this year Lent started on 26 (13) February and so the 21st was the Tuesday of the *maslenitsha* week.[8] This period is dedicated to repentance and religious appeals to God.

Traditionally the message of the Russian rock artists has supported the ruling elite. Their music is political and it has had much to do with Russianness.[9] The Orthodox religion and Slavic history have been themes.[10]

---

ko, An Appeal to Mary: An Analysis of Pussy Riot's Punk Performance in Moscow, in: Journal of the American Academy of Religion 2013, vol. 81: 4, 1061–1092.

[5] The New York Times: A Warning for Americans From a Member of Pussy Riot. Dec. 4, 2016.

[6] *Adele Marie Barker*, Rereading Russia, in: Consuming Russia. Popular Culture, Sex, and Society since Gorbachev. Edited by Adele Marie Barker, Durham / London 1999, 4, *Graeme Gill*, Symbolism and Regime Change in Russia, New York 2013, 200–201, *Wiedlack / Neufeld*, Lost (note 4), 149–150, *Denysenko*, An Appeal (note 4), 1063–1068, *Jukka Korpela*, Holy Russia – the Image of a Thousand-Year-Old Russia as a Tool in Governance, in: Religion – Staat – Gesellschaft. Seit fünfzehn Jahren 21. Jahrhundert – Umbrüche in Gesellschaften und Religionen angesichts neuer politischer und kultureller Herausforderungen Herausgegeben von Gerhard Besier / Hubert Seiwert. Zeitschrift für Glaubensformen und Weltanschauungen 2014, 15:1–2, 209–210, 214–220, Komsomol'skaya Pravda, 21–22.11.2015, p. 5.

[7] Shevzov, Women (note 4), 127–130, *Korte / Zorgdrager / Tolstaya*, Introduction (note 4), 97–98, *Wiedlack / Neufeld*, Lost (note 4), 153, *Denysenko*, An Appeal (note 4), 1062, 1069, 1071–1072.

[8] Pravoslavnyi cerkovnyi kalendar' 2012, Moskva 2011, 36–37, *Wiedlack / Neufeld*, Lost (note 4), 152.

[9] *Julia P. Friedman / Adam Weiner*, Between a Rock and Hard Place: Holy Rus' and its Alternatives in Russian Rock Music, in: Consuming Russia (note 6), 110–137.

[10] *Friedman / Weiner*, Between (note 9), 127–131.

2. Sources of Power in Russia

"Power is the capacity to get others to do things that otherwise they would not do".[11] Legitimacy grants the right to use power and is therefore a resource for power. Despite David Beetham's justified criticism concerning the Weberian concept of legitimacy, for a historian it is enough to think that domination is not possible without a legitimation.[12]

According to Max Weber's typology of power, rational power relies upon laws, traditional upon customs and charismatic upon the leader's personality.[13] Michael Mann has developed this idea to divide the sources of power into four categories: ideological, economic, military and political (the IEMP model). These sources never exist in pure form and their roles differ from one period of time, situation and culture to another.[14]

Soft power is an important dimension of control. Unfortunately, scholars have monopolized it today for traditional diplomatic and other non-military methods of the power use. Historically this concept is much more important for the description of ideological and religious legitimation discussions. I use the term by this way.[15] American brands distribute American hegemony today, because Americanisation means a silent legitimisation of the USA's use of power.[16] Shared ideas are key factors influencing the creation of a sense of right and wrong, from religious fundamentalism to political legacy.[17] In the Cold War period weapons were a core source of power, but this era also saw the heavy ideologisation of everything, leading to the increasingly ideological legitimation of political acts.[18]

Globalisation has limited the options for using power, because nobody is able to control markets. Mann calls the development of weapons technology a lethal boomerang, because it has come up against the planet's limits.[19] The success of capitalism may result in climate change, which limits the possibilities of economic sources of power.[20]

---

[11] *Michael Mann*, Globalizations, 1945–2011. The Sources of Social Power. Volume 4, New York 2013, 1, *Martin A. Smith*, Power in the Global Order. The US, Russia and China, Cambridge 2012, 3–7, 13–14, 33.

[12] *Smith*, Power (note 11), 18, 25–33, *David Beetham*, The Legitimation of Power. Issues in Political Theory, London 1991, 7–11.

[13] *Smith*, Power (note 11), 26, *Max Weber*, Wirtschaft und Gesellschaft: Grundriss der verstehenden Soziologie. Fünfte, revidierte Auflage, besorgt von Johannes Winckelmann, Tübingen 1972, III: 1, 4–5 (pp. 122–124, 140–148).

[14] *Mann*, Globalizations (note 11), 1–2.

[15] I am aware about the theoretical discussion of the soft power (by Joseph S. Nye and others). I use the concept as a tool to understand the practical approach of the Russian administration.

[16] *Smith*, Power (note 11), 21–23.

[17] *Smith*, Power (note 11), 24–25.

[18] *Mann*, Globalizations (note 11), 11,13, 30–36.

[19] *Mann*, Globalizations (note 11), 3, 5–7, 361.

[20] *Mann*, Globalizations (note 11), 361–362.

Moral control is one 'soft' option for using power. There has been much talk about taxation on international financial speculation and regulations against tax evasion. The movement against globalisation and criticism of the market economy has increased.

The medieval period marked the climax of ideological power, implying a unanimous doctrine propagated and control exercised by a centre that owned the channels for distributing the ideology, i. e., Christendom. The reason was the lack of logistical means for controlling huge areas. Although religion has mattered much later, 'ideological power' lost its importance in the late Middle Ages, because economic growth led to the rise of coordinating states.[21] According to Mann, ideological power is a response to the development of the other three power sources. It becomes important when the old structure has collapsed.[22]

Ideology is a device to promise justice to the people. Due to the 'boomerang effect' the influence of other types of power source has recently declined, but the nature of ideology as a power source is different, because it has no fixed form and therefore it cannot reach its limits.

Many scholars view networked power as a new phenomenon demonstrated during the Arab Spring of 2011. It crosses borders and works through social networks such as Twitter and Facebook.[23] Anyhow, the medieval ideological power worked also through networks. Friars, priests and individual Christians distributed it. Networked power is one of the traditional methods of soft power, but it is not a form or source of power.[24]

3. The Traditional Myth of Holy Russia

Sergei Uvarov, the Minister of Nicholas I, declared in 1832 that the Russian nation is identified with *pravoslavie* (Orthodox Christianity), *samoderzhavie* (autocracy) and *narodnost'* (nationality). He placed the story of a Thousand-Year-Old Russia at the heart of Russian nationalism, which is a hybrid construction of nationalism and religious missionarism, and this influenced school curricula from then on.[25]

---

[21] *Michael Mann*, A History of Power from the Beginning to A.D. 1760. The Sources of Social Power. Volume 1. New Edition, New York 2012, 22–24, 301–302, 306–307, 376–390, 416–446.
[22] *Mann*, Globalizations (note 11), 1–2.
[23] *Smith*, Power (note 11), 11–13.
[24] About reach, *Dick Harrison*, Skapelsens geografi. Föreställningar om rymd och rum i medeltidens Europa. Svenska Humanistiska Förbundet, 110, Stockholm 1998, 50–56, *Jukka Korpela*, The World of Ladoga – Society, Trade, Transformation and State Building in the Eastern Fennoscandian Boreal Forest Zone ca. 1000–1555. Nordische Geschichte, 7, Berlin 2008, 203–205.
[25] *Nicholas V. Riassonovsky / Mark D. Steinberg*, A History of Russia. Seventh Edition. New York/Oxford 2005, 302–303, 316, 325–326, *Tobias Köllner*, Patriotism, Orthodox religion and the education: empirical findings from contemporary Russia, in: Religion, State & Society, 44:4, 2016, 367, *Korpe-*

Many scholars deny the uniqueness of Russia and try to explain it in a western mental context.[26] According to Judith Deutsch Kornblatt not all Russians find their identity in the Orthodox Church. Relative support for the church in comparison to evangelical movements and other faiths declined even during the 1990s.[27]

Yet the point may be found in the chaos of the styles and trends so typical for the transition periods of Russian history.[28] The turbulent chaos of the Yeltsin era was short-lived, and soon the new foreign phenomena received a genuine Russian glocalisation. One must also avoid considering the year of 1991 as a watershed, seeing the Soviet Union as a unique phenomenon and speaking about a common CIS post-Soviet religious legacy.[29]

The Russian Orthodox Church and its symbiosis with the Muscovite state is a unique phenomenon in history since the 14th century. The Church has not this status in other CIS countries. Although Russia was multi cultural and multi religious empire, it was also a holy empire as a power formation and not only an ephemeral state, and the Soviet Union continued the tradition with a salvation story that consumed patriotic Russian history. This is also the core aspect today in the Russian power as well as in the Muscow-Kievan-Constantinople discussions about the independent Ukrainian Orthodox Church.[30]

There are also everyday facts which contradict the denial of the Holy Russia concept. The 'multi-vocal Russian Church and Christians' of sociological questionnaires and the share of the population who are church-goers are not the key to church-state relations. To be Orthodox is not a rational choice of world view or a commitment to a rational teaching like the membership of a congregation is for

---

la, Holy (note 6), 218–219, *Marlène Laruelle,* Russian Eurasianism. An Ideology of Empire, Baltimore 2012, 41, 71–72, cf. *Elena Chebankova,* Civil Society in Putin's Russia. BASEES Series on Russian and East European Studies 87, Oxon 2013, 85–86, *Geoffrey Hosking,* Empire and Nation-Building in Late Imperial Russia. Russian Nationalism, Past and Present. Edited by Geoffrey Hosking and Robert Service. School of Slavonic and East European Studies, University of London, London 1998, 19.

[26] *Irina Papkova,* The Contemporary Study of Religion, Society and Politics in Russia: A Scholar's Reflections, in: Religion, State and Society, 41:3, 2013, 244–253.

[27] *Judith Deutsch Kornblatt,* "Christianity, Antisemitism, Nationalism": Russian Orthodoxy in a Reborn Orthodox Russia, in: Consuming Russia (note 6), 414–416, *Eliot Borenstein,* Suspending Disbelief: "Cults" and Postmodernism in Post-Soviet Russia, in: Consuming Russia (note 6), 439–456.

[28] *Barker,* Rereading Russia (note 6), 5–14.

[29] *Irina, Papkova,* The Orthodox Church and Russian Politics, New York 2011, 2–4, 11–12, *Jerry G. Pankhurst / Alar Kilp,* Religion, the Russian Nation and the State: Domestic and International Dimensions: an Introduction, in: Religion, State and Society, 41:3, 2013, 226–227, *Alicja Curanović,* The Post-Soviet Religious Model: Reflections and Relations between the State and Religious Institutions in the CIS Area, in: Religion, State and Society, 41:3, 2013, 330–351.

[30] *Smith,* Power (note 11), 128–129, *Jukka Korpela,* Ukraine: Historical notes on reunification of the Russian lands, in: Gerhard Besier / Katarzyna Stokłosa (eds.), Neighbourhood Perceptions of the Ukraine Crises: From the Soviet Union into Eurasia? London/New York 2017, 248–252, *Kananovich,* Execute (note 2), 378, *Jane Burbank / Frederick Cooper,* Empires in World History. Power and the Politics of Difference, Princeton and Oxford 2010, 1–22.

many Western Christians. Clerical and Orthodox language are part of political argumentation and the Orthodox identity is part of a Russian's self-understanding as a human being. Orthodox wording is central in the lyrics of Russian rock music, the use of Church Slavonic letters is common on the shirts of national sports teams, and Orthodox symbols are used in nationalistic circles and even in the tattoos of high ranking criminals.[31]

The Cathedral of Christ the Saviour is an enormous investment, which the ordinary church-goers do not need. The re-erection of the Church of the Resurrection Gate in Moscow's Red Square merely creates an obstacle for traffic. They are both political demonstrations.[32]

Yeltsin issued a law permitting only registered religions. Putin started the rebuilding of 'patriotic Russia', affirmed the church-state relationship and stabilised society with new laws, which reached the final form in the 'Yarovaya law' of 2016.[33] The Patriarch described Putin as a miracle of God, President Medvedev called the Russian administrative system common rule by state and church, President Putin evaluated Crimea as the Temple Mount of Russia and called Christianity "a powerful spiritual unifying force" that created the Russian nation and state.[34]

The boost to the cult of the Baptist of *Rus'*, Prince Vladimir, has been significant. His relics 'travelled' through Russian in the millennium year of his death 2015 and people participated in the cult in the main cathedrals of Russia. The President has also a Church of St. Vladimir built near his cottage on the archipelago of Valaam. The provocative St. Vladimir statue was erected just outside of the Moscow Kremlin in the neighbourhood of the Savior's cathedral in November 2016. It declares the submission of Kiev and Ukraine to Moscow.[35]

The sacralisation of the monarch is old tradition in Russia. The religion legitimises the rule and God's grace guides him. Therefore rulers play a permanent role in church proceedings; President Putin was at the airport welcoming the cincture of the Mother of God on loan from Mount Athos in October 2011.[36]

The ruler's honour (*slava*) constitutes his reliability, authority and legitimacy. A great leader is fearsome and has *groza*. Since late medieval Muscovy these two

---

[31] *Friedman / Weiner*, Between (note 9), 111–137, *Nancy Condee*, Body Graphics: Tattooing the Fall of Communism, in: Consuming Russia (note 6), 343–347, *Deutsch Kornblatt*, Christianity (note 27), 417–420.

[32] *Gill*, Symbolism (note 6), 200–202, cf. *Kananovich*, Execute (note 2), 378–379.

[33] *Deutsch Kornblatt*, Christianity (note 27), 414, *Borenstein*, Suspending (note 27), 438, *Arto Luukkanen*, Projekti Putin: uuden Venäjän historiaa 1996–2008, Helsinki 2008, 212–214.

[34] Cf. below p. 000, *Kananovich*, Execute (note 2), 422.

[35] *Korpela*, Holy (note 6), 223, Komsomol'skaya Pravda, 21–22.11.2015, 1, 5, https://www.theguardian.com/world/2016/nov/04/vladimir-great-statue-unveiled-putin-moscow.

[36] *Kananovich*, Execute (note 2), 378–382, 422, *Francis Fukuyama*, The Origins of Political Order. From Prehuman Times to the French Revolution, London 2012, 391–392, 427, *Basil Lourié*, Russian Christianity. The Blackwell Companion to Eastern Christianity, 2007, 213, *Gill*, Symbolism (note 6), 2–5.

concepts legitimise the ruler's position better than constitutions or single laws, because they show how the ruler is the God-given shepherd of his people.[37]

The Russian atmosphere is, however, not as Byzantine as the nationalists declare and scholars believe. The actions of the Russian Orthodox Church should not only be evaluated in a dogmatic Orthodox context. Islamic influence has been strong since early medieval times, the Tatarian conquest increased this after the mid-13th century, and Muscovy was, until the late 17th century, more like a Khanate than a European realm. This influence is visible in the communality of Russianness and in the Russian concept of law.[38]

Western medieval scholasticism led to rationalism, which separated philosophy and jurisprudence from theology, while in Orthodox Christian and Islamic culture, divine wisdom was reached in holistic philosophy (Hesychasm and Illuminationism), which presents the truth in mystic allegories and forms of rhetoric. That is why there is no jurisprudence in the east but God, law and wisdom are parts of one phenomenon which is impossible to define, but can be felt.[39] Therefore one should not evaluate the role of religion today by the level of theological education or church attendance. Religion is a part of identity.[40]

Later the culture of enlightenment also did not have much influence on Russian society; individuals never superseded collectives, nor did rationalism overcome mysticism. The Russian mental landscape thus differs from the western one, and it is misleading to analyse it by western rationalism and standards.[41]

The combination of the western concepts and opinions of the western-minded intelligentsia in Saint Petersburg and Moscow is potentially misleading, as it can

---

[37] *Jaakko Lehtovirta*, Ivan IV as Emperor. The Imperial Theme in the Establishment of Muscovite Tsardom, Turku 1999, 239–243.

[38] *Michael Khodarkovsky*, Russia's Steppe Frontier: The Making of a Colonial Empire, 1500–1800, Bloomington 2002, *Charles J. Halperin*, Russia and the Golden Horde. The Mongol Impact on Medieval Russian History, Bloomington, 1985, *Jukka Korpela*, Zwischen einer Gemeinschaft und einer Gesellschaft: Verbindungen zwischen dem russischen "zakon" und einem "östlichen" Reichsdenken, in: Das Gesetz – The Law – La Loi (hrsg. von Andreas Speer). Miscellanea Medievalia 38, 2014, 53–71, *Matthew P. Romaniello*, The Elusive Empire. Kazan and the Creation of Russia 1552–1671, Madison 2012, passim, *Michael Cherniavsky*, Khan or Basileus: An Aspect of Russian Medieval Political Theory, in: Journal of the History of Ideas 1959, 20:4, 464–473, *R. G. Landa*, Islam v istorii Rossii, Moskva 1995, 10–20, 59–63, Gail Lenhoff, Rus'-Tatar Princely Marriages in the Horde. The Literary Sources, in: Russian History 2015, vol. 42:1, 16–31, Jukka *Korpela*, "Abwesende Meister" – Islamische Verbindungen der russischen Gelehrten im späten Mittelalter, in: Vestnik tverskogo gosudarstvennogo universiteta. Seriya istoriya, 2/2018, 4–16.

[39] *Toshiko Izutsu*, Ishrāqīyah, in: The Encyclopedia of Religion. Ed. Mircea Eliade. London, Volume 7, 1987, 296–301, *Kallistos Ware*, Eastern Christianity: Hesychasm. in The Encyclopedia (note 39), Volume 4, 1987, 567, *Korpela*, Zwischen (note 38), 53–56.

[40] *Kananovich*, Execute (note 2), 379, cf. also *Schroeder / Karpov*, The Crimes (note 1), 301–308, *Smith*, Power (note 11), 124–127, *Deutsch Kornblatt*, Christianity (note 27), 415.

[41] Like *Korte / Zorgdrager / Tolstaya*, Introduction (note 4), 96, *Paul Dukes*, The Russian Enlightenment. The Enlightenment in National Context. Edited by Roy Porter / Mikuláš Teich, Cambridge 1981, 188–191, and below p. 84–85, 87, 90–91.

create a western illusion of the reality.[42] The main difficulty with many analyses is their close linkage to the western style political controversies between liberals and conservatives and to the ethos of civil society.[43] According to Smith and other scholars, modern Russia neither uses nor needs soft power. They see the power of Putin's regime as pragmatic, since it stresses sovereignty and the presidential administration does not seek ideological support.[44] However, an image of the bare-chested president riding on polar bear in a picture on a fan shirt is a serious message, but not to members of a western democratic society. The discourse of 'enchurchment' (*votserkovlenie*) means the idea of assimilating society and the state into the church.[45] Its counterpart is the union of the state and church. These are internal discussions about the integration of Russians into power structures.

4. Eternal Truth vs. Empirical Truth

Aleksey Khomiakov admired the internal harmony and togetherness of the Russian peasant society, or *mir'*, described this with the term *sobornost'* and saw in it the idea of Christian catholicity or universality (Greek *katholike*).[46] Nationalists, like Uvarov, idolised the *mir'* and absorbed the concept *sobornost'* into their ideology. The *sobornost'* referred to the togetherness of the members of the *mir'*, their loyalty towards each other and to their leaders.[47] Individuals had no independent value and their autonomous opinions were more of a threat than an asset to the system. Social control encouraged individuals to choose the same opinion as a sign of good behaviour, in order to avoid any threat of violence or revenge. This is still a key element in the modern political system, which stresses the collectivity of Russianness.[48] The concept of *mir'* is close to the Muslim *umma*. Collectivity is also one of the most central characteristics in modern Russian Eurasianist ideology.[49]

---

[42] Cf. *Papkova*, The Contemporary (note 26), 246–249, *Françoise Daucé / Marlene Laruelle / Anne le Huérou / Kathy Rousselet*, Introduction: What Does it Mean to be a Patriot? in: Europe-Asia Studies 67:1, 2015, 1–7.

[43] *Schroeder / Karpov*, The Crimes (note 1), 284–311, *Papkova*, The Orthodox (note 29).

[44] *Smith*, Power (note 11), 124–129.

[45] *Shevzov*, Women (note 4), 135–136.

[46] *Paul L. Gavrilyuk*, Georges Florovsky and the Russian Religious Renaissance, Oxford 2013, 225–231, cf. *Köllner*, Patriotism (note 25), 371.

[47] Cf. *Fukuyama*, The Origins (note 36), 391–393, 399–401, 426–428.

[48] *Igor Chubais*, Ot Russkoi idei – k idei Novoi Rossii, kak nam preodolet' ideinyi krizis, Moskva 1996, 22–36, 44–46, *Schroeder / Karpov*, The Crimes (note 1), 288, *Christer Pursiainen*, Venäjän idea, utopia ja missio. Ulkopoliittisen instituutin julkaisuja nro 6, Helsinki 1999, 15–17, *Irina Karvonen*, Pyhän Aleksanteri Syväriläisen koulukunta–1500-luvun luostarihistoriaa vai 1800-luvun venäläiskansallista tulkintaa? Joensuu 2013, 2–3.

[49] *Tat'yana Andreevna Bulgakova*, Azovskie pokhody Petra I v kontekste filosofii russkoi kul'tury. Avtoreferat dissertatsii. Leningradskogo gosudarstvennogo oblastnogo universiteta: Sankt-Peterburg 2012, 17–18, *Agaltsova*, Collective (note 4), 195–199.

Archpriest Vsevolod Chaplin commented for the press on President Dmitriy Medvedev's and Patriach Kirill's visit to the exhibition on Orthodox *Rus'* on 7 November 2011. In his opinion, the president was right to use the word 'symphony' to describe the relationship between church and state, and this word should not be side-lined, because Russian society is largely made up of Orthodox Christians. According to President Medvedev the traditional values of the state must be promoted. The Orthodox Church is the keeper of these values.[50]

The Greek concept of symphony, meaning a common or the same voice or sound, is central to Orthodox theology in the sense of parish/church unanimity, Christian togetherness and loyalty to the bishop. The idea received legal formulation in the sixth century (Justinian's Novellae VI) in the sense of the common rule of emperor and church; the emperor/king protects the true faith and God blesses the earthly dominion of the ruler. This ideology formed the core of the entire European power system until the late High Middle Ages.[51]

This ideology lost its significance in the west with the development of jurisprudence (natural law) and rational philosophy, leading to the concept of territorial absolute princely power. Today, the church and state are two different organisations in west.[52] Yet the link survived in east, because the state formation took place with a monastic colonisation and not with laws and castle networks. The concept of symphony was introduced into Muscovite law in the Stoglav Council of 1551. The Russian ruler is both a political and a religious (ideological) leader.[53]

According to Weber's categories, the leader is a charismatic ruler in the sense that his power is absolute and based on his ideological position. On 8 February 2012 Patriarch Kirill described the rule of Vladimir Putin as "a miracle of God".[54] In September of the same year, Putin called members of the opposition "weak birds

---

[50] The Russian Orthodox Church will continue creating "symphony" with the state-priest. (http//www.interfax-religion.com/?act=documents&div=218).

[51] *Jukka Korpela*, Prince, Saint and Apostle–Prince Vladimir Svjatoslavič of Kiev, his Posthumous Life, and the Religious Legitimization of the Russian Great Power. Veröffentlichungen des Osteuropa-Institutes München, Reihe: Geschichte, 67, Stuttgart 2001, 13–16.

[52] *Mann*, A History (note 21), 416, 437–440, *Fukuyama*, The Origins (note 36), 245–275.

[53] *Hannan Hunt*, Byzantine Christianity (chapter 4). The Blackwell Companion to Eastern Christianity. Edited by Ken Parry, Oxford 2007, 78–79, *Lourié*, Russian (note 36), 213, Stoglav, edited by E. B. Emchenko, Issledovanie i tekst, Moskva 2000, § 62, *I. U. Budovnits*, Monastyri na Rusi i bor'ba s nimi krest'yan v XIV–XVI vekakh (po zhitiyam svjatykh), Moskva, 1966, 112, 259–260, *Jukka Korpela*, The Christian Saints and the Integration of Muscovy, in: Russia Takes Shape. Patterns of Integration from the Middle Ages to the Present (ed. S. Bogatyrev), Annales Academiae Scientiarum Fennicae, 335, 2005, 44–56, *Kristina Stoeckl*, Community after Totalitarianism. The Russian Orthodox Intellectual Tradition and the Philosophical Discourse of Political Modernity. Erfurter Studien zur Kulturgeschichte des Orthodoxen Christentums 4, Frankfurt am Main 2008, 20.

[54] http://uk.reuters.com/article/2012/02/08/uk-russia-putin-religion-idUKTRE81722Y 20120208, http://theorthodoxchurch.info/blog/news/2012/02/russian-orthodox-patriarch-kirill-calls-putin-era-a-miracle-of-god/, cf. also *Shevzov*, Women (note 4), 125, *Wiedlack / Neufeld*, Lost (note 4), 150, *Kananovich*, Execute (note 2), 378–379.

which do not know how to follow their leader".⁵⁵ A good ruler knows the truth and guarantees the salvation of his subjects.

The story of a unified Holy Russia after the Baptism of St. Vladimir (988/989 AD) was created in Moscow from the 14th century. It legitimated the Muscovite conquests and has been an instrument to wield power ever since, because it declared the unity and uniqueness of Russia (*samobytnost'*).⁵⁶ The honour of ruler, fatherland and army are seen as holy and inviolable values. This sacrosanct history must be presented in the right way. The history of the Russian realm and church have been linked together to form one story. The criteria for the right history are confirmed today by law.⁵⁷ A symbol of this common historical interpretation is Moscow's Cathedral of Christ the Saviour.

5. Minorities are Enemies

The different development of philosophy and state power in the east explains the problematic role of the opposition and minorities. Since the High Middle Ages, western philosophy has been based on a *pro et contra* argumentation and opposing opinions have formed the cornerstone of scientific, political and legal thinking. In the east the ruler knows the truth and law and his grace is the guarantee of justice and peace. A different opinion is an enemy force and indicates the presence of the devil. The concept of *raskol'* (split) describes this state of affairs, and is always a negative concept.⁵⁸

When the opposition leader Aleksey Naval'nyy was given a five year prison sentence as a result of an unclear embezzlement case with the Kirov Timber Company, the spokesman for the Russian police explained on 18 July 2013 that the case was re-opened because Naval'nyy had irritated the authorities, which would be totally an absurd argument in a Western rule-of-law society.⁵⁹

The aim of the Orthodox canons (church law) is to achieve symphony (unanimity) in the church community. Repentance means a reorientation after a transgression of norms. Confession means acceptance and submission to the

---

⁵⁵ http://www.reuters.com/article/2012/09/09/us-russia-putin-opposition-idUSBRE88804R20120909.

⁵⁶ *Korpela*, Ukraine (note 30), 244–252, *Korpela*, Holy, (note 6), 215–220, *Köllner*, Patriotism (note 25), 371.

⁵⁷ http:/minobrnauki.fi/novosti/3485(A Press relies of Russian ministry of education July 2, 2013 "Nachalos' obshchestvennoe obsuzhdenie proekta istoriko-kul'turnogo standard"), http://minobrnauki.fi/dokumenty/3483 (A project document of Ministry July 1, 2013 "Rabochaya gruppa po podgotovke kontseptsii novogo uchebno-metodicheskogo kompleksa po otechestvennoy istorii: Istoriko-kul'turnyy standard"), *Korpela*, Holy (note 6), 212–213, *Köllner*, Patriotism (note 25), 367.

⁵⁸ *Korpela*, Zwischen (note 38), 54, 67, *Korpela*, Holy (note 6), 228.

⁵⁹ http://www.nytimes.com/2013/07/19/world/europe/russian-court-convicts-opposition-leader-aleksei-navalny.html?pagewanted=all&_r=0.

Divine Logos, i. e. the law. The very concept of canons is that they are medicine. They help an errant person to re-orientate to the right path.[60] Because the priest is the shepherd who knows what is best for his flock, he is the prosecutor, judge and law in one person. When the person accepts the punishment and declares his/her acts to be wrong, the medicine takes effect and the person can return to the community. Unanimity is re-established. This understanding of the law is contradictory to the western one.

Cécile Vaissie's idea of connecting the Pussy Riot performance to traditional dissidents like Alexander Solzhenitsyn relies heavily on conspiracy theories. Those, who stress the multivocal character of the modern Russian church do not understand the different character of the opposition in Russia.[61] Opposition movements (such as Judaizers, Non-Possessors, or Old Believers) have existed throughout Russia's entire history, and priests like Feodosiy Pecherskiy (d. 1074), Nil Sorskiy (d. 1508), Maksim Grek (d. 1556), Avvakum Petrov (d. 1682) and Georgiy Gapon (d. 1906) have been in conflict with the ruler. Stalin's relationship with the church and patriarch did not differ much from that of Ivan IV (d. 1584). The position of the KGB was also close to the role of Ivan's *oprishchnina*.

The Russian church serves mystic rituals and is symbiotic with the ruler, similarly to the role of Islam in Muslim countries but totally dissimilar to that of Western Christianity.[62] Although the patriarch and prelates are present in politics, they are not independent social, political and cultural contributors to the debate in the way their western colleagues are. The opposition has never influenced political decision making or church support for the state. Therefore it also does not matter today what individual believers feel, what the nature of current theological debate is, or what kind of people are working in the church. Among the many voices, only the official one counts. The same must be said of the ruler, because, as a member of the collective society, the head of state does not have the freedom to act individually, as most western observers automatically seem to assume. This is typical for all 'Big-Man-Societies'.[63]

Patriarch Kirill said in an interview on 28 January 2013: "There is a real danger of rejecting Christ, rejecting the Orthodox faith. If there is no faith – there is no Russia." The Patriarch listed anti-Christian phenomena as hostility to religion and anti-church actions, campaigns against Christian symbols and insults against the church. He mentioned that such campaigns against Christian symbols in public

---

[60] *John Chryssavgis*, Repentance and Confession in the Orthodox Church, Brookline 1990, 3–9, *Michael Pomanzansky*, Orthodox Dogmatic Theology, Platina (Ca.) 1994, 286–288.

[61] *Vaissie*, Black Robe (note 4), 166–183, *Papkova*, The Orthodox (note 29), 9–10, 18–20, *Elena Volkova*, Mater Nostra: The Anti-blasphemy Message of the Feminist Punk Prayer, in: Religion & Gender 2014, vol. 4:2, 204–205, *Korte / Zorgdrager / Tolstaya*, Introduction (note 4), 97.

[62] *Fukuyama*, The Origins (note 36), 264–272, 279–280.

[63] Cf. *Gerhard E. Lenski*, Power and Privilege. A Theory of Social Stratification, New York 1966, 107–110, 127–128, 135.

places are witnessed in European countries. The criticism of the western pluralism is interesting in relation to President Medvedev's opinion about 'symphony'.[64]

In the early 1990s politicians and the Russian elite were very concerned about foreign faiths, viewing them as a threat to Russia from abroad. In July 1993, foreign missionaries were banned from working. The new counter terrorism law ('Yarovaya law') submits the society under a strong control and stops all non-Orthodox religious work in public.[65]

Foreigners have traditionally been a challenge for Russians, because they have new opinions, which threaten unanimity. A western democratic system is difficult, because critical comments concerning the ruler are viewed as insulting and criminal. This results in a different understanding of civil society, which has the support of the people, however, as the statistics of Schroeder and Karpov show.[66]

In 2009, Patriarch Kirill encouraged celebrating the birthday of Saint Prince Aleksandr Nevskiy (12 June), "the heavenly protector of Russia against the western threat", as a national holiday unifying compatriots in Russia and abroad. The Ulema of the Muslim spiritual directorate of Russia Damir Mukhetdinov supported the proposal because of "St. Aleksandr's union with the Golden Horde". Prince Aleksandr was the Grand Prince of Vladimir who defeated the German and Swedish Crusaders in 1240 and 1242, and is the traditional protector against the western heresies.[67]

In open access orders, which describe the modern western type of political society and state according to Douglass C. North *et al.*, NGOs play a central role in political decision making in civil society. They can easily become political actors and affect the political process with their own agenda.[68] These societies are supposedly based on a mass citizenry and not on elites, unlike Russia, which is a "mature natural state", according to North's taxonomy.[69]

---

[64] http//www.interfax-religion.com/?act=documents&div=218, http//www.interfax-religion.com/?act=documents&div=218), Korpela, Holy (note 6), 215, 223–224, 228–231.

[65] *Borenstein*, Suspending (note 27), 437–439, *Schroeder / Karpov*, The Crimes (note 1), 299, http://www.garant.ru/news/782190/.

[66] *Korpela*, Holy (note 6), 228–231, *Schroeder / Karpov*, The Crimes (note 1), 301–302, *Mihail Korostikov*, Russian Youth and Opposition. A paper at BASEES European Congress "Europe: Crisis and renewal", 5–8 April 2013 Fitzwilliam College / Churchill College, Cambridge, United Kingdom.

[67] http://www.interfax-religion.ru/?act=news&div=29357, http://windowoneurasia.blogspot.fi/2009/03/window-on-eurasia-patriarchs-call-for.html. More about Aleksandr's ideological message: *Jukka Korpela*, Święty Aleksander Newski i jego zwycięstwa nad Newą (1240 r.) oraz na jeziorze Pejpus (1242 r.). Wizerunek bohatera widzianego przez pryzmat polityki, in: Wojna, pamięć, tożsamość. O bitwach i mitach bitewnych. Pod redakcją Jana M. Piskorskiego, Warszawa 2012, 248–271.

[68] *Douglass C. North / John Joseph Wallis / Barry R. Weingast*, Violence and Social Orders. A Conceptual Framework for Interpreting Recorded Human History, New York 2009, 117–118.

[69] *North / Wallis / Weingast*, Violence (note 68), 31, 118.

In Russia, NGOs have been linked to the state administration and have been subject to the Public Chamber (*Obshchestvennaya Palata*) since 2005.[70] The present regime has declared NGOs which have contacts abroad to be foreign agents, because they can transmit ideas and learning which differ from the traditional truth. They must therefore register their work. The restrictions on foreign faiths and NGOs goes together with the tightening legal controls on freedom of speech and independent mass media and the criminalisation of "offending religious feelings".[71]

The Orthodox 'therapeutic' theological interpretation does not view human rights as individual, indivisible, universal, absolute and equal as in the west. The starting point is human value as the image of God. Human rights are intended to increase the divine value of the human person (divinisation, or *theosis*). Because sin destroys this, human rights mean the right to lead a life according to church doctrine. Thus human rights are contextualised, depending on an authority and its opinions, and thus subject to the ruler and society. The modern Russian state follows this line; the ruler is the guarantor of human rights. The criticism by the Russian Ministry of Foreign Affairs concerning the violation of human rights in the EU in January 2014 was a logical action from this perspective.[72] This way of thinking denies any justification of the performance of the Pussy Riot, considering it as contrary to the peace of the ruler and urges the artists to repent.

6. Holy Russia is Global Today

The new Russia took on the international responsibilities of USSR as its successor state, and the Russian Federation came to be the protector of Russians living in the former Soviet republics, which it called the 'near abroad'. Now the first post-Soviet years have passed, many of these Russians no longer consider Russia as their homeland.[73] This means that Russia need to intensify its message in order to renew its ability to wield power in this way. This is also why citizenship and passports are still a live issue between Russia and Ukraine in spring 2019.

---

[70] *Chebankova*, Civil Society (note 25), 83–85, *Françoise Daucé*, NGOs in Russia: between political control and public incentives. A paper at BASEES 2013.

[71] *Kananovich*, Execute (note 2), 372–376.

[72] http://www.mid.ru/bdomp/nsdgpch.nsf/03c344d01162d351442579510044415b/44257b1000 55de8444257c60004a6491, *Alfons Brünning*, Human Dignity versus other dignities – Controversial statements of Orthodox theology on human dignity and rights and western reactions. A paper at BASEES 2013, *Kristina Stoeckl*, The appeal to 'morality clauses' in international human rights instruments in the human rights discourse of the Russian Orthodox Church. A paper at BASEES 2013, *Kristina Stoeckl*, The Russian Orthodox Church and Human Rights, London/New York 2014, passim.

[73] *Lowell W. Barrington / Erik S. Herron / Brian D. Silver*, The Motherland is Calling. Views of Homeland among Russians in the Near Abroad, in: World Politics 55 (January 2003), 390–313.

Metropolitan Hilarion of Eastern America and New York appealed to American Orthodox Christians on 19 June 2013 on the celebration of the 1,025th anniversary of the Baptism of *Rus'*. He stated that all Orthodox Christians are citizens of Holy Russia, which is not the same as the Russian Federation but a community of all Orthodox Russians around the world. Since the Russian Orthodox Church had risen from the ashes after communism, the Russian church abroad was to reanalyse its role.[74]

This argumentation is an expansion of the concept of the near abroad, but also its essential confirmation. If we keep in mind the discussion about 'symphony' and how the state regime has supported this view, this becomes the official policy of the Russian state and is in accordance with the Kremlin's concerns about the cultural and private affairs of Russians abroad. This conceptualisation of Holy Russia resembles the Jewish identity. They both define themselves as global actors according to nationality and religion.[75]

Holy Russia forms a power network for the Kremlin to extend its global influence. Therefore the memory of St. Aleksandr Nevskiy was invoked to unite the Russians against foreigners. The more these messages are disseminated, the further Russian solidarity with the politics of the Kremlin is confirmed. Opponents of the Orthodox Church and Christianity are viewed as enemies whose mission is to undermine the very foundations of Russianness. Thus the violation of (Orthodox) religious feelings must be punished by up to three years in prison, as the new law of 2013 decrees.[76]

7. The Return of the Ideological Power Source: The Crime of the Rock Girls

Schroeder and Karpov have concluded that popular support for the church and condemnation of Pussy Riot's action can be linked to Russia's top-down desecularisation process, which does not oblige Russians to go to church but rather to value the symbiotic church-state domination connected with the social identity theory of the people.[77] I prefer to see the church-state relationship as more factual and real than merely symbolic and rhetorical and to emphasise the entire historical development towards a different understanding of legitimate rule in Russia. Perhaps one could understand Russian society as an ideological collective of its

---

[74] Appeal by the primate of Russian Orthodox Church Abroad on the celebration of the 1,025th anniversary of the Baptism of Rus. (http//www.interfax-religion.com/?act=documents&div=218).
[75] *Deutsch Kornblatt*, Christianity (note 27), 416–417.
[76] *Kananovich*, Execute (note 2), 376, 383–391.
[77] *Schroeder / Karpov*, The Crimes (note 1), 303–307.

unanimous members, while western society is better described as a legalistic and pluralistic community of individuals with their own personal rights.

Pussy Riot knowingly attacked the centre of power using precise forms and words in a very intelligent way. The mainstream society and politicians were against them, and the political response was both decisive and severe. Pussy Riot attacked the legitimation of power and the symphony of state and church, while the other 'enemies of the church' in the study by Schroeder and Karpov merely insulted Christian feelings, kept their views private or concerned about worldly issues such as commercialisation or corruption.[78]

The punishment of Pussy Riot follows the Orthodox canons. The sinner must repent! The court of appeal refused to release Maria Alyokhina on parole on 22 May 2013 and again on 24 July, because she did not show repentance and remained defiant. The other sentenced artist, Nadezhda Tolokonnikova, received a similar decision on 26 July.[79]

In western legislation the condition of repentance is constitutionally illegal, since the core aim is not to create an atmosphere of unanimity but to respect the atmosphere of intellectual pluralism. The crime requires remorse but not repentance. From a Russian perspective these conditions are central, because the core crime is to question the source of power and destruction of unanimity.

According to Michael Mann, ideology was most important as a power source for rising national states and ideologies such as racism, communism, fascism and liberalism, all of which played a decisive global role in and after the two world wars. These ideologies collapsed, however, by the beginning of the 1990s, leading some scholars such as Francis Fukuyama to declare the end of ideology. It is true that modernisation has caused the transformation of ideologies from religious to secular ones and resulted in the victory of less ideological and more pragmatic concepts of reform. Yet the 1990s did not mean the end of ideologies but a rise of new ones such as neoliberalism, environmentalism, and fundamental religious movements in both Christianity and Islam.[80]

There is soft power in Russia, despite the argumentation of Smith. This power is ideological and it aims to organise society's moral values behind the ruler, giving him the means to distribute global messages to boost his own power. This power is religion, patriotism, history and doctrines which declare foreign and other alien influences to be criminal and wrong. The western scholars should see the big difference between western rational and eastern holistic argumentation to be able to understand the role of these. In this context the rhetoric matters!

---

[78] *Schroeder / Karpov*, The Crimes (note 1), 288–292, 297, 299.

[79] http://rt.com/politics/pussy-riot-appeal-rejected-522/, http://www.telegraph.co.uk/news/world news/europe/russia/10204587/Russia-court-rejects-Pussy-Riot-members-appeal-for-freedom.html.

[80] *Mann*, Globalizations (note 11), 403–406, *Francis Fukuyama*, The End of History and the Last Man, London 1992.

The Orthodox religion has a strong position in Russian society and functions as a global distribution channel for political legitimisation messages and influence today. It is an effective weapon against international NGOs such as Greenpeace, international gay rights activists or foreign immigrants, all of which represent what is seen as the most dangerous value: pluralism. The Russian regime is afraid of these challenges to its authority, because they may harm its vital economic and political interests. Traditional means of legislation and international agreements no longer work; instead church doctrine on satanic sin and damnation shapes the togetherness of a national civil society against these new enemies.

The Pussy Riot case shows how seriously religion is taken by the present Russian regime. The punishment was so severe because the performance attacked the heart of the power system. Therefore its explanation is not simply a feminist discourse or theological detail, but a political statement. Religion functions as an instrument of power, because the majority of the people take it seriously. In the broader context, it enables the ruler to both control society within Russia and to reach Russians abroad and thus have global influence. It is like a counterpart to Coca Cola and McDonald's in Americanisation, but much more effective, because the ruler can actively use it for his own political purposes, which the White House cannot do with U.S. brands. Thus the stupid and primitive action of Putin's regime against some young punk rockers was not stupid and primitive but logical and intelligent.

Abstract

The group of punk artists known as Pussy Riot gave a performance in a Moscow Orthodox Cathedral in 2012 which insulted the feelings of many Russians. The performance was a political protest against President Vladimir Putin, and the artists were sentenced to prison. This paper seeks to analyse the case from the perspective of power resources and how the concept of legitimacy has been formed through Russian history. Recent sociological literature stresses that Putin's approach to power in Russia is very pragmatic and not as ideologically based as has previously been thought. Those who understand the symbiosis of the church and state in Russia explain this by the lack of civil society in the country, but they do not consider the historical formation of legitimacy in Russia. Modern rulers face the same problem as their medieval predecessors, who did not have the resources to reach their subjects with armies. Michael Mann's concept of a 'lethal boomerang' implies that the traditional means of control ineffective today, so rulers are forced to distribute their legitimation messages through global networks. Social togetherness and unanimity have been essential to Russian life throughout history. This has been controlled by an ideological power network which consumes religion as a power source. Thus the 2012 Pussy Riot demonstration was not only an act of hooliganism but above all an attack on the core of the modern power system.

"Every Day It Just Gets Worse"

Jehovah's Witnesses Under Ban in Russia Facing Criminal Charges

Wolfram Slupina

1. General Overview

With the collapse of the Soviet regime expectations were high that it would usher in a liberal society in which human rights and democratic values would become a normal way of life for everyone. So, it was no surprise that Jehovah's Witnesses after practising their religion for over 125 years in the territory of the former Soviet Union mainly under ban and underground finally received legal recognition in eleven former Soviet republics. On 27 March 1991, the Russian Federal Soviet Socialist Republic granted legal registration in their State Register of Religious Organisations.[1]

After the establishment of the independent Russian Federation in 1991, a new and progressive constitution was adopted in 1993 based on Western ideals, which would provide more considerable religious freedom.[2] On 29 April 1999, Jehovah's Witnesses were also registered in the Russian Federation by the Ministry of Justice in Moscow as the "Administrative Centre of the Religious Organisation of Jehovah's Witnesses in Russia."[3]

In 2016, there were over 170,000 active Jehovah's Witnesses in the country worshipping in more than 2,300 congregations. Over 290,000 visitors attended the Memorial of Jesus' death, their most important religious holiday.[4] Throughout 71

---

[1] Cf. Wolfram Slupina, Problems Associated with Religious Freedom in the Commonwealth of Independent States – As Shown by the Example of Jehovah's Witnesses, in: Religion – Staat – Gesellschaft [Religion – State – Society] (RSG) 10/2 (2009), 203.

[2] Cf. Russian Federation's Constitution of 1993 with Amendments through 2008, Art. 19 (2), 28 (https://www.constituteproject.org/constitution/Russia_2008.pdf [last accessed: 26 Dec. 2018]); James T. Richardson, Religion in Public Space: A Theoretical Perspective and Comparison of Russia, Japan, and the Unites States, in: RSG 7/1 (2006), 50–51.

[3] Cf. Slupina, Problems (note 1), 204–205.

[4] Cf. 2017 Yearbook of Jehovah's Witnesses (YB), 184–185; https://www.jw.org/en/news/legal/by-region/russia (last accessed: 12 Dec. 2018). This is the last published public report pertaining to the activities of Jehovah's Witnesses in Russia before the official ban in 2017.

regions of the Russian Federation, 395 local religious communities were officially recognised at that time.[5]

However, the constitution of 1993 was never truly applied in full force when it came to the rights of religious minorities.[6] Human rights were trampled on almost daily, particularly freedom of religion. These religious discriminations were especially sanctioned by the Religion Law of 1997, and the 2002 "Law on Combating Extremist Activity." The arbitrary interpretation of these laws by Russian courts amounts to a relapse into the Soviet unjust regime. The situation climaxed on 20 April 2017 when the Russian Federation Supreme Court ruled to criminalise and ban the activity of Jehovah's Witnesses. The Appellate Chamber of the Russian Federation Supreme Court upheld this decision on 17 July 2017. This decision effectively bans the worship of Jehovah's Witnesses throughout the country. The following information provides some insight into the developments which paved the way for the liquidation of this religious organisation.

2.1. Law on Religion (1997)

It was by a large majority that the Russian Parliament (State Duma) passed on 19 September 1997 the new religious legislation "On Freedom of Conscience and Religious Associations" (RelL).[7] Despite international protests, then President Boris Yeltsin signed the law on 26 September 1997, and it took effect on 1 October 1997.[8] The revised version of the restrictive Religion Law can partly be traced back to the initiatives of the Russian Orthodox Church and the "sect hysteria." This was demonstrated by the concerted efforts of anti-cult movements in North America, Western Europe (especially from Germany and Denmark[9]), and Russia itself.[10] This

---

[5] Cf. Slupina, Problems (note 1), 202; Elena Miroshnikova, Religious Intolerance and Discrimination in Russia, in: RSG 12/1 (2011), 67.

[6] Cf. Richardson, Religion in Public Space (note 2), 51.

[7] Cf. http://www2.stetson.edu/~psteeves/relnews/svobodasovesti1709eng.html (last accessed: 23 Jul. 2018); see also http://pravbeseda.ru/library/index.php?page=book&id=571 (last accessed: 23 Jul. 2018).

[8] Cf. Deutsche Tagespost [German Daily Mail], 25 Sept. 1997, 1–2; see also Uwe Kischel, Die Stellung nichttraditioneller Religionen in Russland – Rechtsvergleichende Bemerkungen aus deutscher Sicht [The Status of Non-Traditional Religions in Russia – Comparative Law Comments from a German Perspective], in: Gerrit Manssen/Boguslaw Banaszak (eds.), Religionsfreiheit in Mittel- und Osteuropa zwischen Tradition und Europäisierung, Regensburger Beiträge zum Staats- und Verwaltungsrecht 4 [Freedom of Religion in Central and Eastern Europe Between Tradition and Europeanisation, Regensburg Contributions to State and Administrative Law 4], Frankfurt/Main-Berlin-Bern-Bruxelles-New York 2006, 190; News Release Jehovah's Witnesses (NRJW), 12 Nov. 1998.

[9] In particular with the support by Thomas Gandow, President of the Berlin Dialogue Centre, and Prof. Johannes Aagaard, founder of the Dialogue Centre International in Denmark; cf. Richardson, Religion in Public Space (note 2), 51–52.

[10] Cf. Marat S. Shterin/James T. Richardson, Effects of the Western Anti-Cult Movement on Development of Laws Concerning Religion in Post-Communist Russia, in: Journal of Church and State 42/2

new law demanded that all religious communities wanting to attain legal entity receive registration once again, even if they had already received full rights under the liberal Russian Law between 1990 and 1997 (Art. 8.1 RelL). It only approved the registration of local religious organisations if – among other requirements – the local authorities confirmed that they had already existed in their respective area for at least 15 years (Art. 9 RelL). This posed a problem because it was only religious organisations and churches that had cooperated with the Communist regime during the Soviet era that received full rights. Other religious minorities which had not done so were legally recognised, but were excluded from important rights, among these the right to produce, import and distribute religious media (Art. 17.1 RelL).[11]

A special status was granted to the Russian Orthodox Church and only "symbolic recognition" was given to Islam, Judaism and Buddhism in the new Religion Law (Preamble RelL).[12] Other less favoured religious groups were put in a second-tier status and were denied full rights. The fact that the Russian Orthodox Church is privileged does not necessarily give rise for concern. This is demonstrated by other states such as Denmark, Finland or Poland, which also favour a state religion.[13] The problem lies instead with the new Religion Law being arbitrarily applied by local authorities who seek to control the worship of any given religious group and perhaps label them as non-compliant.[14] This has thrown wide-open the doors to religious discrimination.[15]

(2000), 247–271; idem, The Yakunin vs. Dvorkin Trial and the Emerging Religious Pluralism in Russia, in: Occasional Papers on Religion in Eastern Europe 22/1 (2002), Article 1; Richardson, Religion in Public Space (note 2), 51; see also Emily B. Baran, Contested Victims: Jehovah's Witnesses and the Russian Orthodox Church, 1990–2004, in: Religion, State & Society 35/3 (2007), 262; 271; idem, Jehovah's Witnesses and Post-Soviet Religious Policy in Moldova and the Transnistrian Moldovan Republic, in: Journal of Church and State 53/3 (2011), 429–430; Zoe Knox, Continuities in Soviet and Post-Soviet Religious Policy (with Particular Reference to Jehovah's Witnesses), in: RSG 12/1 (2011), 240–241; idem, Jehovah's Witnesses and the Secular World. From the 1870s to the Present, London 2018, 302; Hubert Seiwert (ed.), Das "Sektenproblem". Öffentliche Meinung, Wissenschaftler und der Staat [The "Sect Problem." Public Opinion, Scientists and the State], in: Massimo Introvigne, Schluß mit Sekten! Die Kontroverse über "Sekten" und neue religiöse Bewegungen in Europa [No More Sects! The Controversy over "Sects" and New Religious Movements in Europe], Marburg 1998, 9–11.

[11] Cf. Kischel, Stellung (note 8), 196–198; see also Knox, Continuities (note 10), 237–238; Heta Hurskainen, The Russian Orthodox Church's Argumentation on Religious Freedom before the 1997 Law on Freedom of Conscience and Religious Associations, in: RSG 18/1, 2 (2017), 172.

[12] Cf. Richardson, Religion in Public Space (note 2), 51.

[13] Cf. Miroshnikova, Religious Intolerance (note 5), 62–65; see also Kischel, Stellung (note 8), 189–205; Zoe Knox, Religious Freedom in Russia: The Putin Years, in: Mark D. Steinberg/Catherine Wanner (eds.), Religion, Morality, and Community in Post-Soviet Societies, Bloomington-Indianapolis 2008, 285; 304.

[14] Cf. Kischel, Stellung (note 8), 204–205; Zoe Knox, Russian Society and the Orthodox Church: Religion in Russia after Communism, Abingdon-New York 2005, 170–172.

[15] Cf. Philip Walters, Religious Freedom in Russia, in: Derek H. Davis/Gerhard Besier (eds.), International Perspectives on Freedom and Equality of Religious Belief, Waco 2002, 129–153; Slupina, Problems (note 1), 202–213.

It is interesting to note that since the new Religion Law entered into force in Russia on October 1997, a similar law was adopted in other post-Soviet republics and autonomous regions. To this day however, the way in which local authorities and courts implement these laws leads to discriminating restrictions of religious minorities or even their ban. The laws are exploited to make a religiously pluralistic society impossible in these states.[16]

On 20 July 2016, an amendment came into force which further restricted the "missionary activity" of religious communities in Russia. The law punished expressions of religious beliefs without state permission, which included the use of the media or the internet by means of high fines.[17] This new law triggered an increase of hostile attacks on religious minorities including Jehovah's Witnesses.[18] During this time, the European Court of Human Rights (ECHR) expressed great concern about the new law and warned against its abuse. Russia was repeatedly urged to bring its laws into harmony with human rights.[19]

2.2. "Law on Combating Extremist Activity" (2002)

The Russian Federal "Law on Combating Extremist Activity" (in short "ExtrLaw")[20] was adopted by the State Duma on 27 June 2002, and approved by the Russian Federation Council on 10 July 2002. When this law was originally passed, it was done with the scope of counteracting any sort of "Islamic extremism," and specifically violent action. Due to an amendment of the law, it was no longer a prerequisite for charges of extremism to be brought forth against any organisation including religious organisations. Article 13 of the law stipulated that the Ministry of Justice post an official "Federal List of Extremist Materials" on the

---

[16] Cf. Wolfram Slupina, Religious Freedom and Jehovah's Witnesses in Putin's Russia, Georgia, and CIS, in: RSG 18/1–2 (2017), 183–222.

[17] Cf. Victoria Arnold, Russia: Putin signs sharing beliefs, "extremism," punishments, in: F18News, 8 Jul. 2016 (http://www.forum18.org/archive.php?article_id=2197 [last accessed: 20 Apr. 2017]).

[18] Cf. Victoria Arnold, Russia: Inconsistency of "anti-missionary" punishments, in: loc. cit., 20 Dec. 2016 (http://www.forum18.org/archive.php?article_id=2242 [last accessed: 20 Apr. 2017]); see also idem, Russia: Ten years' imprisonment for religious meetings?, in: loc. cit., 26 Jan. 2017 (http://forum18.org/archive.php?article_id=2250 [last accessed: 20 Apr. 2017]).

[19] Cf. Victoria Arnold, Russia: European Court repeats calls for Religion Law change, in: F18News, 5 Aug. 2014 (http://www.forum18.org/archive.php?article_id=1982 [last accessed: 24 Apr. 2017]); see also idem, Russia: "Extremism" religious freedom survey, September 2016, in: loc. cit., 13 Sep. 2016 (http://www.forum18.org/archive.php?article_id=2215 [last accessed: 24 Apr. 2017]).

[20] Federal Law no. 114-FZ of July 2002 with amendments of 27 July 2006, 10 May and 24 July 2007, as well as of 29 Apr. 2008; see also Federal Law on Combating Extremist Activity of the Russian Federation, CDL-REF(2012)012, Opinion no. 660/2011, Strasbourg, 24 Feb. 2012; http://www.venice.coe.int (last accessed: 26 Jul. 2012); http://www.rg.ru./printable/2002/07/30/extremizm-dok.html (last accessed: 6 Aug. 2012).

internet. Such a list has been published since 2007.[21] As of May 2014, 2,304 publications or materials were listed which were rated to be extremist. It included at least 65 Islamic books and 70 publications of Jehovah's Witnesses. Among these were various Russian issues of their magazines "The Watchtower" and "Awake!"[22]

Beginning in 2016, an additional 88 publications were banned for being "extremist" and the official website www.jw.org was blocked. Even the New World Translation of the Holy Scriptures (NWT), published by Jehovah's Witnesses in the Russian language, was inspected for "extremist" contents; thousands of Bibles were seized by the Russian customs authority and finally banned by the Leningrad Regional Court on 20 December 2017.[23] In many cases the liquidations of the congregations of Jehovah's Witnesses were based on fabricated evidence in order to charge the Witnesses with extremism. Video recordings and witness testimonies confirmed that Russian authorities themselves had planted banned publications in places of worship and then "found" them during raids.[24]

The new Religion Law of 1997 and the "Law to Combat Extremist Activities" of 2002 were exploited by the authorities to limit freedom of faith and to strengthen the Russian Orthodox Church at the expense of religious minorities. Both laws laid the foundation for arrests of Jehovah's Witnesses, which set in place the basis for their eventual ban.[25]

---

[21] Cf. http://www.minjust.ru/nko/fedspisok (last accessed: 5 May 2014); see also http://minjust.ru/ru/extremist-materials?search= (last accessed: 5 May 2014); Geraldine Fagan, Russia: How the battle with "religious extremism" began, in: F18News, 27 Apr. 2009; Felix Corley, Russia: "An attempt to revive total ideological control," in: loc. cit., 19 Jun. 2012; idem, Russia: More "extremist" books to be banned?, in: loc. cit., 1 Aug. 2012; George D. Chryssides, "Be Not Conformed" – A Historical Survey of the Watch Tower Society's Relationship With Society, in: RSG 18/1–2 (2017), 236–237.

[22] Cf. Corley, "An attempt […]" (note 21); Geraldine Fagan, Russia: "Extremism" religious survey, July 2012, in: F18News, 23 Jul. 2012; idem, Russia: Six-month "extremism" sentence for St Petersburg Nursi reader, in: loc. cit., 6 Sep. 2013, 4–5; Victoria Arnold/Geraldine Fagan: Russia: Two "extremism" bans overturned – but bans, fines continue, in: loc. cit., 27 Jan. 2014, 3; Miroshnikova, Religious Intolerance (note 5), 65–66; Victoria Arnold, Russia: "Tired of the unjust treatment of the books, ourselves, and our loved ones," in: loc. cit., 10 Apr. 2014; Watchtower (WTE) 132 (9), 1 May 2011, 19; YB 2014, 28.

[23] Cf. NRJW, 12 Jan. 2017 (https://www.jw.org/en/news/legal/by-region/russia/decade-long-attack-religious-freedom-intensifies [last accessed: 25 Apr. 2017]); NRJW, 29 Aug. 2017 (https://www.jw.org/en/news/legal/by-region/russia/russia-declares-bible-extremist [last accessed: 16 Mar. 2020]); NRJW, 27 Dec. 2017 (https://www.jw.org/en/news/legal/by-region/russia/court-upholds-ruling-declare-bible-extremist [last accessed: 16 Mar. 2020]).

[24] Cf. Victoria Arnold, Russia: Religious freedom survey, January 2017, in: F18News, 13 Jan. 2017 (http://www.forum18.org/archive.php?article_id=2126 [last accessed: 25 Apr. 2017]).

[25] Cf. Geraldine Fagan/Felix Corley, Russia: 34 Jehovah's Witnesses publications and one congregation banned, in: loc. cit., 8 Dec. 2009; YB 2014, 28.

2.3. Behind the Scenes

On 20 May 1994, an "International Christian Seminar on Totalitarian Sects" took place in Moscow. This seminar was co-supported by some Western anti-cult organisations, and the Russian Orthodox Church. The premise of this meeting was to sound a warning of "imminent danger from totalitarian sects or cults" by implying that they were inherently criminal. This seminar, which was co-sponsored by the Russian Orthodox Church, explicitly condemned religious minorities including Jehovah's Witnesses.[26] That is why the organisers in their final resolution proposed that the Russian government take "tough measures" on how to counter the activities of so-called cults in the whole country.[27]

Some representatives of the Western anti-cult movements have been active supporters in the criminalisation of religious minorities in Russia. Two stand out in particular: Thomas Gandow, who until 2011 was Cult Counsellor of the Protestant Church of Berlin Brandenburg-schlesische Oberlausitz, and is currently head of the Dialog Zentrum Berlin as well as President of the Dialogue Centre International. The second is the late Professor Johannes Aagaard, founder of the Dialogue Centre International in Denmark. In February 1995, Gandow himself was actively involved in the public hearings before the lower chamber of the Russian Federal Assembly (Duma), to discuss law amendments that would counteract the progressive constitution of 1993 that provided important guarantees for religious freedom. A month later "he boasted of the fact that he was 'advising' the Russian government on how to deal with cults."[28] Mikael Rothstein, associate professor of religious history at the University of Southern Denmark, concluded that "effective anti-cult work in Russia and other Eastern European Countries has […] been influenced by the Dialog Center."[29]

Alexander Dvorkin, a self-proclaimed "sect scholar," has spearheaded the opposition against religious minorities as a prominent "anti-sect" activist through cooperation between Western anti-cult-movements, the Russian Orthodox Church, and Russian government officials. Dvorkin immigrated to the United States and returned to Moscow as a clergyman after the collapse of Communism. There he received the blessing of Patriarch Alexy II[30] and set up the first anti-cult organisation

---

[26] Cf. Perry L. Glanzer, The Quest for Russia's Soul. Evangelicals and Moral Education in Post-Communist Russia, Waco (Texas) 2002, 170.

[27] Cf. Shterin/Richardson, Effects (note 10), 263.

[28] Cf. loc. cit., 263–264.

[29] Cf. Mikael Rothstein, Regulating New Religions in Denmark, in: James T. Richardson (ed.), Regulating Religion: Case Studies from Around the Globe, New York 2004, 229.

[30] During Soviet time Alexy II. was a supposed KGB agent under the code name "Drosdow" like his successor Patriarch Kirill under his code name "Michailow;" cf. Gerhard Besier, Expanding religious borders? The new influence of some old state churches: the Russian Orthodoxy, Abington-New York 2017, 229; Awake! 82 (8), 22 Apr. 2001, 11; N.N., Human Rights Without Frontiers International Correspondent in Russia, FECRIS and its Affiliates in Russia: The Orthodox Clerical Wing of

in Russia.³¹ Under the guise of alleged expertise Dvorkin has been very active in his campaign against non-Russian Orthodox religious minorities, including Jehovah's Witnesses, Mormons, Falun Gong, Hare Krishna, the Evangelic, and Pentecostal Church. He has accomplished this by means of the Russian media, his books, and conferences. He even receives support from the Minister of Justice, Alexander Konovalov, who is in office since May 2008. He was Dvorkin's former student at the St. Tikhon Orthodox University in Moscow. A missionary faculty department of this university is the Saint Irenaeus of Lyons Centre for Religious Studies. This Centre also heads a network of anti-associations, called Russian Centres for Study of Religion and Sects. He is President of this association.³² Dvorkin's success as a prominent anti-cultist is also due to the support and backing he has received from the founder of the Dialogue Centre, Johannes Aagaard.³³ In 2009, Dvorkin became vice president of FECRIS, the acronym for the Fédération Européenne des Centres de Recherche et d'Information sur le Sectarisme (European Federation of Centers of Research and Sectarianism). FECRIS was founded in Paris in 1994 and serves as an umbrella organisation connecting 25 anti-sect associations in Europe and 4 in non-European countries as well as 28 European Correspondents Organisations.³⁴ In 2005, FECRIS was granted participative status with the Council of Europe as an NGO. Since 2009 it enjoys ECOSOC (United Nations Economic and Social Council) status.³⁵ It is noteworthy that FECRIS receives most of its financial support from the French government.³⁶ The French constitution guarantees separation of state

---

FECRIS, in: RSG 13/2 (2012), 300; 305. As regards to Patriarch Kirill, he is described as being "a politician first, then a priest and theologian;" cf. Elena Miroshnikova, Religious Intolerance (note 5), 61.

³¹ Dvorkin set up in 1993 the St. Ireneaus of Lyons Information Center which was initially affiliated with the Moscow Patriarchy's Department of Education and Catechization. He is President of this FECRIS member association; cf. Shterin/Richardson, The Yakunin vs. Dvorkin Trial (note 10), 51; Patricia Duval, Anti-sect Movements and State Neutrality, in: RSG 18/1–2 (2017), 144–145.

³² Cf. Regis Dericquebourg, FECRIS: European Federation of Research and Information Centers on Sectarianism, in: RSG 13/2 (2012), 190; Willy Fautré/Regis Dericquebourg, FECRIS: European Federation of Research and Information Centre for Cult Issues, in: RSG 14/1 (2013), 112–113; Duval, Anti-sect Movements (note 31).

³³ Cf. Rothstein, Regulating New Religions (note 29), 229.

³⁴ Cf. Willy Fautré, Introduction, in: RSG 13/2 (2012),12/1, 181–182; Dericquebourg, FECRIS (note 32), 190; https://www.fecris.org/members (last accessed: 14 Nov. 2019).

³⁵ Cf. Fautré/Dericquebourg, FECRIS (note 32), 110; https://www.fecris.org/fecris (last accessed: 2 Apr. 2020).

³⁶ Prof. Sergey Ivanenko writes "that between 2001 and 2010 more than 90 percent of the money came from the Government of France;" cf. Sergey Ivanenko, Ordinary Anti-Cultism, Paris 2013, 9; Dericquebourg, FECRIS (note 32), 185; Patricia Duval, FECRIS and its Affiliates in France. The French Fight Against the "Capture of Souls," in: RSG 13/2 (2012), 199; 256–257. This does not come as a surprise since the French government as early as 1998 imposed a 60 percent tax on all estimated donations made by Jehovah's Witnesses. Their intention was to cause the financial collapse of the national headquarters of the Witnesses. After a 14-year legal battle and a second judgment by the ECHR, the French government had to repay to the religious organisation over 6 million Euros (more than 8 million US dollars); cf. NRJW, 12 Dec. 2012 (https://www.jw.org/en/news/releases/by-region/france/france-returns-funds-collected-illegally [last accessed: 16 Mar. 2020]); Régis Dericquebourg,

and religion thereby guaranteeing the respect of all faiths. Paradoxically, the French Republic has become an accomplice in sponsoring the persecution of religious minorities through its funding of the Russian FECRIS branch headed by Dvorkin, the voice of the Russian Orthodox Church.

A conference entitled "Destructive Cults and Human Rights" took place in St. Petersburg from the 15–16 May 2009, and was mainly orchestrated by Dvorkin. The University of St. Petersburg and the French government supported this conference. Its focus was to combat the threat of totalitarian sects. Notably, the Minister of Justice Aleksander Konovalov and Sergey Milushkin, head of the department in the Ministry of Justice, attended this conference. The latter gave a talk entitled "Possibilities of Coordinating European and Russian Experience in Combating Totalitarian Cults." A special focus was placed on the suppression of the activities of Jehovah's Witnesses under the pretext that they are a totalitarian sect. The German speaker Hans-Werner Carlhoff is director of the Inter-Ministerial Working Group for Cults and Psycho-groups in the German state of Baden-Württemberg. He is also founding member of the German-Vatican Society in Stuttgart, and honorary judge in the Baden-Württemberg State Social Court since 2010. He presented a talk on "Sects and Psycho-groups in Baden-Württemberg: Situation – Endangering Potentials – Challenges." Thomas Gandow also presented a speech entitled "Cults or Foreign Lobby Groups?" Michael Drebing, a former Jehovah's Witness and Chairman of the network Sektenausstieg e. V. (Sect exit), presented the topic "Jehovah's Witnesses and Mental Violation." The goal of the conference was to provide government officials with background information about the dangers of cults and encourage state protection against them.[37]

As early as May 2005, an international conference about "Cults, Education and Training" took place in Vienna (Austria) organised by FECRIS and its Austrian member association (Society against Dangers of Sects and Cults [GSK]).[38] The goal of this conference was "to strengthen resilience against alleged manipulations by sects in the field of education or training […]. On its homepage FECRIS expressed its gratitude to the French government and its Prime Minister Raffarin for its financial contribution to that conference. FECRIS' activities in general and that conference in particular are questionable and problematic."[39]

Jehovah's Witnesses in the Twentieth-Century France, in: Gerhard Besier/Katarzyna Stokłosa, Jehovah's Witnesses in Europe – Past and Present, vol. I/1, 69–70.

[37] Cf. https://www.fecris.org/uncategorized/destructive-cults-and-human-rights (last accessed: 12 Nov. 2019); Miroshnikova, Religious Intolerance (note 5), 74; Gerhard Besier, FECRIS and Its Affiliates in Germany: The Country with Most Anti-sect Organizations, in: RSG 13/2 (2012), 351.

[38] In 1977 this organisation was founded as "Verein zur Wahrung der geistigen Freiheit" [Association for the Protection of Intellectual Freedom]. In 1992 it was renamed as "Gesellschaft gegen Sekten- und Kultgefahren" [Society against Dangers of Sects and Cults] (https://www.sektenberatung.at [last accessed: 12 Feb. 2020]).

[39] Christian Brünner/Thomas Neger, FECRIS and its Affiliates in Austria. State and Mainline Religions against Religious Diversity, in: RSG 13/2 (2012), 312. According to the authors the GSK

FECRIS and Dvorkin have managed to export anti-cult hate speech through the Orthodox Churches and their parishes of European countries as well as to other countries by means of organised international conferences or lectures against religious minorities in the following places: China (Beijing 2008),[40] Italy (Pisa 2008), Ukraine (Kiev 2008 and 2009, Lugansk City and Alchevsk 2009), Bulgaria (Varna City 2009), Kazakhstan (Astana 2009), Armenia (Erevan 2010), England (London 2010), Greece (Veria 2010), Denmark (Copenhagen 2013), France (Marseille 2004 and 2015), Belgium (Brussels 2017), and Latvia (Riga 2018).[41]

FECRIS also has close ties with certain information centres and advisory offices in Germany, such as the Federal State Parliament of Baden-Württemberg, and the Sect-Info North Rhine-Westphalia in Essen (Sekten-Info Nordrhein-Westfalen e. V., a member association of FECRIS). These centres and institutions provide regular support to schools and other information centres in Baden-Württemberg and other German federal states. The Sect-Info North Rhine-Westphalia receives 300,000 Euros in financial support from the Federal State of North Rhine-Westphalia.[42]

2.4. Developments Leading to Restrictions by Russian Authorities

Two anti-cult organisations, the "Committee for the Rescue of Youth from Totalitarian Cults"[43] in Moscow (an NGO closely connected with the Orthodox Church) and the "St. Petersburg Committee for the Protection of the Family and the Individual,"[44] filed four charges against Jehovah's Witnesses with the public prosecutor's office in Moscow between 1995 and 1997.

---

received approximately €210,230 in financial support from the city of Vienna from 1992–2008 (cf. loc. cit., 320).

[40] Influences by Russian propaganda to restrict the activities of Jehovah's Witnesses and other religious minorities has resulted in deportation and imprisonment of some of their members also in China; cf. Bitter Winter. A Magazine on Religious Liberty and Human Rights in China (https://bitterwinter.org/tag/jehovahs-witnesses).

[41] Cf. N.N., Human Rights (note 30), 284–288; Dericquebourg, FECRIS (note 32), 191; https://www.fecris.org/our-activities/conferences (last accessed: 12 Nov. 2019).

[42] Cf. Landtag von Baden-Württemberg [Federal State Parliament of Baden-Württemberg], Drucksache 16/6046, 04.04.2019, 20 (https://www.landtag-bw.de/files/live/sites/LTBW/files/dokumente/WP16/Drucksachen/6000/16_6046_D.pdf [last accessed: 10 Jul. 2019]).

[43] Komitet po spaseniju molodjoschi ot totalitarnych sekt; nowadays, the anti-cult organisation "Committee for the Rescue of Youth from Totalitarian Cults" (Komitet po spaseniju molodjoschi ot destruktiwnych kultow) is active in Moscow; cf. Baran, Contested Victims (note 10), 271. A detailed account of the cooperation of the Orthodox Church and anti-cult organisations in regards to church apologetics and the battle against religious minorities in Russia can be found in: Miroshnikova, Religious Intolerance (note 5), 53–78; N.N., Human Rights (note 30), 267–301. Further articles in later issues of the journal highlight the international cooperation between anti-cult organisations.

[44] Sankt-Peterburgski Komitet saschtschity semi i litschnosti.

Several Russian provinces initiated on a local level restrictive anti-missionary laws and regulations. Based on the foregoing, the Archbishop's Council of the Russian Orthodox Church pronounced a very strong statement that the sectarian "views [...] threaten the integrity of our national consciousness and our cultural identity."[45]

On 13 April 1998, Jehovah's Witnesses were exonerated and proceedings ended due to lack of evidence. Nevertheless, the investigator recommended that the prosecutor responsible for the Northern Administrative Division of Moscow strive to dissolve the community concerned, and ban their activities by means of a civil action. Thus, the public prosecutor pressed civil action with the Moscow District Court Golovinsky endeavouring to terminate the Moscow community of Jehovah's Witnesses, and charged them with violation of both national and international law.[46]

Despite the continuation of the lawsuit from the Moscow District Court Golovinsky, Jehovah's Witnesses were registered on 29 April 1999 by the Ministry of Justice as a religious community under the Religion Law of 1997. They were acknowledged as a Christian religion in the whole of Russia. The state registration did not, however, bring about a positive turn in the trial. Paradoxically, the Russian Federation had already signed the European Convention of Human Rights (ECnHR) on 28 February 1996 and ratified it on 5 May 1998.[47]

The representative of the prosecution for the Northern Administrative Division of Moscow accused the religious community of having violated Article 14 of the Religion Law of 1997 – quite in contrast to the above-mentioned registration. This Article states that religious organisations or groups which break adopted state laws will be dissolved as a legal entity and their activities banned.[48] Due to a lack of evidence, after nearly three years, on 23 February 2001 all the charges of the Moscow prosecution against Jehovah's Witnesses were dropped.[49] However, because the plaintiff filed an appeal, the Court of Appeal ordered a retrial.[50] Subsequently, Jehovah's Witnesses' religious beliefs became the object of the re-

---

[45] Shterin/Richardson, Effects (note 10), 263.
[46] Cf. Case of Jehovah's Witnesses of Moscow v. Russia, Application no. 302/02, First Section, ECHR, Strasbourg, 10 Jun. 2010, 3–4 (16–22); see also Charlotte Wallace, The Jehovah's Witnesses Case: Testing the 1997 Law "On Freedom of Conscience and Religious Associations" and the Russian Legal Process, in: California Western International Law Journal 32 (2001), 44; Gerhard Besier, Der Status und die Rolle von Religion in Staat und Gesellschaft [Status and the Role of Religion in State and Society], in: RSG 11/2 (2010), 128–129; Shterin/Richardson, Effects (note 10), 266–267; Slupina, Problems (note 1), 202; 205; Knox, Religious Freedom (note 13), 299; WTE 132 (14), 15 Jul. 2011, 4–5.
[47] Cf. Slupina, Problems (note 1), 204–205; see also WTE 132 (14), 15 Jul. 2011, 5–6.
[48] Cf. Knox, Continuities (note 10), 243; see also idem, Religious Freedom (note 13), 301–302.
[49] Cf. NRJW-G (German NRJW) 12/01, 8 Jun. 2001; see also WTE 132 (14), 15 Jul. 2011, 7.
[50] Concerning the course of the trial from 1996 to 2001, cf. http://www.jw-russia.org/legal/moscowa.html (last accessed: 30 Oct. 2012); Wallace, The Jehovah's Witnesses Case (note 46), 43–83; Walters, Religious Freedom (note 15), 137–138; 145; Baran, Contested Victims (note 10), 271–273.

trial, not their religious activities. Three years later, Golovinsky's District Court banned the activities of the religious community in Moscow. Even though the accusations could not be supported by facts, the court announced the ban of the legal entity of Jehovah's Witnesses in Moscow in a judgment dated 26 March 2004. The ban was justified by valid judgments on religious beliefs, and then used to legitimise a flood of harassments. The objective was clear, to spread the ban to entire Russia. On 16 June 2004, the Moscow Court of Appeal, the City Court, upheld the judgment to ban the activities of the legal entity of the Moscow community of Jehovah's Witnesses and dissolve them. The ban and the dissolution entered into force immediately. Jehovah's Witnesses' appeal against this sentence was rejected.[51] High ranking religious dignitaries of the Russian Orthodox Church and the Jewish community welcomed the ban, and the press stigmatised the religious community as a dangerous sect.[52]

From then on, Jehovah's Witnesses were increasingly attacked and treated unjustly both by authorities and individuals. In many cases, such assaults reached completely new dimensions. Because of the discriminating court sentence, a growing flood of religious intolerance ensued, either incited by Russian authorities or tacitly tolerated by them: Religious meeting places of Jehovah's Witnesses were destroyed by arson and other acts of vandalism against their Kingdom Halls were committed; their worship services were massively disrupted by raids carried out by officials of the FSB and the Office for Combating Extremism (oftentimes these were accompanied by illegal body searches and fingerprinting); larger religious conventions were broken up or had to be cancelled due to the intervention by the police and authorities; violence was used against members of the community, who were unjustifiably arrested and whose houses were unlawfully and randomly searched; numerous Jehovah's Witnesses were surveyed by means of hidden video cameras, which were illegally installed in their homes, and their phones were tapped;[53] their literature was confiscated and later on destroyed by court order;[54] they were not allowed to rent premises for their worship nor to construct church buildings of their own; landlords were threatened with consequences should they continue to offer their property to Jehovah's Witnesses. In some regions, the religious community was refused local registration.[55]

---

[51] Cf. Case of Jehovah's Witnesses of Moscow v. Russia (note 46), 8 (54); see also Slupina, Problems (note 1), 205; WTE 132 (14), 15 Jul. 2011, 7.
[52] Cf. Knox, Religious Freedom (note 13), 300–301; idem, Russian Society (note 14), 169.
[53] Cf. Geraldine Fagan/Felix Corley, Russia: Raids, literature confiscations and criminal case in Tambov, in: F18News, 22 Oct. 2010; Slupina, Problems (note 1), 209–211.
[54] Cf. Fagan/Corley, Russia: Raids (note 53).
[55] Cf. NRJW-G 06/00, 15 Mar. 2000; NRJW-G 42/10, 10 Jun. 2010; NRJW-G 62/10, 23 Sep. 2010; NRJW-G 80/10, 17 Dec. 2010; NRJW-G 38/11, 5 Sep. 2011; WTE 132 (14), 15 Jul. 2011, 8.

2.5. ECHR Cases Involving Jehovah's Witnesses in Russia

Jehovah's Witnesses for their part lodged a complaint against the Moscow Court decision with the ECHR. On 10 June 2010, the ECHR unanimously passed a judgment stating that the rights of the community of 10,000 believers in Moscow had been violated severely. Alongside, the ECHR sentence requested Russia to protect religious freedom and reverse the dissolution of the legal entity of Jehovah's Witnesses in Moscow. Based on Article 41 of the ECnHR, the Court ordered that the Moscow community of Jehovah's Witnesses receive a total of € 70,000 ($ 84,480 U.S.) in compensation.[56] Thereupon, Russia requested the referral of the case to the Grand Chamber of the ECHR on 9 September 2010. On 13 December 2010, a panel of judges of the Great Chamber announced that the request had been rejected. Therefore, the original sentence of the ECHR protecting religious freedom was legally binding and an end was finally put to a lawsuit which had for over 13 years occupied several courts.[57]

Similar court cases before the ECHR occurred: On 11 January 2007, the court reached a unanimous decision against human rights officer Yekaterina Viktorovna Gorina and the Russian police. They had violated the right to religious freedom when they stormed and broke up a legal Christian meeting of 150 hearing-impaired Jehovah's Witnesses in Chelyabinsk (Ural) in April 2000. The judgment of the ECHR in favour of the religious community reinforced the right to freedom of faith in Russia.[58]

Another favourable outcome involved a case brought up to the ECHR in violation of the "fundamental privacy rights" in disclosing private information to public officials. Public health care representatives asked medical institutions to forward to the prosecutor's office "every refusal of transfusion of blood or its components" by Jehovah's Witnesses without the consent of the patient. On 9 March 2009 and on 6 June 2013, the ECHR ordered that damages be paid to the concerned Jehovah's Witnesses.[59]

On 26 June 2014, the ECHR ruled in favour of four Jehovah's Witnesses, who on 12 April 2006, were raided by the police during a religious service. Their right to worship without unlawful interference from the Russian authorities was ac-

---

[56] Cf. Case of Jehovah's Witnesses of Moscow v. Russia (note 46), 55; see also NR (News Release) ECHR 472, 10 Jun. 2010; NRJW-G 42/10, 16 Jun. 2010.

[57] Cf. NR ECHR 959, 13 Dec. 2010, 3; see also NRJW-G 62/10, 23 Sep. 2010; NRJW-G 80/10, 17 Dec. 2010.

[58] Cf. Case of Kuznetsov and Others v. Russia, Application no. 184/02, First Section, ECHR, Strasbourg, 11 Jan. 2007; see also NR ECHR 20, 11 Jan. 2007; NRJW, 11 Jan. 2007; Slupina, Problems (note 1), 211.

[59] Cf. Case of Avilkina and Others v. Russia, Application no. 1585/09, First Section, ECHR, Strasbourg, 6 Jun. 2013; see also NR ECHR 171 (2013), 6 Jun. 2013; NRJW, 2 Jul. 2013 (https://www.jw.org/en/news/releases/by-region/russia/european-court-protects-privacy-rights [last accessed: 16 Jul. 2013]); YB 2014, 35.

knowledged. In its unanimous judgment, the Court found that Russia had violated Articles 5 (the right to liberty and security) and 9 (freedom of thought, conscience, and religion). The Court ordered Russia to pay damages to the Witnesses.[60]

There are approximately about 40 cases pending before the ECHR. Despite the decisions of the ECHR, the Russian Government continued to defy the judgments of the Court. Hundreds of cases are proof of this fact.[61] While the penalties imposed and compensations ordered by the ECHR were paid, religious discrimination and intolerance from citizens, authorities, judicial institutions, in school and at work were commonplace for Jehovah's Witnesses. Not even ECHR judgments have made a change in this respect. Other religious minorities face a similar situation.[62]

On the 14 December 2015, President Putin signed a Federal Law amendment which basically gives the Constitutional Court of the Russian Federation the freedom to apply or not the judgments passed by the ECHR. This in effect not only contradicts the Russian Constitution, but sets a precedence in breaking away from international law and human rights in Europe.[63]

Over 25 years ago, thousands of Jehovah's Witnesses were rehabilitated by the Russian State as "victims of political repression" due to their experiences in Communist prisons, penitentiaries, forced labour camps, and their forced displacement in special settlements. Today, they are being stigmatised as "extremist" by the same authorities and courts.[64] The police have been complacent in punishing religious discrimination against Jehovah's Witnesses, which constitutes a serious crime against human rights. Moreover, an alarming increase of inhuman discrimination of members of the religious community by the police has been observed. Jehovah's Witnesses have been harassed in all ways possible – just as it was in Communist times. Even the official websites of Jehovah's Witnesses' were blocked by court order.[65]

---

[60] Cf. Case of Krupko and Others v. Russia, Application no. 26587/07, First Section, ECHR, Strasbourg, 26 Jun. 2014; see also NRJW, 1 Jul. 2014 (https://www.jw.org/en/news/legal/by-region/russia/echr-judgment-freedom-of-religion [last accessed: 17 Jul. 2017]); cf. Slupina, Problems (note 1), 210.

[61] Cf. Miroshnikova, Religious Intolerance (note 5), 67; see also NRJW-G 30/09, 18 Jun. 2009; NRJW-G 50/11, 14 Dec. 2011.

[62] Cf. Miroshnikova, Religious Intolerance (note 5), 67–68; Geraldine Fagan, Russia: Religious freedom survey, July 2012, in: F18News, 19 Jul. 2012; Felix Corley, Russia: Shock at Moscow church demolition, in: F18News, 6 Sep. 2012.

[63] Cf. Bill Bowring, Russia's cases in the ECtHR and the question of implementation, in: Lauri Mälksoo/Wolfgang Benedek (eds.), Russia and the European Court of Human Rights. The Strasbourg Effect, Cambridge (UK)-New York 2018, 188–191.

[64] Cf. Miroshnikova, Religious Intolerance (note 5), 67; NRJW-G 15/08, 25 Jul. 2008; WTE 132 (9), 1 May 2011, 18–19; WTE 132 (14), 15 Jul. 2011, 4.

[65] Cf. NRJW, 27 Jul. 2015 (https://www.jw.org/en/news/legal/by-region/russia/bans-jw-org-website-blocked [last accessed: 24 Apr. 2017]).

2.6. Ban of Jehovah's Witnesses and Its After-Effects

On 20 April 2017, after 6 days of hearings, the Supreme Court ruled to uphold the claim of the Ministry of Justice to liquidate Jehovah's Witnesses in Russia. The verdict came into effect immediately. The lawyers of the defendants, in turn, appealed against the verdict at once and were also prepared to bring the case before the ECHR.[66] The entire property of the 395 local religious communities – including their buildings – was seized.

On 17 July 2017, the Supreme Court decided to confirm its earlier ruling, which criminalised the activity of Jehovah's Witnesses in Russia. The decision effectively bans the worship of Jehovah's Witnesses throughout the country. Despite further appeals, the decision of 20 April entered into legal force and came into effect across the country.

Since then the authorities have progressively seized 131 of the properties owned by Jehovah's Witnesses, with an additional 60 properties subject to confiscation. The total value of the properties is estimated to be over €51 million ($57 million U.S.). One of the seized properties was the former Russia branch complex in Solnechnoye – a property that was owned by the Watch Tower Bible and Tract Society of Pennsylvania. This property alone has an estimated value of € 26 million ($ 30 million U.S.). An additional 43 of the properties that were seized belong to foreign legal entities existing in Austria, Denmark, Finland, the Netherlands, Norway, Portugal, Spain, Sweden, and the United States. The seizures are illegal, since the Supreme Court's decision banning Jehovah's Witnesses did not give the government a legal basis for taking foreign-owned properties. It is the largest nationalisation of private property.[67] Jehovah's Witnesses have filed a claim with the ECHR and with the UN Human Rights Committee (HRC) concerning the illegal seizure of the former Russia branch property. So far the judgments pronounced by the ECHR were unable to halt the ban of a peaceful religious minority and to grant religious freedom in Russia.

This verdict has impacted the lives of approximately 170,000 Jehovah's Witnesses in Russia. Even the peaceful exercise of their faith such as praying in a private setting and conducting religious services has led to prosecution. The participation in religious activities could be punished with a fine of up to 600,000 roubles (over € 8,660; $ 10,600 U.S.), and prison terms of up to ten years.[68]

---

[66] Cf. Administration Centre of Jehovah's Witnesses v. Russia, no. 10188/17, introduced 3 Feb. 2017; NRJW, 21 Apr. 2017 (https://www.jw.org/en/news/legal/by-region/russia/supreme-court-rules-to-criminalize-jehovahs-witnesses-activity [last accessed: 29 Apr. 2017]); see also Victoria Arnold, Russia: Jehovah's Witnesses banned, property confiscated, in: F18News, 20 Apr. 2017 (http://www.forum18.org/archive.php?article_id=2274 [last accessed: 2 May 2017]).

[67] Cf. NRJW, 4 Jul. 2019 (https://www.jw.org/en/news/jw/region/russia/Russia-Continues-to-Seize-Properties-of-Jehovahs-Witnesses-Valued-at-Over-57-Million [last accessed: 21 Oct. 2019]).

[68] Cf. HRWF (Human Rights Without Frontiers), 5 May 2017 (http://hrwf.eu/russia-jehovahs-witnesses-banned-in-russia-human-rights-organizations-appeal-to-russias-supreme-court-and-presidential-administration [last accessed: 11 May 2017]).

The judgment was followed by an increase of violent attacks as religious buildings were demolished or set on fire. The private homes of Jehovah's Witnesses have not been spared, such was the case of a family in Belgorod whose home was burned down.[69] In the Moscow region, on 30 April 2017 a neighbour set fire to the house of a Witness, and was not prosecuted. On 24 May 2017, in the village of Zheshart (Republic of Komi, Northwest Russia), unidentified persons set fire to a residential building where Jehovah's Witnesses held religious services.[70]

Even before the Supreme Court's decision entered into force, the bank accounts of some members were frozen, and children of Jehovah's Witnesses faced pressure in schools. Some of them were humiliated before the whole class because the teachers called their parents terrorists. In addition, many Witnesses lost their jobs and some were even attacked by individuals or groups in the streets.

The ban on Jehovah's Witnesses has affected also their right to perform civilian service as an alternative to military service. Previously, Russian authorities had recognised the rights of Jehovah's Witnesses as conscientious objectors. It is ironic that these so-called "extremist" are forced to be trained as soldiers with weapons by this very regime! As of September 2018, there were at least ten cases in which the Russian authorities denied young Witness men alternative civilian service.[71] Now these young men face a prison sentence.[72] The Washington Post commented on Russia's treatment of conscientious objectors: "Russia remains very much like the Soviet Union in one respect: It still has prisoners of conscience, incarcerated for their beliefs and subject to criminal prosecution for what they say."[73] One of these

---

[69] Cf. NRJW, 21 Apr. 2017 (https://www.jw.org/en/news/legal/by-region/russia/supreme-court-rules-to-criminalize-jehovahs-witnesses-activity [last accessed: 29 Apr. 2017]); see also Victoria Arnold, Russia: Jehovah's Witnesses banned, property confiscated, in: F18News, 20 Apr. 2017 (http://www.forum18.org/archive.php?article_id=2274 [last accessed: 2 May 2017]); NRJW-R (Russian NRJW), 25 Apr. 2017 (https://www.jw-russia.org/news/17042512-150.html [last accessed: 2 May 2017]); NRJW-R, 5 May 2017 (https://www.jw-russia.org/news/17050516-157.html [last accessed: 10 May 2017]); NRJW-R, 8 May 2017 (https://www.jw-russia.org/news/17050817-158.html [last accessed: 10 May 2017]).

[70] Cf. Russia: Religious Freedom Concerns, Statement by the European Association of Jehovah's Christian Witnesses, OSCE Human Dimension Implementation Meeting, Warsaw, 11–22 Sept. 2017, 6.

[71] Cf. Jehovah's Witnesses, Interim Report: Negative Impact of Russia's Ban on Jehovah's Witnesses, 26 May 2017, 9; Russia: Religious Freedom Concerns, Statement by the European Association of Jehovah's Witnesses, OSCE Human Dimension Implementation Meeting, Warsaw, 10–21 Sept. 2018, 12.

[72] Cf. NRJW-R, 11 May 2017 (https://www.jw-russia.org/news/17051113-160.html [last accessed: 11 May 2017]); see also HRWF, Russia: Supreme Court's Decision About "Extremism" Threatens Right of Conscientious Objection, 15 May 2017 (http://hrwf.eu/russia-supreme-courts-decision-about-extremism-threatens-right-of-conscientious-objection [last accesses: 6 Jun. 2017]).

[73] The Washington Post, 18 Jan. 2020 (https://www.washingtonpost.com/opinions/global-opinions/russias-prisoners-of-conscience-are-an-ugly-continuity-of-the-soviet-union/2020/01/17/bd6d71a0-28d1-11ea-ad73-2fd294520e97_story.html [last accessed: 4 Mar. 2020]).

cases dealing with the denial of alternative service was brought before the ECHR and is still pending.[74]

Since February 2019, the Russian authorities have vigorously increased their home searches, which by 7 August 2019 had reached more than 600 home raids.[75] As of March 2020, the number of home raids increased to over 740. Three years have elapsed since the ban went into effect resulting in at least 325 criminal cases against Jehovah's Witnesses launched throughout Russia and Crimea, 35 are in detention, 18 under house arrest, and over 117 are under different restrictions. In 2019, 18 were convicted and in 2020, 24 have already been convicted.[76]

The raids usually take place late in the evening or in the early hours of the morning and involve several agencies, such as the FSB, riot police or the Investigative Committee. The victims are forced to lie face down on the floor or against the wall while the authorities search their homes and confiscate personal items. The Witnesses are then taken in for questioning, which can take hours. The year 2019 has seen an alarming number of cases opened against Jehovah's Witnesses initially called in for questioning.[77]

In a continued crackdown on the religious community, the authorities have placed more than 200 Witnesses on the Federal Financial Monitoring Service of the Russian Federation (Rosfinmonitoring) list register of extremists and terrorist. As a result, innocent Witnesses on this list are denied access to their bank accounts and pensions loosing their livelihoods, jobs, and businesses.[78]

On the 28 February 1998, the Russian Federation became the 39th Member State of the Council of Europe whose aim is to protect and promote human rights. The Russian Federation has failed to uphold the rights of religious minorities. Willy Fautré, Director of Human Rights Without Frontiers International, comments:

---

[74] Cf. Office of Public Information, World Head Quarters of Jehovah's Witnesses (OPI WHQ), Special Report, Russia: State-Sponsored Persecution of JW Continues, May 2019, 15; 27.

[75] Cf. NRJW, 7 Aug. 2019 (https://www.jw.org/en/news/jw/region/russia/Number-of-Witness-Homes-Raided-By-Russian-Agents-Tops-600/#?insight[search_id]=4b433962-ddec-4f10-8a93-0e93f0331119&insight[search_result_index]=0 [last accessed: 19 Aug. 2019]).

[76] Cf. NRJW, 10 Jan. 2020 (https://www.jw.org/en/news/legal/by-region/russia/imprisoned-infographic-20200110 [last accessed: 12 Feb. 2020]); Pekka Vanttinen, in: HRWF, 21 Feb. 2020 (https://hrwf.eu/helsinki-jehovahs-witnesses-getting-a-cold-shoulder [last accessed: 2 Mar. 2020]); see also loc. cit., 31 Mar. 2020 (https://hrwf.eu/russia-special-bi-monthly-digest-on-forb-16-31-march-2020 [last accessed: 1 Apr. 2020]).

[77] Cf. NRJW, 7 Aug. 2019 (https://www.jw.org/en/news/jw/region/russia/Number-of-Witness-Homes-Raided-by-Russian-Agents-Tops-600 [last accessed: 19 Feb. 2020]); Victoria Arnold, Russia: Jehovah's Witness criminal cases-list, in: F18News, 11 Oct. 2019 (http://www.forum18.org/archive.php?article_id=2512 [last accessed: 21 Oct. 2019]).

[78] Cf. NRJW-R, 6 Feb. 2020 (https://jw-russia.org/en/news/2020/02/15.html [last accessed: 24 Feb. 2020]); see also https://www.voanews.com/europe/russia-blacklists-more-200-jehovahs-witnesses (last accessed: 24 Feb. 2020).

"Russia is the only country in the European continent that imprisons people for peacefully exercising their rights to freedom of religion."[79]

On his Twitter account, on 20 February 2020, U.S. International Religious Freedom Ambassador, Sam Brownback, expressed his concern over the manner in which authorities in Russia are treating Jehovah's Witnesses. He pointed to the physical abuse and imprisonment associated with the simple exercise by this community of their religious beliefs.[80]

The ripple effect of the ban impacts all aspects of life for Jehovah's Witnesses throughout Russia. There is a reminiscent feeling which echoes a past era ruled by a monistic ideology where conformity was imposed and freedom of thought and personal conviction was inadmissible. And the instrument behind this tragic development is the Russian Orthodox Church.

With the ban of Jehovah's Witnesses in Russia a consorted international effort can be observed in the spread of "fake news" about this religious organisation. In his analysis, Prof. Massimo Introvigne commented on this current trend:

> "During these last years we have observed [...] a systematic distribution of 'fake news' about religious movements which were not organised by private, but rather by public players. In 2017 for example, Jehovah's Witnesses were banned and 'dissolved.' The Putin administration was obviously perturbed by the unanimous condemnation of these measures as expressed by international organisations, western states, academics, prominent NGOs in Russia, and foreign nations [...]. One consequence of this situation was the creation of media blogs, groups and pages in social networks that flourished thereby accusing Jehovah's Witnesses of numerous offenses. Most of these blogs, groups and pages were supposedly managed by individuals that claimed to be former Witnesses. Without doubt some of these websites reflected the real frustration of indignant, angry former members. The appearance of such news at the same time throughout the world in the weeks following the Russian decision to 'liquidate' could not merely be a coincidence."[81]

An example of this is seen in the German online news of "Russia Today." When discussing the ban in Russia, Prof. Dr. Michael Utsch, leading speaker of the Evangelische Zentralstelle für Weltanschauungsfragen (Evangelical Headquarters for Religious Worldviews) in Berlin, is quoted together with two apostates of Jehovah's Witnesses in supporting the Russian ban of Jehovah's Witnesses. He

---

[79] Cf. Willy Fautré, Russia: Over a hundred believers of several faiths behind bars, in: Our World, 18 Dec. 2019 (https://www.ourworld.co/Russia-over-a-hundred-believers-of-several-faiths-behind-bars [last accessed: 1 Jan. 2020]); see also https://www.coe.int/en/web/portal/russian-federation (last accessed: 1 Jan. 2020).

[80] Cf. Pekka Vanttinen, HRWF, 21 Feb. 2020 (https://hrwf.eu/helsinki-jehovahs-witnesses-getting-a-cold-shoulder [last accessed: 2 Mar. 2020]).

[81] Massimo Introvigne, Fake News: Die MacDonalds-Morde von 2014 [The MacDonald's Murder of 2014], in: RSG 19/1–2 (2018), 72.

went on to criticise Chancellor Angela Merkel for condemning the ban on Jehovah's Witnesses before President Vladimir Putin in Sochi May of 2017.[82]

Another alarming development occurred on 14 November 2017, when the Supreme Court Plenum of the Russian Federation passed Resolution No. 44, in which parental rights could be stripped if a court deems that the religious education children receive is potentially harmful and considered extremist. Russia's Ministry of Education recommended that children that are exposed to so-called extremist ideology be reconditioned. Children of Isis members and Jehovah's Witnesses were identified. In Russia there are tens of thousands of children and adolescents whose parents are Jehovah's Witnesses. Currently no children have been removed from their parents; however, the potential to separate families is a real threat.[83]

2.7. Danish Citizen and Others Incarcerated

Following the 20 April 2017 Russian Federation Supreme Court's decision to ban Jehovah's Witnesses in the whole of Russia, Danish Citizen Dennis Christensen was arrested on 25 May 2017 in Oryol. This occurred when armed police officers stormed and disrupted a religious service taking place in Oryol, Russia. Christensen was charged with organizing the activity of an "extremist" organisation.[84] This was the first time that a Jehovah's Witness was arrested since Soviet times. It is noteworthy to mention that Christensen was never a foreign missionary. He was self-employed and moved to Oryol for personal reasons, not at the invitation of any organisation. After spending more than 20 months of pre-trial, his trial began on 19 February 2018 and on the 6 February 2019 the Russian District Court in Oryol pronounced Dennis Christensen to be guilty of "organising the activity of an extremist organization." After being sentenced to six years in prison an appeal was filed.[85] The prosecution of the state charged Christensen with "evidence" that supposedly substantiated their claim of criminal activity. Such activities included opening the gate of the local Kingdom Hall in Oryol, removing snow from the premises, and greeting fellow believers into the hall for worship.[86]

---

[82] Cf. https://deutsch.rt.com/gesellschaft/57363-rt-spezial-seltener-einblick-in-die-welt-der-zeugen-jehovas-freiheit-missbrauch-und-verbote (last accessed: 13 Nov. 2019).

[83] Cf. Russia Religious Freedom Issues, Statement by the European Association of Jehovah's Witnesses, OSCE Human Dimension Implementation Meeting, Warsaw, 16–27 Sept. 2019, 13.

[84] Cf. NRJW, 21 Jan. 2020 (https://www.jw.org/en/news/legal/by-region/russia/jehovahs-witnesses-in-prison/#?insight[search_id]=99a8ebfc-2f47-4fc3-98ad-6730c6d26973&insight[search_result_index]=3 [last accessed: 24 Feb. 2020]).

[85] Cf. NRJW, 6 Feb. 2019 (https://www.jw.org/en/news/jw/region/russia/Russian-Court-Declares-Dennis-Christensen-Guilty-and-Imposes-Six-Year-Prison-Sentence/#?insight[search_id]=c481118e-8cf3-4a2c-896d-baaca6f05b28&insight[search_result_index]=4 [last accessed: 24 Feb. 2020]).

[86] Cf. OPI WHQ, Special Report (note 74), 3.

Outcry and concern over Dennis Christensen's sentence is evidence of a blatant disregard for religious freedom. According to Human Rights Watch (HRW) this sentencing is a result of a nationwide crackdown against Jehovah's Witnesses.[87] This case was extensively covered by the world news.[88]

On 23 May 2019, a three-judge panel of the Oryol Regional Court denied Dennis Christensen's appeal and upheld the six-year prison sentence he previously received.[89] Two weeks after he lost his appeal, Christensen was relocated to Penal Colony No. 3 in the city of Lgov which is approximately 200 kilometers (124 miles) from Oryol. Upon his arrival he was subjected to insults and pressured to break his resolve.[90]

Following in the footsteps of Christensen, is another case of the foreign citizen Andrzej Oniszczuk from Poland who was put in pre-trial detention on the 9 October 2018. During his detention, his wife was not permitted to visit him despite repeated requests. When he was arrested, he was forced to sign a document wherein he had to agree not to receive any visits from representatives of the Polish Embassy.[91] He was kept in solitary confinement for almost one year and was released on 3 September 2019. His case is still under investigation and strict restrictions have limited his possibility to travel.[92]

In the city of Saratov, on 19 September 2019 the Leninsky District Court sentenced six men to prison terms ranging from two years to three years and six months simply because they are Jehovah's Witnesses. They were arrested on 12 June 2018 when Russian authorities raided their homes. Two of them spent almost one year in pre-trial detention. Russia continue to convict and sentence to prison innocent believers simply for their faith.[93]

---

[87] Cf. HRW, 6 Feb. 2019 (https://www.hrw.org/news/2019/02/06/russia-jehovahs-witness-convicted [last accessed: 27 Feb. 2019]).

[88] Among the many news outlets were: The New York Times, 6 Feb. 2019; The Washington Post, 6 Feb. 2019; Le Monde, 7 Feb. 2019; Frankfurter Allgemeine Zeitung, 7 Feb. 2019, 5; 8 Feb. 2019, 3; https://www.aljazeera.com/news/2019/02/dane/jailed/jehovahs-witness/link/russia (last accessed: 27 Feb. 2019).

[89] Cf. NRJW, 23 May 2019 (https://www.jw.org/en/news/jw [last accessed: 24 Feb. 2020]).

[90] Cf. NRJW, 31 July 2019 (https://www.jw.org/en/news/jw/region/russia/UPDATE-Dennis-Christensen-Remains-Steadfast-After-Transfer-to-Penal-Colony [last accessed: 7 Aug. 2019]).

[91] Cf. OPI WHQ, Special Report (note 74), 5.

[92] Cf. NRJW, 6 Sept. 2019 (https://www.jw.org/en/news/jw/region/russia/Brother-Andrzej-Oniszczuk-Freed-From-Prison-After-11-Months-in-Solitary-Confinement [last accessed: 2 Oct. 2019]).

[93] Cf. NRJW, 23 Sept. 2019 (https://www.jw.org/en/news/jw/region/russia/Six-More-Brothers-Convicted-and-Imprisoned-in-Russia [last accessed: 2 Oct. 2019]).

2.8. Further Incarcerations and Brutal Torture

Rather than fight extremism, Russia is persecuting its own citizens for their peaceful worship. In the early morning hours, on 15 February 2019, mass searches in Surgut (West Siberia) took place. Worshippers were taken to the Investigative Committee offices located on the first floor of the Russian Investigative Committee's building at ul. Ostrovskogo, d. 47, in Surgut. At least, seven Jehovah's Witnesses were subjected to torture. Officers used brutal force when interrogating the Witnesses and demanded to know where their religious meetings were and the names of those present at these meetings. Moreover, they wanted to know the names of the elders and the passwords of their cell phones.

Agents put a bag over the victims' heads, sealed it with tape, tied their hands behind their backs, and beat them, even attempting rape. Then, after stripping the Witnesses naked and dousing them with water, the agents shocked them with stun guns. This sadistic torture lasted for about two hours. Additionally, after the mass searches were completed, the Russian authorities initiated criminal cases against a total of 19 Witnesses for so-called "organising an extremist organisation." Those who have been released have had their injuries documented by medical professionals, and have filed complaints with supervisory agencies. During the Soviet era, Jehovah's Witnesses experienced already this type of brutal torture with the difference being that most likely the tormenters are now members of the "Christian" Orthodox Church. The Witnesses will pursue all available legal remedies for this crime, since such a horrible abuse of authority is punishable under the Russian Criminal Code.[94] Due to the threat of cruel treatment and out of fear for their own safety and that of their children, hundreds of Witnesses have already fled to other countries.[95] Since the ban's implementation in 2017, many Witnesses have applied for asylum in Finland. Regrettably, the Finnish Immigration Office has rejected most of the applications. Many Witnesses have been repatriated back to Russia where they will most likely face criminal charges and prison terms. Others are uncertain of their status in Finland.[96]

On February 25, 2019, the ECHR ordered the Russian government to immediately release 57-year-old Sergey Loginov – one of seven Jehovah's Witnesses who reported torture in the building of the Investigative Committee – for an inde-

---

[94] Cf. NRJW-R, 19 Feb. 2019 (https://jw-russia.org/en/news/19021923-622.html [last accessed: 27 Feb. 2019]); https://www.jw.org/en/news/jw/region/russia/Jehovahs-Witnesses-Tortured-in-Surgut-Russia [last accessed: 9 Apr. 2020]).

[95] Cf. The New York Times, 16 Jul. 2018 (https://www.nytimes.com/2018/07/16/world/europe/putin-trump-russia-jehovahs-witness.html [last accessed: 6 Mar. 2019]); Independent, 22 Aug. 2018 (https://www.independent.co.uk/news/world/europe/jehovahs-witness-russia-finland-asylum-seekers-religion-a8503326.html [last accessed: 6 Mar. 2019]); Frankfurter Allgemeine Zeitung, 8 Feb. 2019, 3.

[96] Cf. Pekka Vanttinen, in: HRWF, 21 Feb. 2020 (https://hrwf.eu/helsinki-jehovahs-witnesses-getting-a-cold-shoulder [last accessed: 2 Mar. 2020]).

pendent medical examination. According to the order handed down by the court in Strasbourg, the government of Russia had to respond. On 9 April 2019, all of the torture victims were released from their pre-trial detention.[97] In the meantime, one of the torture victims fled with his family out of Russia. The German national broadcast "Deutschlandfunk" aired a program entitled "Putin's Empty Words" which included the testimony of one of the victims who was quoted as saying the following:

> "They bound my hands together and with a hard object they beat me across my thighs, which was very painful. Then, they subjected me to electric shocks on my thighs, legs and in between my legs. They then poured water on my legs and once again I was subjected to electric shocks on these same areas."[98]

These terrible developments were also reported in the "Süddeutsche Zeitung" under the title "Every Day It Just Gets Worse."[99]

Mikhail Fedotov, Chairman of the Presidential Council for the Development of Civil Society and Human Rights, met with Jehovah's Witnesses in Surgut, 14 August 2019. During this meeting the Witnesses elaborated on the torture inflicted on them by police officials. There were a total of 28 Jehovah's Witnesses present which included victims and family members. Among those in attendance, the head of the Investigative Committee in Yugra, the first deputy prosecutor of Yugra, the deputy chief of the Ministry of Internal Affairs in Yugra, and the mayor of the city of Surgut were present. In his concluding comments Fedotov emphatically stated the importance of "getting to the bottom of the truth." He added President Putin's negative sentiments on the facts concerning the torture that took place. He lastly stated that he recalled his words "that this is an absolutely unacceptable practice."[100] In response to a question with regard to the current status of Jehovah's Witnesses in Russia by political scientist Ekaterina Shulmana, member of the Presidential Council for Civil Society and Human Rights, President Putin commented:

---

[97] Cf. NRJW, 1 Mar. 2019 (https://www.jw.org/en/news/jw/region/russia/ECHR-Quickly-Responds-to-Application-Filed-on-Behalf-of-Brother-Tortured-in-Russia/#?insight[search_id]=985f2633-79df-4446-9a81-2e2da22da469&insight[search_result_index]=0 [last accessed: 4 Mar. 2019]); Fränkischer Tag, Bamberg, 12.11.2018, 9; OPI WHQ, Special Report (note 74), 6.

[98] Thielko Grieß, Unterdrückung der Religion in Russland: Putins leere Worte [Suppression of Religion in Russia: Putins Empty Words, 14 Mar. 2019 (https://www.deutschlandfunk.de/unterdrueckung-der-religion-in-russland-putins-leere-worte.886.de.html?dram:article_id=443370 [last accessed: 9 Apr. 2020]).

[99] "Es wird jeden Tag schlimmer". Russland geht mit Haftstrafen gegen die Zeugen Jehovas vor ["Every Day It Just Gets Worse." Russia Is Serving Out Prison Terms Against Jehovah's Witnesses], Süddeutsche Zeitung, 2/3 Mar. 2019, 8.

[100] NRJW, 15 Aug. 2019 (https://jw-russia.org/en/news/19081514-1070.html [last accessed: 24 Feb. 2020]).

"This certainly does not mean that we should label representatives of religious communities as members of destructive, much less terrorist, organisations. Of course, this is complete nonsense. It is necessary to deal with this attentively. […] Jehovah's Witnesses also are Christians, for which they are persecuted, and I don't understand that well. So this should be looked into, this must be done."[101]

Further incidents of torture continue throughout different regions of Russia. On 6 February 2020, prison guards assaulted and beat with clubs five male Witnesses being held in Penal Colony No. 1 in Orenburg, Russia. One of the Witness prisoners, Feliks Makhammadiyev, sustained severe injuries, which included a broken rib, a punctured lung, and a damaged kidney. He subsequently underwent surgery for accumulation of fluid in his lungs. He was only allowed to go to the hospital after consenting to sign a document stating that he had "slipped in the bathroom and fell." While hospitalized, tests revealed that Makhammadiyev was suffering from malnutrition because the prison personnel withheld the special food used to treat his celiac disease. After their beatings, the other four Witnesses were placed in a punishment cell based on unsubstantiated allegations, which included the smoking of cigarettes – a habit shunned by the religious community.[102] The use of electric shocks has become a prevalent form of sadistic torture by law enforcement officials. Vadim Kutsenko, a Witness from Chita, was handcuffed, strangled, repeatedly beaten and had electric shocks to his stomach and leg as officers demanded information of fellow believers. The torture took place in a forest on 10 February 2020. He was placed in pre-detention, and released since investigators did not have sufficient evidence to bring charges forward.[103]

Authorities are also resorting to involuntarily psychiatric commitment of individuals who due to their religious beliefs are considered to be possibly mentally unstable. This occurred on 16 January 2020 to a resident of Surgut, Timofey Zhukov, a Jehovah's Witness and an experienced lawyer who was forced to undergo a psychiatric examination for 30 days (equivalent to pre-detention). He has been active in defending the rights of victims who have been targeted by the security forces due to their religious beliefs. He pointed to his placement in a psychiatric hospital as an act of repression against him and other citizens who practice the religion of Jehovah's Witnesses. During his preliminary outpatient examination, it was determined that his refusal to answer some questions put into question his

---

[101] At a meeting of the Council for Civil Society and Human Rights, 11 Dec. 2018; cf. https://hrwf.eu/?s=Russia+Putin+promises+to+talk+about+Jehovah%27s+Witnesses&print=pdf-search (last accessed: 4 Mar. 2019); The Washington Post, 18 Dec. 2018; OPI WHQ, Special Report (note 74), 2; NRJW-R, 17 Dec. 2018 (https://jw-russia.org/en/news/18121716-544.html [last accessed: 27 Feb. 2019]).

[102] Cf. NRJW, 17 Feb. 2020 (https://www.jw.org/en/news/jw/region/russia/Prison-Guards-Beat-Five-Brothers-in-Orenburg-Russia [last accessed: 24 Feb. 2020]).

[103] Cf. NRJW, 18 Feb. 2020 (https://www.jw.org/en/news/jw/region/russia/Officers-Torture-Brother-Vadim-Kutsenko-in-Chita-Russia [last accessed: 24 Feb. 2020]); HRWF, 31 Mar. 2020 (loc. cit., 31 Mar. 2020 (https://hrwf.eu/russia-special-bi-monthly-digest-on-forb-16-31-march-2020 [last accessed: 1 Apr. 2020]).

sanity. He came to the realization that the investigator and the judge involved in the case reacted negatively to his legal exercise of article 51 of the Russian constitution in which no one shall be obliged to give evidence incriminating themselves. There are approximately 21 residents in Surgut that are awaiting trials because of their religious convictions as Jehovah's Witnesses.[104]

3. Concluding Remarks

The evidence presented in this analysis is proof of a growing religious intolerance of government agencies in Russia in cooperation with the Russian Orthodox Church – in spite of the fact that the Russian Constitution guarantees the fundamental right to religious freedom based on international agreements. In 2007, faithful adherents witnessed the Canonical Communion and Reunification of the Russian Orthodox Church in Moscow, which would become the bridge between Russia's political aspirations, and its core values. In the last decade the Russian Orthodox Church has promoted nationalism as an integral part of the Orthodox faith.[105] Because of this, Western anti-cult concepts were introduced to de-legitimise unpopular religious minorities like Jehovah's Witnesses. As HRWF explains on their website, the way minorities are dealt with in Russia is justified with the "concept of spiritual security." After the collapse of the Soviet Union, this concept replaced communism in an attempt to protect the traditional and cultural values of the Russian society. The Orthodox Church was closely linked to this concept. Therefore, any religious organisation that is not Orthodox is labelled as "non-traditional" and "anti-social." The "Law on Combating Extremist Activity" gave this concept the legal basis to fight religious diversity.[106] The rising concern by international onlookers and human rights activists over Russia's curtailment on freedom of speech, information, and religion has done very little to improve the situation. Instead, as highlighted in this analysis, "every day it just gets worse." The hope for a pluralistic and democratic society seems unattainable, thus ushering in the end of civilisation, and human rights in Russia.

---

[104] Cf. NRJW-R, 27 Jan. 2020 (https://www.jw-russia.org/en/news/2020/01/38.html [last accessed: 25 Mar. 2020]).

[105] Cf. Yuri Zarakhovich, Putin's Reunited Church, in: Time Magazine, 17. May 2007 (www.content.time.come/time/world/article/0,85599,1622544,00.html [last accessed: 2 Mar. 2020]).

[106] Cf. HRWF, 12 Jun. 2017 (fhttps://hrwf.eu/wp-content/uploads/2017/06/FECRIS-Russian-branch-behind-the-persecution-of-non-Orthodox-minorities-in-Russia.pdf [last accessed: 24 Feb. 2020]).

Abstract

This analysis focusses on the developments that led to the ban of Jehovah's Witnesses on 20 April 2017. The religious life of approximately 170,000 Jehovah's Witnesses throughout Russia were affected by this verdict. What led to this tragic event was basically the enactment of two laws: the Law on Religion (1997) which prevented the legal re-registration of religious minorities and the "Law on Combatting Extremist Activity" (2002). Both laws gave the authorities the license to arbitrarily apply them on religious minorities. In the background for over two decades the Russian Orthodox Church and the "sect hysteria" movement throughout Europe and North America pushed the implementation of these laws. The Russian government has arbitrarily misapplied laws meant to protect their national security, and subsequently stripped religious minorities of their fundamental rights: freedom of belief, conscience, and thought.

Religious minorities including Jehovah's Witnesses have been repressed and denied their right to belief. The Russian Orthodox Church and FECRIS have aligned themselves with the common objective to safeguard the core values of Putin's Russia. The FSB has systematically coordinated house raids with armed and masked officers to roundup Witnesses. These raids have led to pre-detention interrogations that have at times involved brutal torture as in former Communist times by the KGB. There has been a nationwide escalation of criminal prosecutions and convictions of Jehovah's Witnesses because of their religious activities. Prosecutors have pushed for maximum sentences of up to six or more years of incarceration for the peaceful practice of the Jehovah's Witness faith. Despite the sanctions imposed on Russia by the ECHR, and public outcry, gross human rights violations against Jehovah's Witnesses continue. Putin himself exclaimed his dismay when questioned over the plight of Jehovah's Witnesses in Russia since they "also are Christians." For Jehovah's Witnesses in Russia it can be said that "every day it just gets worse."

The Invention of the French Notion of "Sectarian Therapeutic Drifts" (*Dérives Sectaires Thérapeutiques*)

Régis Dericquebourg

1. The beginning of the anticult fight: the argument at that time

The anticult movement in France began in 1977, when the Association for the Welfare of Families and Individuals who are victims of sects (ADFI) and the Center Against Mental Manipulations (CCMM) were created. The ADFI had a catholic and conservative ideology and the CCMM established by the Freemason Roger Ikor was imprinted with the radical socialist ideology, which finds its origins in Combes's antireligious atheism. The ADFI was created by young people's parents converted to minority religious groups, mainly at that time to the Unification Church and the Children of God. Those Catholic parents did not accept that their children leave their family religion and feared that the family inheritance would be left to the so-called sects by mean of donations. Roger Ikor would have established the CCMM just after his son supposedly died from an inappropriate feeding regime, without involving a religious matter. One of his friends published a book[1] explaining that R. Ikor gave a false version of his son's life and death. Facing the journalists' questions, the anticultists had to build an argumentation to justify their anticult fight by developing a theory about the so-called sects. Meanwhile, the "Jonestown Massacre" (Guyana) gave them visibility and some form of credibility. Thus, the journalists accepted more easily the idea of the dangers of the sects. When the coalition of the left-wing party won the elections in France in 1981, the antireligious radical socialists supported the anticult associations and then created in 1998 the Interministerial Anticult Mission (MILS) to fight the sects. This was established under the prime minister's authority, instead of the authority of the Cults Office (*Bureau des cultes*) of the Ministry of Home Affairs that is traditionally in charge of religious matters in France. This committee has changed its name many times and it was recently called the "Interministerial Mission for Vigilance and Combating Sectarian Aberrations" (MIVILUDES, 2002). It includes politicians hired through their network of friends, or sometime

---

[1] Waguet J. P., *"C'est la faute à Arsène"*. Paris, Les Lettres libres. 1983.

to retrain politicians who were defeated in previous elections or were for some reason forbidden by the court of justice to run for election, as it was the case for Georges Fenech (2008) and for the socialist deputy mayor of the 13th district in Paris Serge Blisko (2012). The latter had ceased his office as a deputy and mayor to pass it on to an ecologist allied to the socialist party. The fact that Serge Blisko was a doctor enticed the MIVILUDES to look upon the health sector.

That kind of committees gave a negative definition of "The Sect" in 10 features (of which it is not necessary to recall here[2]) that reproduced the same definition of the anticult associations. At that time, none of these points included references to health care or therapy. And then, in the wake of the victimology issued from the psychology of justice, victims of the sects started to be spoken of as well.

Philippe-Jean Parquet, Professor of psychiatry at the Faculty of Medicine of Lille, who became member of the MIVILUDES, gave a list of 10 specific criteria, which according to him show how a person becomes a victim of a sectarian organization. In his mind, five of the ten criteria must be identified to diagnose a mental control, similarly to the check-lists of the Diagnostic and Statistical Manual of Mental Disorders (DSM) in psychiatry.

But the main characteristic feature of the movements involving a sectarian risk is the psychological destabilization of the adept, that can be considered as a major criterion (pathognomonic sign) of a mental illness in a psychopathological diagnostic. But this psychological destabilization is unknown in psychology and psychiatry. It is a pure invention of the French anticultists who are unable to define it correctly. They only give a tautologic definition: psychological destabilization is deduced from criteria which in return prove a psychological destabilization. Pr. Parquet gives a list of criteria which reflects the anticultists's definition of a sect rewritten in a pseudo-scientific language. (It seems useless to quote this here.) However, if we read the written grounds of the judgment in cases of trials of minority religious groups, the criterion of psychological destabilization have not been accepted by the judges. We hear this expression only in the speeches of the journalists and the politicians who merely repeat the anticultists's rhetoric. After that, the anticultists proposed the expressions of "mental domination" and "mental enslavement", which were registered as an infraction to the law and could be punished by the judges. However, the judges seem to be reluctant to apply these charges because they are not clearly defined and they are used to relying on experts who generally have opposite points of view. In the facts, it seems difficult to find material and obvious proofs of "mental enslavement" or "mental domination". On another side, the French anticultists have not succeeded to register their obscure and negative definition of a sect. Their definition could also be applied to political parties or to the main churches. Having failed to register in the law

---

[2] Gast Philippe, "Analyse critique de la situation des mouvements religieux en droit positif francais", in: Massimo Introvigne, Gordon Melton ed. *"Pour en finir les sectes"*. Paris, Dervy. 1996, 190.

the word "sect", the French anticultists have proposed to register in the law the notion of "sectarian drifts". Ironically, that expression is even more unclear than the notion of sect, because it adds the imprecise notion of drifts to the imprecise notion of sect. Thus, it is difficult to make a law out of it, because a law must define clearly the facts in order to find evident proofs of an offence. The notion of "sectarian therapeutic drifts" is built on this unclear definition and includes the word "therapeutic" which is apparently clear at first sight but becomes problematic when we analyze it deeply. It seems to be an unclear alternative to the "illegal practice of medicine". The judges and the professional order of doctors may sue in justice an unofficial healer. According to their judgment, the judges and the associations of doctors don't have the same opinion. The ancient case of Louis Antoine (1846–1912), a Belgian spiritual healer, and a friend of his Martin Jeanfils, a local healer at that time, proves it. They were suited in law by doctors for illegal practice of medicine but the judges released them. Thus, Louis Antoine's movement was definitively accepted as an element of the religious Belgian landscape in Belgium, and thereafter in France. To take legal action against a movement or a person for illegal practice of medicine is risky because if the defendant wins the trial, its practice becomes then legal by jurisprudence. The notion of "sectarian therapeutic drifts" is a mean to circumvent the risky accusation of "illegal practice of medicine."

2. The "who's who" of the sectarian therapeutic drifts

The history repeats itself. In the past, a parliamentary report[3] has listed 172 supposed dangerous sects. That included groups that were not religious at all, such as associations that deliver methods of self-improvement that the public liked to practice at this time. Most of the 172 "dangerous sects" are now included in the list of sectarian therapeutic drifts. The anticultists seem to re-use always the same data.

The list included: 1. All sort of methods of psychology and self- improvement mentioned in a previous report of dangerous sects, even if they are not spiritual, nor religious, or are not shaped into an organization such as reiki, transactional analysis (Eric Berne), EMDR (Eye Movement Desentization and Reprocessing, by Francine Shapiro), enneagram, kinesiology, False Memory Syndrome (Peter Freyd), rebirth (Leonard Orr), Simonton method, the neurolinguistic program (John Grinder and Richard Bandler, 1976); 2. Alternative medicines such as Ryke Geerd Hamer method (diet to cure cancer), Simoncini method (also to cure cancer), Scohy method (lemon juice to cure cancer), Rudolf Breuzes method (vegetable juice to cure cancer), urinotherapy, instinctotherapy, new shamanism; breath-

---

[3] Gest Alain, Guyard Jacques, *Commission d'enquête sur les sectes*, 22 décembre 1995, n° 2468.

arianism; 3. Religious movements such as the Twelve Tribes because of the case of a young child who died of a cardiac abnormality (1997). Recently, the anticultists have also included in the list of sectarian therapeutic drifts anti-vaccination leagues whose leaders were called "*guru*" such as the Pr. Henri Joyeux.[4]

As we can see, this list is a salmagundi of methods and groups yet listed as dangerous sects in a previous report, various practices of psychology and self-improvement, and alternatives medicines. It seems to be a rush work done to justify the existence of the MIVILUDES and its subsidy.

3. The case of Doctor Guéniot

Let us recall the case of Dr. Guéniot as an example of a professional problem mixted with his belonging to a spiritual movement (*Mouvement International du Graal*). It illustrates what the MIVILUDES calls sectarian therapeutic drifts and how the court of justice manages this kind of problem.

Dr. Guéniot was a doctor in the towns of La Madeleine and Tourcoing (North of France). In addition to the allopathic medicine, he practiced homeopathy and naturopathy. He was a member of the Movement of the Graal that is considered as a dangerous sect in the report Gest-Guyard (1995). The Dr. Guéniot received a female patient who had a breast cancer. This woman took the decision to stop all her medical treatments and she consequently died. Thus, the Dr. Guéniot was accused by the patient's family to breach his obligation of safety required by the law or the rule of the conventional medicine, out of clumsiness, imprudence, carelessness. He was also accused of giving wrong medical advice that could entice the patient to give an appropriate treatment up, exposing herself to a dramatic and lethal consequences, of which Dr. Guéniot was perfectly aware of. So, he would be responsible of the death of his patient. These facts are sanctioned by the articles 221–6, 221–8, 221–10 of the penal code.

Dr. Guéniot was also accused of voluntarily not advising the patient to give her inappropriate care up.

In sum, the court had to judge a classical case of supposed malpractice. But the accusation was parasitized by the ADFI, by being aware of Dr. Guéniot's belonging to the Movement of the Graal and by joining the criminal proceedings arguing that the malpractice in that case was a result of Dr. Guénot's believes. They informed the media about a sectarian therapeutic drift and the media echoed this. In the first instance at the Court of Lille, Dr. Guéniot was cleared of the charges of negligent homicide of his patient, but he still was condemned for failing to help a person in danger. The ADFI was dismissed of the criminal proceeding.

---

[4] *Aujourd'hui en France*, jeudi 21 juin 2018, website.

Dr. Guéniot appealed in justice and the Court of Appeal in the city of Douai cleared completely Dr. Guéniot of all the accusations. The Court confirmed the dismiss of the criminal proceeding. The judges explained their judgment in a very long report.[5]

So, what could have been an accusation of sectarian therapeutic drift was processed in the light of the penal code, and it was proved that the notion of sectarian therapeutic drifts in that case was irrelevant.

However, politicians and anticultists still spread the notion of sectarian therapeutic drifts, although they know this judgment, through which Dr. Guénot's spiritual believes were brought on the public place before and during the inquiry and the trial.

4. The case of the emergency doctor in Caen

The daily medical newspaper *"Le quotidien du médecin"* (May 21,2019) for the French doctors related another case of accusation of a doctor who works in the University Hospital of the town of Caen and who is also president of the group *"Notre Dame de la Lumière"* which proclaims to be in the Charismatic Renewal stream. He was accused of having founded a sectarian community where a dozen of women and men lived separately in two houses. They give half of their income to this community. Formerly recognized by the bishop, this community was afterward rejected because of "theological drifts", i. e. heresy, and also because of negative rumors about itself. According to the journalists, the judges accused this doctor to practice exorcism during meetings in which the participants live "deep mystical experiences". Furthermore, the justice accused the doctor of organizing sessions of healing prayers and reproached him his rough speech to his adepts. We notice that most of the members of his group do not consider themselves as victims.

In this trial, the Departmental Section of the Order of Doctors filed a civil action.

In the trial, the judges declared the doctor non guilty and dropped all charges against him (Tribunal de Caen, 11 juillet 2019). It is easy to explain the judges' decision. Having theological divergence with the catholic bishop and practice of exorcism are not condemned by law in France, and even certain Catholic priests are exorcists. Furthermore, the French legislation does not forbid the healing prayer and does not forbid to have deep mystical experiences. That is not the unique privilege of monks and nuns. We may explain that the local section of the Order of Doctors filed a civil action because it stands up against malpractices of doctors. But in this case, it lost the case probably because the judges have considered this doctor could correctly separate his spiritual believes from his professional occupation.

---

[5] Arrêt de la cour d'appel de Douai du 17 février 2001, 6ème chambre 09/283. *Tribunal correctionnel.*

5. Conclusion

Sociologists have often emphasized that the theory of the sects constructed by the French anticultists is a false theory and it is easy to destroy it. However, it carries on because it is repeated incessantly by politicians, journalists and persons who speak about minority religious groups without having studied it objectively. This false theory also lasts because anticultists demonize those who try to analyze the phenomena objectively like in the inquisition time. In that sense, it can be considered as a kind of McCarthyism.

Globally, the anticultists' argumentation avoids precise legal accusations included in the criminal code, because they can not prove it in justice. In fact, their arguments are often vague and unproved. But they are demagogic.

The anticultists' definition of "The Sect" was an invention, and the judges and legislators did not accept it. So, the anticultists proposed the expression of "sectarian drifts" and "sectarian therapeutic drifts", that neither convinced the judges. In doing so, the anticultists tried to prove they were useful and needed to be sponsored by the authorities. Globally the scholars and the jurists do not give credit to their argumentation. But we may also notice that in a conference "*Corps, nouvelles religions et dérives sectaires*"[6] ("Body, New religions, and Sectarian Drifts") to which some scholars participate, some of them accredited the notion of "sectarian therapeutic drifts". For example, the attendee Abdelkader Behtame (University of Guelma and of Franche-Comté) and Houari Maidi (University of Franche-Comté) delivered a speech entitled "The Sectarian Drifts: A Clinical and Psychopathological Study". Scholars are also able to describe what doesn't exist, in that way, anticultists have found their valet.

Abstract

France share with most of the authoritarian nations a high level of intolerance with the minority religious groups. Since the rise of the anticultist groups, official or unofficial and sponsored by the successive governments after 1983, many arguments to justify a fight against the sects (pejorative word) were developed. When an argument becomes obsolete, another one is invented. In this article I expose how the pejorative notion of "sectarian therapeutic drifts" emerged in France. I show the cases of persons to whom it was applied as a way of prosecution.

---

[6] "*Corps, Nouvelles religions et dérives sectaires*", Paris, 24 juin, 25 juin, 18 octobre 2019, UFR Staps, *Maison des sciences de l'homme, Maison des cultures du monde*.

RELIGION – WHAT DOES THIS MEAN TODAY?

GERHARD BESIER

When the concept of religious freedom is discussed in Europe, it quickly becomes apparent that it is the understanding of religion that divides opinion, not the fundamental right to freedom of religion.[1] Quite a narrow understanding of religion prevails in Europe. Frequently, it is almost as if there is a desire to preserve the fundamental insights of Émile Durkheim (1858–1917) – the clear separation of the "profane" and "sacred", together with the basic question of religion's function in society. As a reminder, religion for Durkheim is about the separation of the sacred from the profane. On the one hand, the sacred refers to collective representations that are set apart from society, or those things which transcend the humdrum of everyday life. The profane, on the other hand, is everything else, all those mundane things like our jobs, our bills, and our rush hour commute. Religion is the practice of marking off and maintaining the distance between these two realms. Rituals, for example, reaffirm the meaning of the sacred by acknowledging its separateness, such as when religious devotees pray to a particular statue or symbol.[2] It is Durkheim's belief that religion creates a realistic and effective picture of the society in which it is practised – or, in other words, a genuine sense of reason within the relationships of that precise society corresponds to the beliefs found in the specific religion. According to Durkheim, religion consists of three core components: religious beliefs, rites and the church. Collectively, all three components form the stable structure of religion as a social institution.[3]

In the 1920s, a number of political scientists and sociologists spoke of quasi-religions with reference to the totalitarian political-systems of the era. They were

---

[1] Cf. Rosalind Gottfried, My Sociology. An Introduction for Today's Students, New York and London: Routledge, 2019, 513–534 (religions in Society); John E. Farley & Michael W. Flota, Sociology, New York and London ⁷2018, pp. https://www.routledge.com/Sociology-7th-Edition/Farley-Flota/p/book/9781138694682 (Religion); Anthony Giddens & Philip W. Sutton, Sociology, Cambridge: Polity Press, 2016, 720–763; Christian Smith, Religion: What It Is, How It Works, and Why It Matters, Princeton, NJ: Princeton University Press, 2017.

[2] Cf. Durkheim, Die elementaren Formen des religiösen Lebens [1912], Frankfurt am Main: Suhrkamp, 1981.

[3] Cf. Thomas M. Schmidt & Annette Pitschmann (eds.), Religion und Säkularisierung. Ein interdisziplinäres Handbuch, Berlin: J. B. Metzler, 2014. See also Robert Yelle, Sovereignty and the Sacred. Secularism and the Political Economy of Religion. Chicago: University of Chicago Press, 2018.

quickly confronted with fierce opposition and protests because such ideologies, it was felt, lacked any holy or sacred element, which is considered a basic condition for the recognition of a belief-system as a religion. Nevertheless, these ideologies did incorporate what could be considered religious beliefs, rites and also, in the broader sense, a church. This concept comes to the fore if one considers, for example, the Nazi Party's Nuremberg Rallies.

Luther's Large Catechism states, "Whatever your heart clings to and confides in, that is really your God."

Even if the Reformer, Luther, did not necessarily understand the concept in this way, his formulation gets to the heart of a religious belief that illustrates precisely the notion that forms the fundamental essence of religion: It does not matter which elements are contained in a belief system. If a group of people profess a specific religious belief, then society should regard this as worthy of protection – provided that it does not disturb the peace in that society. If this sentence were to be respected without exception, then it would not be possible for anti-cult movements or authoritarian governments to assert with reference to particular religions that this or that faith community or belief system is not genuinely a religion, but that they are dealing with something else completely – namely an extremist movement that is likely to harm members of society. It is for this reason that followers of what might be deemed to be a repugnant or objectionable movement still need to be protected if and when that faith community is confronted with condemnation and disparagement.

Patterns of argument like these are not only put forward by anti-cult movements and authoritarian governments, but also by the established, mainstream churches, which have effectively lost all those previous modes of social pressure that they freely utilised to bind people to the church and to prevent them from straying onto their own unconventional life paths.

For far too long, people had no alternative but to participate in various church rituals if they didn't want to risk being excluded from society. If an individual did not regularly attend church worship services, they were considered to be an infidel or disbeliever and were forced to endure significant disadvantages. Even outside the confines of the church, churchgoers would turn their back on such a person, would not trust them and would avoid conducting business with them. Because it was a definite advantage in worldly trading and day to day relationships to take an active role in church events and functions, very little attention was actually paid to people's religious motives as they participated in various religious rituals. Belief was a public affair, while crises of faith were expected to remain a private matter that was never discussed publicly. Consequently, it was not important whether the interpretation of belief – how people understood their faith – was convincing or not because there simply was no alternative to publicly practised religion. There was no need for the religious doctrine proclaimed by the Church to be acceptable to the majority, nor did it need to be fundamentally attractive.[4] As a result, leaders in theological thought scaled dizzying heights in the field of scholasticism well into the 20th century, even though very few outside the esteemed priestly circles had any genuine comprehension of these studies.

In our modern society, however, church membership does not instantaneously open doors or automatically ensure personal success. Attending church does not lead to a natural promise of social advantage, and non-participation in traditional church rites no longer entails sanctions. Belief has become a personal affair. Because the social pressure has fallen away, religious indifference is running increasingly rampant in and around the churches and clergy.

Does that logically mean that those people who still hold firm to their church membership do this primarily for religious reasons? And conversely: Do we look deeper into the motives of those who have chosen to leave the church to establish if they simply didn't find the church's teachings sufficiently attractive and engaging, meaning that this teaching really requires a contemporary reinterpretation?

The churches themselves see the joining and leaving of their members as an effective statement of belief. But is this actually justified? The fact alone that so many members of the church do not actively participate in congregational life – only 3.3% of members of the Protestant Church actually attend Sunday worship on a regular basis – and yet the majority do not renounce their church membership. This statistic raises serious doubts about whether it is reasonable to draw such conclusions from the membership of a church. Moreover, surveys indicate that church members generally describe the meaning of their faith in such a way that there is almost no overlap between their beliefs and the official church doctrine. Ultimately, the religious differences existing within a Mainstream Church [*Volkskirche*] are no less than those between different denominations. If it is the case that many church members are not actually familiar with and don't have a genuine understanding of the official teachings of the church, then the coming and going of these members should not become a criterion for the quality of their beliefs. The external borders of the church system are, in fact, quite fluid and offer only a handful of information about what form of belief genuinely exists within those borders.

It is against this background that Niklas Luhmann proposes that members of the clergy should undertake exploratory conversations with active members of their church, and raise questions about which interpretations of belief equate most closely to their understanding of faith. Different forms of belief would then be available within a church. Admittedly, this solution would mean that the ques-

---

[4] Cf. Niklas Luhmann, Die Organisierbarkeit von Religionen und Kirchen, in: Ernst Lukas & Veronika Tacke (eds.), Schriften zur Organisation, Vol. 3: Gesellschaftliche Differenzierung, Wiesbaden: Springer, 2019, 3 ff.

tion of truth would be suspended and individual religious taste would assume priority.

Detlef Pollack, Professor of Sociology and Religion from Münster, picked up on Luhmann's considerations in quite a unique manner at the 2017 Synod of the Evangelical Church in Germany (EKD). He described the Church's problem as a religious question and advocated the belief that Luther's faith most likely needs to be "modified" to adapt to the modern age.[5] To this extent, he offered the following examples of which central elements of faith potentially need to be discarded in the interests of a new interpretation of faith.[6] According to Pollack, "Nowadays, we can no longer believe in the fundamental sinfulness of humanity." In the contemporary perspective, it is no longer appropriate to see people as essentially corrupt or depraved, but as capable of changing and worthy of improvement. Likewise, the personal concept of God really needs to be changed. "We no longer think of God as an authority figure, who stands in judgement over our sins. On the contrary, He is perceived as a far away, yet good-hearted power who does not grieve over every one of our small sins, but who has our well-being at his core." This image of the Church should express that it is liberal minded, open to dialogue and ready to reform. The Church should concentrate foremost on those already within the circle of the Church, as well as looking to those on the fringes and those seeking religion – some ten percent of the German population. It could hardly be said that there is a sense of religious longing in these modern times. The number of people who are seriously considering a return to the church do not even add up to one percent of the secular community. The Church would be well advised to invest in religious education for children, because it is a marked reality that the likelihood of belonging to a church community as an adult bears a significant relationship to whether an individual received religious instruction as a child.

This perspective is consistent with that of Thies Gundlach (Hannover), principal theologian of the Protestant Church in Germany and Vice-President of the Church Office of the EKD, who is actively advocating for greater freedom on the issue of whether Sunday services of worship absolutely need to be held in the Protestant churches. Speaking with the German media service, Deutschlandfunk, he clarified that Sunday worship is, without a doubt, a central event in congregations, but it is not the only function. "And that is something that needs to be considered locally, in a spirit of genuine Protestant freedom."[7] Pastors should not be "placed

---

[5] Cf. Detlef Pollack, Herausforderungen für eine reformbereite Kirche (https://www.ekd.de/Synode-2017-4-schwerpunktthema-prof-dr-detlef-pollack-muenster-30298.htm); see also idea spektrum, No. 46, dated 15/11/2017, 9.

[6] Cf. "Study into Church membership retention" [*Kirchenverbleibstudie*] undertaken by the Evangelical Church of Westphalia. According to this study, 65 % of church member respondents in Westphalia said that Christians could still live their belief without the Church. Quoted from idea Pressedienst, dated 05/11/2019.

[7] Quoted according to idea Pressedienst, No. 262, dated 01/11/2019, 2.

under undue pressure: You are absolutely required to preside over services of worship every single Sunday, regardless of whether anyone attends or whether they find it relevant and important. That is a form of ideology that I cannot and do not share." In the face of growing secularism in communities and congregations, let alone within the international liberal order[8], Gundlach endorses services of worship targeted at specific groups. "That would be an intelligent response on the part of our church to the differentiation within our society."

How a religious politician might envisage a pro-social form of religion can be seen in Berlin.[9] In this city, a unique initiative, the "House of One", is presently under construction – a church building designed for Catholics, Jews and Muslims to share and jointly use from 2023. This project is supplemented by the opening of a Faculty for Islamic Theology and another for Catholic Theology at the Humboldt University in Berlin. Even though the three religions – Judaism, Christianity and Islam – currently operate as three separate entities, the concept is unequivocally being considered as a possible future perspective that the religions will seek reconciliation with one another and with the secular world in the spirit of enlightened, historically-critical thinking. Benedikt Schmidt, Professor of Catholic Ethics for the Institute for Catholic Theology at the Humboldt University in Berlin, gets to the heart of the Metropolitan Project when he speaks of an "anthropologically directed" form of theology.

There seems to be little or no protest among various anti-cult organisations and other critics of religion with regard to such projects espousing a "religion of the middle way". Even atheists might be able to accept such a form notions of religion.[10] The mainstream churches are also assuming an active role. However, attitudes are fermenting on the margins. The reality is that "fundamental truths" that previously divided the churches increasingly seem to be disappearing in this new outlook. This is, however, not because the theologians have somehow agreed on or reached a unifying position on these previously divisive doctrinal differences – this hasn't even been the case between different denominations within the Christian Church. Individuals in positions of leadership and representatives from Theology Faculties supporting an "anthropologically directed" form of theology are, in fact, pursuing an "empirical turn" that would also like to give theological disciplines a more material orientation in the form of social sciences.[11] This mode of access is essentially dealing with the "enlightenment of religious practice" on

---

[8] Cf. Brian D. Weigelt, Understanding the Impact of Secularism Within the Liberal International Order. In: Journal of Church & State 61 (2019), 106–123.

[9] Cf. Reinhard Bingener & Daniel Deckers, Religion der Mitte, FAZ, No. 255, dated 02/11/2019, 3.

[10] Cf. Tim Crane, Die Bedeutung des Glaubens. Religion aus der Sicht eines Atheisten, Berlin: Suhrkamp, 2019.

[11] Cf. Ulrich Riegel, Stefan Heil, Boris Kalbheim & Alexander Unser (eds.), Understanding Religion. Empirical Perspectives in Practical Theology, Münster and New York: Waxmann, 2019.

"the social presence of religion in modern, secular society" and the "public significance of religion".[12]

There is absolutely nothing wrong with this perspective. But what is the situation with those religious groupings on the margins of the mainstream churches and the various religious congregations that have been leading an increasingly independent existence for some time as spin-offs from the mainline churches? These evangelical or fundamentalist circles have shut themselves off to any form of "anthropologically oriented" theology; they continue to believe in the inspired nature of the Bible as Holy Scripture, cultivating and cherishing traditional piety, and evidently enjoying great popularity among their members. In these circles, there is no challenge whatsoever to the concept of a God whose very existence and intention involves a personal concern for each individual. And no one initiates any form of protest to this belief. Certainly, conflicts with the rule of law have arisen since the Holy script is no longer in consonant with modern ethical norms.[13] So, it might be impossible for a fundamental Christian to bless a marriage of homosexuals by their pastor or to accept a minister who is an avowed homosexual.[14]

For this reason, the law passed by the German Federal Government in 2020 mandating against so-called "conversion therapies" is interesting because it saw the triumph of a sexual minority over a religious minority. In a press release, the Chairman of the Bible Society [*Bibelbund*], Michael Kotsch (Detmold), stated that the proposed law would "provide left-wing and Green activists with another instrument to bring criminal actions against Evangelical Christians and congregations". In future, according to the drafted law, any person who might dare to offer spiritual counsel to a homosexual or transsexual individual seeking to change their feelings would be considered a criminal offender. According to Kotsch, "This highly intolerant legislation must and should be viewed as the beginning of state sponsored discrimination against Evangelical Christians."[15]

Realistically, those who choose not to respect the current rules for social coexistence and interaction can anticipate consequences to the detriment of their career. To celebrate "LGBT Pride Month" in June – a commemorative day, orig-

---

[12] Ibid., 5. See also Jürgen Habermas, Auch eine Geschichte der Philosophie 2 vls., Berlin: Suhrkamp, 2019; Ulrich H. J. Körtner, Rainer Anselm & Christian Albrecht (eds.), Konzepte und Räume öffentlicher Theologie. Wissenschaft – Kirche – Diakonie, Leipzig: EVA, 2020.

[13] Cf. William N. Eskridge, Jr. & Robin Fretwell Wilson (eds.), Religious Freedom, LGBT Rights, and the Prospects for Common Ground, New York: Cambridge University Press, 2018.

[14] Cf. idea Pressedienst, dated 22/11/2019. According to this report Pastor Jörg Uwe Pehle had to leave his parish Saint Stephan in Vlotho because of "hostilities" on the part of parishioners who had been upset by his homosexuality. Following a resolution calling for tolerance, signed by more than one thousand citizens, the pastor changed his mind and remained – as he explained in an interview with the news magazine, Der Spiegel, No. 2, dated 04/01/2020, 42

[15] Idea Pressedienst, No. 304, dated 19/12/2019, 4.

inating in the USA, seeking greater tolerance for the LGBT community – the Swedish international furniture group IKEA circulated an article to its employees in Poland. The article carried the headline "The inclusion of LGBT is mandatory for everyone". In response to this, an IKEA employee and committed Catholic took to the company's Intranet (the in-house communication portal) and cited Bible passages from the Old and New Testaments condemning homosexual activities. According to Ordo Iuris, IKEA then terminated the employee's employment on the grounds that the man had violated the concern's internal regulations and acted in a manner contrary to the "fundamental rules of social co-existence", resulting in a loss of confidence in the employee.[16]

The USA Evangelist, Franklin Graham, had intended to travel to Great Britain in the spring of 2020 to conduct a preaching tour.[17] When the proposed tour met with increasing resistance, all of the contractually agreed events across a number of British cities were cancelled. The Mayor of Liverpool, Joe Anderson, put a positive spin on the increasing public pressure when he declared that we should not allow hate and intolerance to remain unchallenged. Graham's wrongdoing lies in the fact that he quotes and advocates statements from the Bible that pronounce practising homosexuality to be a sin. On the heels of Great Britain, a further protest ensued in Germany where Graham had planned to preach in the Lanxess-Arena in Cologne on June 20, 2020.[18]

In April 2020, the Evangelical "Network Bible and Faith" [*Netzwerk Bibel und Bekenntnis*] in Württemberg published an alternative handout specifically for parish councils on the subject of the blessing of homosexual couples. This handout referred to an official handout published by the Württemberg Senior Church Council in November 2019 under the title "What God does not bless cannot be blessed by the Church!" In the same month, the Tübingen Protestant Theology faculty expressed their opposition to this evangelical perspective. According to the scholars, "a series of theologically untenable assertions" were laid out in the text, "with the aim of condemning public church services that celebrate the marriage of same-sex couples, and discriminating against homosexuals by referring to the alleged will of God". Set against the background of the "long history of marginalisation and persecution that people in homosexual partnerships" have had to endure, it is "intolerable when attitudes, promoting such open discrimination continue to be advocated in the Protestant Church today". It would appear that the network had issued this handout as "an attempt to justify acts of discrimination again same sex couples on the basis of Scripture". However, it was not in a position to appeal to the different denominations of the Church because these did

---

[16] Ordo Iuris Institute for Legal Culture, Warsaw, July 1, 2019.

[17] Cf. idea Pressedienst, No. 25, dated 03/02/2020, 17.

[18] Cf. idea Pressedienst, No. 27, dated 05/02/2020, 4. See also idea Pressedienst, No. 41, dated 24/02/2020, 2 f.

not take precedence "over a reasonable understanding of biblical witness". The alternative handout was "based on the erroneous conviction that its own prior understanding of an allegedly reasonable interpretation of Holy Scripture represents the sole guideline of church doctrine and action". It was claimed that the authors had singled out "various specific Bible passages, which they had interpreted as supposed Biblical findings and as the Word of God without any consideration of their literary of historical context". In this way, they had, however, misappropriated the "historical character of Biblical texts and their integration in contemporary world views and cultures". For this reason, the Augsburg Confession, the central Lutheran denominational document, emphasises, "that ministry is to be used for the communication of the Gospel – and not to be understood as a means for merely reciting Scripture". Furthermore, the signatories to this letter explain their appreciation of the fact that, "in the light of the powerfully increasing realisation in other academic disciplines, God's creation is far more diverse" than was ever able to be perceived "in earlier centuries". It is consistent with "the nature of God's good creation, as in the Scriptures, that same-sex relationships should be freely and openly shared, just as occurs in all other partnership relationships". Assertions that such relationships are sinful and to "deprive them being blessed" demonstrated a "failed approach towards the Biblical text". Therefore, they are simply "theologically untenable".

The Network Bible and Faith's Chairman in Württemberg, Pastor Tobias Eissler (Ostfildern), responded to the Open Letter on 29 April with a statement that was published on the Network's website. The statement claims that is incomprehensible why the Network's position should be untenable so long as the "law and regulations of the Regional Church countenance the stance of the majority of church congregations", which oppose the blessing of same-sex couples. He raises the question of exactly who, and based on what criteria, ought to be allowed to decide, "What exactly is considered to be 'sinful' and what should be understood as 'discrimination'," if the definition of sin, as specified by the Apostle Paul in Romans 1: 26–32, is rejected as discriminatory: "University professors? Synod? The vast majority?" It is completely unreasonable to suggest that the alternative handout places the Lutheran Confessions above the Bible. Luther himself insisted that, on the contrary, the writings of a false tradition ought not to be given priority. In any case and without question, the "practice of homosexuality has been understood at all times and everywhere as sinful and immoral misconduct from the first century to the modern day". This understanding has been consistently held by the Catholic Church, the Orthodox Churches, a clear majority of Protestant Churches and larger Free Churches, and "in solidarity with Israel and its Scripture-faithful Jewish theology". It is difficult to find another example that illustrates so clearly the depth of the rift that divides the Evangelical Church into a conservative-Biblical-Evangelical group and a liberal-historical-critical group.

Further examples abound of how assuming a conservative religious standpoint can increasingly have a negative impact on career prospects.[19] The Swiss corporation Läderach Chocolatier has been frequently criticised for its longstanding commitment to the right to life "March for life" [*Marsch fürs Läbe*] and has had to contend with acid attacks on its products. The Swiss Air airline recently ended their commercial relationship with the company because of its stance. Similarly, a Swedish mid-wife has been banned from practising her profession because she refuses to undertake abortions as part of her obstetric responsibilities. She pursued the matter in the legal courts, claiming the right to freedom of conscience, but she was not successful in pleading her case.

In Finland, police officers interrogated the Lutheran cleric Juhana Pohjola (Helsinki) for five hours – on the grounds that he had preached and incited hatred against homosexuals.[20] Pohjola is a pastor for the Evangelical Lutheran Mission Diocese of Finland – an independent denomination that preaches a traditional understanding of the Bible and adheres strongly to the 16th century Lutheran Confessions. According to Pohjola, criminal proceedings have been instituted against him, because he published a brochure on the Church website decrying homosexuality from a Christian perspective in 2006. Because another theologian had registered an official complaint, Finland's Attorney General, Raija Toivianen, initiated investigations into his actions on October 31, 2019. The brochure's author was a Member of Parliament and former Finnish Minister of the Interior, Päivi Räsänen. Criminal proceedings have also been initiated against her, the wife of a minister and mother of five children, accusing her of dissemination of hatred. In September 2019, she was also subjected to four hours of police interrogation. A further criminal investigation is being pursued into critical statements from a politician of the Christian Democrats [*Kristillisdemokraatit, KD*] (Finland) after she had used social networks to criticise the participation of the Evangelical Lutheran Church of Finland in a homosexual parade. According to its own records, the Evangelical Lutheran Mission Diocese of Finland has 37 congregations and around 2,200 members. It is a member of the International Lutheran Council and maintains relations with the Independent Evangelical-Lutheran Church (SELK) in Germany. Of the 5.5 million citizens of Finland, approximately 70 % are members of the Evangelical-Lutheran Church. In addition, 27 % are non-denominational and 1.1 % are Orthodox.

Modern western liberal societies are increasingly practising intolerance. They are taking an axe to fundamental questions of freedoms of speech, religion and conscience. Those who do not adapt to the modern zeitgeist, who do not conform

---

[19] See, for instance, the case of pastor Olaf Latzel Bremen, whose church instituted a disciplinary procedure against him. Idea Pressedienst, No. 107, dated 20/05/2020, 10–13, and idea Pressedienst, No. 136, dated 02/07/2020, 2.

[20] Cf. idea Pressedienst, No. 34, dated 14/02/2020, 3.

to the spirit of the modern age, need to anticipate realities such as humiliating interrogation, exclusion, loss of business and even denunciation and dismissal. In Germany, Evangelical pastors can still invoke a safeguard of conscientious objection based on belief if they choose not to marry same-sex partners. However, it can be anticipated that this safeguard of conscientious objection is also likely to crumble soon in the face of ongoing pressure from the general public. Theologically founded beliefs are typically interpreted as "hate-speech" or "stirring up hatred", conservative Christians are being perceived as opponents who need to be silenced through verbal humiliations. Freedom of speech still exist "on paper". However, consequences are becoming increasingly drastic. Harassment is steadily increasing.

The quarrel as to how Christian communities should deal with the issue of homosexuality is not just raging in marginal conservative Christian groups. It has also developed into a destructive wedge, dividing members within the mainstream churches. It is anticipated that the General Conference of the United Methodist Church (UMC) planned for May 2020, which represents some 25 million Christians around the world, will come to a decision whereby members of the church who find homosexuality to be incompatible with the Christian Church will withdraw from the UMC and establish a new, conservative Methodist Church. To this end, the UMC will provide start-up financing of 25 million dollars.[21]

The very much bigger Worldwide Anglican Church has deferred its Lambeth Conference from 2018 to 2020, and now the summer of 2021, following the threat from conservative bishops that they would boycott the conference on the basis of the homosexual issue.[22]

Thus far, the Evangelical Church in Germany has been spared such threats of separations and internal division. However, on the pietistic margins of the Church, the issue is festering; homosexuality is considered contrary to the will of God, in contradiction of creation theology and the theology of the cross. Furthermore, the church is churning over internal disputes about gender, abortion, migration and the question of the relationship to Islam. Modern social-political demands are pushing many Christian religious communities into a state of crisis. Conservative groups are no longer prepared to follow what they consider to be a leftist, liberal humanistic agenda, which they believe is directly opposed to Holy Scripture.

The crucial question remains; has this mode of religion overstepped the boundaries of religious freedom – simply because it has rejected outright any concept of religious compromise and a historically critical perspective of enlightenment? It is quite understandable that a society – bearing a striking resemblance to

---

[21] Cf. FAZ, No. 39, dated 15/02/2020, 8.
[22] Ibid.

pre-Christian Rome – which has to deal with a whole range of religions and gods, might find it easiest for its political actors to maintain a spirit of gentle mutual tolerance in all temples, churches and mosques. However, the rejection of such an attitude by conservatively pious communities, combined with their insistence on specific "fundamental truths" must also not give rise to a situation where various social media denounce them as extremists, where they are effectively equated with terrorists and banished from the very centre of society.

It is completely logical and understandable that the mainline churches are proceeding in this manner, in an attempt to defend their traditionally predominant position in the open market of religions. The reality is that the evangelicals are implicitly fostering and nurturing the church's so-called "crisis" ad absurdum. Their members are not fleeing in droves, they have no serious doubts about the teachings of their religious congregations, they are not suffering any form of "crisis of faith", and their members attend the community meetings of the respective denominations on a regular basis. However, they do not belong to the well-tempered religions of the centre; they see heresy and delusions in other religious communities and they will fight passionately for their own beliefs. Not least for this reason, they keep their religion alive and flourishing.

Lastly, it was also religious leaders from the realm of mainstream churches[23] who essentially channelled, or even undermined, traditional Church values and norms. This was effectively accomplished, in the first instance, through the Universal Declaration of Human Rights, declared in mid-December 1948, together with its precursors, as well as later regulations based on these – even though these same leaders had shared in the inspiration for and work towards the Declaration.[24] By placing universal human rights in the place of God, they created a new religion,

---

[23] Cf. John Foster Dulles und die Einigung Westeuropas, in: Die Christen und die Entstehung der Europäischen Gemeinschaft, published by Martin Greschat und Wilfried Loth (= Konfession und Gesellschaft. Beiträge zur Zeitgeschichte, Bd. 5), Stuttgart: Kohlhammer 1994, 159–187. See also Anna Fries, Warum die Kirche gegen die Menschenrechtserklärung war (Berlin, 10/12/2018) https://www.katholisch.de/artikel/19912-warum-die-kirche-gegen-die-menschenrechtserklaerung-war; ACK (ed.), Kirchen erinnern an 70 Jahre Allgemeine Erklärung der Menschenrechte: https://www.oekumene-ack.de/aktuell/aktuelle-meldungen/mitgliederversammlung/artikeldetails/kirchen-erinnern-an-70-jahre-allgemeine-erklaerung-der-menschenrechte/

[24] Cf. Paul Gordon Lauren, The Evolution of International Human Rights. Visions seen. University of Pennsylvania Press, Philadelphia 2011; Hans-Georg Ziebertz (ed.), Menschenrechte, Christentum und Islam, Münster: Lit, 2010; Stefan-Ludwig Hoffmann (ed.): Moralpolitik – Geschichte der Menschenrechte im 20. Jahrhundert, Göttingen: Wallstein, 2010; Yvonne Donders & Vladimir Volodin, Human Rights in Education, Science, and Culture – Legal Developments and Challenges. Aldershot: Ashgate, 2008; Hans Joas, Die Sakralität der Person. Eine neue Genealogie der Menschenrechte, Berlin: Suhrkamp, 2011; Hans Joas, Sind die Menschenrechte westlich? München: Kösel, 2015; Wilhelm Gräb & Lars Charbonnier (ed.), Religion and Human Rights. Global Challenges from Intercultural Perspectives, Berlin-Boston: De Gruyter, 2015; Judith Schmidt and Niels Rochlitzer, Tradition oder Mimese? Die Katholische Kirche und die Menschenrechte, in: Menschenrechtsmagazin Heft 1/2006, 47–62.

which would now become a benchmark of what traditional Christian groups are allowed to teach and how they can shape their beliefs. When, for example, practising homosexuality is considered a human right,[25] then religious communities must comprehend this as a normative principle, which they are not permitted to contradict. Liberal-theological mainstream churches generally do not have a problem with this, unlike evangelical and other groups who see their claim for freedom of religion as being challenged in this process.

The democratic constitutional state must not be allowed to stand by the considerations and requests from the established churches and other critics of the fundamentalist forms of piety; the state should not allow moderate religions to assume a one-sided position of privilege – among other things, because it is also pursuing the mostly peaceable political middle ground. The contents and substance of a religious community and its rituals are not incumbent upon state supervision. So long as there is no infringement of state laws, all religious communities should be able to live according to their faiths and practise their religion. They all stand, without discrimination, under the umbrella and protection of the state. This means freedom of religion in all its fullness and this is also prescribed by the constitutions of modern democratic constitutional-states.

Abstract

Christian churches, with their conservative Biblical-evangelical oriented character are increasingly coming into conflict with the legal and social-ethical principles of liberal societies that are far more concerned with universal human rights. When Christian religious communities use selective explicit wording from Holy Scripture to justify not wanting to implement new legal rules and regulations within their community, and openly articulate their rejection, then they will increasingly have to anticipate corresponding sanctions. Within western societies, tolerance is steadily decreasing towards the exercise of religiously motivated intolerance. Does this mean that religious freedom is reaching its limits with the reality of universal human rights taking effect in legal norms and standards? In any case, reactions emanating from liberal societies and the liberal mainstream churches are certainly causing a contraction of pluralism within the structure of the Church to the detriment of Evangelical spirituality and devotion.

---

[25] Cf. Hans-Joachim Mengel, Homosexualität und internationaler Menschenrechtsschutz, in: Aus Politik und Zeitgeschichte (APuZ 15–16/2010); Dreilinden gGmbH Gesellschaft für gemeinnütziges Privatkapital (ed.), Menschenrechte fördern! Deutsche Unterstützung für lesbische, schwule, bisexuelle, trans* und inter* (LSBTI) Menschenrechtsarbeit im Globalen Süden und Osten, Hamburg 2011, esp. 29 f.; Robert Aldrich (ed.), Gleich und anders. Eine globale Geschichte der Homosexualität, Hamburg: Murmann Verlag, 2007.

The Religious Scene After the End of the Swedish State Church Since 2000

Non-transparency and Confusion

Anders Jarlert

1. The changed relations between Church and state and its pastoral and administrative consequences

Contrary to what one would presume from the outside, the circumstances might be clearer and more transparent in a State Church, as in Sweden before the year 2000, than – as it is now – with an independent, yet by the State regulated Church. With a State Church it is self-evident that the Church has a privileged position. However, under current conditions in Sweden, the impression is much more obscure and unclear, which is, or should be a problem for both Church and State.

Since the year 2000, Church and State in Sweden have been separated or, rather, they got changed relations. This change or dissolution cannot be described as a divorce, neither as a full separation. As early as 2001, I described the new position of the Church of Sweden deliberately contradictory as a "Free State Church".[1] Since 2000, the Church is being regulated by a separate Law on the Church of Sweden, decided by Parliament only. The general Law on faith-communities does not include the Church of Sweden, but all other churches and religious communities. There, a religious community is defined as "a community for religious activities, including arranging religious services"[2], which is a rather open wording, necessary for the public registration of a religious community, thus getting a public status, including so-called sects, but excluding atheist and other organisations that do not arrange religious services.

The special Law on the Church of Sweden, however, is much more detailed. It states that

---

[1] Anders Jarlert, "Kirche, Staat und religiöse Minderheiten in Schweden", in: Religion – Staat – Gesellschaft 2. Jg., 2001/1, 141–152, here 151.

[2] https://www.riksdagen.se/sv/dokument-lagar/dokument/svensk-forfattningssamling/lag-1998 1593-om-trossamfund_sfs-1998-1593.

1 The Church of Sweden is an Evangelical-Lutheran religious community appearing as congregations and dioceses. The Church of Sweden also has national institutions.
2 The Church of Sweden is an open folk church (*folkkyrka*), which in co-operation between a democratic organisation and the ecclesiastical office conducts a nationwide activity.
---
4 The congregation (*församling*) is a local entity within the Church of Sweden. It includes those who belong to the Church of Sweden and reside in the area of the congregation.

The basic task of the congregation is to celebrate worship, conduct teaching, and practice deaconry and mission.[3]

This is a rather problematic document. First, the Parliament has decided about the confessional character of the Church of Sweden, that it should be Evangelical-Lutheran. This is from a historical point of view not undisputed. The Lutheran Church of Finland is named the Evangelical-Lutheran Church of Finland, indicating that there is also an Orthodox national Church. In Sweden, "Evangelical" only is sometimes – contrary to in Germany – regarded as more open towards Catholic perspectives, while "Lutheran" is being regarded as narrower. However, the label "Evangelical-Lutheran" alone does not provide enough space for the special, episcopal character of the Church of Sweden, where more of the medieval heritage has been kept than in most other Lutheran churches.

Simultaneously, the Church is described as "an open folk church" with a nationwide activity. This might sound uncontroversial, but since the membership in a certain congregation is totally dependent on where you live, this in practice means that the stately, local tax authorities decide in which congregation you should be a member. You are of course free to participate in the services and community life of any congregation, but your Church taxes are distributed to the congregation and parish where you live, and you have no possibility to take formal responsibility in another congregation. A somewhat similar system was changed in Austria in 1981. There, a Jewish believer who wanted to enjoy the freedoms and rights in connection with his religion, had to belong to the *Israelitische Kultusgemeinde*. An orthodox Jew had complained that he had either to belong to a liberal confession or leave the denomination entirely. In the decision of the court, freedom of religion as an individual right was placed before the corporate law concept that had formed the foundation of the *Israelitengesetz*. The order that every Israelite should belong to the congregation where he resided was considered

---

[3] https://www.riksdagen.se/sv/dokument-lagar/dokument/svensk-forfattningssamling/lag-1998 1591-om-svenska-kyrkan_sfs-1998-1591.

unconstitutional and was therefore repealed.[4] However, this has not been the case in Sweden.

Further, the prescribed "cooperation between a democratic organisation and the ecclesiastical office" is of course not without its problems. A continuous, fundamental problem is that the clergy is now not only appointed by the local parishes, but the Bishops have no formal opportunity to intervene when difficulties arise between the "democratic organisation" and "the ecclesiastical office". During the times of the State Church, the Bishops and Diocesan Chapters had the possibility to move a certain priest to somewhere else in the diocese, now they have to be "bought out" like other employees.

That the Church of Sweden has a nationwide activity has during the last two decades not excluded extensive structural changes with strong mergers of several congregations. This implies that the activity of the Church still is nationwide. However, there is no guarantee that there in practice is any continuing, ecclesiastical activity within several miles of the place where you live. This has, of course, always partly been the case in the sparsely populated far North of the country, but now also the Southern parts have in many places been strongly concerned.

I will mention one example of the problematic character of these structural changes. In Malmö, Sweden's third city, sixteen parishes (*pastorat*) were 2014 fused into one only, with just six congregations. (To make the situation understandable, I translate the most local, legal level, *församling*, with "congregation", and the bigger level, *pastorat*, containing one or several congregations, with "parish".) This division corresponds with a communal division in use between 2013 and 2017. The borders between the six congregations were redrawn – without historical or pastoral considerations – to get about the same size of membership in them all. A result of this is that the basic pastoral unit is now limited to the local church and the area around it, a district which is only a smaller part of what is officially named "congregation". This might perhaps not be a bad idea; however, the problem is that such a system does not exist in the Church ordinance, where the congregation only is the fundamental local unit. These changes have also in different parts of Sweden led to a number of new clerical titles between vicar and curate, such as "congregational vicar" (*församlingsherde*), or the more secularized "managerial curate" (*arbetsledande komminister*), none of which are mentioned in the Church ordinance. This means that the local Church authorities feel themselves free to adopt new pastoral and administrative systems, not regulated or even predicted in the Church ordinance. As far as they fulfil the regulations of the stately Law on the Church of Sweden, this seems to pass without any inter-

---

[4] Richard Potz & Brigitte Schinkele, Religionsrecht im Überblick, Wien 2005, 178. Anders Jarlert, "Individuell eller institutionell religionsfrihet?", in: A. Singer, M. Jänterä-Jareborg, A. Schlytter (eds.), Familj – religion – rätt. En antologi om kulturella spänningar i familjen – med Sverige och Turkiet som exempel. Uppsala 2010, 113–126, here 119.

vention. The Bishop might play a role, but now more based on personal authority than on formal proxies. In a very episcopal Lutheran church, like the Church of Sweden, this system is extremely congregationalist, inspired from the local civil communities. The pastoral and administrative structure is much less transparent and much more confused than in the times of the State Church, where everything was clearly defined by Ecclesiastical Law, approved by both the General Synod and the Parliament.

2. The Diocesan chapters as judicial courts

In an interesting article in 2016, Sven-Erik Brodd in a slightly tapered way named the Diocesan chapters (*domkapitel*) in the Church of Sweden "judicial courts of inquisition". He starts in the criticism against the processes in the chapters already during the 1940s, when they were accused of "suffering from all the weaknesses of the inquisitorial process". A main point was, and still is, that prosecutor and judge are the same person, with limited and unclear possibilities for the accused one to defend him- or herself.[5] However, at that time the Diocesan chapters were stately authorities, and their decisions could be appealed to the High Court.

According to Brodd, the inquisitorial elements remain after the changes of Church-State relations in the year 2000. The diocesan chapters consist of the Bishop, the Dean, one member elected by the priests and deacons, three elected laymen, and – only in disciplinarian matters, an elected judge. The results of these processes are that priests or deacons may be declared unauthorized to practice their offices or get a trial period or a serious reminder. These decisions may be appealed to a separate, national Board of appeal for Clergy, regulated by the Church ordinance. This Board of appeal has two parties and an independent judge. It does not initiate its own investigations. This means that it is not part of the inquisitorial system.[6]

As Brodd clearly shows, the ecclesiastical terminology after the so-called separation between Church and State, does not mention prosecution, trial or judgment, but instead uses mild words like "notified" and "decision". The Diocesan chapters do not seem to regard themselves as courts, and discipline is often labelled as "supervision" only.[7]

The existence of ecclesiastical courts working in parallel with stately courts is by no means unique to Sweden. The problem is rather the lack of regulations how a notification to the Chapter should be made, and the important point that the

---

[5] Sven-Erik Brodd, "Domkapitlen i Svenska kyrkan som inkvisitionsdomstolar", in: Martin Berntson & Anna Minara Ciardi, Kyrklig rätt och kyrklig orätt – kyrkorättsliga perspektiv. Festskrift till professor Bertil Nilsson. Skellefteå 2016, 245–274, here 247.
[6] Ibid., 248.
[7] Ibid., 249.

court itself initiates different cases.⁸ A big problem is the parallel process of soul-care or support from the bishop to the accused priest or deacon, regulated differently in the Church ordinance. The emphasis on the bishop as *pastor pastorum* is in a sense stronger in the new Church ordinance. This is a striking example of the non-transparency and confusion in the new situation.

An alternative would be an accusatory process, where the accused does not stand before an institution that simultaneously is police, prosecutor, and judge. Then it would be a negotiation between prosecutors and defendants with an unruly judge.⁹

In his conclusion, Brodd states, that "as there is no detailed ecclesiastical law in the Church of Sweden, the courts are judging according to general regulations found in the Church Order. Subsequently, the diocesan chapters handle the cases differently."¹⁰ As mentioned above, this is a problem already present in the State Church, but more non-transparent and confused after the changed relations.

3. The "secularization" of the concrete Church buildings

As Svante Beckman states in a book on conservation, religion, and politics in the Church, the changed relations between Church and State in Sweden meant a secularization of the state, while the concrete Church buildings simultaneously went through a "secular musealization", when these buildings were placed under the supervision of the county administrative boards.¹¹

In a concluding article on a concrete example, Madeleine Sultán Sjöqvist asks the critical question if the Cultural Act (*Kulturmiljölagen*) is legally contrary to religious freedom. Her example is a Lutheran church building, belonging to the Church of Sweden, that was sold to the Roman Catholic Church, but was still included in the strong cultural protection of the buildings in the Church of Sweden. She does this from the obvious fact that the legally protected church-cultural heritage includes only the Church buildings of the Church of Sweden, and not the material heritage in other churches, denominations, and religions.¹²

The financial support of the state for the restoration of the churches of the Church of Sweden is regulated by agreement. The Church of Sweden is regarded as

---

⁸ Ibid., 253f.
⁹ Ibid.
¹⁰ Ibid., 270.
¹¹ Svante Beckman, "Svenska kyrkan – ett nationellt kulturminne?", in Magdalena Hillström, Eva Löfgren & Ola Wetterberg (eds.), Alla dessa kyrkor. Kulturvård, religion och politik, Göteborg 2017, 103–125, here 117, 120.
¹² Madeleine Sultán Sjöqvist, "En luthersk kyrka blir katolsk – Nacksta kyrka i Sundsvall", in: Magdalena Hillström, Eva Löfgren & Ola Wetterberg (eds.), Alla dessa kyrkor. Kulturvård, religion och politik, Göteborg 2017, 311–321, here 319.

the nations's greatest cultural heritage manager. Here, the Church of Sweden has got a role as a national, social institution, and in its obligation to report its Church antiquarian activities to the Government, the Church is being treated like any other public authority. In this field, the Church of Sweden is acting on behalf of the state.[13]

However, that the Church of Sweden gets financial support from the state for the antiquarian additional costs of keeping the old Church buildings, is not as strange as it may sound. In a formally totally secularized country like France, all Church buildings from before 1905 are owned by the municipalities for the use of the Church. The 87 cathedrals are owned by the State. Even Church buildings owned by the Church may get financial support from the State, though only for the restoration of the building, not for its religious use.[14] Only Roman Catholic churches are being supported.[15] The difference is that the state and the municipalities, respectively, are more directly active in the Church restorations in France, whereas the Swedish state is directing the Church of Sweden's restoration work with the Church buildings, a system which instrumentalizes the local Church authorities as tools of the State.

4. The Church of Sweden's responsibility for the cemeteries

In all communities, except Stockholm and Tranås, the Church of Sweden still has the full responsibility for the planning, maintaining and care of the public cemeteries, whether they are located next to a church or not, and including, for example, Moslem cemeteries. Whereas the Jews have always taken care of their own cemeteries, nowadays often in some co-operation with the Church of Sweden, the Moslems have never been able to do so. Every citizen pays a certain fee for this service, which for the members of the Church of Sweden is included in their church tax. The local Church administrations fulfil their common responsibility for the cemeteries through this special fee, which is being directed to them by the State, through the *Kammarkollegium*, which also handles the registration of religious communities. Funeral services and anything connected with them, on the other hand, is being paid directly by the church taxes. This is a more transparent order than in many other parts of the ecclesiastical activity. However, the terminological confusion is total. The fee that is paid by every citizen is named "funeral fee", but the only thing that is not included in this fee is what in everyday language is described as a "funeral", i.e. the funeral service. It would have been easier in English, but in Swedish "funeral" and "burial" is generally the same word.

---

[13] Beckman, Svenska kyrkan (n. 11), 114.
[14] Eva Löfgren, "Franska kyrkor som kulturarv", in: Magdalena Hillström, Eva Löfgren & Ola Wetterberg (eds.), Alla dessa kyrkor. Kulturvård, religion och politik, Göteborg 2017, 41–57, here 46f., 50.
[15] Löfgren, Franska kyrkor (n. 14), 54f.

Proposals have been made to transfer the cemeteries into communal hands, but the local communities have not been interested in taking over this responsibility. That this responsibility is an assignment from the government becomes very clear when conflicts arise about where a certain person is to be buried, or if a coffin or ashes are to be moved. If the mediation by the ecclesiastical cemetery management does not become successful, a decision is made by the public county government.

5. Conclusion

In my overview of the religious scene after the end of the Swedish State Church since 2000, I have characterized the changed situation as non-transparent and confused. This is clearer in some areas than in others. The special legislation with a separate Law on the Church of Sweden remains a problem since it differs so much from the general Law on religious communities, and since it regulates the inner, confessional character of the Church as well. That members of the Church of Sweden cannot register as members of a congregation after their own choice but are compulsory members of the congregation where they live, based on a decision of the tax authorities, is a relic of the State Church system. The structural changes of the last decade have brought along a confusion in the differences between the Church ordinance and the factual, local circumstances. The Diocesan chapters remain in practice "judicial courts of inquisition", though they do not seem to regard themselves as courts, and discipline often is labelled as "supervision" only. Different chapters handle the cases in a different way. This is an old problem that has grown more non-transparent after the year 2000. That the Swedish State directs the Church of Sweden's restoration work with the Church buildings is a significant example of changed relations that seem rather to be some sort of reverse relationships. The local Church is being instrumentalized by the State. Also, in the responsibilities of the cemeteries, the State has left the care to the Church of Sweden, but keeps in a certain sense, an ultimate responsibility. In this area, a terminological confusion adds to an otherwise transparent system.

To sum up, the changed relations between the State and the Church of Sweden cannot be described as a divorce or a separation, but rather as a new structure of cooperation, promoting, instrumentalization, and supervision, partly as a result of the structural development of the Church of Sweden during the last decades. Especially in its non-transparent and confused parts this remains a problem for both Church and State.

Concluding, I would state that religious freedom in Sweden is somewhat limited both for the members of the Church of Sweden and for the members of other churches and denominations, which, of course, adds to the confused impression of a "free State Church". History will regard the present system as a new and different chapter of the State Church era.

Abstract

With the changed relations between Church and state, the pastoral and administrative structure is less transparent than in the times of the State Church, where everything was clearly defined by Ecclesiastical Law, approved by both the General Synod and the Parliament. The problem with the Diocesan chapters as judicial courts was already present in the State Church, but is more non-transparent after the changed relations. The concrete Church buildings has gone through a process of "secular musealization", in which the state is now directing the Church's restoration work, a system which instrumentalizes the local Church authorities as tools of the State. The Church of Sweden's responsibility for the cemeteries is an assignment from the government, which becomes very clear when conflicts arise. If the ecclesiastical mediation is not successful, a decision is made by the public county government. Concluding, the result is that religious freedom in Sweden is somewhat limited both for the members of the Church of Sweden and for the members of other churches and denominations, which, of course, adds to the confused impression of a "free State Church".

We're Happy to Talk, But Dialogue …?

Courteous Discrimination in Establishment Parlance

Eileen Barker

… nor is religion manifold because there are various sects and heresies in the world. When I mention religion I mean the Christian religion. Not only the Christian religion, but the Protestant religion, and not only the Protestant religion but the Church of England.[1]

1. Prolegomenon

The English gentleman is terribly polite. His manners are impeccable. He is well versed in the Queensbury Rules – that is, one doesn't hit a man when he is down – and certainly not below the belt. The English gentleman is – well, he's a gentleman.[2]

The English gentleman is polite to servants and foreigners. He knows he is generous to his inferiors and would not dream of being rude to the men and women who toil on his estate, to the servants who wash his clothes, prepare his food and clean the sewers – he may well address the poacher caught stealing a rabbit from his country estate as 'my good man'. He smiles briefly but graciously at the *maître d'hôtel* who shows him to his favourite table. He even gives a curt nod to the bedraggled man who offers to sell him matches in the street – but keeps his distance as it is clear the man has not bathed for some considerable time.

The English gentleman will agree, perhaps insist, that all men are born equal – even those who clean the sewers and sweep the streets, and nowadays he will include the foreign doctors and nurses who keep our National Health Service just about functioning. True English gentlemen insist that they believe in the equality of men and women – although women are, of course, 'different'. They abhor anyone who is a racist – Conservative gentlemen are shocked at the anti-Semitic tendencies to be found within the Labour Party, and Labour gentlemen – yes,

---

[1] Mr. Thwackum in *The History of Tom Jones, a Foundling*, by Henry Fielding.

[2] It should be noted that throughout this chapter, unless indicated otherwise, England almost always refers to England, not to Britain (which includes both Scotland and Wales), nor yet to the United Kingdom (which further includes Northern Ireland).

even Labour party members can be gentlemen – abhor the Islamophobia to be found within the Conservative party.

And this brings us to religion.

2. Religion populations in England

Most of Pagan, heathenry and folkloric practices having been squashed, if not entirely eliminated, by the start of the second millennium CE, England, like most of the rest of Europe had become a majority Christian country – there have been exceptions such as Spain in what the English refer to as the Dark Ages, and parts of Eastern Europe during the time of the Ottoman Empire. Until the Reformation, Western European religion was almost entirely Roman Catholic, though Greece, like Eastern Europe, followed the Eastern rite. England's Reformation, as every school child is taught, was the result of Henry VIII (1491–1547) wanting to marry Ann Boleyn. With the 1534 Act of Supremacy, Henry proclaimed himself "the only supreme head on Earth of the Church of England". His daughter, Mary Tudor (1516–1558), attempted during her reign (1553–1558) to restore Catholicism but merely succeeded in fanning the flames of the Reformation. One of the first actions of Mary's half-sister, Queen Elizabeth I (1533–1603), was to secure a Protestant future for England, and since 1559 the Church of England has been 'by law established.'

Once established, the Church of England was opposed not only by Roman Catholics but also by Protestants who wanted to purify the Church even further. Some of these Puritans worked for reform within the Church, others formed small separatist movements, later known as the English Independent or Congregationalist movement. The Separatist Puritans found a more tolerant reception in The Netherlands, and the Pilgrim Fathers emigrated from Leiden, via Plymouth, to New England in 1620. Since then, the Church of England has survived as the Established Church in the face of a continuing history of religious dissent.

The early English Baptists from Holland settled in London in the first half of the seventeenth century; in 1650 the name 'Quaker' was applied to George Fox (1624–1691) and his followers, who were later known as the Society of Friends. With the turbulence of the Civil Wars, there was a mushrooming of relatively short-lived millennial movements (such as the Ranters, the Levellers, and the Fifth Monarchy Men). Around the 1730s, a surge of revivalism (the Awakening) was witnessed and in 1738 John Wesley (1703–1799), an Anglican priest who was to found the Methodist movement, experienced a spiritual conversion that reinforced his evangelical fervour. The nineteenth century saw the arrival of a number of new sects, some of which (such as the Plymouth [exclusive] Brethren and the Salvation Army) were home-grown; others (such as the Seventh-day

Adventist Church; the Church of Christ, Scientist; the Church of Jesus Christ of Latter-day Saints and the Jehovah's Witnesses) arrived from the United States of America. Towards the end of the century, one or two other movements, such as Madame Blavatsky's Theosophical Society, began to introduce ideas from the East to sections of upper-middle-class England.

The early twentieth century witnessed the arrival of several Pentecostal sects from the United States, followed by the further appearance of 'foreign' religions. Successive waves of migrants (particularly West Indians in the 1950s and people of South Asian origin from the 1960s onward; then, as they joined the European Union, increasing numbers of Eastern Europeans) arrived and changed – there are those who would say 'diluted' – not only the ethnic but also the religious composition of England.

The 2011 census recorded the population of England as 53.0 million, Scotland having 5.3 million, Wales 3.1 million, and Northern Ireland 1.8 million. Of the 56.1 million population of England and Wales, 80.5 % reported their ethnic group as White British; 4.4 % reported themselves to be 'Any Other White'. Indians were the next largest minority group (2.5 %), followed by Pakistanis (2 %); those of mixed ethnic backgrounds (2.2 %); black Caribbeans (1.1 %); black Africans (1.8 %); Bangladeshis (0.8 %); Chinese (0.7 %); 'black other' (0.5 %); 'other Asian' (0.4 per cent); and 'other' (1 %).

Over the past two and a half decades, there has been a dramatic decline in identification with Christian denominations, particularly the Church of England, from 67 % in 1983 to 38 % in 2018. But whilst it and other major denominations were undergoing a steady decline in church attendance and membership, there was a growth (which by no means compensated for the loss in the traditional churches) in Charismatic and Pentecostal Christianity, especially among Afro-Caribbeans who frequently found themselves unwelcome in predominantly white churches. Sunni, Shi'a and Ahmadiyya mosques, Hindu and Buddhist temples, Sikh Gurdwaras, and a few Shinto shrines are now becoming an increasingly visible part of the English landscape. The geographical distribution of the minority ethnic groups has, however, been very uneven, tending to concentrate in large urban conurbations.

A further development has been the emergence of both indigenous and imported new religious movements (NRMs), which became increasingly visible from the late 1960s. Among those originating in the United Kingdom were the Aetherius Society, the School of Economic Science, the Emin, the Jesus Fellowship, and the Findhorn Foundation in the north of Scotland, which is regularly visited by New Age seekers from around the world. Other new religions that were to become household names included the Unification Church (popularly known as the Moonies) from Korea; the Church of Scientology and The Children of God (later known as The Family International) from the USA; the followers of Bhagwan Rajneesh (later known as Osho) from India; the International Society for Krishna Consciousness from India via the USA; and the Rastafarians from Jamaica.

By 2019, Inform (see below) had records on well over 5,000 different religious organisations, more than 1,000 of which had appeared since the Second World War and were currently active in England. There were also a few 'anti-cult' and 'counter-cult' movements which had been established to warn the population about the perceived theological and practical dangers of heresies and alien spiritual movements. Sometimes referred to as England's first anti-cult group, FAIR was founded by a Member of Parliament in 1976 and, at various times, had one other Member of Parliament, one member of the House of Lords and two Church of England priests as its Chair. FAIR was originally an acronym for Family, Action, Information, and Rescue, and several of its members were involved in 'deprogrammings', when adult converts were illegally kidnapped and held against their will until they managed to escape or persuade their captors that they had renounced their faith (Barker, 1989; Bromley and Richardson, 1983). After one of its committee members was convicted in Germany in 1987 of kidnapping and causing bodily harm to a German Scientologist, it changed the acronym to Family, Action, Information and Resource (Arweck, 2006). More recently, FAIR has evolved into The Family Survival Trust.[3]

During the 1970s and '80s, academics who had been studying the new religions were becoming increasingly concerned about the harmful effects brought about through the ignorance and misinformation that was being disseminated through the media, who were frequently being fed stories by the anti-cultists. As one such academic, I founded Inform (Information Network Focus on Religious Movements)[4] in 1988 with the support of the then-Archbishop of Canterbury, Dr Robert Runcie, and the Home Office. The idea behind Inform was then, and still is, to carry out original research and to draw on an international network of scholars and others with professional and personal experience of minority religions so as to provide information that is as objective, contextualised and up-to-date as possible (Barker, 2001). As well as academics and others professionals, Inform's Board of Governors has at least one representative of the Church of England, the Roman Catholic Church and the Free Churches Group (originally the Free Church Federal Council).[5] The first Vice Chair of Inform and the person who helped me most in the early days when Inform was being attacked quite viciously by the anti-cult movement and certain sections of the media (Barker, 1995), was an ecumenically-minded Church of England priest, the late Canon Martin Reardon. Over the years, Inform has responded to thousands of enquiries about hundreds of different minority religions, the

---

[3] https://www.thefamilysurvivaltrust.org.
[4] www.Inform.ac.
[5] https://www.freechurches.org.uk/what-we-do.

questions ranging from those of concerned relatives trying to discover what has happened to a loved one who has 'disappeared into a cult', to the media seeking background for a story, to the police investigating an unexplained murder, to a parish priest worried about letting his church hall to 'a strange group' – and much else beyond. Whilst not involved in lobbying or counselling, Inform holds regular open seminars addressing a wide range of issues related to minority religions, in which the participants include members of a wide range of old and new religions, 'anti-cultists', civil servants, police, lawyers, social workers, relatives and friends of new religions and interested members of the general public. Speakers have included both Dr Runcie and his successor, Dr George Carey (both of whom were Inform's Patrons), as well as a variety of representatives of the minority religions.[6] Inform also publishes a series of edited volumes, in which, often drawing from the seminars, a variety of contributors, including both scholars and members of minority religions, discuss a particular issue from their particular perspective.[7]

The National Secular Society had been founded by Charles Bradlaugh in 1866, and the British Humanist Association appeared in 1928. But England has not experienced the virulent anti-clericalism found in some other parts of Europe; even the recent rise of 'New Atheists' has involved attacking the beliefs and practices of religion in general terms, rather than the Church of England or its clergy in particular. When, in January 2003, The Sunday Assembly, a congregation for atheists and nonbelievers began to meet for monthly services at a deconsecrated church in north London, the overflowing crowds who attended, did so in the spirit of offering an alternative to the friendship and fellowship to be found in churches, while just leaving out references to any supernatural Being.

3. The Law, The Church and Other Religions

The 1534 Act of Supremacy was followed by the Dissolution of the Monasteries (1536–41), one of the first of sweeping 'reforms' under the Church of England. There were also several executions for heresy, which by then was frequently indistinguishable from treachery. During Mary Tudor's reign (1553–1558), the Act of Supremacy was repealed and England was formally re-united with Rome. Then, when Elizabeth I became Queen, England once again became a non-Catholic country with her 1558 Act of Supremacy re-establishing the Church of England's independence from Rome. Elizabeth adopted the title of Supreme Governor of the Church of England. The 1558 Act of Uniformity decreed that church services

---

[6] https://inform.ac/pastevents.
[7] For a list of titles, see https://www.routledge.com/Routledge-Inform-Series-on-Minority-Religions-and-Spiritual-Movements/book-series/AINFORM?pg=&so=pubdate&pp=12&view=list&pd=published.

should adhere to the English Book of Common Prayer, and that everyone had to attend church once a week (or face a fine of 12 pence).[8] To this day, when Parish priests are inducted, they are given spiritual responsibility for everyone in the Parish, whatever their faith or lack thereof.

In 1571 (in response to Pope Pius V's 'Regnans in Excelsis' Bull of the previous year which had not only excommunicated Elizabeth and anyone who obeyed her, but also required all Roman Catholics to rebel against her), Parliament passed an Act declaring it treasonable to be under the authority of the Pope, or to harbour a Catholic priest. The standard penalty for those convicted of treason was execution by being hanged, drawn and quartered. A law decreeing the burning at the stake of heretics remained in force in England until 1676, although the last person burned for heresy was executed in 1612; Witches had been burned or, more frequently, hanged in Britain from the time of the Middle Ages, but witch-hunts reached a peak in the seventeenth century. The last witchcraft trial in England was held in 1712 (1722 in Scotland). In 1736 Parliament passed an Act repealing the laws against witchcraft, but imposing fines or imprisonment on people who claimed to be able to use magical powers. This was not repealed until the 1951 Fraudulent Mediums Act, which was itself repealed in 2008.

In 1689 the Act of Toleration had granted freedom of worship to Nonconformists or Free Churches (that is, Protestants refusing to conform to the doctrines or authority of the Established Church), who were then allowed their own ministers and places of worship, subject to their taking an oath of allegiance to the Crown. However, the Act did not apply to Roman Catholics or Unitarians, who remained subject to civil and religious constraints until the nineteenth century. The 1701 Act of Settlement stated that the crown could only be passed to a Protestant and anyone who became a Roman Catholic, or who married one, became disqualified from inheriting the throne. Today (2020), Queen Elizabeth is the Supreme Governor of the Church of England and 'Defender of the Faith', a title Parliament had conferred on Henry VIII and his successors in 1544. It is, moreover, she who appoints archbishops, bishops and deans of cathedrals – on the advice of the Prime Minister. The Archbishop of Canterbury ranks next in precedence to the Royal Family.[9] Interestingly, there was a time when it was widely circulated that the current Queen's son, the Prince of Wales, had said that, rather than having the title of Defender of the Faith when he acceded to the throne, he would prefer to be known as 'Defender of Faith' because he was concerned "about the inclusion of other people's faiths and their freedom to worship in this country". He had, however, eventually decided that this desire

---

[8] This would be the equivalent of around US $ 30 in 2019, roughly a day's wages for a skilled worker.

[9] Next is the Lord Chancellor, followed by the Archbishop of York. https://www.debretts.com/expertise/forms-of-address/professions/religion/.

was compatible with the original, traditional wording, and that he would keep the 'the' for the coronation ceremony.[10]

The Test Act of 1673 had required anyone taking civil or military office to take the oaths of supremacy and allegiance and subscribing to swear that they did not believe in transubstantiation. In 1678, the requirement was extended to Peers and Members of the House of Commons. Such laws, barring Catholics and others who were not members of the Established Church from holding public office, remained in force until the second half of the nineteenth century. Religious tests for academics in the universities of Oxford, Cambridge and Durham were abolished in 1871. The Roman Catholic hierarchy was eventually restored in England and Wales in 1850, giving rise to a 'no popery' furore over 'Papal Aggression' (Ralls, 1974).

A small community of Jews, who had settled in England after the Norman Conquest, was expelled by Edward I (1239–1307), and then readmitted during Cromwell's Protectorate (1653–1659). Confessing Jews were sufficiently integrated into British society to be admitted to Parliament in 1858. Although there have been waves of Jewish refugees, such as those exiled by the Russian pogroms in 1881 and those fleeing from Nazi persecution in the 1930s, a high rate of intermarriage has meant that the Jewish community has never been statistically (as opposed to socially) very significant in England. On a few isolated occasions outbreaks of anti-Semitism have hit parts of Britain: anti-Semitic riots occurred, for example, in the Welsh valleys in 1911 and in several large English towns in 1947. And, as intimated above, the Labour Party under the leadership of Jeremy Corbyn (2015–2020), was accused of an anti-Semitic bias.

Whilst, compared to some other parts of the world, the UK has enjoyed a relatively peaceful coexistence among its many religious communities during the past three or so centuries, there have been some serious clashes, the most critical of which were in Northern Ireland, where tensions have existed between the Protestant majority, who enjoyed relative economic and political advantage and who want to stay part of the United Kingdom, and the Catholic minority, who want to be reunited with the Republic of Ireland. Despite being defined in religious terms, the conflict had little to do with religion, and far more with politics and economics. The tensions erupted into violence in 1968, with over 3,500 'troubles-related deaths' (including some lethal bombings in England). After a series of short-lived cease-fires throughout the mid-1990s, a fragile peace agreement was eventually brokered in 1998. This has resulted in a generally non-violent situation, despite occasional eruptions by small schismatic groups.

Ironically, although discrimination on grounds of sex or race became illegal in the 1970s, Northern Ireland was the only part of the UK in which discrimination

---

[10] https://www.secularism.org.uk/news/2015/02/charles-vows-to-keep-defender-of-the-faith-title-as-king.

on religious grounds was an offence. There had been an interesting case in 1982, *Mandla v Dowell-Lee*, in which a father lodged a complaint with the Commission for Racial Equality when his son was refused entry to a school unless he would cut his hair and stop wearing a turban. In the Court of Appeal, Lord Denning ruled that, under the 1976 Race Relations Act,

> You can discriminate for or against Roman Catholics as much as you like without being in breach of the law. … But you must not discriminate against a man because of his colour or of his race or of his nationality, or of "his ethnic or national origins." … You can discriminate against the Moonies or the Skinheads or any other group which you dislike or to which you take objection. No matter whether your objection to them is reasonable or unreasonable, you can discriminate against them - without being in breach of the law.[11]

An appeal was then made to the House of Lords, where Lord Fraser ruled that the Sikhs could be defined as an ethnic group (although they were not biologically distinguishable from the other peoples of the Punjab) rather than just a religion and, as such, could be protected in law under the Race Relations Act.

It was not until 1998 that Parliament was to introduce the Human Rights Act, allowing cases concerning those rights which had been established under the European Convention of Human Rights to be handled in British courts. This enabled cases of religious discrimination to be judged according to Article 9, giving all individuals an absolute right to hold or change a particular religion or belief, and a qualified right to manifest that religion or belief. And then, in 2010, the Equality Act made it unlawful to discriminate against someone because of religion or belief, or because of a lack of religion or belief (Equality and Human Rights Commission, 2016).

Unlike the situation in many other countries in Europe and elsewhere, England does not require a religion to be registered. The Church of England, as the Established Church, has been the only religion for which there have been special laws. In theory at least, one could expect the law to apply equally to any individual or organisation irrespective of religious affiliation. The law has not, however, always been obeyed to the letter and there can be no doubt that some religions have been 'more equal than others' (Barker, 1987). If they wish to be eligible for special tax exemptions, religions can apply to register with the Charity Commissioners who will grant them charitable status so long as they can demonstrate that they are a religion (now relatively widely defined) and that they operate 'in the public interest'.[12] This is entirely voluntary, and some minority religions prefer not to register as a charity because they do not wish to be constrained by charity law. Others have not succeeded in being granted charitable status because they have been deemed not to be a 'real' religion and/or not operating for the public benefit.

---

[11] https://www.sikhiwiki.org/index.php/Mandla_v_Dowell_Lee.
[12] https://www.gov.uk/setting-up-charity.

But even if they are not classified as a charity, they are still free to operate in any way they wished, so long as they do not contravene the laws of the country.

However, one of the consequences of 'the Troubles' in Northern Ireland was that between 2000 and 2015 the British Parliament passed a series of Terrorism Acts, which extended in their scope beyond the situation in Northern Ireland. These opened up an opportunity for the introduction of laws that banned any group that 'glorified terrorism'.[13] In 1998, a consultation paper, *Legislation Against Terrorism*, had argued that although the original Prevention of Terrorism Act, which had been a direct response to Irish terrorism, had been extended to cover international terrorism (such as that conducted by Islamic extremists), it was now judged necessary to widen it to include domestic terrorism, such as that currently or potentially threatened by animal activists, objectors to homosexuality and abortion clinics (Secretary of State, 1998). Perhaps inevitably, the outcome was that, starting with the 2000 Terrorism Act, a number of movements have been proscribed on the grounds that they are believed (by the Home Secretary) to be involved with terrorism for the purpose of advancing a political, religious, racial or ideological cause. As well as the 14 organisations in Northern Ireland that had been proscribed under previous legislation, 75 international terrorist organisations were proscribed under the Terrorism Act 2000 and the numbers have increased over the years (Home Office, 2020). Not infrequently, the increase in numbers has been due to a proscribed organisation reinventing itself under a new name.[14] The majority, but by no means all, of those with a religious affiliation consider themselves to be Islamic.

However, banning certain religions because they are associated with terrorism has nothing to do with established religion. Indeed, despite the fact that 26 of its senior Bishops (known as the Lords Spiritual) sit in the House of Lords,[15] the Church has little or no say in the legal status of other religions. There is certainly nothing like the current, apparently cosy, relationship between the Kremlin and the Russian Orthodox Church, or even the relationship that, until recently, the five state-sanctioned Patriotic Religious Associations had with the Chinese Communist Party. In so far as the Church of England has any influence on the situation of 'traditional' minority religions, this now tends towards enhancing, rather than constraining, their lot. At several of the ceremonial events that have in the past been exclusively attended by the Church of England, today one can see, alongside the Archbishop of Canterbury and/or the Bishop of London, the Head of the Roman Catholic Church in England and the Moderator of the Free Churches Group (who might be a member of the Methodist Church, the Baptist

---

[13] The 2006 Terrorism Act Part 1. 1 (3) http://www.legislation.gov.uk/ukpga/2006/11/.

[14] Al-Muhajiroun, then Al Ghurabaa, The Saviour Sect, Islam4UK, Muslims Against Crusades, Need4Khilafah and the Shariah Project have, at different times, borne a remarkable resemblance to each other so far as beliefs, practices and personnel are concerned.

[15] https://publications.parliament.uk/pa/ld/ldcomp/compso2010/ldctso04.htm#a3.

Union or the Salvation Army). One might also see the Chief Rabbi, one or more of the more prominent Muslim leaders, a turbaned Sikh and perhaps a Hindu Swami and Buddhist monk with a shaved head and brightly coloured robe, likely to be representatives of the 'major religions' with membership of the Inter Faith Network (see below).

But, as Bob Dylan has observed, "the times, they are a'changin".

On 17 October 2018, a government press release reported:

> Seven more faith and belief groups are to be permanently represented during the National Remembrance Service at the Cenotaph from this year.[16]

For the first time, Baha'i, Coptic, Humanist, Jain, Mormon, Spiritualist and Zoroastrian representatives were to stand alongside leaders from 'the main religions' at the Cenotaph as spots reserved for clerics on Armistice Day were opened up both to non-believers and to smaller faiths.

4. The Church of England in Recent Times

While in the earlier part of the twentieth century the Church of England was referred to as the Conservative party at prayer, from around the 1960s it appeared, both theologically and politically, to become less compliant with the establishment (with a small e). The publication of *Honest to God* in 1963 by the Bishop of Woolwich, John Robinson (1919–1983), the introduction of the Anglican Alternative Service Book in 1980, and a series of provocative statements by David Jenkins (1925–2016), who was the Bishop of Durham from 1984 to 1994, all led to acute anxiety among traditionalists about the undermining not merely of the Established Church but also of the very fabric of British society. Tensions between Church and State – as represented, respectively, by the then Archbishop of Canterbury, Robert Runcie (1925–2000) and the Prime Minister, Margaret Thatcher (1925–2013) – were exacerbated when Dr Runcie commissioned a report on urban poverty (published as *Faith in the City* in 1985), and insisted on praying not only for the British but also for the relatives of Argentines who died in the 1982 Falklands War. The final crunch for some Anglicans came when, in 1992, the General Synod agreed to the ordination of women to the ministry, and the then Bishop of London, Graham Leonard (1921–2010), led a small exodus of clergy into the Roman Catholic Church. Yet further tensions surrounding gender have continued to erupt over various incidents involving homosexuality among the clergy and same-sex marriages.

---

[16] https://www.gov.uk/government/news/more-faith-and-belief-groups-to-join-the-national-service-of-remembrance.

Another development in the twenty-first century has been associated with the biologist Richard Dawkins (2006) who, through a television series and a best-selling book, *The God Delusion*, has been popularising atheism for the British public. This has resulted, on the one hand, in a strong reaction from theologians such as Alister McGrath and, on the other hand, by the establishment of the 'Richard Dawkins Foundation for Reason and Science'.[17] Around the same time there was a revivalism in organizations such as the British Humanist Association, now called Humanists UK,[18] resulting in such high profile campaigns as the Atheist Bus Advertisements, with posters on buses throughout Great Britain proclaiming "There's probably no God. Now stop worrying and enjoy your life".[19] Initially, this had been in response to a "Quote Jesus" campaign that had been advertising verses from the New Testament on sides of London buses in June 2008.[20]

4.1. Some Statistics

Measuring religiosity is well known to be fraught with problems. One can reach very different conclusions whether one is asking questions about religious membership, affiliation, beliefs, and/or practice. However, there can be little doubt that, throughout the twentieth century, England witnessed an increasing overall decline in all these aspects. Introducing the data collected by The National Centre for Social Research, David Voas and Steve Bruce (2019, 3) have commented,

> In Britain, church attendance has declined steadily since at least 1851, when a government count showed about half the population in church on a particular Sunday. The figure derived from recent clergy counts is around 6%. In 1900 church membership was around 25%; it is now less than 10%. In 1900 more than half the age-relevant population attended Sunday schools; now it is less than 4%. Similar declines are visible in the use of religious offices to mark rites of passage. … In 2012 there were more humanist than Catholic weddings. Before the Second World War, the Church of England was baptising three-quarters of the English population; the figure now is 15%.

The British Social Attitudes survey also indicated that most of the shift in the religious profile has been towards non-affiliation, with 52% of the public now saying they do not regard themselves as belonging to any religion. Two-thirds (66%) of people in Britain never attend religious services, apart from special occasions such as weddings, funerals and baptisms. However, while most people show little enthusiasm for institutionalised religion, there is evidence that the public are, in general, prepared to be tolerant of the faith of others (op. cit., 2).

---

[17] https://www.richarddawkins.net/.
[18] https://humanism.org.uk/.
[19] https://humanism.org.uk/campaigns/successful-campaigns/atheist-bus-campaign/.
[20] https://www.churchtimes.co.uk/articles/2017/7-april/news/uk/london-buses-to-carry-jesus-s-words/.

According to the 2011 government census, 59.4% of the English population declared itself affiliated with Christianity. This had been 71.7% in the 2001 census. Affiliation to other religions was as follows (the first percentage being that in the 2011 census and the one in brackets being that of the 2001 census): Islam 5.0 (3.1); Hinduism 1.5 (1.1); Sikhism 0.8 (0.7); Judaism 0.5 (0.5); Buddhism 0.5 (0.3); other religion 0.4 (0.3); no religion 24.7 (14.6) religion not stated 7.7 (7.2).

Taking Christianity alone and comparing the breakdown of the response to questions about religious identity in 2018 with that in 1983, of the 66% in 1983 (and 32% in 2018) who reported that their religious identity was Christian, 12% were Church of England/Anglican in 2018 (and 40% in 1983); 7% (10%) Roman Catholic; 2% (5%) Presbyterian; 1% (4%) Methodist; less than 1% (1%) Baptist; 13% (3%) Christian 'no denomination'; and 1% (3%) 'other Christian' (Voas and Bruce, 2019, 5).

In short, although some Christian churches, most notably those of a Pentecostal or nondenominational nature have seen a rise in membership, the Church of England would seem to have been decreasing its hold on the English population on practically every count over the past century (Church of England, 2019). Furthermore, Church of England affiliation has been ageing for some time, so any hope for a robust future membership is looking somewhat slim for the immediate future (Day, 2017).

One consequence of the changing scene has been that questions are increasingly being asked about why the Church of England should hold a privileged place in society when it no longer represents the majority.[21] Why, for example, should it receive state funding for its schools?[22] Why should the tradition of Bishops sitting in the House of Lords be continued?[23] At the same time, however, it would seem that although there is now a majority of individuals belonging to the category of 'nones', a significant number of these will still consider themselves 'spiritual but not religious', and/or still believe in what Grace Davie (2007) has referred to as vicarious religion – that is, the belief that religion in general and perhaps Church of England in particular has a role to play in society even if the rank-and-file are minimally involved. The priests should do the praying, and the Archbishop of Canterbury should crown the monarch.

The Church itself, whilst not giving any sign of wanting to give up its position as the Established Church, let alone welcome the laicity of its French neighbour, has, nonetheless, increasingly sought to be partnering (as, perhaps, the first among equals), with other Christian religions (though not non-Trinitarians), and then (some) other faiths.

---

[21] https://leftfootforward.org/2018/09/new-figures-show-its-time-to-end-the-privileged-position-of-religion-in-public-life/.

[22] https://humanism.org.uk/education/.

[23] https://www.electoral-reform.org.uk/why-are-there-bishops-in-the-house-of-lords/.

5. With whom does the Church of England Dialogue?

The Church of England is part of the Anglican Communion, which, starting with Canada in 1578, has grown through missionary work into a community of tens of millions of members in more than 165 countries around the globe.[24] Anglicanism includes the Episcopalian Churches of Scotland and the USA, and a number of religious orders of laity and/or clergy. Each Anglican Province is autonomous, with its own Primate and its own canon law.[25] Since 1867, every ten years or so, Bishops from the various Provinces are invited by the Archbishop of Canterbury to attend the Lambeth Conference for collaborative consultation on issues of the time. These Conferences have not always demonstrated a meeting of minds, some of the African Provinces being more conservative, theologically and socially, than some Western Anglicans. The decision of the American Church to persist in ordaining, first, an openly gay bishop in 2004, and then a lesbian bishop in 2010 was the cause of not a little tension, and at times it looked as though the results might be split in the Communion.[26]

Although most commonly Holy Communion in the Church of England is offered to members who have been confirmed into an Anglican Church, others, such as Methodists, "baptised persons who are communicant members of other Churches which subscribe to the doctrine of the Holy Trinity" may receive communion.[27] This clearly excludes non-Trinitarian religions such as the Church of Jesus Christ of Latter-day Saints, Jehovah's Witnesses, Christadelphians and Christian Scientists. It might be noted that although the Church of England does not exclude the possibility of administering the Eucharist to a Roman Catholic, the Catholic Church itself strictly forbids its members to receive communion in an Anglican church.[28]

Regardless of whether or not the members of different religions share the holy Communion with each other, the Church of England has been actively involved in ecumenical dialogue with other Christian world communities in the hope of working towards Christian unity. Those with whom it has entered into formal dialogue include Baptists, Lutherans, Methodists, Eastern Orthodox, and, especial-

---

[24] https://www.anglicancommunion.org/.

[25] Together with the other Churches of the Anglican Communion, the Church of England is 'in communion with' the Old Catholic Churches of the Union of Utrecht, the Philippine Independent Church and the Mar Thoma Church. http://www.anglicancommunion.org/ecumenism/churches-in-communion.aspx.

[26] http://edition.cnn.com/2010/US/05/15/episcopal.lesbian.bishop/index.html.

[27] https://www.churchofengland.org/more/policy-and-thinking/canons-church-england/section-b#b28.

[28] It might be added that there are Church of England clergy who offer a blessing as part of the communion service to anyone who would like to receive it, without making any enquiries as to that person's belief or lack of belief.

ly, since the conclusion of Vatican II in 1965, the Roman Catholic Church.[29] The Church of England is actively involved in a number of ecumenical organisations, the Churches Together in Britain and Ireland being but one example.[30] Furthermore, the Anglicans and Episcopalians have been actively involved in interfaith dialogue with senior figures in the Muslim and Jewish communities and play a central role in formal organisations such as the Council of Christians and Jews (CCJ), which has held events at Lambeth Palace, the official London residence of the Archbishop of Canterbury. Membership of the CCJ is open to people of all faith traditions and none who wish to promote positive relations between Jews and Christians in the UK, although serving in official capacities locally or nationally is usually restricted to members of *recognised* Jewish and Christian faith traditions.[31] The Archbishop of Canterbury is an active patron of the Christian Muslim Forum, which refers to itself as the leading national forum for Christian-Muslim engagement. It too has meetings at Lambeth Palace.[32]

Dialogue with Asian religions has been less formal, although not entirely ruled out. In 2010, the then Archbishop of Canterbury, Rowan Williams, paid a visit to India. In an hour-long interview with *The Hindu,* when asked about dialogue with Hindus, he responded:

> We can't pray publicly together, for many reasons. Prayer follows conviction. But we can sometimes keep silence together. We can certainly look together at the sacred texts of one or another tradition. ... It doesn't mean I say, 'Oh well, you must be right.' But I can at least say, 'I know you're serious.' And that's dialogue for me – the recognition of the serious. And therefore if we find we can do things together after all in servicing, witnessing, peace-making, then it will come out of depths, not shallows ...
>
> ... For many reasons in the U.K., it's tended to be the Christian-Muslim dialogue that has filled the horizon. It's politically the more pressing in some ways. But I'm very conscious of the way in which a number of Hindus in the U.K. say, 'Nobody ever talks to us, everyone's interested in Muslims.' So of course we try to pursue a dialogue as best we can. I made two or three visits to Hindu centres and welcome the opportunity of hearing from well-placed Hindus during [these] visits.[33]

One is, however, more likely to hear terms such as Anglican-Hindu conversations or studies than Anglican-Hindu dialogue. This, of course, leads us to the question as to what is meant by 'dialogue'. Until a few years ago, I had thoughtlessly assumed that the concept was a synonym for discussion, conversation, interchange – or talk. I first realised that there might be a more nuanced understanding of the concept of which I had been unaware when in July 2012 I attended

---

[29] https://www.anglicancommunion.org/ecumenism/ecumenical-dialogues.aspx.
[30] https://ctbi.org.uk/.
[31] http://www.ccj.org.uk/members/become-a-member/.
[32] http://www.christianmuslimforum.org/.
[33] http://aoc2013.brix.fatbeehive.com/articles.php/553/the-hindu-interview-dialogue-for-me-is-recognition-of-the-serious @ 49.41.

a debate between the then Prime Minister, Tony Blair, and the then Archbishop of Canterbury, Rowan Williams, on Religion in Public Life. In the Question and Answer session, I asked whether there were certain religions which it could be unsafe or inadvisable for the government or the Established Church to dialogue with. Blair's answer was that he was pretty broad-minded and saw no reason why government shouldn't talk with religious groups, although there might be some that were so far out on the further shores of common sense that one wouldn't dialogue with them – but generally it would not be a problem – though if they were harmful, that would be a different matter.

It was, however, the Archbishop's response that got me thinking and led to the title of this paper. What he said was:

> There are different kinds of dialogue – different kinds of engagement. And there's virtually nobody that I would feel we ought not to talk to, but there are questions, I think, about how much legitimacy you want to give to some groups if there are groups … that have what you might call a proven record of internally abusive or corrupt behaviour … You don't particularly want to deal with a leadership that is compromised by a solid record of bad behaviour, and we know there are some religious groups like that – (I guess some would draw the net quite widely!) That's my baseline: I think if there is a group where, as I say, there is a proven record of internally abusive or corrupt behaviour, I would not want to give any extra credence to that by publicly engaging and sharing a platform. On the other hand, there are other kinds of dialogue, other kinds of more private engagement – we find ways of doing that.[34]

Clearly, both these figures at the head of the English establishment believed strongly in democracy, freedom of speech and the rights of all citizens. But it was also clear that certain ideas and practices, even if they were not criminal in any legal sense, could not be given the legitimacy that would be awarded to the vast majority of the English population. Somewhere, a line had to be drawn separating the sheep from the goats, although the goats would certainly be entitled to be fed and protected by the law and, up to a point, be treated with respect as fellow human beings. The question posed by the title of the conference which instigated this paper was 'Where is that line?'

It has been said by Dr Anne Richards (2014, 4), that "policy relating to New Religious Movements is called 'Boundaries not Barriers'".[35] Perhaps it is not surprising that the boundary in contemporary England is a fuzzy one, drawn in different positions by different individuals and by different hierarchs at different times. The same is true so far as the state is concerned; I have had a number of civil servants asking me to mediate between a perfectly law-abiding but unpopular minority

---

[34] http://faithdebates.org.uk/debates/2012-debates/religion-and-public-life/religion-public-tony-blair-rowan-williams/.

[35] Dr Richards is the National Adviser for mission theology, alternative spiritualities and new religious movements in the Mission and Public Affairs Office of the Church of England. She attends Inform's Governor's meetings as the Church of England Observer.

religion and themselves on the grounds that they did not want to be compromised by giving any official standing to the movement. There are members, including clergy, of the Church of England who have expressed horror when they have learnt that I am on visiting terms with members of certain new religions and have, on occasion, invited 'such people' into my home. On the other hand, there are members, including clergy, of the Church of England who have themselves dialogued in the full sense of the term with what others would term 'cults' and 'sects'. Some have friendly relations with certain minority religions, but not with others. But, the question I was asked to address concerned 'The' Ecclesia.

It has already been intimated that the Church of England currently has cordial relations with pretty well all the traditional religions, despite the fact that they may disagree not only on theological but also on social and political positions. The rest of this paper will focus primarily on the Church of England's relationship with those minority religions that are often referred to as new religious movements (NRMs), 'cults' or 'sects'.

6. Interfaith organisations and NRMs

NRMs of what Roy Wallis (1984), following Max Weber, called the world-rejecting type are likely in their early days to draw a sharp boundary between themselves and the wider society. Within a generation or so, however, many of these movements frequently adapt to many of society's ways and seek to become part of the accepted religious community. It should, however, be noted that there are a number of multi-generational minority religions, the Plymouth Brethren Christian Church being but one example, which reject the idea of partaking in formal inter-religious dialogue, perhaps quoting Paul's injunctions: "Do not become unevenly yoked with unbelievers."[36] or "Therefore, get out from among them, and separate yourselves".[37]

There are several local, national and international forums in which different religions partake in a variety of activities such as organising formal conferences, visiting each other's places of worship, going on rambles or just sitting together in a church hall or some other convenient location and chatting over a cup of tea. Some local interfaith groupings have welcomed members of NRMs to join their ranks, but these have been relatively few and far between. Quite a few attempts have been made to found an interfaith organisation by one or other of the new religions in the hope of getting some recognition from mainstream religions; the Unification Church and the Church of Scientology have been among the most active, and to some extent successful, in this respect, especially when the group

---

[36] 2 Corinthians 6:14
[37] 2 Corinthians 6:17.

has focussed on issues of religious freedom. For example, it was a Unificationist, Peter Zoehrer (forthcoming), who was responsible for the founding of the Forum for Religious Freedom Europe (FOREF). One of FOREF's objectives is to support "civil society's ability to pro-actively find solutions to inter-religious conflicts".[38] Another example would be the Freedom of Religion or Belief Roundtable Brussels-EU, which describes itself as "a convenor of NGOs and individuals from any or no faith that work for freedom of religion or belief",[39] and has as one of its Co-Chairs the Rev Eric Roux, an ordained minister of the Church of Scientology. Rev Roux is also Chair of the European Interreligious Forum for Religious Freedom, the International Steering Committee of which includes a hierodeacon of the Bulgarian Orthodox Church, a member of the Church of Jesus Christ of Latter-day Saints, a teacher at Leo Baeck Rabbinical College, a Sikh, a Catholic priest, and a member of the Ahmadiyya Community.[40]

Although the occasional Anglican might participate in such organisations, the Church itself has no formal connections with them, and there have been occasions when clergy have been warned by their bishop against getting involved in such associations. A further problem militating against inclusiveness has been that NRM X is quite likely not to want to be involved in an organisation connected with NRM Y – and *vice versa*.

One of the oldest and most inclusive interfaith bodies is the World Congress of Faiths (WCF), which traces its roots back to the first Parliament of World Religions, held in Chicago in 1893, and the Religions of Empire Conference, held in London in 1924. Inspired by these meetings and his own spiritual experience, the explorer, Sir Francis Younghusband, organised two international conferences in London, which led to the WCF becoming established as an independent body in 1936. Sir Francis believed it was important that the Congress should be called the World Congress of *Faiths* as faiths would apply to individuals, whereas the concept of religions had organisational connotations. Whilst some of the early speakers at WCF meetings were clearly of the opinion that their own religion ought to be accepted throughout the world, Prof John Scott Haldane (1860–1936) was to write:

> Many Christians entertain the ideal of converting non-Christian peoples to Christianity. I think that a much higher ideal is to understand and enter into sympathy with the religions which exist in other countries and to use this understanding and sympathy as a basis for higher religion.[41]

One of the WCF's offerings is a poster of the Golden Rule: versions from the Scriptures of twelve of the world religions that are variants of the Christian injunction

---

[38] https://foref-europe.org/about/.
[39] https://www.forbroundtable.org/.
[40] https://www.eifrf-articles.org/The-steering-committee-of-EIFRF_a86.html.
[41] http://www.worldfaiths.org/our-history/.

"Do unto others as you would have them do unto you." (Matthew 7:12).[42] Membership of the WCF is open to any individual who pays a nominal subscription and agrees not to proselytise or use it for political purposes.[43] Although there is no group membership, the WCF website does have links to other interfaith groups, including the International Association for Religious Freedom (IARF), which has its roots in Unitarianism,[44] and the Inter Religious Federation for World Peace (IRFWP), which owes its origin to the Rev Sun Myung Moon, the founder of the Unification Church.[45]

Dadi Janki (1916–2020), the spiritual leader of the (relatively) new religious movement the Brahma Kumaris,[46] was, until her recent death, one of WCF's Patrons, along with the Anglican Bishop Desmond Tutu, the Dalai Lama and Harvard Professor Diana Eck.[47] The Joint Presidents are Dr Jackie Tabick, the first woman to be ordained as a rabbi in the UK, and the Rev Dr Marcus Braybrooke, a retired Anglican priest.[48] Dr Braybrooke is one of those members of the established Church who has devoted his life to inclusive interfaith work. He joined WCF in 1964 and was the Executive Director of the Council of Christians and Jews from 1984–8. In 1997, together with Sir Sigmund Sternberg and Sheikh Dr Zaki Badawi, he founded the Three Faiths Forum with the aim of encouraging friendship, goodwill and understanding between people of different faiths, especially between Muslims, Christians and Jews. However, over the years the work of the Forum expanded to include people of all faiths and beliefs, both religious and non-religious, and in 2018, the name was changed to the Faith & Belief Forum to better reflect this inclusive ethos.[49]

Arguably the most influential interreligious organisation in England is the Inter Faith Network for the UK (IFN). This was founded in 1987 by Brian Pearce, a member of the Anglican laity and the IFN's first Director, "to advance public knowledge and mutual understanding of the teachings, traditions and practices of the different faith communities in Britain".[50] In direct opposition to the WCF, the IFN has no individual members, but only organisations. The founding member organisations were representatives of the Baha'i, Buddhist, Christian, Hindu, Jain, Jewish, Muslim and Sikh communities, with the Zoroastrian community joining in 1989 (Pearce, 2012, 151). For several years, the IFN resisted applications

---

[42] http://www.worldfaiths.org/wp-content/uploads/2015/08/Golden-Rule-Poster.pdf.

[43] In theory anyone trying to push their own faith would be expelled from membership, but, I have been told, this has never happened.

[44] http://www.iarf.net/.

[45] https://www.irfwp.org/wp/.

[46] The Brahma Kumaris is a Hindu-based spiritual movement founded by Dada Lekhraj Kripalani, a retired Indian businessman, in 1937. https://www.brahmakumaris.org.

[47] http://www.worldfaiths.org/our-patrons/.

[48] The Chair and Editor of the WCF's Journal *Interreligious Insight* is another Anglican priest, the Revd Canon Dr Alan Race. http://www.worldfaiths.org/journal/.

[49] https://faithbeliefforum.org/about/history/.

[50] https://www.interfaith.org.uk/about/history.

from other religious organisations to join its network. I was told on more than one occasion that the Christians were strongest in their opposition to any minority religion calling itself Christian; the Sikhs did not want to see Sikh sects join the network and the Hindus opposed membership of other Hindu sects. Drawing on the work of the anthropologist, Mary Douglas (1961), it is not surprising that those who have a vested interest in demonstrating that they are 'the real' Christians, Buddhists, Muslims or Hindus are those who are most likely to want to secure the most impermeable boundary between themselves and 'others' who claim to belong to their category (Barker, 2006).

As the IFN went from strength to strength, becoming the main body representing the traditional religions and the one with which the Church of England and the government appeared to have the most connection (Dawson, 2016; van Eck Duymaer van Twist, 2020),[51] a number of minority religions started to complain about their exclusion (Weller et al, 2013, 68–69).

In May 2012, the Druid Network, which, after a four-year struggle, had been granted charitable status in 2010 (Harvey and Vincent, 2012), formally applied to join the IFN. After seeking legal advice which had suggested it was within its right to refuse the request, the IFN Executive decided it could not recommend the application for approval at its AGM. The Druid Network, together with others, including a group named Religious Freedom UK,[52] started to organise a campaign against the IFN's stance.[53] Representatives of a score or more religions, including Christians, Druids, Hindus, Humanists, Jews, Muslims, Pagans, Scientologists and Sikhs, gathered in the House of Lords to raise a joint protest in defence of religious freedom (Home Office, 2012). The meeting was chaired by the Revd Peter Owen, referred to as "our esteemed and greatly loved Anglican friend" in a letter from Religious Freedom UK to the *Church Times* (Wilson, 2012).

The IFN also came under fire from a Jewish-Muslim interfaith organisation called 'Stand for Peace',[54] which accused it of having received millions of pounds of taxpayers' funds when, apart from denying the Druid Network, the IFN had, it was claimed, among its membership a number of individuals and organisations who were anti-Semitic or associated with terrorism (Westrop 2013, 11–14).

---

[51] To my surprise, a senior civil servant once told me that the nine religions of the IFN were those that the government officially recognised. In fact, of course, Parliament does not officially recognise any religion apart from the Church of England. However, there was enough truth in his statement to make a telling point.

[52] Religious Freedom UK described itself as "people from 'traditional' religions (Muslims, Christians, Hindus…) together with people from Minority Religions ('New Religious Movements' or NRMs) who strive together to end the persecution and discrimination against people from New Religious Movements". http://www.religiousfreedom.org.uk/about.html.

[53] For a compilation of some of the correspondence and other documents associated with the campaign, see Anon (2012).

[54] http://standforpeace.org.uk/about/.

More cogently perhaps, the Druids secured the support of one of England's foremost human rights law firms, Bindmans LLP, which produced a 20-page Advice. This found the IFN "to have practised discrimination on grounds of religion or belief, contrary to the Equality Act 2010 and other law, in its membership policies against particular faith communities in Britain" (Halford, 2012, 1). Among the points made in the Advice (which are too numerous to be dealt with in detail here) are the arguments that the IFN's objective "to advance *public* knowledge and mutual understanding of the teachings, traditions and practices of *the different faith* communities in Britain" (italics added), implies that it would be wrong to exclude the Druids (who are statistically more numerous than some of those faiths included in its membership); that its aims are not primarily for the advancement of the membership, but the public at large; and that the Government ought to cease funding the IFN as it is bound by section 149 of the 2010 Equality Act (op. cit., passim).

Rather than risk facing an expensive legal battle that neither side wanted, the IFN underwent a strategic review of its membership policies and, at its 2014 AGM, voted to accept the membership of not only the Druid Network, but also (among others) the Church of Jesus Christ of Latter-day Saints (Great Britain); the Pagan Federation; and the Spiritualists' National Union (Inter Faith Network, 2014, 20).

It is possible that the hierarchy of the Church of England was to some extent influenced by the situation in which the IFN had found itself, and wished to clarify its own, independent position (Van Eck Duymaer van Twist, 2020, 10; 13). In the letter to the *Church Times* mentioned above, Religious Freedom UK not only complained about the IFN's rejection of the Druid Network, it also took a shot at the Church of England's position with regard to new religions:

> … It, therefore, appears wholly contrary to scripture and the Christian gospel that the Church of England hierarchy should have manufactured an official 2009 policy document to denigrate and exclude from equal dialogue "New Religious Movements and Alternative Spiritualities" (go to www.churchofengland.org/our-faith/mission/engaging-with-new-religious-movements.aspx and click on the right on "NRM Policy Document"),[55] without any biblical foundation whatsoever, but rather in breach of the Christian injunction to love one's neighbour as oneself. (Wilson et al, 2012)[56]

---

[55] The website referred to no longer exists. In June 2013 it announced that the Church of England had placed 'under review' its policy document "The Church of England in Relation to New Religious Movements and Alternative Spiritualities" and had removed it from its website. This post is itself no longer available, but a link to the original website is, at the time of writing, still obtainable on the Churches Together in England website. https://www.cte.org.uk/Articles/172922/Home/Photo_Stock/Extra_photos/Resources_and_Information.aspx.

[56] The offending document has, in fact, been commended in other quarters by, for example, Frank Cranmer (2014) when he compared it to the Council of Europe's draft document on sects.

7. The Church of England and NRMs

The policy document to which the *Church Times* letter referred, (Church of England, 2009), states in its introduction,

> The Church of England encourages openness, welcome and hospitality towards people of other faiths and none. However, the religious scene is changing in Britain, such that, in addition to established other faiths such as Judaism and Islam, there are many so-called New Religious Movements (NRMs) and alternative spiritualities now also present in Britain. The Church of England has two strands of work in relation to people of other faith and these are distinguished from each other. One strand of work relates to the inter-faith portfolios and the other to New Religious Movements and Alternative Spiritualities. This document relates to the work done in relation to NRMS and Alternative Spiritualities.

In other words, the Church was drawing a clear distinction between its relationship with world religions and that it has (or does not have) with NRMs. Its 'interfaith portfolios' relate to "major faiths other than Christianity" and these include Judaism; Islam; Buddhism; Hinduism; Sikhism; Jainism; Zoroastrianism; and the Baha'i.[57] These, it claims, are characterised by a significant and identifiable history of the faith; significant scripture or holy text; identifiable theology, mythic structure or philosophy within a developed tradition; accountable authority or leadership, upholding right behaviour in practice within the community; and cultic integrity – the formation and sustaining of an identifiable faith community. Through its interfaith portfolios, the Church could, it stated, have formal dialogue, advocacy, representation and sharing and exchange.

The Church sees NRMs as being less easy to define, but generally characterised as being less than 200 years old; changing from one to several generations; sometimes changing in style, name, theology or character; often derivative of established faiths; and/or possessing a religious character or processes. Specific NRMs may reinvent an ancient practice, be a science fiction or personal development movement, or they may be small esoteric groups. Alternative spiritualities are seen as more functionally religious and may include a sense of the sacred; they maybe new-age groups, or a variety of therapies and practices. A number of examples were given, including the Unification Church; the Church of Jesus Christ of Latter-day Saints; Jehovah's Witnesses; the International Society for Krishna Consciousness; the Brahma Kumaris; the Rajneeshees; Scientology; Freemasonry; Transcendental Meditation; Shamanism; Druidry; and Witchcraft. Examples of alternative spiritualities included Reiki; Mind/Body/Spirit practices; belief in the powers of psychics; Astrology; and some forms of Yoga.

Although it concedes that many NRMs want nothing from the Church of England, it warns that others may want the same kind of relationship as the Church has

---

[57] It admits that there could be some confusion over the status of the Baha'i, which could fall into either category.

with the major historic religions; they may also be looking for acceptance, advocacy, dialogue, access, and/or money. Some could want the Church to intervene on their behalf with the government or other agencies to help them gain credibility; some might invite the Church to join them on issues such as the environment or peace initiatives.

The document then states Church of England policy towards NRMs and alternative spiritualities. This is that it does not have formal dialogue or provide services to such groups; it does however attempt to listen, to encourage and to support informal local contacts with groups, and to provide pastoral assistance where this is requested. It adds that it uses and supports Inform for knowledge about the movements and that Inform can provide access to legal and counselling services. It is stressed that the Church of England does *not* act to suppress groups, either directly or by supporting anti-cult or counter-cult groups.

The document ends by explaining that work pertaining to NRMs is staffed by the Archbishop's adviser and the national adviser, along with a network of diocesan advisers. These can provide information and educational material; guidance for families who have people in NRMs; the use of church buildings and church halls by NRMs; and specialist advice on ecclesiastical law in relation to the movements. They can also provide pastoral care for people facing an NRM issue; negotiation, support for family members and clergy; access to special ministries, such as the deliverance ministry; they can, furthermore, investigate complaints about churches or Christian groups exhibiting 'cult-like' behaviour, and offer advice about compatibility issues, such as "can I be both Christian and Pagan?"

However, as intimated above, this document has now been superseded by a new website of the position of the Church of England (2017). The current website does not draw a stark distinction between NRMs and 'major faiths'. It is far more pragmatic than the earlier policy statement in its approach, and less likely to give offence to law-abiding NRMs that are behaving in a socially acceptable manner. It warns of some of the problems known to be associated with some NRMs and gives practical advice as to what might be done when these arise. Some helpful guidance is given on NRM-related advertisements in church communications,[58] letting church premises;[59] Halloween,[60] and responding to a situation in which a family member has joined an NRM.[61] Revised guidelines for good practice for exorcisms are also provided.[62]

---

[58] https://www.churchofengland.org/sites/default/files/2017-11/New%20Religious%20Movements%20-advertisements.pdf.

[59] https://www.churchofengland.org/sites/default/files/2017-11/%20New%20Religious%20Movements%20-%20advice%20about%20hiring%20church%20premises%20and%20halls.pdf.

[60] https://www.churchofengland.org/sites/default/files/2017-11/New%20Religious%20Movements%20-%20Halloween.pdf.

[61] https://www.churchofengland.org/sites/default/files/2017-11/New%20Religious%20Movements%20-%20family%20advice.pdf.

[62] https://www.churchofengland.org/sites/default/files/2018-01/House%20of%20Bishops%E2%80%99%20Guidelines%20for%20Good%20Practice%20in%20the%20Deliverance%20Ministry%201975%20%28revised%202012%29.pdf.

In addition, the site provides examples of enquiries that could promote discussion and reflection about various issues – rather than arriving at 'right' answers.[63] It offers special guidance for chaplains engaging with minority religions and alternative spiritualities in hospital.[64] Finally, it recommends twelve general principles to Anglicans when engaging with people from NRMs. These include honesty, knowledge respect, empathy and vigilance. Hardliners might be surprised to see that it suggests: "we should look for evidence of God's work in others and not try to second guess what God is doing." They might (or might not) be reassured to read that it also states "be clear about the distinctiveness of Christian faith. The richness, variety and depth of what is offered in Christ should satisfy every part of a person's spiritual need and life pathway. If that does not happen, our mission and evangelism may be at fault."[65]

8. Concluding Remarks

The Church of England is a broad Church – a very broad Church. Its members may see it as a central part of their lives and their identity, or they may, if asked, merely assume they are CoE as a birth-right. Its services range from Low Church, enthusiastic 'happy-clappy' Evangelicalism to High Church liturgically formal Anglo-Catholicism. Amongst its clergy one can find believers in the literal truth of the Bible and the Thirty-Nine Articles, and one can find men and women who don't really seem to believe in God at all. As an institution, the Church is privileged enough to be able to afford to be generous and gracious, but insecure enough to be nervous of becoming too cosy with dubious newcomers. On the one hand, there are those who consider the Church of England to be in *loco parentis*, with a responsibility of serving the whole nation; on the other hand, an Anglican priest could recently comment, "We are now a domestic, members-only Church, with nothing to say to the nation about death, sacrifice, or charity, and nothing to plead before God on behalf of us all" (Tilby, 2020).

This chapter has attempted to sketch something of the history of the Established Church in England and its relationship with other religions over the past four and a half centuries. Concentrating on the current situation, it has indicated that there are many ways in which the Church of England has not only tolerated but developed excellent relationships with the other traditional religions in the country, in many cases facilitating their existence as part of a multi-faith society.

---

[63] https://www.churchofengland.org/sites/default/files/2020-03/nrm_scenario_group_work_sheet_march_2020.pdf.

[64] https://www.churchofengland.org/sites/default/files/2020-03/guidance_for_chaplains_minority_religions_-notes.pdf.

[65] https://www.churchofengland.org/sites/default/files/2017-11/New%20Religious%20Movements%20-%20principles%20and%20practice.pdf.

It has also been suggested that the Church is wary of associating with new religious movements, particularly those that have been labelled a cult or sect in the popular media. Whilst certainly not campaigning against their existence, so long as they obey the law of the land, there is undoubtedly a feeling that he who sups with the devil should have a long spoon.

Finally, it could be argued with good reason that were a minority religion to want to be accepted by society (although not a few of them have virulently rejected society in its present form) contemporary England (together, perhaps, with parts of northern Europe) could be one of the least unwelcoming countries in which to settle. Not only is the law of the land open to law-abiding citizens of all faiths and none, but the Established Church, if not enthusiastically welcoming, tends towards courteous toleration and, in some of its manifestations, it will even celebrate the religious kaleidoscope that is part of the make-up of England in the twenty-first century.

References

All websites were accessed in May 2020

Anon. (2012): 25th Anniversary of the Inter Faith Network for the United Kingdom: The Inter Faith Network and Illegal Religious Discrimination in Treatment of Membership Applications. http://www.theinterfaithnetwork.org.uk/.

Arweck, E. (2006): Researching New Religious Movements: Responses and Refinements, London.

Barker, E. (1987): The British Right to Discriminate, in: T. Robbins and R. Robertson (eds.), Church-State Relations: Tensions and Transitions, New Brunswick.

Barker, E. (1989): New Religious Movements: A Practical Introduction, London.

Barker, E. (1995): The Scientific Study of Religion? You Must be Joking! In: Journal for the Scientific Study of Religion 34 (3), 287–310.

Barker, E. (2001): INFORM: Bringing the Sociology of Religion to the Public Space, in P. Côté (ed.), Frontier Religions in Public Space, 21–34. Ottawa.

Barker, E. (2006): We've got to Draw the Line Somewhere: An Exploration of Boundaries that Define Locations of Religious Identity, in: Social Compass 53 (2), 201–213.

Bromley, D. G. and J. T. Richardson, eds. (1983): The Brainwashing/Deprogramming Controversy: Sociological, Psychological, Legal and Historical Perspectives. Vol. V, Studies in Religion and Society, New York.

Church of England, The. (2009): The Church of England in relation to New Religious Movements and Alternative Spiritualities, London. https://www.cte.org.uk/Articles/172922/Home/Photo_Stock/Extra_photos/Resources_and_Information.aspx

Church of England, The. (2017): New Religious Movements. London. https://www.churchofengland.org/more/policy-and-thinking/our-views/new-religious-movements

Church of England, The. (2019): Statistics for Mission 2018. London: Church of England Research and Statistics, London. https://www.churchofengland.org/sites/default/files/2019-10/2018StatisticsForMission_0.pdf/

Cranmer, F. (2014): The Council of Europe's draft document on sects: one Quaker's perspective, in: Law & Religion UK, 26 March. https://www.lawandreligionuk.com/2014/03/26/the-council-of-europes-draft-document-on-sects-one-quakers-perspective/

Davie, G. (2007): Vicarious Religion: A Methodological Challenge, in: N. Ammerman (ed.), Everyday Religion: Observing Modern Religious Lives, 21–36, New York.

Dawkins, R. (2006): The God Delusion, Boston.

Dawson, A. (2016): Religious diversity and the shifting sands of political prioritization: reflections on the UK context, in: A. Dawson (ed.), The Politics and Practices of Religious Diversity: National Contexts, Global Issues, 133–52. Abingdon, Oxon.

Day, A. (2017): The Religious Lives of Older Laywomen: The Last Active Anglican Generation, Oxford.

Douglas, M. (1966): Purity and Danger: An Analysis of Concepts of Pollution and Taboo, London.

Equality and Human Rights Commission. (2016): Religion or Belief: A Guide to the Law, London. https://www.equalityhumanrights.com/sites/default/files/religion-or-belief-guide-to-the-law.pdf/

Fielding, H. (1994) (1st edition 1749): The History of Tom Jones, A Foundling, London.

Halford, J. (2012): Legal Guidance on Religious Discrimination under The Equality Act 2010 and The Statutory Public Sector Equality Duty of Government Departments, Local Authorities and Other Public Bodies in Relation to Awarding of Public Funding to Interfaith and Faith-Based Organisations: The Case of "The Inter Faith Network for the United Kingdom" and Religious Discrimination Contrary to Law, 20 November, London. http://www.religiousfreedom.org.uk/guidance.pdf

Harvey, G, and G. Vincett. (2012): Alternative Spiritualities: Marginal and Mainstream, in: L. Woodhead and R. Catto (eds.), Religion and Change in Modern Britain, 156–172, London.

Home Office. (2020): Proscribed Terrorist Organisations, London. https://assets.publishing.service.gov.uk/government/uploads/system/uploads/attachment_data/file/869496/20200228_Proscription.pdf

Inter Faith Network for the United Kingdom. (2014): Annual Review 2013/14, London. https://www.interfaith.org.uk/uploads/low_res_annual-review-2013-14.pdf

Jacob, P. (2010): Dialogue for me is recognition of the serious: Rowan Williams, in: The Hindu, 29 October. https://www.thehindu.com/opinion/interview/Dialogue-for-me-is-recognition-of-the-serious-Rowan-Williams/article15795596.ece

Pearce, B. (2012): The Inter Faith Network and the Development of Interfaith Relations in Britain, in: L. Woodhead and R. Catto (eds.), Religion and Change in Modern Britain, London.

Ralls, W. (1974): The Papal Aggression of 1850: A Study in Victorian Anti-Catholicism, in: Church History, 43 (2), 242–56.

Richards, A. (2014): New Religious Movements in the UK: adapting to a changing society, in: Materialdienst der Evangelischen Zentralstelle für Weltanschauungsfragen (EZW) 77, 44–53. https://www.ezw-berlin.de/downloads/MD_2_2014_Anne_Richards_NRM_in_the_UK.pdf

Secretary of State for the Home Department and the Secretary of State for Northern Ireland. (1998): Legislation Against Terrorism: A consultation paper, Cm 4178, London. https://assets.publishing.service.gov.uk/government/uploads/system/uploads/attachment_data/file/265689/4178.pdf

Tilby, A. (2020): The C of E has become member-only, in: Church Times, 8 May.
van Eck Duymaer van Twist, A. 2020. Who can we dialogue with? Seeking effective interfaith development: the Inter Faith Network for the UK, in: K. Knott and M. Francis (eds.) Minority Religions and Uncertainty, Abingdon, Oxon.
Voas, D, and S. Bruce. (2019): Religion: Identity, behaviour and belief over two decades, in: J. Curtice et al (eds,), British Social Attitudes: Religion, London. https://www.bsa.natcen.ac.uk/media/39293/1_bsa36_religion.pdf
Wallis, R. (1984): The Elementary Forms of the New Religious Life, London.
Weller, P., K. Purdam, N. Ghanea and S. Cheruvallil-Contractor. (2013): Religion or Belief, Discrimination and Equality: Britain in Global Contexts, London.
Westrop, S. (2013): The Interfaith Industry, London: Stand for Peace: Counter-Extremism; Social Cohesion, Counter-Terrorism. http://standforpeace.org.uk/wp-content/uploads/2013/11/Interfaith-Industry.pdf
Wilson, G. et al. (2012): The Druid Network and the Inter Faith Network, in: Church Times, 14 December. https://www.churchtimes.co.uk/articles/2012/14-december/comment/letters-to-the-editor/the-druid-network-and-the-inter-faith-network
Zoehrer, P. (Forthcoming): Legal Challenges Posed to the Unification Church in Europe – Perspectives from a Unificationist Advocate for Religious Freedom, in: J. T. Richardson and E. Barker (eds.), How Minority Religions React to the Law: Case Studies and Theoretical Applications, Abingdon, Oxon.

Abstract

The Anglican Church of England broke away from Rome in the middle of the 16th century and, apart from a short five-year return to Catholicism, it has been accepted as the Established Church in England, with the ruling monarch at its head, ever since. This chapter describes some of the ways in which the Church has managed to keep its supremacy, originally by force and law, but gradually through an acceptance that England has become a multi-ethnic and multi-religious society, through cordial relations. It is argued that by the 21st-century, the Church of England had become a very broad church, encompassing a wide range of attitudes towards other religions. The Church's hierarchy has, however, cemented good relations firstly with Trinitarian Christians, then with the other major religions. While it remains wary about too close a relationship with new religions and alternative spiritualities, it does affirm their right to some respect and a place in contemporary English society.

PARTICIPATION OF STATE PRIVILEGED RELIGIONS IN THE FIGHT AGAINST RELIGIOUS MINORITIES

PATRICIA DUVAL

1. Freedom of Religion or Belief and International Human Rights Law

International Human Rights Treaties – and more specifically the European Convention on Human Rights and Fundamental Freedoms (ECHR) Article 9 and the International Covenant on Civil and Political Rights (ICCPR) Article 18 – provide for the right to freedom of religion or belief. It encompasses both the right to believe and the right to manifest one's beliefs in the private but also public sphere.

The UN Human Right Committee elaborated a detailed Opinion (General Comment 22) on how this right should be interpreted.[1]

It stressed that the freedom to manifest religion or belief in worship, observance, practice and teaching encompasses a broad range of acts. The observance and practice of religion or belief may include not only ceremonial acts but also such customs as the observance of dietary regulations, the wearing of distinctive clothing or head coverings.

As an example, refusal of a blood transfusion by the Jehovah's Witnesses or a head covering by Muslim girls or Sikh children in the French public schools are expressions of the right to manifest their religious beliefs and fall under the protection of Article 18 ICCPR or Article 9 ECHR. Courts have had to decide whether the limitations to such right were proportionate and necessary in a democratic society. The Jehovah's Witnesses won many cases over the years on the right to refuse a blood transfusion and the right of control over one's own body, and the Sikhs obtained rulings of the UN Human Rights Committee asking France to review its law prohibiting the wearing of conspicuous religious symbols in public schools. But it is not the subject of this paper.

The practice and teaching of religion or belief also includes acts integral to the conduct by religious groups of their basic affairs, such as the freedom to choose

---

[1] HRC General Comments provide orientation for the practical implementation of human rights and form a set of criteria for evaluating the progress of states in their implementation of these rights. https://www.institut-fuer-menschenrechte.de/en/topics/development/frequently-asked-questions/9-what-are-general-comments/.

their religious leaders, priests and teachers *and the freedom to prepare and distribute religious texts or publications.*

The Committee made it clear in this regard that Article 18 is not limited in its application to traditional religions or to religions and beliefs with institutional characteristics or practices analogous to those of traditional religions. It expressed that it viewed "with concern any tendency to discriminate against any religion or belief for any reason, including the fact that they are newly established, or represent religious minorities that may be the subject of hostility on the part of a predominant religious community".

However, the question of dissemination of religious literature and proselytism by minority religions has given rise to heated discussions and harsh reactions by some States, including "democratic" ones, and traditional religions.

1.1. Right to proselytize

Article 18.2 ICCPR provides for the right to adopt or change one's religion and freedom and be free from coercion in relation thereto.

In its Comment 22, the Committee observed that the freedom to "have or to adopt" a religion or belief necessarily entails the freedom to choose a religion or belief, including the right to replace one's current religion or belief with another as well as the right to retain one's religion or belief. Article 18.2 prohibits coercion that would impair the right to have or adopt a religion or belief, *including the use of* threat of physical force or *penal sanctions to compel believers* or non-believers to adhere to their religious beliefs and congregations, *to recant their religion or belief* or to convert.

Policies or practices having the same intention or effect, such as those restricting access to education, employment or public service, as well as preventing individuals from taking part in public affairs, are similarly inconsistent with article 18.2.

This would apply for example to the practice of so-called "sect-filters" in Germany, whereby some municipalities have applicants to civil servant positions fill in a form where they must attest not belonging to a so-called sect, in particular to the Church of Scientology. This practice will be addressed later in this paper.

This would apply also to the situation in Russia where Jehovah's Witnesses and members of other religious communities have been subject to criminal charges and imprisonment for proselytizing.

The UN Rapporteur's Digest on Freedom of Religion or Belief gives a summary of the findings of the successive Rapporteurs from 1986 to 2011 on the subject of the right to proselytize.[2]

---

[2] Rapporteur's Digest on Religion or Belief, 31–33.

The question of missionary activities and other forms of propagating one's religion has been at the centre of the mandate on freedom of religion of Special Rapporteur Amor since the beginning[3].

In one of his reports[4], he considered "constitutional provisions prohibiting proselytism to be inconsistent with the 1981 Declaration[5] and stresse[d] the need for greater respect for internationally recognized human rights norms, including freedom to convert and freedom to manifest one's religion or belief, either individually or in community with others, and in public or private, except where necessary restrictions are provided for by law".

He added that, while not explicitly including religious rights, article 19 of ICCPR, which protects freedom of expression, is formulated in a way that also covers missionary activities: "[T]his right shall include freedom to seek, receive and impart information and ideas of all kinds, regardless of frontiers, either orally, in writing or in print, in the form of art, or through any other media of [one's] choice". The Human Rights Committee's constant jurisprudence has deemed the protection afforded by article 19 extremely strong.[6]

However, certain limitations can be imposed in accordance with article 18.3 of the Covenant. It should be underlined though that this article allows for restrictions only in very exceptional cases.[7]

In particular, limitations to proselytism through criminal sanctions should be strictly applied to actual offences according to the Special Rapporteur. He explained:[8]

> Certain acts may constitute an offence under the criminal code of the State concerned and should therefore be prosecuted. In view of the Special Rapporteur, however, it would not be advisable to criminalize non-violent acts performed in the context of manifestation of one's religion, in particular the propagation of religion, including because that might criminalize acts that would, in another context, not raise a concern of the criminal law and may pave the way for persecution of religious minorities. Moreover, since

---

[3] Mr. Abdelfattah Amor (Tunisia), April 1993 – July 2004.

[4] Report of the Special Rapporteur to the General Assembly after his visit to Greece, 7 November 1996, A/51/542/Add.1/para. 134.

[5] The 1981 Declaration of the UN General Assembly provides:
Art. 6 (d): The right to freedom of thought, conscience, religion or belief includes the freedom, "To write, issue and disseminate relevant publications in these areas".
Art. 6 (e): The right to freedom of thought, conscience, religion or belief includes the freedom, "To teach a religion or belief in places suitable for these purposes."

[6] See Manfred Nowak, UN Covenant on Civil and Political Rights, CCPR Commentary (2nd revised ed.), 2005, pp. 450–452.

[7] Article 18.3 ICCPR provides: "Freedom to manifest one's religion or beliefs may be subject only to such limitations as are prescribed by law and are necessary to protect public safety, order, health, or morals or the fundamental rights and freedoms of others."

[8] Rapporteur's Digest, 32.

the right to change or maintain a religion is in essence a subjective right, any concern raised with regard to certain conversions or how they might be accomplished should primarily be raised by the alleged victim.

Indeed, the European Court of Human Rights (ECtHR) confirmed the right to convert consenting adults in its landmark decision *Jehovah's Witnesses of Moscow v. Russia* of 10 June 2010.

The case was initiated in 1995 by the Committee for the Salvation of Youth from Totalitarian Cults ("the Salvation Committee"), a non-governmental organisation aligned with the Russian Orthodox Church.

After four unsuccessful complaints to the Prosecutor's office, the Salvation Committee finally obtained an official investigation against the applicant community under the accusation that the Witnesses alienated their followers from their families, intimidated believers and controlled their mind, as well as incited them to civil disobedience and religious discord.

Subsequently, the Russian courts ordered its dissolution and the banning of the Witnesses' activity by holding, inter alia, that the applicant community breached the right of citizens to freedom of conscience by subjecting them to psychological pressure, "mind control" techniques and totalitarian discipline. The European Court found:

> 129.   Leaving aside the fact that *there is no generally accepted and scientific definition of what constitutes "mind control"* and that no definition of that term was given in the domestic judgments, the Court finds it remarkable that the courts did not cite the name of a single individual whose right to freedom of conscience had allegedly been violated by means of those techniques. Nor is it apparent that the prosecution experts had interviewed anyone who had been coerced in that way into joining the community. On the contrary, the individual applicants and other members of the applicant community testified before the court that they had made a voluntary and conscious choice of their religion and, having accepted the faith of Jehovah's Witnesses, *followed its doctrines of their own free will*. [emphasis added]

The European Court ruled that the findings of undue proselytism by the Russian courts were based on conjecture uncorroborated by fact. It held that there had been a violation of Article 9 of the Convention read in the light of Article 11 on account of the dissolution of the applicant community and the banning of its activity.

In his 1996 Report mentioned above, Special Rapporteur Amor already stressed that the fact that Article 18.3 mentions the protection of "fundamental rights and freedoms of others" as a legitimate ground for restriction of the right to freedom of religion or belief indicates a stronger protection than for some other rights whose limitation clauses refer simply to the "rights and freedoms of others". In his view if the freedom of religion or belief of others can be regarded as such a fundamental right and freedom which would justify limitations to missionary activities, however *the freedom of religion and belief of adults basically is a question* of individual choice, so any generalized State limitation (e.g. by law) conceived to protect "others'" freedom of religion and belief by limiting the right of individuals to conduct missionary activities should be avoided.

Such an abuse is particularly topical with the so-called extremism laws in Russia, adopted to favor the Orthodox religion and which prohibit dissemination of religious literature listed as extremist publications by the Ministry of Justice of the Russian Federation.

In this regard, the European Court of Human Rights adopted a ruling last year against the Russian Federation in the case of Nursi followers and the ban of their publications. In a landmark decision *Ibragim Ibragimov and others v. Russia* of 28 August 2018,[9] the Court has invalidated the Russian Extremism Law as far as the Law's definition of extremism allows the ban of religious publications in the absence of any violence or hate speech.

The decision is extremely significant as the Human Rights Court found that any application of the Extremism Law must be based on actual incitement to hatred or violence in order to justify any restriction of freedom of expression of religious beliefs.

As the ban concerned the distribution of books, which contained a commentary on the Qur'an, the Court deemed the followers' claim had to be examined under Article 10, interpreted in the light of Article 9 of the Convention (the right to freedom of expression in the light of the right to freedom of religion or belief).

The European Court reiterated that freedom to manifest one's religion *includes the right to try to convince one's neighbour, for example through "teaching"*, failing which "freedom to change [one's] religion or belief", enshrined in Article 9 ECHR, would be likely to remain a dead letter, and stressed that, in the absence of improper proselytism, e.g. through the use of violence, *the mere fact that the author's intention was to convince the readers to adopt his religious beliefs was insufficient, in the Court's view, to justify banning the book*". [emphasis added]

In particular, the Court could not discern any element in the domestic courts' analysis which would allow it to conclude that the book in question incited violence, religious hatred or intolerance, that the context in which it had been published was marked by heightened tensions or special social or historical background in Russia or that its circulation had led or could lead to harmful consequences. The Court concluded that it was not necessary, in a democratic society, to ban the book in question.

Those findings should entail further developments since the Russian authorities have qualified numerous religious texts as "extremist materials" in recent years and numerous applications are pending at the European Court, filed by various religious groups such as Jehovah's Witnesses, Scientologists and others.

---

[9] *Ibragim Ibragimov and others v. Russia*, Nos 1413/08 and 28621/11.

1.2. Privileges granted to certain religions

In their policy towards religious groups, governments have a duty to remain neutral. They may be allowed to grant privileges to certain religions, in particular predominant or traditional religious denominations but they must in doing so ensure that they do not discriminate against minority religions.

In General Comment 22, the Human Rights Committee stated:

> "If a set of beliefs is treated as official ideology in constitutions, statutes, proclamations of ruling parties, etc., or in actual practice, this shall not result in any impairment of the freedoms under article 18 or any other rights recognized under the Covenant nor in any discrimination against persons who do not accept the official ideology or who oppose it."

The Committee explained more specifically:

> "The fact that a religion is recognized as a State religion or that it is established as official or traditional or that its followers comprise the majority of the population, shall not result in any impairment of the enjoyment of any of the rights under the Covenant, including articles 18 and 27,[10] nor in any discrimination against adherents to other religions or non-believers. In particular, certain measures discriminating against the latter, such as measures restricting eligibility for government service to members of the predominant religion or giving economic privileges to them or imposing special restrictions on the practice of other faiths, are not in accordance with the prohibition of discrimination based on religion or belief and the guarantee of equal protection under article 26.[11]"

The European Court of Human Rights constantly affirmed the duty of neutrality of the State in religious matters. In particular, in an important ruling *Metropolitan Church of Bessarabia v. Moldova* in 2001, the Court formulated as a principle that "the right to freedom of religion for the purposes of the Convention excludes assessment by the State of the legitimacy of religious beliefs or the ways in which those beliefs are expressed."

The Court ruled:

> "1. However, in exercising its regulatory power in this sphere and in its relations with the various religions, denominations and beliefs, *the State has a duty to remain neutral and impartial* (see Hasan and Chaush, cited above, § 78). What is at stake here is the preservation of pluralism and the proper functioning of democracy, one of the principle characteristics of which is the possibility it offers of resolving a country's problems

---

[10] Article 27 provides: "In those States in which ethnic, religious or linguistic minorities exist, persons belonging to such minorities shall not be denied the right, in community with the other members of their group, to enjoy their own culture, to profess and practise their own religion, or to use their own language."

[11] Article 26 provides: "All persons are equal before the law and are entitled without any discrimination to the equal protection of the law. In this respect, the law shall prohibit any discrimination and guarantee to all persons equal and effective protection against discrimination on any ground such as race, colour, sex, language, religion, political or other opinion, national or social origin, property, birth or other status."

through dialogue, without recourse to violence, even when they are irksome (see United Communist Party of Turkey and Others v. Turkey, judgment of 30 January 1998, Reports 1998-I, p. 27, § 57). Accordingly, *the role of the authorities in such circumstances is not to remove the cause of tension by eliminating pluralism*, but to ensure that the competing groups tolerate each other (see Serif v. Greece, no. 38178/97, § 53, ECHR 1999-IX)."

And the Court found that *"where the exercise of the right to freedom of religion or of one of its aspects is subject under domestic law to a system of prior authorisation, involvement in the procedure for granting authorisation of a recognised ecclesiastical authority cannot be reconciled with the requirements of paragraph 2 of Article 9."*

The Organization for Security and Cooperation in Europe (OSCE) has tackled the issue of privileges granted to certain religions in its Guidelines for the Review of Legislation Pertaining to Religion or Belief.

The Guidelines distinguish between "basic rights" which States are bound to grant equally to minority or majority religious groups, and additional "benefits or privileges" which may be granted but without discrimination:

> *"Privileges and benefits of religious/belief organizations.* In general, out of deference for the values of freedom of religion or belief, laws governing access to legal personality should be structured in ways that are facilitative of freedom of religion or belief; at a minimum, access to the *basic rights associated with legal personality – for example, opening a bank account, renting or acquiring property for a place of worship or for other religious uses, entering into contracts, and the right to sue and be sued* – should be available without excessive difficulty. In many legal systems, there are additional legal issues that have substantial impact on religious life that are often linked to acquiring legal personality – for example, obtaining land use or other governmental permits; inviting foreign religious leaders, workers, and volunteers into a country; arranging visits and ministries in hospitals, prisons, and the military; eligibility to establish educational institutions (whether for educating children or for training clergy); eligibility to establish separate religiously motivated charitable organizations; and so forth. In many countries, a variety of financial benefits ranging from tax-exempt status to direct subsidies may be available for certain types of religious entities. *In general, the mere making available of any of the foregoing benefits or privileges does not violate rights to freedom of religion or belief. However, care must be taken to assure that non-discrimination norms are not violated."* [emphasis added]

Cole Durham, member of the Panel of Experts of the OSCE Office for Democratic Institutions and Human Rights (ODIHR) on Freedom of Religion or Belief, elaborated on this concept in a paper submitted by ODIHR at the OSCE Review Conference in September 1999.[12] He explained:

---

[12] Organization for Security and Co-operation in Europe (OSCE), *Freedom of Religion or Belief: Laws Affecting the Structuring of Religious Communities*, 1 September 1999, ODIHR Background Paper 1999/4 by Cole Durham.

"In many of the legal systems of OSCE participating States, there are two or more levels of legal status available to religious organizations for carrying out their affairs. The first level includes what can be called *"base level"* entities. These include entities that religious associations can use to acquire rudimentary forms of legal personality that are sufficient to carry out their affairs, but typically lack significant additional benefits (other than the advantages of the entity form itself). Beyond the base level are a diverse range of often very country-specific *"upper tier"* entities which are eligible for direct and indirect financial benefits from the State, and various other privileges. For example, in countries such as Italy and Spain, which have a system of agreements with major Churches or with federations of religious associations, significant benefits flow from being eligible to participate in a state agreement, and not all religious organizations are eligible to do so. In Germany, a number of benefits, as well as heightened prestige, flow from achieving status as a public corporation (*Körperschaft des öffentlichen Rechts*). In Austria the "recognized" Churches have more privileges and greater public status than "publicly registered belief communities" or than religious communities that have not been recognized." [emphasis added]

He added that "It is of course important that such "upper tier" schemes be implemented in ways that are sensitive to the rights and equality concerns of smaller religious groups."

Actually, the European Court has had to decide on the granting of such privileges in particular in Austria.

Austria has a two-tier system whereby religious groups can obtain registration as religious community (base level status) whereas recognition as religious society grants an upper level status with additional privileges.

In the case *Religionsgemeinschaft der Zeugen Jehovahs and others v. Austria*,[13] the religious community of Jehovah's Witnesses in Austria and four of its members submitted that the status of a religious community, a private-law entity, finally conferred upon the community in 1998 was inferior to the status held by religious societies, public-law entities, as religious communities were subject to more severe State control in respect of their religious doctrine, their rules on membership and the administration of their assets pursuant to the 1998 Religious Communities Act.

The applicants complained in particular of the discriminatory nature of section 11 of the 1998 Religious Communities Act, which introduced further requirements for recognition as a religious society. In particular, it required the existence of the religious association for at least twenty years in Austria and for at least ten years as a registered religious community.

The Court first observed that under Austrian law, religious societies enjoy privileged treatment in many areas, such as exemption from military service and ci-

---

[13] *Religionsgemeinschaft der Zeugen Jehovas and Others v. Austria*, no. 40825/98, §§ 37–55, 31 July 2008.

vilian service, reduced tax liability or exemption from specific taxes, facilitation of the founding of schools, and membership of various boards. Given the number of these privileges and their nature, in particular in the field of taxation, the advantage obtained by religious societies is substantial and this special treatment undoubtedly facilitates a religious society's pursuance of its religious aims. Therefore, the obligation under Article 9 of the Convention incumbent on the State's authorities to remain neutral in the exercise of their powers in this domain requires therefore that *all religious groups must have a fair opportunity to apply for this status and the criteria established must be applied in a non-discriminatory manner.*

As concerns the ten-year existence as registered religious community requirement, the Court accepted that, "in exceptional circumstances", a period might be necessary before the granting of such more consolidated status, "such as would be in the case of newly established and unknown religious groups".

However, it found that it hardly appeared justified "in respect of religious groups with a long-standing existence internationally which are also long established in the country and therefore familiar to the competent authorities, as is the case with the Jehovah's Witnesses". In respect of such a religious group, the authorities should be able to verify whether it fulfils the requirements of the relevant legislation within a considerably shorter period.

In addition, the JW maintained that the government did not really deem that waiting period necessary since the Coptic Orthodox Church was granted the status of religious society by a specific law in 2003 whereas this Church had only existed in Austria since 1976 (so 17 years of existence instead of 20 per the law) and had been registered as a religious community in 1998 (5 years of registration instead of 10 per the law). The Court found that this fact showed that the Austrian State did not consider the application on an equal basis of such a waiting period to be essential in the pursuance of its policy in that field and concluded to a violation of Articles 9 and 14.

From this case law, the Jehovah's Witnesses obtained further ECHR decisions finding violations of Articles 9 and 14 on the same basis.

In the cases of *Lang v. Austria*,[14] *Gütl v. Austria*[15] and *Löffelman v. Austria*,[16] the refusal of exemption from military and alternative civilian service was likewise based on the ground that the applicant was not a member of a religious society within the meaning of the 1874 Recognition Act. Given its findings in the above case law, the Court considered that the very same criterion – whether or not a person applying for exemption from military service is a member of a religious group which is constituted as a religious society – cannot be understood differ-

---

[14] Lang v. Austria, no. 28648/03, 12 March 2009.
[15] Gütl v. Austria, no. 49686/99, 12 March 2009.
[16] Löffelman v. Austria, no. 42967/98, 12 March 2009.

ently and its application must inevitably result in discrimination prohibited by the Convention.

In the case of *Jehovahs Zeugen in Österreich v. Austria*,[17] a Jehovah's Witnesses religious community established in Austria under the Religious Communities Act 1998 complained that it had been subject to laws concerning the employment of foreigners and tax from which recognised religious societies had been exempted.

The Court similarly considered that the same criterion identified in the above case law – whether or not the applicant community was a recognised religious society – could not be understood differently in this case and its application inevitably resulted in discrimination prohibited by the Convention.

The Court therefore concluded that the relevant part of the Employment of Aliens Act, which provides for exemptions from the scope of application of that Act in respect of the employment of aliens for pastoral work as part of a recognised religious society, is discriminatory and that the applicant community was discriminated against on the basis of religion as a result of the application of this provision. There had therefore been a violation of Article 14 taken in conjunction with Article 9 of the Convention.

This case law is precious for religious minorities to fight for their rights and should be extended to other groups and countries.

2. Participation of privileged religions in the fight against religious minorities

Some States, although signatories of the ICCPR and the ECHR and considered democratic States, not only maintain privileges for traditional or predominant religions but they also rely on them to fight against religious minorities.

The case of two of these States will be examined here: Germany and Russia.

2.1. Germany

As Gerhard Besier explained in the German chapter of the book Anti-sect movements and State neutrality,[18] freedom of religion in Germany is guaranteed by the Basic Law. Religion and state are separate but a special partnership exists between the State and those religious communities that were given the *born* status of a "corporation under public law" (PLC) in 1919 – namely the two mainstream Churches: the former Protestant State Church (until 1918) and the Roman Catho-

---

[17] Jehovahs Zeugen in Österreich v. Austria, no. 27540/05, 25 September 2012.
[18] Freedom of religion or belief, anti-sect movements and State neutrality, a case study: FECRIS, Journal for the study of beliefs and worldviews, 13. Jahrgang (2012) / Heft 2.

lic Church. Since 1949, the decision to grant PLC status has been made at the level of the *Länder* on the basis of certain requirements: a guarantee of permanence, the membership of the organization, and the respect of the constitutional order and fundamental rights.

2.1.1. Privileged religions and their anti-sect activities

This special status of mainstream Churches has enabled them to benefit from substantial financial privileges. Gerhard Besier explains:

> "The most important source of income for the mainline Churches in Germany is constituted by the church tax and additional payments by the State to compensate expropriations that took place in 1803. Taxpayers, whether Roman Catholic, Protestant or members of other tax-collecting communities, pay between 8% (in Bavaria and Baden-Württemberg) and 9% (in the rest of the country) of their income tax to the Church or other community to which they belong. In 2008, the tax provided the Roman Catholic Church with a net income of 5.1 billion Euros (£ 4.79bn)[19] and provided the Protestant Churches (Lutheran, Reformed and United) with a net income of 4.7 billion Euros. Moreover, the additional payments by the State amount to 9 billion Euros per year. Finally, the State forbears from raising taxes and other rates from the Churches to the amount of 10 billion Euros annually. These extensive privileges have made the two German mainstream Churches the wealthiest in the world."

This becomes particularly problematic under international human rights law when this money is used to combat religious minorities, with the blessing of the State. Gerhard Besier reports:

> "The Catholic Church and the Lutheran Church have created more than a hundred agencies to warn against sects at the regional and local level. Numerous ministries and public institutions at the federal level and at the level of the *Länder* have also put in place similar agencies. Anti-sect organizations are therefore well-funded in Germany."

The fact that mainstream Churches use financial privileges granted to them by the German State to combat religious minorities they see as competitors cannot be reconciled with international human rights treaties and the German Constitution.

The UN Human Rights Committee laid out in General Comment 22:

> Article 18 protects theistic, non-theistic and atheistic beliefs, as well as the right not to profess any religion or belief. The terms "belief" and "religion" are to be broadly construed. Article 18 is not limited in its application to traditional religions or to religions and beliefs with institutional characteristics or practices analogous to those of traditional religions. The Committee therefore views with concern any tendency to discriminate against any religion or belief for any reason, including the fact that they are newly established, or represent religious minorities *that may be the subject of hostility on the part of a predominant religious community*. [emphasis added]

---

[19] See http://www.secularism.org.uk/germanys-outrageous-church-tax-u.html.

If the German State gives financial support to mainstream Churches and declares them Public Law entities, then these should be bound in their use of public moneys by the same duty of neutrality as the State itself. Otherwise the State is evading its obligation by financing separate entities to carry out its ideological battle.

Pursuant to the principle, *"Nemo potest facere per alium, quod per se non potest"*: No one can do through another what he cannot do himself, a State cannot do, through public law corporations and private organizations created by them, what it cannot do itself.

The German Federal Administrative Supreme Court confirmed this principle when it ruled on 27 March 1992 in favour of the Osho movement: "Further it must be considered that the State itself – when it makes public statements to warn against the activities of certain religious or philosophical communities – is subject to the obligations of reserve and objectivity to protect constitutional rights. The State cannot evade these legal obligations by obtaining the assistance of a private association which can make use of its own constitutional freedom of speech and expression up to the limit of malicious criticism."[20] On this basis the Court prohibited the Federal Republic of Germany to fund the anti-sect association AGPF, Action for Mental and Psychological Freedom.

Nevertheless, the Catholic Church and the Lutheran Church, which are the wealthiest Christian Churches in Europe thanks to the tax church system and are administratively managed by the State, have put in place a whole network of local "advisory centres" warning against religious minorities they label "sects".

During the 70ies and 80ies some factions in the established two mainstream Christian Churches endeavoured to halt the expansion of religious minorities. They established so-called "sect Commissioners" in all their dioceses or bigger parishes and "Parents Initiatives" under their control who spread all kinds of baseless rumours about sects.

These Churches are closer to the State because they have the legal status of "corporation governed by public law" and are considered to have expertise in religious matters. This materializes, for example, in the fact that their sect Commissioners were members of the Inquiry Commission on Sects and Psychogroups appointed by the German Parliament in 1996, or the fact that the Government regularly refers to their publications as authoritative on sects.

All in all, the anti-sect policy of the German State contributes to the strengthening of the Catholic Church and the Lutheran Church. This constitutes a direct violation of Germany's duty of neutrality under international human rights norms.

---

[20] Decision p. 19–20 (BVerwG 7 C 21.90/OVG 5 A 584/86).

2.1.2. Anti-sect filters and discrimination

Another contentious practice in various German Länders is that of so-called "sect filters". A number of municipalities and public entities have had applicants to civil servant positions fill in a pre-designed form where the applicants have to declare that they are not followers of the Church of Scientology as a condition for employment or contracting with the State.

In 1995 the then sect Commissioner of the City of Hamburg invented the first sect filter, called "Scientology protection declaration" or "Technology declaration", to prevent the "infiltration" of the German business world by Scientologists – an accusation which was later found to be false by a task force of the Federal Office for the Protection of the Constitution (OPC), the domestic secret service, as publicly confirmed in an interview of its President on 2nd September 1999.[21]

By way of background, an OPC surveillance of the Church of Scientology was started based on a resolution adopted on 25 April 1997 by the Bavarian Lutheran Church synod at the initiative of its synod member politician Mr. Beckstein, who also held the Bavarian Minister of Interior post at that time. This resolution stated that the Lutheran Church could no longer cope with the Church of Scientology issue and that it called upon the State to take charge of it. It accused Scientology of not being a religion but a business enterprise and of being a threat to the individual and to society. But the main concern it formulated was that Scientology intended to eradicate the Christian belief from the minds of people. It concluded that it was *a Christian duty* to take action against that.

A few weeks later, on 5 June 1997, the Conference of the Ministers of Interior for Germany, under the pressure of Bavarian Minister of Interior Beckstein and his counterpart in the State of Baden-Württemberg Thomas Schäuble, ruled that the Church of Scientology should be subject to OPC surveillance throughout Germany, both by overt and covert means of surveillance.

To this day, the OPC has been unable to find any evidence of the alleged intention of Scientology to overthrow democracy despite using these various measures. In fact, the OPC has issued several reports to the contrary.[22]

However, the practice of sect-filters has been justified by these unfounded accusations.

---

[21] Stern magazine, 2 Sept 1999, "No case for spies", an interview of the President of the State OPC of Northrhine-Westfalia, Mr. Fritz-Achim Baumann, who had been the Chairman of a special national OPC Task Force to determine whether Scientology should be put under OPC surveillance.

[22] File inspections enforced on government agencies by the Courts under the Freedom of Information Act in 2015 have established evidence of prior government internal reports that such facts do not exist, despite 20 years of surveillance. OPC representatives have actually issued public statements that there was no basis for the insinuation of "infiltration" of the business world nor politics as had been alleged in the 90s to justify it. See Die Welt, report of 19 Feb 2013, "Scientology – no second Power in the State", an interview of the President of the State OPC of Hamburg, Mr. Murck.

Such filters have required an individual to reveal any connection to or affiliation with the Church of Scientology by asking whether or not the person ever attended or currently attends a course or seminar that contained the "Technology of L. Ron Hubbard". In addition, the individual has had to declare that he would not practice, disseminate such "technology" nor attend any such seminars/courses in the future and for the time of his employment or service contract. The same declaration has been required from the General Manager of any business or company in relation to his employees or subcontractors involved in the service provided by the business or company.[23]

The sect filter therefore requires both the revelation of any Scientology membership and/or affiliation and discontinuation of membership or resignation from Scientology as a contractual necessity otherwise no employment contract, service contract or invitation to a government bid would be granted. A refusal to fill out such a filter results in being automatically disbarred from the prospective employment, service contract or invitation to bid for a government contract.

Undoubtedly, this entails serious consequences and results in personal, professional, social, economic or other disadvantages being imposed on any Scientologist solely by reason of his or her religious membership and affiliation. Sect filters not only result in outright and organized discrimination, but they also violate the protected right to freedom of religion or belief, which includes the right to internal conviction (*forum internum*), which is not subject to limitation. No one can be coerced to reveal one's beliefs under international Human Rights Law.

The UN Human Rights Committee spelled out in General Comment 22:

> "Article 18 distinguishes the freedom of thought, conscience, religion or belief from the freedom to manifest religion or belief. It does not permit any limitations whatsoever on the freedom of thought and conscience or on the freedom to have or adopt a religion or belief of one's choice. These freedoms are protected unconditionally, as is the right of everyone to hold opinions without interference in article 19.1.[24] In accordance with articles 18.2 and 17,[25] *no one can be compelled to reveal his thoughts or adherence to a religion or belief.* [emphasis added]

Many legal conflicts resulted throughout the years across Germany between individual members of the Scientology religion and individual corporations of public law and private organisations which were ordinarily settled before or out of court on the basis of severance payments to the employed Scientologists.

---

[23] "Scientology in Germany – Sect Filters", submission by the European Office of the Church of Scientology at the Human Dimension Implementation Meeting, Warsaw September 2019.

[24] Article 19.1 ICCPR:
Everyone shall have the right to hold opinions without interference.

[25] Article 17 ICCPR:
No one shall be subjected to arbitrary or unlawful interference with his privacy, family, or correspondence, nor to unlawful attacks on his honour and reputation.
Everyone has the right to the protection of the law against such interference or attacks.

The campaign of the City of Hamburg resulted in several Scientologists losing a contract or business deals by reason of the City having promoted their anti-Scientology "protective declaration" to their prospective customers or business contractors. This resulted in several court cases against the City of Hamburg where the Hamburg State Administrative Court of Appeal held that the promotion of the sect filter was illegal and represented an interference with the right to freedom of religion or belief of individual Scientologists.[26]

As the City appealed, the case went up to the Federal Supreme Administrative Court which finally issued a ground-breaking decision on 15 Dec 2005 that the distribution and promotion of the sect filter to exclude Scientologists from a business relationship was unconstitutional as it violated the freedom of religion or belief guaranteed by Article 4 of the German Constitution and that the interference by the City of Hamburg with this right was illegal.[27]

However, the City of Hamburg and other German States such as Bavaria refuse to apply the principles of the above decision and they still require a sect filter to be signed such as in the context of service contracts with private companies or the sale of state owned real property to any prospective buyer, or in the context of employment contracts between state agencies or state organisations and private individuals.

Recently in 2018, the City of Munich adopted a city-funded incentive programme to subsidise individuals or certain professions in purchasing a so-called e-bike (a bicycle with an electrical engine to support riding the bicycle) for use in professional contexts as an incentive to reduce pollution from car traffic. Anyone who applies for participation in this program can obtain a support of up to € 500 for the purchase of such an e-bike but has to sign a declaration that he/she does not adhere to Scientology.

The declaration form provides:

> "By way of her/his signature the applicant declares that she/he does not apply, teach or otherwise disseminate any contents or methods and also no technology of L. Ron Hubbard and that she/he does not attend any courses or seminars according to this Technology."

A woman from Munich applied for such funding but she refused to sign the above declaration as it would have implied her resignation from the Church of Scientology. As a consequence, the City rejected her application. A suit was filed with the Bavarian Administrative Court against this denial in 2019 and the City argued that it did not grant the support because it did not want to be associated to Scientology as such a bike could be used by the applicant "for promotional purposes of the Church" (though the applicant clearly intended to use it only for professional

---

[26] Hamburg State Administrative Court of Appeal, 17 June 2004, file no. 1 Bf 198/00.
[27] Federal Supreme Administrative Court 15 Dec 2005, file no. 7 C 20.04.

purposes). The suit was dismissed by the ruling of the Munich Administrative Court on 28 August 2019, which has been appealed.

This practice undoubtedly violates Article 18.2 ICCPR and the right to be free from coercion to recant one's religion or belief.

The case of Scientologists is typical. Although they won some 14 cases to date where the German Courts found that they have been the victim of discrimination, the leaders of the anti-sect groups of the mainstream religions, mainly the Lutheran Church, continue exerting media and political pressure to make this practice persist.

2.2. Russia

The current critical situation of religious minorities in Russia traces back to the 1990s with the opening of the country to freedom of religion or belief and the fear of the Orthodox Church that they would lose their traditional status in society.

2.2.1. The concept of "Spiritual Security" – Background

In October 1990, a Law on Freedom of Religion was adopted under the Gorbachev regime, which was one of the last and most decisive liberalizing legislative reforms introduced in the old Soviet system. For the first time in Russian history, practicing religion was declared "the unalienable right of Russian citizens". This right also applied to all those residing in Russia, irrespective of their citizenship. The law maintained strict separation between Church and State, provided State ideological neutrality and guaranteed equal rights for all faiths, regardless of their origins and size.

As an immediate consequence of the Law, Russia's religious landscape started to become significantly modified. There was a resurgence of the Russian Orthodox Church and other "traditional" religions, Muslim, Catholic, Jewish and Buddhist and their missionary activities from abroad, as well as proselytizing efforts of religions that were new to Russia.

This evolution gave rise to a strong anti-cult movement, focused in the Moscow Patriarchate of the Russian Orthodox Church, which started to push the concept that Russia's "spiritual security" and traditional values were somehow at risk.

In November 1996, then Orthodox Bishop Kirill, who was subsequently elected in 2009 as the Patriarch of Moscow and all Russia, publicly spoke about the problem of proselytism the Russian Orthodox Church (ROC) was facing. He noted that once the 1990 law allowed for freedom of conscience, "hordes of missionaries dashed in, believing the former Soviet Union to be a vast missionary territory."

According to him, instead of aiding the ROC in its missionary endeavors, these proselytizing groups worked against the Church "like boxers in a ring with their pumped-up muscles, delivering blows." He added that the blows were against the "people's national and religious sentiments", leading to a state where for many Russians, "'non-Orthodox' means those who have come to destroy the spiritual unity of the people and the Orthodox faith – spiritual colonizers who by fair means or foul try to tear the people away from their Church".

In the eyes of the religious leaders of the ROC, Russia was losing its cultural identity as an Orthodox nation. In this atmosphere, where the ROC believed itself as well as the Russian culture to be under attack, Boris Yeltsin passed a new religion law in September 1997, differentiating traditional from nontraditional religions in Russia.

The 1997 Law on Freedom of Conscience and Religious Associations provided serious restrictions on the registration of religious organizations and thus on the activities of religious groups of foreign origin. Religious communities registered earlier under the 1990 law were submitted to the obligation of re-registration; many were denied the right to re-register and challenged the negative decision before domestic courts and then the European Court of Human Rights, in particular the Salvation Army, the Jesuits, Jehovah's Witnesses and the Church of Scientology.

The 1997 law, as well as the ideological stand and repressive laws which were thereafter adopted by the Russian authorities, were all inspired by the desire to ensure the "spiritual security" of Russia, a new concept expressing the purported role of the Russian Orthodox Church in safeguarding national values and security.

2.2.2. Extremism Law and Extremist Religious Literature

The Suppression of Extremism Act ("Extremism Law") enacted in 2002[28] defined "extremist activities" as, among others: (i) incitement of social, racial, ethnic or religious discord; (ii) propaganda about the exceptional nature, superiority or deficiency of people on the basis of their social, racial, ethnic, religious or linguistic affiliation or their attitude to religion; (iii) violation of human and civil rights and freedoms, and of lawful interests in connection with a person's social, racial, ethnic, religious or linguistic affiliation or attitude to religion; and (iv) public appeals to commit the above-mentioned acts, or mass dissemination of material known to be extremist, as well as the production or storage of such material with the aim of mass dissemination.

The Act further defined "extremist material" as documents intended for publication, or information disseminated via other media, calling for extremist activity to be carried out or substantiating or justifying the necessity of carrying out such activity.

---

[28] Federal Law no. 114-FZ of 25 July 2002.

Those extremely vague provisions were revisited by the European Human Rights Court in the previously mentioned Nursi followers' case. The Court, like the European Commission for Democracy through Law (the Venice Commission) had done,[29] invalidated those provisions in that they contain no requirement of violence or incitement to hatred to define extremist activities or extremist publications.

The Court ruled that in order to qualify religious publications as extremist on the basis that they were "stirring up religious discord"', the national courts had to demonstrate that the publications in question, when read as a whole and in their context, could be seen as promoting *violence*, hatred or intolerance.

It also found that the expression of the belief in the superiority of one's worldview over all other world-views, which makes it necessary to substantiate the choice of that world-view, in particular by claiming that it was better than the others, is common to all religions and does not suffice for accusing religious publications of being an "extremist activity" (as per (ii) of the definition above).

In particular, it found that the Russian courts should have taken into account the fact that, according to the experts, the impugned statements were common in religious texts because any monotheistic religion was "characterized by a psychologically based belief in the superiority of its world-view over all other world-views, which made it necessary to substantiate the choice of that world-view", in particular by claiming that it was better than the others.

In its 2008 Opinion, the Venice Commission stated:

In the view of the Venice Commission, to proclaim as extremist any religious teaching or proselytising activity aimed at proving that a certain worldview is a superior explanation of the universe, may affect the freedom of conscience or religion of many persons and could easily be abused in an effort to suppress a certain church thereby affecting not only the freedom of conscience or religion but also the freedom of association. The [European Court of Human Rights] protects proselytism and the freedom of the members of any religious community or church to 'try to convince' other people through 'teachings'. The freedom of conscience and religion is of an intimate nature and is therefore subject to fewer possible limitations in comparison to other human rights: only manifestations of this freedom can be limited, but not the teachings themselves.

Unfortunately, the Russian authorities did not care to follow the Opinion of the highest Constitutional expert body in Europe and maintained their Extremism Law in force to strengthen the State Church (ROC) position and repress non-traditional beliefs.

---

[29] Venice, 17–18 October 2008.

They have deemed the religious literature of various religious groups extremist, have prohibited their teachings and dissolved their associations.

This is the case in particular of the Jehovah's Witnesses. The SOVA Centre in Moscow[30] reported for the sole month of February 2020:

> In February, several sentences were issued for continuing activity of Jehovah's Witnesses communities and a number of new cases were opened. The charges have been brought against believers in connection with the fact that, in April 2017, the Supreme Court of Russia recognized the Jehovah's Witnesses Administrative Center in Russia and 395 of their local religious organizations as extremist. We believe that this decision, which let to mass prosecutions against believers under Article 282.2 of the Criminal Code, had no legal basis, and regard it as a manifestation of religious discrimination.[31]

There followed a long list of cases of police arrest, massive house searches and various instances of torture of Witnesses, performed pursuant to Article 282 of the Criminal Code which represses incitement of hatred or enmity.

Typical is that, in the second half of February, a District Court of the Russian Federation found a Witness guilty under this Article and issued a two-year suspended sentence with restriction of liberty for six months for reading the Bible in the Jehovah's Witnesses translation during a religious meeting.

2.2.3. Yarovaya Law on missionary activities

Furthermore, adoption of repressive legislation escalated. In July 2016, the so-called "Yarovaya package" was enacted, which comprised a series of legislative amendments ostensibly designed to combat terrorism. It included a ban on the performance of "missionary activities" in non-religious settings.

The package consisted of two laws: No. 374-FZ amended certain federal laws and regulations, and No. 375-FL amended the Criminal and Criminal Procedure Codes.

Some amendments introduced a new definition of "missionary activity" (Federal Law No. 125-FZ on Freedom of Conscience and Religious Associations, Chapter III.1), which was quite broad and applied to virtually any religious practice, including rituals, sermons, reading of religious literature, and sharing religious views online.

Missionary activities were restricted to premises occupied by religious organizations. In order to be allowed to engage in mission work elsewhere, the new law required individuals to carry authorization from their religious association and

---

[30] SOVA Center for Information and Analysis is a Moscow-based Russian nonprofit organization founded in October 2002. SOVA Center conducts research and informational work on nationalism and racism, relations between the churches and secular society, and political radicalism. They are also interested in human rights issues, especially government misuse of counter-extremism measures.

[31] See https://www.sova-center.ru/en/misuse/news-releases/2020/03/d42228/.

proof of the organization's registration. Proselytizing in residential areas – except for prayer and ritual – was specifically forbidden, and violators could face fines of up to one million rubles.

In an article published on 27 November 2016 on the Yarovaya Laws, the SOVA Centre expressed that:[32]

> "the law is actively enforced, in particular against Protestants: in August [2016], those charged and fined included Ebenezer Tuah, head of the Christ Embassy Evangelical (Pentecostal) group in Tver, Baptist preacher Donald Ossewaarde in Orel, and pastors Alexey Teleus in Noyabrsk, Yamalo-Nenets Autonomous District, and Alexander Yakimov in the Republic of Mari El.
>
> In September, those fined for "illegal missionary activity" included Sergey Zhuravlev, archbishop of the Ukrainian Reformed Orthodox Church of Christ the Saviour and the Russian Orthodox Reformed Church, in St. Petersburg, and Irina Tishchenko, leader of the Family and Women's Ministry in the New Generation movement, in Kemerovo."

2.2.4. The Orthodox Church anti-sect activities

To a large extent, the responsibility for the increasing religious tensions that culminated in the adoption of the 1997 Law (and the subsequent repressive legislation) must be borne by the Russian anti-cult movement, and by leading anti-cult crusader Aleksandr Dvorkin in particular. Dvorkin has been the key agitator responsible for popularizing the new term "totalitarian sects" that he uses against peaceful religious minorities.

Aleksandr Dvorkin is the vice-President of FECRIS, the European Federation of Centres of Research and Information on Sectarianism[33]. He is at the head of the FECRIS member association in Russia, the anti-sect centre *Saint Ireneus of Lyons Centre for Religious Studies* which was founded in 1993 with the blessing of the Patriarch of Moscow and All Russia Alexy II and is a missionary faculty department of St Tikhon's Orthodox University in Moscow.

Dvorkin and the FECRIS chapter as part of the Missionary Department of the Orthodox University have been engaged in hate speech and disparagement against the so-called "sects" or "cults" for the last twenty years, fueling suspicion and prejudice that lead to repression such as banning and imprisonment, not to mention incitement of hatred that lead to physical violence, threats, vandalism and similar aggression.

Another aspect of the activity of the Missionary anti-sect Department in Moscow is the referral of followers of religious minorities to so-called "Rehabilitation Centers".

---

[32] See http://legal-dialogue.org/russias-controversial-yarovaya-package-targets-missionaries-threatens-privacy.

[33] The above-mentioned anti-sect association AGPF in Germany is also a member of FECRIS.

The Saint Ireneus of Lyons anti-sect Centre operates with a network of so-called "parents' initiatives" and other similar organizations in Russia.

On the Centre's advice, families who disagree with the choice of one of their relatives to adhere to a non-traditional religion take them to so-called "rehabilitation centres" where they are "enlightened" about the danger of sects and how sects manipulate one's mind, then persuaded by a priest or catechist to accept the Orthodox religion because, according to them, if one really believes in Christ he is protected from various sects.

The Saint Ireneus of Lyons Centre posted an article on its website explaining how to deal with people "caught in sects": The process of exit through an external influence involves a psychologist, relatives and a "sect-specialist", to arouse critical thinking towards the "sect" and get rid of emotional dependency towards it. Then it involves connecting the person to the Orthodox catechist, preferably a priest offering the true religious and ideological alternatives.

This approach recalls the much-criticized practice of "deprogramming" which has been found to be illegal as it involved abduction and violence to have followers recant their faith, and to violate the followers' right to freedom of religion or belief.

The religious "rehabilitation" performed with the blessing of the Russian authorities does not apparently include abduction, but it still includes pressure and psychological constraint to convert followers of religious minorities to the politically correct religion. This alone constitutes a violation of the followers' right to be free to adhere to the beliefs of their own choosing and to be free from coercion to recant their faith under Article 18.2 ICCPR.

In consideration of the above, the whole policy of the Russian government designed at protecting the interests of the Russian Orthodox Church constitutes an outright violation of its duty of neutrality in religious matters, and a violation of the rights of the Russian people to freedom of thought and belief.

3. Conclusion

Limitations to freedom of religion or belief cannot be legitimately justified under international human rights norms by reasons of "national security", a justification however claimed by both the German and Russian authorities to limit the rights of certain religious minorities.

Article 18.3 ICCPR provides that "Freedom to manifest one's religion or beliefs may be subject only to such limitations as are prescribed by law and are necessary to protect *public safety*, order, health, or morals or the fundamental rights and freedoms of others." [emphasis added]

Public safety has nothing to do with "national security" or "spiritual security" of the Nation.

The UN Human Rights Committee addressed this issue in General Comment 22:

> "The Committee observes that paragraph 3 of article 18 is to be strictly interpreted: *restrictions are not allowed on grounds not specified there*, even if they would be allowed as restrictions to other rights protected in the Covenant, *such as national security*. Limitations may be applied only for those purposes for which they were prescribed and must be directly related and proportionate to the specific need on which they are predicated. Restrictions may not be imposed for discriminatory purposes or applied in a discriminatory manner." [emphasis added]

States have a duty of neutrality in matters of religion or belief under the Human Rights obligations they have committed to.

They cannot favor a religious denomination to the detriment of others, and even less can they repress minority religions to protect the interests of mainstream or State Churches.

Much remains to be done to protect the right to freedom of religion or belief even in democracies and alleged human rights countries.

Abstract

The right to freedom of religion or belief, protected by international human rights treaties, implies the free dissemination of religious beliefs, even though they belong to minority and non-traditional denominations.

States can grant privileges to mainstream religions providing they do not discriminate against minority religions in doing so.

States have a duty of neutrality in religious matters and cannot finance or support mainstream religions to fight against religious minorities seen as competitors and labeled as "sects".

Two study cases, Germany and Russia, show that these human rights obligations can be overlooked in the name of "national security" or "spiritual security".

"YOUR HUMAN RIGHTS, YOUR FUNDAMENTAL FREEDOMS ARE IN DANGER!"

Crusade Against Christianity, Jehovah's Witnesses, and the Fight for Religious Freedom

TIM B. MÜLLER

To Simone Arnold Liebster

1. What freedom?

When German-Jewish philosopher Theodor W. Adorno, whose theoretical fame is not primarily owed to his reflection on everyday political life, gave his lecture series on the philosophy of history in the winter of 1964/65 at Frankfurt University, he remarkably abstained from any abstract definition of freedom. Definitions of freedom were in vogue in the early Cold War period. But when this émigré from Nazi Germany, whose family had been severely affected by the Holocaust, was asked what freedom is, he simply pointed to an existential and transformative political experience: You know what freedom is when the Gestapo wakes you up early in the morning, searches your home, mistreats you, and seizes your work and books.[1]

Hannah Arendt, another émigré from Nazi Germany and one of the first and most perceptive thinkers on the impact of totalitarianism and the Holocaust on the human condition, stated in a famous postwar lecture in Germany in 1959 that freedom starts with the freedom of movement (*Bewegungsfreiheit*), as the historically most ancient and the most elementary form of freedom. She called the freedom to move and leave (*Aufbrechen-Können*) the original gesture of being free.[2]

Jehovah's Witnesses are at the forefront in today's battle over religious freedom, as they have been in so many cases and places throughout the 20th century. And religious freedom, for many reasons, some of which will be touched upon

---

[1] *Theodor W. Adorno*, Zur Lehre von der Geschichte und von der Freiheit (Nachgelassene Schriften, series 4, vol. 13), Frankfurt am Main 2001, 28 f.

[2] *Hannah Arendt*, Von der Menschlichkeit in finsteren Zeiten: Rede über Lessing, München 1960, 14; see also *eadem*, Essays in Understanding 1930–1954: Formation, Exile, and Totalitarianism, ed. Jerome Kohn, New York, 1994; *eadem*, Elemente und Ursprünge totaler Herrschaft: Antisemitismus, Imperialismus, totale Herrschaft (1951), München 1996.

later on, is also one of the historically most ancient and most elementary forms of freedom, closely related to the freedom of movement. With Adorno and Arendt in mind, let us have a glimpse at Sergei Klimov. According to a 21 October 2019 news report on *Kavkazskii Uzel*, "the representative of the European Association of Jehovah's Witnesses, Yaroslav Sivulsky, said that since 2017, more than 600 searches in homes of believers in Russia have been conducted, 40 persons are behind bars, and seven have been convicted."[3] Soon thereafter, Sergei Klimov became the eighth person belonging to this group to serve actual time in prison. His experience does not differ much from historical experience in authoritarian and totalitarian regimes, as a statement by Jehovah's Witnesses in Russia shows:

On 5 November 2019, Judge Dmitry Borisov of the October district court of Tomsk announced the verdict for a local resident, Sergei Klimov, who was convicted of professing an 'incorrect' religion: six years imprisonment in a correctional labor colony of general regime.

> The judge concluded that the guilt of the 49-year-old believer for serious crimes against the constitutional structure of Russia was fully proven [...]. The only grounds for such a severe sentence are the religious convictions of the defendant [...]. After serving the prison term, the believer will be given additional punishments: prohibition to engage in educational activity in all types of educational institutions and to post materials on the internet and other social networks for a period of five years, and also another year of restrictions of liberty (he is prohibited to attend cultural events including festivals, religious holidays, and ceremonies and prohibited to leave the boundaries of Tomsk and to change his place of residence without the permission of supervisory agencies).[4]

As Zoe Knox has argued, the current persecution of Jehovah's Witnesses in Russia signals the repudiation of European human rights norms by Russian governmental authorities, lawmakers, and religious elites.[5] Limitations or restrictions of religious freedom, more often than not supported by privileged state religions, are violations of fundamental rights and of freedom as such – this is not just a recent insight, but also a lesson of the 20th-century experience with authoritarian and totalitarian regimes. Among those who made this claim and gave ample evidence of it in the first half of the 20th century were Jehovah's Witnesses. Their understanding of freedom and of the Nazi assault on freedom was surprisingly close to the thinking of émigré intellectuals. One of their most visible statements in this regard was the important and impressive book *Kreuzzug gegen das Christentum*. This is the subject of the last part of this article. But there are questions to be addressed before discussing this book.

---

[3] https://www2.stetson.edu/~psteeves/relnews/191021a.html (18 March 2020).
[4] https://www2.stetson.edu/~psteeves/relnews/191105a.html (18 March 2020).
[5] *Zoe Knox*, Jehovah's Witnesses as Extremists: The Russian State, Religious Pluralism, and Human Rights, in: The Soviet and Post-Soviet Review 46, 2019, 128–157.

2. The Jehovah's Witnesses' exposure of the Nazi crusade against Christianity and intellectual history

Kreuzzug gegen das Christentum, or *Crusade Against Christianity,* as an English translation of the book title would read, is among many other things a book that invites a more nuanced reading of the position of Jehovah's Witnesses on religious freedom and the arguments they brought forward in support of religious freedom in the historical contexts of the 1930s. However, we have to leave the level of documentary history and engage in an intellectual history of the texts produced by Jehovah's Witnesses to understand and appreciate these arguments.

This approach is rather rare in research on Jehovah's Witnesses. For example, the recent, important book by Zoe Knox on Jehovah's Witnesses and the secular world is not particularly strong on intellectual nuance and historical contexts of arguments.[6] While there is substantial literature on Jehovah's Witnesses in Nazi Germany, few are the examples of readings of the religious texts and public interventions of Jehovah's Witnesses that are sensitive to theologico-political arguments and intellectual contexts.[7] Among those that paved the way for an intellectual history of Jehovah's Witnesses are Gerhard Besier and Jolene Chu. And of course, Detlef Garbe's classical and unsurpassed account of the Nazi persecution

---

[6] *Zoe Knox,* Jehovah's Witnesses and the Secular World: From the 1970s to the Present, London 2018.

[7] Among the most important contributions on the persecution and resistance of Jehovah's Witnesses in Nazi Germany and Nazi-occupied Europe are, in addition to the volumes discussed below, *Falk Bersch,* Aberkannt!: Die Verfolgung von Jehovas Zeugen im Nationalsozialismus und in der SBZ/DDR, Berlin 2017; Gerhard Besier and Clemens Vollnhals, eds., Repression und Selbstbehauptung: Die Zeugen Jehovas unter der NS- und der SED-Diktatur, Berlin 2003; *Gerald Hacke,* Die Zeugen Jehovas im Dritten Reich und in der DDR: Feindbild und Verfolgungspraxis, Göttingen 2011; Hans Hesse, ed., "Am mutigsten waren immer wieder die Zeugen Jehovas": Verfolgung und Widerstand der Zeugen Jehovas im Nationalsozialismus, Bremen 1998; Marcus Herrberger, ed., Denn es steht geschrieben: "Du sollst nicht töten!": Die Verfolgung religiöser Kriegsdienstverweigerer unter dem NS-Regime mit besonderer Berücksichtigung der Zeugen Jehovas (1939–1945), Wien 2005; Winfried Nerdinger and Christoph Wilker, eds., Die Verfolgung der Zeugen Jehovas in München 1933–1945, Berlin 2018; important remarks on texts and contexts in the Nazi era are also included in some of the best work on the communist post-war persecution of Jehovah's Witnesses, above all by *Emily B. Baran,* Dissent on the Margins: How Jehovah's Witnesses Defied Communism and Lived to Preach About It, Oxford 2014; see also *Hans-Hermann Dirksen,* "Keine Gnade der Feinden unserer Republik": Die Verfolgung der Zeugen Jehovas in der SBZ/DDR 1945–1990, Berlin 2001; *Waldemar Hirch,* Die Glaubensgemeinschaft der Zeugen Jehovas während der SED-Diktatur: Unter besonderer Berücksichtigung ihrer Observierung und Unterdrückung durch das Ministerium für Staatssicherheit, Frankfurt am Main 2003. Utterly useless, albeit unfortunately widely known in the Anglophone book market, is *M. James Penton,* Jehovah's Witnesses and the Third Reich: Sectarian Politics under Persecution, Toronto 2004. Besides factual errors, dubious interpretations and open hostility towards its subject, this book also shows a severe lack of understanding of the history of Nazi Germany and German history before 1933. See also *Detlef Garbe,* Between Resistance and Martyrdom: Jehovah's Witnesses in the Third Reich, Madison 2008, xix–xx; *Baran,* Dissent on the Margins, 259.

of Jehovah's Witnesses and their resistance against the genocidal German dictatorship includes highly perceptive readings of the theological positions of the International Bible Students or, after 1931, Jehovah's Witnesses.[8] This article will also pursue an intellectual history approach to the history of Jehovah's Witnesses and (religious) freedom in the 1920s and 1930s, but it will abstain from any summary of basic religious beliefs or the general history of this minority Christian group and for this purpose instead refer to the authors mentioned.[9]

3. Narratives of the fight for religious freedom

Jehovah's Witnesses have for many years engaged in the fight for religious freedom, one of the fundamental freedoms according to UN and European conventions and most national constitutions. There is a growing historiography of these endeavors to which a number of historians and legal experts, including lawyers and writers related to institutions of Jehovah's Witnesses, have contributed. As a consequence, perhaps a standard historical account has been established. Key elements of this narrative are featured as early as in a June 10, 1942 editorial of the *New York Times* on the wartime persecution and the legal battles of Jehovah's Witnesses in the United States. This article includes three remarkable sentences which also serve as epigraph to one recent example of this historiography, Jennifer Jacobs Henderson's *Defending the Good News*: "The minorities whose civil rights are threatened are always small and, to many, obnoxious. They may or may not be unworthy. Yet their treatment is the test, and will always be the test, of the sincerity with which we cling to the Bill of Rights."[10]

---

[8] Gerhard Besier and Katarzyna Stokłosa, eds., Jehovas Zeugen in Europa – Geschichte und Gegenwart, 3 vol.s, Berlin 2013–2018; *Jolene Chu*, "No Creed but the Bible": The Belief System of Jehovah's Witnesses, in: Religion – Staat – Gesellschaft 16, 2015, 109–175; *eadem*, God's Things and Caesar's: Jehovah's Witnesses and Political Neutrality, in: Journal of Genocide Research 6, 2004, 319–342; *Detlef Garbe*, Zwischen Widerstand und Martyrium: Die Zeugen Jehovas im "Dritten Reich", München 1997.

[9] For a historiographical review of scholarly work as well as personal memoirs and polemical literature regarding Jehovah's Witnesses, see *Zoe Knox*, Writing Witness History: The Historiography of the Jehovah's Witnesses and the Watch Tower Bible and Tract Society of Pennsylvania, in: Journal of Religious History 35, 2011, 157–180. This review, however, is clearly methodically committed to a top-down approach, privileging events at the American "center" of the Christian group, and focused almost exclusively on the United States and Great Britain, with little attention given to the social, intellectual, and everyday life history of this diverse global movement. These lacunae have been acknowledged by Knox's review of recent historiography which has started to fill this gap, most notably *Baran*, Dissent on the Margins (note 7); see *Knox*, The History of the Jehovah's Witnesses: An Appraisal of Recent Scholarship, in: Journal of Religious History 41, 2017, 251–260.

[10] *Jennifer Jacobs Henderson*, Defending the Good News: The Jehovah's Witnesses' Plan to Expand the First Amendment, Spokane 2010, 15.

Behind this statement is clearly a pluralist conception of freedom. Jehovah's Witnesses as a particularly visible and vulnerable Christian minority have indeed since the mid-1930s become a test case of modern religious freedom and fundamental rights. The legal arguments advanced in these contexts have come to define in very general and far-reaching terms what religious freedom means in constitutional, liberal, democratic, and pluralist states. The religious freedom arguments and decisions in which Jehovah's Witnesses were involved have shaped broader understandings of fundamental rights and the rule of law in Western societies and beyond, for they tested and defined the limits of religious freedom already guaranteed in the U.S. Bill of Rights as well as in many constitutions and international conventions.

There are different historical explanations why Jehovah's Witnesses have become this test case of modern religious freedom and related fundamental rights. Some point to key features of the 20th and 21st century "dark side" of modernity, such as national war efforts, mobilization, nationalism, racism, the creation of the national security state, the strategies of forced consensus and homogeneity. These phenomena, in varying degrees and extremely different in their effects, characterized, at least at times, the history of Europe, the United States, and other places before 1945 and possibly even thereafter. A pacifist and antiracist group such as Jehovah's Witnesses embodied the opposite of this streak of modern politics and hence became the object of repeated attack.[11]

Other scholars, who do not fully share this bleak vision of (early) 20th century history, emphasize the expansion of the modern state and its institutions as key structural feature of modernization in the 20th century. As result of this large-scale process, the relationship of the state and the individual citizen and his or her individual rights had to be re-negotiated. Jehovah's Witnesses as publicly visible evangelizing group, international, heterogeneous and multiracial in its character and vehemently claiming the rights of free speech, of conscientious objection, and other individual elements of religious freedom, then more or less by default – and not so much by design – became the group around which a number of the legal and political issues of the day crystallized.[12]

Going further in this direction, Shawn Francis Peters and others have argued that the legal battles in which Jehovah's Witnesses were involved, and also the

---

[11] See, e.g., *Richard J. Evans*, Social Outsiders, in: *idem*, The Third Reich in History and Memory, London 2015, 59–84; *Garbe*, Widerstand und Martyrium; *Ira Katznelson*, Fear Itself: The New Deal and the Origins of Our Time, New York 2013, 48; for "dark side" interpretations *Michael Mann*, The Dark Side of Democracy: Explaining Ethnic Cleansing, Cambridge 2005; *Mark Mazower*, Dark Continent: Europe's Twentieth Century, London 1998.

[12] This is, couched in abstract terms, more or less the interpretation for the United States running through, e.g., *William E. Leuchtenburg*, The Supreme Court Reborn: The Constitutional Revolution in the Age of Roosevelt, Oxford 1995; *James F. Simon*, FDR and Chief Justice Hughes: The President, the Supreme Court, and the Epic Battle Over the New Deal, New York 2012.

concerted mass activism and grass-roots legal techniques Jehovah's Witnesses deployed in the United States, ushered in the "dawn of the rights revolution".[13] This means that Jehovah's Witnesses and their fight for religious freedom in a broader sense were crucial for the emergence of the postwar understanding of civil and human rights that since the 1960s revolutionized western thinking about individual and fundamental freedoms. The 1940s trials of Jehovah's Witnesses paved the way for the African-American civil rights movement in the 1950s and 1960s: "African Americans pressed courts at all levels, including the Supreme Court, to safeguard the basic democratic freedoms that were guaranteed to all Americans by the Bill of Rights. [...] The seeds of this revolution had been sown decades earlier, when Jehovah's Witnesses repeatedly tested the boundaries of the Bill of Rights."[14] There are similar, even less familiar, stories to be told for other nations. In postwar West Germany, the constitutional right to conscientious objection established in the 1949 *Grundgesetz* was to a large degree an acknowledgement of the hundreds of Jehovah's Witnesses who had been executed for resisting the Nazi war. How this constitutional right was to be put into practice was defined in legal cases involving Jehovah's Witnesses.[15] The European dimension of this legal fight for religious freedom and for conscientious objection has been researched in particular by James T. Richardson, an expert for the European Court of Human Rights (ECHR) jurisdiction. He shows that the long and enormously successful effort of Jehovah's Witnesses that has shaped the European legal system and the European understanding of fundamental rights is still going on in the present day,[16] and that it could be understood as a continuation of earlier legal strategies developed in the United States and Canada.[17]

---

[13] *Shawn Francis Peters*, Judging Jehovah's Witnesses: Religious Persecution and the Dawn of the Rights Revolution, Lawrence 2000; *Jacobs Henderson*, Defending the Good News.

[14] Peters, Judging Jehovah's Witnesses, 292–293.

[15] *Hans Hesse*, "Dann wäre der Krieg gleich zu Ende": Die Kriegsdienstverweigerer im NS-Staat und das Grundgesetz der Bundesrepublik Deutschland, in: Nerdinger and Wilker, eds., Verfolgung der Zeugen Jehovas (note 7), 20–31.

[16] *James T. Richardson*, Update on Jehovah's Witnesses before the European Court of Human Rights. Implications of a Surprising Partnership, in: Religion, State & Society 45 (2017), 232–248; *idem*, The European Court of Human Rights: Changes and Challenges in the Social Construction of Religious Freedom, in: Religion – Staat – Gesellschaft 18, 2017, 13–34; *James T. Richardson and Mihai Popa*, The role of Jehovah's Witnesses case law in the jurisprudence of the European Court of Human Rights, in: Effie Fokas, ed., The European Court of Human Rights on the Ground: Grassroots Level Impact of Religious Freedoms Jurisprudence (forthcoming 2020). See also, e. g., Jeroen Temperman, T. Jeremy Gunn and Malcolm Evans, eds., The European Court of Human Rights and the Freedom of Religion or Belief: The 25 Years since Kokkinakis, Leiden 2019.

[17] *Pauline Coté and James T. Richardson*, Disciplined Litigation, Vigilant Litigation, and Deformation: Dramatic Organization Change in Jehovah's Witnesses, in: Journal for the Scientific Study of Religion 40, 2001, 11–25; *William Kaplan*, State and Salvation: The Jehovah's Witnesses and Their Fight for Civil Rights, Toronto 1989.

In the historical accounts published by Jehovah's Witnesses themselves, they assert that their contribution to the definition and expansion of religious freedom plays a major role.[18] The legal strategies of leading attorneys Joseph Rutherford, Hayden Covington, and Glen How as well as the courage of the average Witness of Jehovah, are highlighted. But these accounts not only enumerate the good results for their own religious community. "Strengthening the Guarantees of Freedom" and "Shaping of Constitutional Law" are claimed as effects of the religious group's legal battles.[19] Based on references from legal studies, an official history explains:

> The activity of Jehovah's Witnesses has, in some lands, been a major factor in shaping the law. Every American law student well knows the contribution made by Jehovah's Witnesses to the defense of civil rights in the United States. [...] Their court cases make up a significant portion of American law relating to freedom of religion, freedom of speech, and freedom of the press. These cases have done much to preserve the liberties not only of Jehovah's Witnesses but also of the entire populace.[20]

With regard to the legal history of Canada, the same account quotes approvingly from the seminal study by law professor William Kaplan: "The Jehovah's Witnesses taught the state, and the Canadian people, what the practical content of legal protection for dissenting groups should be." Kaplan's conclusion quoted here is that the Jehovah's Witnesses court cases "made an important contribution to Canadian attitudes about civil rights, and they constitute the bedrock of civil-liberties jurisprudence in Canada today."[21] "'One of the results' of the Witnesses' legal battle for freedom of worship 'was the long process of discussion and debate that led to the Charter of Rights', which is now part of the fundamental law of Canada."[22] Thus the enormous impact these cases and strategies had on legal and political culture in western democracies is acknowledged and emphasized in official statements by Jehovah's Witnesses.

What is largely beyond dispute then, no matter which serious scholar is taken into consideration, is the enormous impact that the legal work of Jehovah's Witnesses had over the decades. However, most accounts, including those of repre-

---

[18] For a critical review of both the public image and the self-image of mid-century Jehovah's Witnesses and their legal battles in the United States, see *Zoe Knox*, Jehovah's Witnesses as Un-Americans? Scriptural Injunctions, Civil Liberties, and Patriotism, in: Journal of American Studies, 47, 2013, 1081–1108.

[19] Jehovah's Witnesses: Proclaimers of God's Kingdom, ed. Watch Tower Bible and Tract Society of Pennsylvania, New York 1993, 683, 698. See also, e.g., *Victor Blackwell*, O'er the Ramparts They Watched, Aurora 1976; *A. H. Macmillan*, Faith on the March, Englewood Cliffs 1957; *W. Glen How*, "The Battle Is Not Yours, but God's", in: Awake, 22 April 2000, 18–24, https://wol.jw.org/en/wol/d/r1/lp-e/102000287 (18 March 2020). Glen How's law office is still operating for Jehovah's Witnesses around the globe, https://wghow.ca (18 March 2020).

[20] Jehovah's Witnesses: Proclaimers of God's Kingdom (note 19), 698–699.

[21] Ibid., 699; *Kaplan*, State and Salvation (note 17), xii.

[22] Jehovah's Witnesses: Proclaimers of God's Kingdom (note 19), 699; the quotation inside the quotation is from *Kaplan*, State and Salvation (note 17), 270.

sentatives of Jehovah's Witnesses, tend to give what I would call a functionalist reading of this impact on legal systems and the evolution of fundamental rights understandings: By deploying all the legal instruments at their disposal and in not giving up, neither in their legal nor in their religious activities, and by defending their beliefs and their way of life, Jehovah's Witnesses spear-headed a legal revolution they never had intended to start in the first place. Their "Strenghtening the Guarantees of Freedom" for all or their "Shaping of Constitutional Law" for every citizen would then be more or less the unintended consequence of the legal self-defense of their own community and religious practices.

One of the few scholarly voices that would ascribe more than a functionalist agency to Jehovah's Witnesses, and rather speak of intentional efforts to shape and expand international law and fundamental rights regimes is probably James Richardson, whose analysis of ECHR cases depicts this religious community, their lawyers and legal corporations as human rights activists having established a working partnership with the court. In a process of division of labor religious freedom-related cases are prepared that have the potential for strengthening or expanding fundamental rights in general – in particular, but not only with a view to, Central Eastern and Eastern European states. Sometimes additional human rights NGOs are involved in these cases. This means Jehovah's Witnesses' legal activism in these cases gives a voice to all victims of human rights abuses and fights for fundamental freedoms in general. In the way these cases are structured from the very beginning, not only their own community is in view, but the fundamental rights of every human being.[23]

4. The political ethics of a non-political community

If it is beyond dispute that Jehovah's Witnesses had a significant impact on the 20th and 21st century human rights (r)evolution, it remains a riddle why the discussion on their resistance against the National Socialist regime in Germany and Nazi-occupied Europe is sometimes still stuck in obsolete views denying the stand Jehovah's Witnesses, as individuals or as a group, have made for human rights. Even the otherwise unsurpassed historical account by Detlef Garbe, notwithstanding many later editions originating from a 1989 dissertation, engages in a critical discussion on the "exemplary" character of the Jehovah's Witnesses' resistance that today reads more like an affirmation of 1980s political certainties than like an adequate appreciation of Jehovah's Witnesses in the Nazi era. After words of recognition for the persecuted and resisting Jehovah's Witnesses, Garbe states that Jehovah's Witnesses

---

[23] *Richardson*, Update on Jehovah's Witnesses (note 16); *idem*, The European Court of Human Rights (note 16), 21–24.

fought for their (own) freedom of religion and community organizing, but not for the freedom (of all) in a more general and political sense. Their resistance to dictatorship was not motivated by a democratic attitude. Insofar their courageous stand in the "Third Reich" deserves respect and recognition, but they do not qualify as role models (*Leitbild*) in a democratic society. This, however, holds true for many victims of Nazi persecution and even for many political resistance fighters [...] They [Jehovah's Witnesses] cannot claim an exemplary function (*Vorbildfunktion*) in a pedagogical sense.[24]

From today's historical perspective, there are three things wrong with this statement: First of all, even the politics of the "good examples" Garbe goes on to mention do not at all match democratic ideals of the postwar consensus in western democracies, as further research on crucial members of the resistance such as Dietrich Bonhoeffer or Claus Graf Stauffenberg has shown.[25] So what degree of democratic consciousness has to be reached before a person resisting the Nazi regime can be classified as a "role model"? And to what kind or school of democratic ideas did they have to be committed? There is no ideal 1980s democracy outside time and forever uncontested.

Secondly, this clearly shows that the whole set of underlying assumptions bears witness to the claim of a 1980s West German historiography which, in a "whiggish" way, thought itself to be in a superior position from which to heap political judgment on historical actors even in extreme historical situations. But there are good reasons that this is not the task of history, but an anachronism, an error of category.[26] We can today appreciate the enormous courage and humanity of the resistance against the Nazi regime without measuring it against the assumedly fixed, but in fact constantly changing, democratic ideas and practices of an age in which no one ever had to muster the same courage.[27] And this is not only a historical issue, but also a question of political theory. The time since the 1980s has shown that even today democracy can be manipulated for authoritarian and totalitarian purposes, and that there are competing and contradictory visions of democracy. Democracy can be a mere slogan that does not guarantee humane and human rights-oriented behavior. Democracies need both shared procedures

---

[24] *Garbe*, Widerstand und Martyrium (note 8), 554. All translations from the German, if not otherwise noted, are by the author. For a slightly different, somewhat mitigating translation of this quotation, see *Garbe*, Resistance and Martyrdom (note 7), 540–541.

[25] See, e. g., *Sabine Dramm*, V-Mann Gottes und der Abwehr: Dietrich Bonhoeffer und der Widerstand, Gütersloh 2005; *Peter Hoffmann*, Claus Schenk Graf von Stauffenberg und seine Brüder, Stuttgart 1992.

[26] See, e. g., *Tim B. Müller*, Von der "Whig Interpretation" zur Fragilität der Demokratie: Weimar als geschichtstheoretisches Problem, in: Geschichte und Gesellschaft 44, 2018, 430–465.

[27] See, e. g., *Dramm*, V-Mann Gottes (note 25); *Linda von Keyserlingk-Rehbein*, Nur eine "ganz kleine Clique"? Die NS-Ermittlungen über das Netzwerk vom 20. Juli 1944, Berlin 2019; *Ulrich Schlie*, Claus Schenk Graf von Stauffenberg: Biografie, Freiburg im Breisgau 2018; see also *Karl Heinz Bohrer*, Die Entlarvung des 20. Juli: Man darf Stauffenberg nicht als einen Helden unserer heutigen Zeit sehen, in: Süddeutsche Zeitung, 30 January 2009, https://www.sueddeutsche.de/kultur/debatte-um-stauffenberg-die-entlarvung-des-20-juli-1.483411 (18 March 2020).

and shared values to work properly according to western, human and civil rights-based standards.²⁸

Thirdly, these values may be cultivated and put into practice by the most unexpected quarters in society. In the situation of Nazi dictatorship, the defense of human rights and human dignity may have mattered even more than political maneuvering. Jehovah's Witnesses rendered silent but steadfast opposition to totalitarianism, extreme nationalism, racism, violence and war, while large parts of German society, including the churches and even a number of the later resisters, supported the war in the first place. While Jehovah's Witnesses had never intended to topple the Nazi system, this regime would have collapsed immediately if everyone in German society had believed and lived like them. German mainline churches, rather than acknowledging without hesitation and without any qualification the courageous and humane resistance of Jehovah's Witnesses, and rather than apologizing for their own involvement in the Nazi persecution of Jehovah's Witnesses,²⁹ still engage in belittling or denigrating this resistance as selfish, or a result of group-pressure, or not properly Christian. This is an almost unheard-of phenomenon in a Germany society that is proud of its coming to terms with the Nazi past: the successor institutions of those complicit in Nazi crimes against a certain group assume the right today to judge that very same group of victims of Nazi persecution, and as a hopefully unintended consequence, downplay Nazi crimes.³⁰ The situation is reminiscent of a 1950s Federal Republic, when German society was still perpetuating National Socialist propaganda against Nazi vic-

---

[28] For analysis of contemporary developments, see, e.g., *Francis Fukuyama*, Political Order and Political Decay: From the Industrial Revolution to the Globalization of Democracy, New York 2014; Ivan Krastev, Europadämmerung: Ein Essay, Berlin, 2017; *Joshua Kurlantzick*, Democracy in Retreat: The Revolt of the Middle Class and the Worldwide Decline of Representative Government, New Haven 2014; *Steven Levitsky and Daniel Ziblatt*, How Democracies Die, New York, 2018; *Yascha Mounk*, The People vs. Democracy: Why Our Freedom Is in Danger and How to Save It, Cambridge, MA 2018. For contradictions in the history of democracy, see, e.g., *Margaret Lavinia Anderson*, Practicing Democracy: Elections and Political Culture in Imperial Germany, Princeton 2000; Joris Gijsenbergh et al., eds., Creative Crises of Democracy, Brussels 2012; Joanna Innes and Mark Philp, eds., Re-imagining Democracy in the Age of Revolutions: France, America, Britain, Ireland 1750–1850, Oxford 2013; Jussi Kurunmäki et al., eds., Democracy in Modern Europe: A Conceptual History, New York 2018; idem and Johan Strang, eds., Rhetorics of Nordic Democracy, Helsinki, 2010; *Jan-Werner Müller*, Contesting Democracy: Political Ideas in Twentieth-Century Europe, New Haven 2011; Tim B. Müller and Adam Tooze, eds., Normalität und Fragilität: Demokratie nach dem Ersten Weltkrieg, Hamburg 2015.

[29] See, e.g., with further references, *Gerhard Besier*, Jehovas Zeugen in Deutschland, in: idem/Stokłosa, eds., Jehovas Zeugen in Europa – Geschichte und Gegenwart, vol. 3, Berlin 2018, 129–268, at 166–169; *Garbe*, Widerstand und Martyrium (note 8), 70–76, 83–84, 96–99, 118–119.

[30] *Besier*, Jehovas Zeugen in Deutschland (note 29), 231–233; *Patrick Bahners*, Zeugen Jehovas: Keine Beweiskraft, in: Frankfurter Allgemeine Zeitung, 29 March 2005, https://www.faz.net/aktuell/feuilleton/zeugen-jehovas-keine-beweiskraft-1211886.html (18 March 2020); for a recent example: Michael Utsch, ed., Jehovas Zeugen: Eine umstrittene Religionsgemeinschaft (EZW Texte 255), Berlin 2018; more on this issue below.

tims such as Sinti and Roma, but it is certainly not appropriate in the historically enlightened Federal Republic of today.[31] In fact, as we will see below, Jehovah's Witnesses were in the 1920s and 1930s more committed to pluralism and human rights than their mainline church-based opponents, whose heirs in today's churches continue to collaborate with authoritarian, if not totalitarian, regimes.[32]

The oft-repeated insinuation of group-pressure, totally inappropriate for the courageous course of such a diverse group of so many different individuals – young and old, male and female, with and without family, physically firm and handicapped, German and non-German – shows also historical ignorance vis-à-vis life in a totalitarian society. As we are reminded by an insightful contribution to the recent and impressive volume of the NS-Dokumentationszentrum München on the persecution of Jehovah's Witnesses between 1933 and 1945, the peaceful, non-violent resistance of Jehovah's Witnesses demanded every day a huge number of individual decisions in a coordinated totalitarian society: "The pressure they were subject to was caused by the Nazi regime and its supporters, not by the own religious community. The many individual decisions taken as a result of the confrontation with the Nazi regime show individual differentiation and nuance. The individual spiritual and moral condition was the decisive factor for how far individuals would go" as resisters. This resistance was clearly religiously motivated, but it included also opposition to war and racism as well as the fight for the equality of all humans.[33]

This is acknowledged by voices who can claim to speak for the few and isolated resisters in the Nazi-era churches – outsiders isolated from their official churches, churches supporting a war of extermination – such as Bonhoeffer's nephew Klaus von Dohnanyi, son of key organizer of the military-political resistance, Hans von Dohnanyi. He portrays a totally different picture of Jehovah's Witnesses in National Socialist Germany and even has argued that Jehovah's Witnesses displayed qualities without which democratic civilization would not work. The former leading German social-democratic politician, in a more ethical than political way, pointed to Jehovah's Witnesses as role models for a democratic society:

---

[31] See, e.g., *Karola Fings*, Schuldabwehr durch Schuldumkehr: Die Stigmatisierung der Sinti und Roma nach 1945, in: Oliver von Mengersen, ed., Sinti und Roma: Eine deutsche Minderheit zwischen Diskriminierung und Emanzipation, Bonn 2015, 145–164.

[32] See, e.g., the 2012 (13, no. 2) issue of Religion – Staat – Gesellschaft on "Freedom of Religion or Belief: Anti-Sect Movements and State Neutrality: A Case Study: FECRIS"; *Patricia Duval*, Anti-Sect Movements and State Neutrality: The Case of FECRIS, in: Religion – Staat – Gesellschaft 18, 2017, 133–146; or the contribution by *Wolfram Slupina* to this issue. On Putin's Russia as a novel form of totalitarian regime: *Masha Gessen*, The Future Is History: How Totalitarianism Reclaimed Russia, New York 2017.

[33] *Christoph Wilker*, Der religiös motivierte Widerstand der Zeugen Jehovas gegen das NS-Regime, in: Nerdinger/Wilker, eds., Verfolgung der Zeugen Jehovas (note 7), 32–39, at 37; similarly, for the Soviet Union, *Baran*, Dissent on the Margins (note 7), 41, 52–53, 68–69, 251.

> They were steadfast opponents of the Hitler regime because of their belief and the humaneness and brotherly love for their fellow humans resulting from their Christian belief. […] The substances on which a modern society can be made safely democratic and humanistic are tolerance, decency, reliability, moral courage. […] Only nations in which social dealings with each other are based on simple, direct, and humane foundations of decency […] are safe as democracies. […] The resistance of Jehovah's Witnesses against the Nazis reminds us of this simple truth. No antifascist party in the Weimar Republic – including my own Social Democratic party – can point to such a high percentage in their ranks of determined resistance as can the seemingly apolitical Jehovah's Witnesses. They showed us that faith and decency, humanistic values and committed humaneness have little to do with political party positions of the left or the right, but with the education and practice of religious and ethical values.[34]

In this view, notwithstanding their non-political perspective and Christian neutrality in political affairs that are recognized also by Dohnanyi, Jehovah's Witnesses are seen as political actors in an ethical sense. Their political agency, and Dohnanyi is not the only one to make this point, is understood as agency in a field beyond the political issues of the day, a realm which may be called political ethics; "political" in the fundamental sense of living together and interacting in a "city" (*polis*), a community or society for which every individual citizen assumes responsibility. This view, 30 years after the peaceful revolutions in many of the former Soviet-dominated nations in Europe, might resonate with the political ethics in the dissident underground which claimed for itself a "parallel polis" beyond the political systems of their present and a way of "living in truth" characterized by values and ethics that are not political in themselves but would fundamentally change the realm of politics if translated into reality.[35]

Not surprisingly, some politicians and intellectuals emerging from the dissident underground of the cold war, just as members of the "supra-political" resistance movements against Nazi Germany before them, have highlighted this particular political-ethical quality in the conduct and concepts of Jehovah's Witnesses. Their common experience seems to have been that ethics had become politics in totalitarian regimes. Some examples: Dutch law professor and conservative politician Isaac Arend Diepenhorst stated in an official survey of the Dutch state on the resistance

---

[34] *Klaus von Dohnanyi*, Vergessene Werte und unsere Zukunft, in: Hamburger Abendblatt, 7 April 1999, 14. See *Hans von Dohnanyi*, "Mir hat Gott keinen Panzer ums Herz gegeben": Briefe aus Militärgefängnis und Gestapo-Haft 1943–1945, ed. Winfried Meyer, München 2015; *Eliabeth Chowaniec*, Der "Fall Dohnanyi" 1943–1945: Widerstand, Militärjustiz, SS-Willkür, München 1991; *Marikje Smid*, Hans von Dohnanyi – Christine Bonhoeffer: Eine Ehe im Widerstand gegen Hitler, Gütersloh 2002.

[35] *Tim B. Müller*, Die Verfolgung der Zeugen Jehovas im Nationalsozialismus, in: H-Soz-Kult, 11 July 2019, https://www.hsozkult.de/publicationreview/id/reb-27190 (18 March 2020); *Baran*, Dissent on the Margins (note 7), 42: Jehovah's Witnesses lived "as though Soviet power did not exist for them". For a prominent example of such dissident thought, see *Václav Havel et al.*, The Power of the Powerless: Citizens against the State in Central-Eastern Europe, ed. John Keane, Armonk, NY 1985.

against Nazism in 1950 that Jehovah's Witnesses were part of the Dutch resistance and that the "religiously motivated willingness to make sacrifices" of these "religious, fanatically good-natured, non-revolutionary anarchists" had benefited the "fatherland", even if, as a follow-up 1954 assessment elaborated, their resistance was in the service the "kingdom of God, not the kingdom of the Netherlands".[36] Correspondingly, also individual Jehovah's Witnesses after the war expressed their sense, in spite of all differences, of being part of a larger resistance against National Socialism. Concentration camp survivor Karl Pützmann fought in 1950 against a German Democratic Republic decree to deprive him and all other Jehovah's Witnesses of their status as victims of the Nazi regime and wrote to state institutions:

> By trying to exert pressure on us, to force us to advocate a certain political position, to advocate politics in general, the freedom of conscience and other basic rights of free humans are abolished. Everyone who stood with us in Nazi times in the united front of resistance, who was incarcerated under the same conditions, knows that we were neutral towards political issues even back then. Back then we all, Bible Students, Communists, or others, were all opponents of the Nazi regime, and we were all acknowledged equally. Is it democratic now to deprive a human being, by disregarding the torment he suffered, of his right to be a [victim of fascism]? Is it not one of the virtues of democracy to respect the opinion of others, even if one does not agree with them?[37]

We may add some examples from the post-1989 world. A member of East German dissident circles and minister in the state of Brandenburg, Steffen Reiche, remarked in a 1998 speech that has been quoted by Jehovah's Witnesses themselves: "The conduct of Jehovah's Witnesses in the camps and prisons embodies virtues that are as essential today as they were in the past for the existence of a democratic constitutional state: namely, their steadfastness against the SS and their human sympathy toward their fellow prisoners. Given the increasing brutality against foreigners and against political or ideological dissenters, these virtues are a must for every citizen of our country."[38] Following this line of thought, Austrian law professor Reinhard Moos added with regard to World War II war resisters:

> The attitude of Jehovah's Witnesses went far beyond the pacifist prohibition of killing. [...] The tragic dilemma was that on the one hand Jehovah's Witnesses denied blind loyalty to the state because of their political neutrality, while on the other hand by this very political neutrality they became political opponents of the regime which claimed total submission. [...] The subjective neutrality of Jehovah's Witnesses resulted in objective political resistance.[39]

---

[36] *Tineke Piersma*, Ihrem Glauben treu: Die Verfolgung von Jehovas Zeugen in den Niederlanden während des Zweiten Weltkriegs, in: Besier/Stokłosa, eds., Jehovas Zeugen in Europa – Geschichte und Gegenwart, vol. 1, Berlin 2013, 433–511, at 500–502.

[37] *Bersch*, Aberkannt! (note 7), 221.

[38] Lila Winkel – die "vergessenen Opfer" des NS-Regimes: Die Geschichte eines bemerkenswerten Widerstandes, ed. Wachtturm Bibel- und Traktatgesellschaft, Deutscher Zweig, Selters 1999, 3.

[39] *Reinhard Moos*, Vorwort, in: Herrberger, ed., Denn es steht geschrieben (note 7), 5–9, at 8–9.

The clearly anti-totalitarian and to a certain degree even democratic political ethics of Jehovah's Witnesses are also emphasized by a legal advisor to the Central European Office of Jehovah's Witnesses, Armin Pikl. In a recent radio interview he explained that democracy means mostly living together in society, so democracy is also a way of life, a form of everyday living, and not only about politics and elections. Pikl referred to the famous dictum coined by German legal scholar and constitutional court judge Ernst-Wolfgang Böckenförde, who had at the start of his distinguished career debunked some of the legends of alleged Catholic resistance against the Nazi regime, that the liberal state is dependent on preconditions which it cannot guarantee by itself. Jehovah's Witnesses, in this understanding, contribute to the well-being of modern, liberal, constitutional states, to a polity defined by freedom and the rule of law, simply by living according to their beliefs.[40]

Thus, according to many testimonies and voices, the non-political religious way of life of Jehovah's Witnesses seems to correspond particularly well to societies and polities characterized by the rule of law, fundamental rights, and liberal ideas of democracy. Their way of life may even be thought of as a stabilizing force in rule of law-based democracies. The political ethics of Jehovah's Witnesses, which do not contradict their political neutrality, lead then, depending on historically changing political contexts, both to resistance against totalitarian politics and to a qualified consent with liberal states. Neutrality then is not tantamount to equidistance to any political order, but a reflected and consistent Christian position in changing historical constellations.[41]

5. The Bible Students' struggle for religious freedom in interwar Germany

The landmark court cases of Jehovah's Witnesses in the United States since the 1930s, in Canada in the 1940s and 1950s, or before the ECHR since 1993 have received much attention.[42] However, there is a modest and almost overlooked German prelude. The small group of Bible Students in Imperial Germany had hardly come into conflict with the state, until the number of conscientious objectors from the Bible Students' ranks decisively rose in World War I.[43] After the

---

[40] Neutralität in einer zerstrittenen Welt, Bayern 2 Positionen, 14 January 2018, ca. 08:20–11:15 min, https://jwconf.org/sendungen/mp3/20180114_Bayern2%20Positionen_Neutralität%20in%20einer%20zerstrittenen%20Welt.mp3 (18 March 2020).

[41] This includes resistance against racism and rescuing humans from genocide even at the price of their own life also in more recent periods such as in the 1994 Rwandan genocide, see, e. g., *Tharcisse Seminega*, No Greater Love: How My Family Survived the Genocide in Rwanda, Davenport, IA 2019.

[42] *Coté/Richardson*, Disciplined Litigation (note 17); *Richardson*, Update on Jehovah's Witnesses (note 16).

[43] *Marcus Herrberger*, Die deutschen Bibelforscher im Ersten Weltkrieg: Zwischen militärischem Ungehorsam und christlichem Gewissen, in: Religion – Staat – Gesellschaft 16, 2015, 33–74; see also *Besier*, Jehovas Zeugen in Deutschland (note 29), 134–146.

war, Germany became the second-largest center of the international Bible Students movement after the United States. The democratic Weimar Republic granted religious freedom, and the pluralist Weimar society was a field of intense Bible Student activity and increase. This development also brought the Bible Students' opponents to the scene, not only radical nationalists and National Socialists, but also conservative and church circles. The Protestant churches of Germany, which lost many of their state-church privileges in the German revolution of 1918 and rejected the new democracy, founded a new institution in 1921, the Apologetische Centrale, for monitoring and combating minority religions, which were derogatorily called "sects".[44]

The result of increased Bible Student activity and visibility on the one hand and rising opposition from nationalists and conservative church circles on the other hand was a growing number of lawsuits before German courts. These were mostly free-speech cases. Often instigated by church representatives or politicians close to the mainline churches, some municipalities and in the late Republic even the State of Bavaria tried to inhibit the Bible Students' missionary activities by categorizing them as illicit door-to-door peddling. Bible Students fought for their religious freedom, and the courts most of the time followed their arguments and found in favor of them: in 1926, in 421 of 460 court rulings. From 1927 to 1929, the German Bible Students participated in 4,523 lawsuits. The number of cases kept increasing with the instability of the democratic republic. In 1932, 2,335 Bible Students' court cases were pending.[45] But even in the existential crisis of democracy in Weimar Germany, higher courts such as the Administrative Court of the State of Baden on 15 June 1932 held in favor of the Bible Students and against the state government.[46] As mentioned, the situation in the State of Bavaria proved different, where the otherwise mutually hostile Nazi Party (NSDAP) and the conservative-Catholic government party BVP (*Bayerische Volkspartei*) joined forces in 1931 in order to prohibit the Bible Students' activities in the public realm – a Bavarian forerunner of things to come in all of Germany in 1933.[47]

The large number of court cases and the severe state measures in Bavaria, however, are just one part of the story. In spite of lobbying by anti-Bible Student, church-related forces, the German government upheld the religious freedom guaranteed by the Weimar constitution. This included the government led by the last

---

[44] *Besier*, Jehovas Zeugen in Deutschland (note 29), 146–167; *Garbe*, Widerstand und Martyrium (note 8), 58–85.

[45] *Bersch*, Aberkannt! (note 7), 25–26; *Besier*, Jehovas Zeugen in Deutschland (note 29), 166–167; *Garbe*, Widerstand und Martyrium (note 8), 78–79.

[46] *Garbe*, Widerstand und Martyrium (note 8), 84. The decision is also archived by Jehovas Zeugen in Deutschland Archives (JZDA), Selters, Dok. 1932/06/15–01/02. I would like to thank Debora Adler and Rebekka Schmidt from JZDA for providing me access to these records.

[47] *Garbe*, Widerstand und Martyrium (note 8), 82–84; *Besier*, Jehovas Zeugen in Deutschland (note 29), 167.

democratic chancellor of the republic, Heinrich Brüning of the Catholic Center Party.[48] Public authorities of the Weimar Republic came out in support of religious freedom, such as the police commissioner (*Polizeipräsident*) of the city of Magdeburg in the Prussian province of Saxony, where the national office of the German section of the International Bible Students was located, as well as other officials in the State of Prussia which was governed by a social-democratic prime minister. Against attempts to lump the Bible Students together with communist activities, Magdeburg police commissioner Menzel confirmed in 1928 that the *Internationale Bibelforscher-Vereinigung* (IBV) was an "entirely religious community which is concerned with religious matters only. In particular, political tendencies and activities are far from their minds". So did his successor in 1932, as did the police commissioner and the criminal investigation department of the city of Berlin in 1929. In 1930 the Prussian minister of the interior sent an enactment to all police offices in the state. He admonished that the police should not take any action against the Bible Students, as this was a legally registered, entirely religious association. Their missionary work and distribution of religious book was fully legal and not economically motivated, and court cases had "always ended with acquittal".[49] Also in 1930 the Prussian minister of education and culture intervened on behalf of the German International Bible Students Association in 1930 in Hungary, where the Bible Students were facing state repression.[50] And even in Bavaria, the seizure of publications of Jehovah's Witnesses was stopped by the police in October 1932.[51]

The Bible Students seem to have devised a rudimentary legal strategy of their own to counter the rising number of lawsuits pressed by their opponents. A legal office (*Rechtsbüro*) was established in the German headquarters in Magdeburg in 1926.[52] As records from the archives of Jehovah's Witnesses in Germany demonstrate, not only did the legal office, headed by Hans Dollinger, intervene with public authorities, but also individual Bible Students were helped to file their complaints and defend themselves in court. Similar wording was used, which indicates a coordinated legal strategy, perhaps a first step towards "disciplined litigation".[53]

---

[48] *Garbe*, Widerstand und Martyrium (note 8), 84; *Besier*, Jehovas Zeugen in Deutschland (note 29), 167.

[49] Beglaubigte Abschrift, 28 April 1928, JZDA, Dok. 28/04/28; Bescheinigung, 19 March 1929, JZDA, Dok. 19/03/29; excerpt, Ministerial-Blatt für die preußische Innere Verwaltung, Runderlass des Ministers des Innern, 30 April 1930, JZDA, Dok. 30/04/30; *Bersch*, Aberkannt! (note 7), 26; *Garbe*, Widerstand und Martyrium (note 8), 79.

[50] *Annegret Dirksen*, Religionsfreiheit in Ungarn: Verfassungspolitik und -wirklichkeit am Beispiel kleiner Religionsgemeinschaften in Ungarn 1845–1945 unter besonderer Berücksichtigung der Horthy-Zeit, Berlin 2016, 263–264.

[51] Polizeidirektion, Beck, to Bayerische Bezirksämter, 14 October 1932, JZDA, Dok. 1932/10/14.

[52] *Garbe*, Widerstand und Martyrium (note 8), 79.

[53] See, e.g., JZDA, Dok. 1932/01/19–01; 1932/02/06–01; 1932/02/16–03; 1932/02/19–02; 1932/04/19; 1932/04/20; 1932/08/16–01; on the later legal strategy, *Coté/Richardson*, Disciplined Litigation (note 17).

The Bible Students received support in their legal work from the prominent Jewish lawyer Jacques Abraham, a Berlin defense lawyer, leading expert on administrative and civil service law and a member of the left-liberal German Democratic Party (*Deutsche Demokratische Partei, DDP*). Abraham and his wife became later victims of the Holocaust. They were deported and killed in Riga in 1942.[54] In Switzerland, among the impressive group of legal counsels to the Central European Office of Jehovah's Witnesses in Berne in the interwar years, some of them social-democratic politicians, was Georges Brunschvig, not only a distinguished lawyer involved in the trial about the "Protocols of the Elders of Zion", but future President of the Jewish Community of Switzerland. Brunschvig offered words of praise for his clients, for "they offered absolute, categorical resistance" against National Socialist totalitarianism.[55]

There was also in-house legal counsel in the German office. The seemingly ubiquitous and energetic Hans Dollinger, who fought in the early years of Nazi dictatorship against the expropriation of German Bible Students Association and American Watch Tower Society property (whether or not he had a professional legal background), later distanced himself from the religious community.[56] But the judge and lawyer Alfred Mütze, born in 1869, defended his fellow believers in court after 1933 and was also active as an underground organizer of the community. Mütze, a legal advisor to the Magdeburg office of Jehovah's Witnesses, operated together with his brother, fellow believer and fellow lawyer Camille Mütze from his Dresden law office. Alfred Mütze served briefly as a member of the board of directors of a short-lived North German Bible Students Association in 1933. He was the responsible "elder" for the Dresden congregation of Jehovah's Witnesses, one of the largest anywhere. Jehovah's Witnesses subject to accusation and persecution kept seeking his advice and help. A Bible Student since 1917 and a judge in the State of Saxony until 1931, the now-aged Mütze was arrested several times by the Gestapo, not only for defending fellow Jehovah's Witnesses in court, but also for organizing illegal meetings and underground missionary activity, as well as for not participating in Nazi elections and other political activities. He had also

---

[54] Jacques Abraham to Prussian Minister of science, culture and education, 21 October 1929, JZDA, Dok. 1929/10/29; *Dirksen*, Religionsfreiheit in Ungarn (note 50), 263. On Abraham, *Hellmuth Günther*, Dr. Jacques Abraham, Beamtenrechtler der Weimarer Republik: Lebensbild, Gedenkblatt, in: Zeitschrift für Beamtenrecht 53, 2005, 221–244.

[55] *Esther Martinet*, Jehovas Zeugen in der Schweiz und im Fürstentum Liechtenstein, in: Besier/Stokłosa, eds., Jehovas Zeugen in Europa, vol. 3 (note 29), 571–702, at 631, 633–634 (quotation), 682; *Max Wörnhard*, Rechtskämpfe und rechtliche Stellung der Zeugen Jehovas in einer Demokratie wie der Schweiz, in: Katarzyna Stokłosa und Andrea Strübind, eds., Glaube – Freiheit – Diktatur in Europa und den USA, Göttingen 2007, 501–515; on Brunschvig, without reference to his role as legal counsel to Jehovah's Witnesses, *Hannah Einhaus*, Für Recht und Würde: Georges Brunschvig: Jüdischer Demokrat, Berner Anwalt, Schweizer Patriot (1908–1973), Zürich 2016.

[56] *Garbe*, Widerstand und Martyrium (note 8), 92–96, 109–112, 131–135; *Besier*, Jehovas Zeugen in Deutschland (note 29), 215.

reproduced prohibited Bible Student leaflets in his office. Between 1933 and 1936, he served at least 14 months in prison. Arrested again in 1938, the court attested that Mütze "adhered with incomprehensible stubbornness to the ideas of the IBV". As with many Jehovah's Witnesses cases, his acquittal due to health reasons led to immediate arrest by the Gestapo under the guise of "preventive detention", which usually meant by this time incarceration in a concentration camp. This is the last trace of Mütze; it is most likely that, frail and almost 70 years of age, he died in Nazi imprisonment. His wife Johanna, born 1878, seems to have survived; she appears in a 1946 list of group organizers of Jehovah's Witnesses in the Soviet Occupation Zone, where she directed a group of the religious community in the city of Brandis close to Leipzig.[57]

6. Crusade against Christianity and the anti-totalitarian fight for human rights

A key quotation from *Crusade Against Christianity: The Modern-Day Persecution of Christians: A Collection of Documents*, published in Switzerland in 1938, gets to the heart of the argument for religious freedom advanced in this book:

> These reports are an ear-piercing alarm call. Not merely to come to the aid of those who fight for the Christian freedom of thought and conscience and who are threatened in Germany by extermination through murder, torture, ostracism and psychological torment of any kind. To their rescue will come the One whom they are standing up for: Jehovah God. Rather, this alarm call is sounded to the remainders of the world that are not yet enchained but surrounded everywhere by dictatorship: Your human rights, your fundamental freedoms are in danger! What you think you achieved in centuries of cultural development can collapse over night.[58]

How do we deal with this claim? Is it simply instrumental, in order to raise attention to the case and persecution of Jehovah's Witnesses? Or is there more behind it – a deliberate, intentional fight for human rights and fundamental freedoms,

---

[57] *Jens-Uwe Lahrtz*, Nationalsozialistische Sondergerichtsbarkeit in Sachsen: Das Beispiel der Verfolgung der Zeugen Jehovas in den Jahren von 1933 bis 1940, Frankfurt 2003, 150–152 (quotation); *Garbe*, Widerstand und Martyrium (note 8), 88–89; JZDA, Alfred Mütze file; Verzeichnis der Ortsgruppen in der SBZ, Dok. 1946/04/01. I thank Falk Bersch for bringing this document to my attention. The present author engages in a research project on Alfred Mütze and his legal activities.

[58] *Franz Zürcher*, Kreuzzug gegen das Christentum: Moderne Christenverfolgung: Eine Dokumentensammlung, Zürich 1938, 194. The original German reads: "Diese Berichte sind ein gellender Alarmruf. Nicht allein, um jenen Kämpfern für christliche Geistesfreiheit zu Hilfe zu eilen, die dort in Deutschland durch Mord, Folterung, Boykott und seelische Martern aller Art mit Ausrottung bedroht werden. Ihnen wird der helfen, für den sie einstehen: Jehova Gott. Vielmehr gilt dieser Alarmruf aller übrigen, von Diktaturfesseln noch nicht geknebelten, aber überall umsponnenen Welt: Eure Menschenrechte, Eure elementarsten Freiheiten sind in Gefahr! Was Ihr in Jahrhunderten kultureller Entwicklung errungen zu haben glaubt, über Nacht kann es zusammenbrechen!" – Further references to this book (abbreviated: *Kreuzzug*) are given in the main text in brackets.

even based on a distinctive understanding of modern dictatorship and the fragility of modern civilization?

The way to approach such issues is by historical contextualization. It is important to note that *Crusade Against Christianity* is not a one-off, and it is not a purely local event. As research on the production and the reception of the book by Detlef Garbe, Esther Martinet and Johannes Stephan Wrobel has shown, *Crusade Against Christianity* was compiled and written in Switzerland in the Central European Office (*Zentraleuropäisches Büro*) of Jehovah's Witnesses in Berne, but with full support from the world headquarters of Jehovah's Witnesses in the United States. The book itself is an important document of German literature in exile. It presented mainly press coverage and underground reports by persecuted German Jehovah's Witnesses, clandestinely smuggled out of the Nazi Reich. The collection of these reports is deeply impressive. Comparing it to a well-known and influential 1933 report on the Nazi persecution of the political left and communist anti-Nazi propaganda coup, the Gestapo called it the "Brown Book" of the International Bible Students Association ("Braunbuch der IBV"). It was published by Europa-Verlag, a house that published books by Thomas Mann and other leading literary figures exiled from Nazi Germany. Thomas Mann met with the head of the Central European Office, Martin Christian Harbeck, and supported the publication of the book. He even wrote a letter as an endorsement that was appeared in later editions and French and Polish translations of the book. Although published by Europa-Verlag, the book was printed in the Watchtower printery, and 11,000 of the 15,000 copies of the first edition were bought by the Central European Office of Jehovah's Witnesses in Berne. The book was again advertised and distributed by Jehovah's Witnesses after World War II. There were about 30,000 books printed altogether. *Crusade Against Christianity* received substantial contemporary attention in the Swiss, French and American media.[59]

Swiss press reports called *Crusade Against Christianity* in 1938 a "book of martyrs" and "one of the very best collections of material on the Third Reich," comparing it to the most famous examples of underground and concentration camp literature known at that time. One article even stated: "Had European statesmen and party leaders shown just a small fraction of the courage of Jehovah's Witnesses, the world would have been spared the appalling crimes of the demons of our age." However, the book was, like other publications of Jehovah's Witnesses, banned and confiscated in 1940 by Switzerland in fear of Nazi invasion and not without Nazi sympathizers of its own. Harbeck left Switzerland for the United

---

[59] *Garbe*, Widerstand und Martyrium (note 8), 35–36, 260; *Johannes Stephan Wrobel*, Eine "empörende Faktensammlung": Das Buch "Kreuzzug gegen das Christentum" 1938 als Zeitdokument der NS-Verfolgung von Zeugen Jehovas, http://www.jwhistory.net/text/wrobel-zuercher1938.htm (18 March 2020). I want to thank Johannes Stephan Wrobel for providing me a footnoted version of his important and indispensible article.

States. Only at the end of September 1944 were the books returned and all restrictions on Jehovah's Witnesses in Switzerland lifted again.[60]

Crusade Against Christianity attracted most attention and praise for its detailed documentation of Nazi crimes, including diagrams of concentration camps drawn by Jehovah's Witnesses camp inmates such as Arthur Winkler, one of the coordinators of the German and later the Dutch underground of the Christian community. Harbeck's deputy, the Swiss citizen Franz Zürcher was named as editor, but the German-American Harbeck was the main author. He used about 80 underground reports from Jehovah's Witnesses in Germany and Nazi-governed Danzig. These reports, collected by Erich Frost and other key organizers of Jehovah's Witnesses in Germany, were smuggled out of the Nazi realm by secret couriers risking their lives. In addition, official documents and news reports were used to document the brutal persecution. The Central European Office in Berne had become the hub of the transnational network of the Jehovah's Witnesses' legal and underground activity in many European countries after 1933. Not only were reports on persecution and underground information of any kind as well as printed religious material sent or smuggled in and out of Switzerland, the Swiss office also was a safe haven for refugees from other European countries, including Germany.[61] The Central European Office even published some of the farewell letters written by German conscientious objectors shortly before their execution. These letters were circulated in the German underground and had a great impact on the German Jehovah's Witnesses by giving them examples of martyrs to emulate, thereby strengthening their courage and perseverance. Some of these letters were smuggled into Switzerland.[62]

The book *Crusade Against Christianity* was addressed to the public, even the global public, but from many sources it is obvious that it had also a major impact on Jehovah's Witnesses themselves. It was smuggled out of Switzerland and soon read by believers inside Nazi Germany and Austria. For young believers in particular, reading *Crusade Against Christianity* was a formative or even transformative experience, as memoirs from Hermine Schmidt (living in Danzig) or Simone Arnold Liebster (in Alsace) reveal. By prompting a level of reflection that transcended adolescence, it strengthened their religious conviction and their determination to follow the course of Christian martyrs, if Nazi dictatorship forced them to do so.[63] Simone Arnold Liebster writes how closely her parents and fellow Jehovah's Wit-

---

[60] *Wrobel*, Eine "empörende Faktensammlung" (note 59); *Martinet*, Jehovas Zeugen in der Schweiz (note 55), 663–665, 674–677, 681–683.

[61] *Wrobel*, Eine "empörende Faktensammlung" (note 59); *Martinet*, Jehovas Zeugen in der Schweiz (note 55), 620–691.

[62] *Johannes Wrobel*, "Auf Wiedersehen!": Abschiedsbriefe von zum Tode verurteilten Zeugen Jehovas im NS-Regime, in: Herrberger, ed., Denn es steht geschrieben (note 7), 237–326, at 273–288.

[63] *Wrobel*, Eine "empörende Faktensammlung" (note 59); *Hermine Schmidt*, Die gerettete Freude: Eine junge Frau geht mutig ihren Weg in einer Zeit bitterer Verfolgung (1933–1945), Kopenhagen 2007, 89–91.

nesses in Alsace were reading the book already in 1938, and that she intended to re-read it when her father was deported to a concentration camp in late 1941, soon before her own ordeal of incarceration inside Nazi Germany began.[64]

7. Inside a book from inside Nazi Germany

Few historians or religious studies scholars have engaged in a close reading of the book itself. In one sympathetic analysis, the apologetic intention, the religious perspective on persecution in Nazi Germany, of the introductory chapters is emphasized: "The aim is not a objective, historical account".[65] So it seems to the present-day reader, even the theologically informed. But it is striking that contemporary readers, Thomas Mann being only the most prominent one, did not have the impression that the religious perspective overshadowed the historical account. Among them were journalists, politicians in exile, and clergymen. They compared the book to the best and most famous reports on Nazi Germany of the day, as we have just seen above. It was treated as a factual report, while no one complained about the religious perspective in the first part of the book. How can this be? The answer is the book itself.

A close reading of the book and additional sources will also offer further insight into the political-ethical concepts and conduct of Jehovah's Witnesses in the 1920s and 1930s. Contexts matter again: The fight for religious freedom and human rights was in this period much more couched in political terms rather in technical legal language. An important reason for this is that the technical legal language of human rights, the whole international legal framework with institutions and professional careers in the field, did not yet exist as it did in the Cold War or later periods, but was still in the process of emerging.[66] And in this process the political ethics of what it meant to be a Christian, the anti-totalitarian dimension of the Christian belief and way of life of Jehovah's Witnesses, was openly argued, without ignoring or compromising the doctrine and practice of Christian political neutrality, which was both in doctrine and practice well-developed at that time and never called into question.

This historical constellation is crucial. The confrontation over religious freedom and human rights took place in intellectual or discursive contexts different from later periods. Terminology was different: As a positive evaluation of "religion" was uncommon among Jehovah's Witnesses at that time (see, e. g., *Kreuzzug*, 16, 17–20, where "religion" is opposed to "Christianity"), they rather defended the freedom

---

[64] *Simone Arnold-Liebster*, Allein vor dem Löwen: Ein kleines Mädchen widersteht dem NS-Regime, Esch-sur-Alzette 2013, 98, 180, 379.

[65] *Gabriele Yonan*, Jehovas Zeugen: Opfer unter zwei deutschen Diktaturen, 1933–1945, 1949–1989, Berlin 1999, 30.

[66] See, e. g., *Samuel Moyn*, The Last Utopia: Human Rights in History, Cambridge, MA 2010.

of conscience and belief (e. g., *Kreuzzug*, 27, 66–67, 194, 213), thereby following contemporary intellectual and political parlance,[67] but occasionally the term "religious freedom" (*Religionsfreiheit*), which is deployed in this article as equivalent term, was used as well (*Kreuzzug*, 91). As Samuel Moyn and other scholars have shown, human rights language was in the 19th and early 20th centuries by and large a post-revolutionary language, the language of the left and liberals, the language of democracy (and occasionally the language of communist imitations of democracy). Human rights, however, were also the medium by which Christian thinkers and politicians started to approach, and finally embrace, democracy. This proved particularly true for Catholic thinkers and politicians who created an early version of Christian democracy. They would speak repeatedly of human rights and human dignity in the 1920s and 1930s.[68]

To be sure: Jehovah's Witnesses were not part of this development. They never supported any political party nor any specific political order or political program. But their demand for religious freedom included an appreciation of human rights in general and even of democracy in a very broad, ethical sense, as *Crusade Against Christianity* and additional texts indicate in several aspects:

1. There was a contemporary discussion on human rights that traced the origins of human rights back not to the French Revolution, but to the fight for religious freedom by dissenting Christian groups in early modern Britain and most notably in colonial America. The leading proponent of this reading in Germany, Georg Jellinek, portrayed religious freedom and the freedom of conscience as the historically first and the most fundamental of all human rights, and his evidence included texts by Christian dissenters who used the divine name Jehovah.[69] Jellinek's argument included an appreciation of democracy: "the principle of religious freedom", which received "constitutional recognition" first in America, was "most intimately intertwined with the great religious-political movement from which American democracy originated".[70] While there is no evidence that Jehovah's Witnesses had read Jellinek or other contributions to this debate, which had

---

[67] The most important German text on fundamental and human rights of the age, published in new editions in 1919 and 1927, called religious freedom "Denk-, Glaubens-, Gewissensfreiheit" (freedom of thought, belief and conscience) and considered it to be the very first individual right to freedom; *Georg Jellinek*, Die Erklärung der Menschen- und Bürgerrechte, in: Roman Schnur, ed., Zur Geschichte der Erklärung der Menschenrechte, Darmstadt 1964, 1–77, at 57, see also 49–50; the term religious freedom is used as well, 42, 44, 50–51.

[68] See, e. g., *Samuel Moyn*, Christian Human Rights, Philadelphia 2015; *Hans Joas*, Die Sakralität der Person: Eine neue Genealogie der Menschenrechte, Berlin 2015; *Müller*, "Whig Interpretation" (note 26), 461–465.

[69] *Jellinek*, Erklärung (note 67), 45, 57. This and other key texts of that time are collected by Schnur, ed., Geschichte der Erklärung (note 67); see also Hans Carl Nipperdey, ed., Die Grundrechte und Grundpflichten der Reichsverfassung: Kommentar zum zweiten Teil der Reichsverfassung, 3 Bde., Berlin 1929–1930.

[70] *Jellinek*, Erklärung (note 67), 52.

started in the early 1900s and continued in the 1920s, it is obvious from *Crusade Against Christianity* and other texts of that time that religious freedom was considered to be the first and foremost of human rights, the foundation of the fundamental freedoms which were God-given.

2. In their literature, both in magazines and tracts running a circulation of millions even in German, Jehovah's Witnesses showed a cautious religious appropriation of the idea of democracy that was so much in vogue in those days.[71] For example, an article in the German November 1, 1929 edition of *The Watchtower* on postwar reconstruction stated: "The world war of 1914 to 1918 was fought to make the world safe for democracy. Democracy means the political, social, and legal equality of human beings. This is the ideal condition intended by God."[72] This article then goes on to explain that only God's Kingdom can create true and lasting democracy.[73] But it is obvious from this and other Bible Student writings that they saw a connection between a political order that guarantees religious freedom and respects the rule of law and democracy in a broad and nonpartisan sense.

3. *Crusade Against Christianity* adds more nuance to this understanding. It is a deeply Christian, apolitical, politically neutral book – but it is at the same time, as a result of Christian conduct and belief, a deeply anti-totalitarian book. Democracy becomes the umbrella term for non-totalitarian political order. In this 1938 book, the world is divided in a totalitarian camp, the camp of dictatorship and fascism, which is also called "the fascism assaulting all freedom" or "the European fascist conspiracy" (*Kreuzzug*, 42, 69), similar to what Hannah Arendt named it a few years later,[74] on the one side and the democratic camp on the other side (*Kreuzzug*, 25, 27, 39–71). The enemies of Jehovah's Witnesses were also labeled enemies of democracy (*Kreuzzug*, 58, 65). While communist crimes were not totally ignored, the book prominently criticized anti-Bolshevism as a fascist

---

[71] For Bible Students in interwar Germany and the circulation of their publications, see *Besier*, Jehovas Zeugen in Deutschland (note 29), 146–167; *Garbe*, Widerstand und Martyrium (note 8), 58–85. The Bible Student magazine "The Golden Age" (*Das goldene Zeitalter*) was advertised in 1926 as "philanthropic journal", a circulation of 270,000 for each issue was stated; Das Photo-Drama der Schöpfung: Wissenschaft, Geschichte, Philosophie, aufgebaut auf das Wort Gottes, 6th edition, ed. Internationale Vereinigung Ernster Bibelforscher, Magdeburg 1926.

[72] Wiederaufbau der Welt: Warum, wie und wann?, in: Der Wacht-Turm, 1 November 1929, 333–335; the German original reads: "Der Weltkrieg von 1914–1918 wurde gekämpft, um die Welt für die Demokratie zu sichern. Demokratie bedeutet politische, gesellschaftliche und gesetzliche Ebenbürtigkeit der Menschen. Das ist der ideale und von Gott beabsichtigte Zustand."

[73] That stable and good government can only be guaranteed by God was also the message of a book that discussed different systems of government, *Joseph F. Rutherford*, Regierung, ed. Internationale Bibelforscher-Vereinigung and Wachtturm Bibel- und Traktat-Gesellschaft, Magdeburg 1928.

[74] *Arendt*, Approaches to the "German Problem" (1945), in: *eadem*, Essays (note 2), 106–120; *eadem*, The Seeds of a Fascist International (1945), in: ibid., 140–150; *eadem*, Elemente und Ursprünge (note 2), 529–558.

strategy (*Kreuzzug*, 43, 53–54, 59) to excite the masses and attract the European bourgeoisie and receive the support of the Catholic Church.

4. The anti-totalitarian nature of the book becomes obvious by many brief but highly insightful observations on the nature of National Socialism. There are a number of observations that are more than faintly reminiscent of analyses and depictions of totalitarianism by contemporaries such as Hannah Arendt, Bruno Bettelheim, or George Orwell. Some aspects include how totalitarianism turned lies into truth, how it developed strategies such as the *Hitlergruß* to force people to demonstrate daily their political loyalty to the dictator, and thus aimed at the totalitarian deformation of their souls and the "control of conscience" (*Kreuzzug*, 88, 134).

5. Also the book analyzes the way the Nazi regime exploited the instruments of the *Rechtsstaat*, the rule of law, to create an *Unrechtsstaat*, a state of injustice and despotism, offering lucid comments that sound like Ernst Fraenkel's 1938 dissection of the Nazi *Dual State* in a nutshell. Bible quotations, in particular Psalm 94:20 about a "throne of iniquity […] which frameth mischief by a law" (*King James Bible*), were used to support this analysis. The Nazi state gave itself the appearance of law and order and legality, but it made injustice its basic rule and started to persecute religious dissenters by systematic terror (*Kreuzzug*, 28, 112, 115, 123). The 28 February 1933 decree "for the protection of the people and the state" is singled out as the key instrument to destroy the rule of law and constitutional rights in Germany (see, e.g., *Kreuzzug*, 75, 112). This corresponds to research starting with Fraenkel, who called this *Reichstagsbrandverordnung* the "constitutional charter of the Third Reich", and, as is not widely known, the outlawed Jehovah's Witnesses play an important role in Fraenkel's argument.[75] According to Karl Dietrich Bracher, the decree marked the replacement of the Weimar constitution by the permanent state of emergency and the framework for *Gleichschaltung* (co-ordination) and permanent terror.[76] Jehovah's Witnesses had lived experience as evidence, for the *Reichstagsbrandverordnung* was the framework for the prohibition and persecution, for the imprisonment and "preventive custody" of Jehovah's Witnesses ever since 1933.[77]

6. The recurring statements in *Crusade Against Christianity* on religious freedom, human rights, and fundamental freedoms clearly show a pluralist understanding of modern society. The book proposes a strong notion of minorities;

---

[75] *Ernst Fraenkel*, The Dual State: A Contribution to the Theory of Dictatorship, New York 1941, 3 (quotation), 17, 53–55, 117. Large parts of the book where finished by the time of Fraenkel's exile in 1938; *Ernst Fraenkel*, Der Doppelstaat, ed. Alexander von Brünneck, Hamburg 2001.

[76] *Karl Dietrich Bracher et al.*, Die nationalsozialistische Machtergreifung: Studien zur Errichtung des totalitären Herrschaftssystems in Deutschland 1933/34, Wiesbaden 1962, 87.

[77] *Garbe*, Widerstand und Martyrium (note 8), 90–93, 136–146, 150–152, 266. Only after the beginning of World War II did additional wartime decrees become as crucial for legally justifying the persecution as the 28 February 1933 decree had been before, see ibid., 346.

minorities are to be protected. The treatment of minorities is the key criterion that distinguishes the rule of law from dictatorship. Fascism is opposed to individual freedom and aims to destroy minorities, while the book defends the individual rights and freedom of every human being (*Kreuzzug*, 27, 42, 197). The idea of a racially homogenous *Volksgemeinschaft* finds no support by true Christians: racism and colonial violence by Europeans in Africa are condemned (*Kreuzzug*, 41, 106, 135, 213), and the book approvingly quotes the words of a Catholic anti-fascist from Spain that "fascism is the negation of everything Christian" (*Kreuzzug*, 48). This indicates that Jehovah's Witnesses embraced multi-cultural, multi-religious, pluralist society for religious reasons. The spread of "the fascist ideology", which justified violence and terror against minorities and dissenters, could result in a *Völkermorden*, a notion that means here a new total war and not yet genocide, as well as in "self-destruction" and in the assault on life as such (*Kreuzzug*, 71).

It is an irony of history that some of the fiercest critics of Jehovah's Witnesses today still reveal a deeply anti-pluralist and anti-minority understanding of society, even in German mainline churches, that is reminiscent of the homogenous *Volksgemeinschaft*, as a recent publication on Jehovah's Witnesses demonstrates. These critics bring forward arguments in the tradition of their anti-democratic, anti-pluralist predecessors of the 1920s and 1930s and seem to have avoided a proper "denazification" and "re-education" of their field. The understanding of democracy in these polemics is not liberal-pluralist, while Jehovah's Witnesses in the 1930s defended religious and cultural pluralism against Nazi attacks and ideas of national and racial homogeneity and superiority. Institutions and ideas perpetuating the spirit of the anti-pluralist forces of the 1920s and 1930s are obviously in need of unsparing historical reflection and relentless (self-)criticism.[78]

---

[78] A particularly revealing, recent example is the official Protestant church text by Utsch, ed., Jehovas Zeugen (note 30), a collection of essays that, in ignorance of the bulk of serious research, constructs the enemy stereotype of a Jehovah's Witnesses collective without room for individual differences. This dubious and unscientific procedure disregards the individual believer and his or her human dignity and singularity as a human being (37). "Conflict" is seen in an anti-pluralist perspective as the odium of the other, the "sect", while any pluralist thinker or politician would welcome conflict as a medium of democratic debate and integration. To ask the polemical and denigrating question whether Jehovah's Witnesses are the object of "total control", even if answered to the negative, to a degree at least, by some of the authors, is discriminatory, as the language insinuates a proximity to totalitarianism, to which the Bible Students/Jehovah's Witnesses were opposed like no mainline church. One of the authors even speaks of the "totalitarianism" of Jehovah's Witnesses (3–4, 15, 25). Group pressure (the possibility of authentic, individual faith does not even occur to the author) is implied as the main motivation of Jehovah's Witnesses (10), an insinuation which has time and again been disproved by history (see above, section V), of which the author is unaware. Personal fashion preferences of authors replace research, and historical evidence is disregarded (5–6). Just as the enemies of religious pluralism in the 1920s did, so are Jehovah's Witnesses again wrongly blamed to run economic enterprises (7). The victims of discrimination, including children, are treated as the true perpetrators, because they do not adapt far enough to the majority of society. Anti-pluralism, anti-minorities- and anti-fundamental rights-thinking is stated bluntly by way of an affirmation

7. While totalitarianism in *Crusade Against Christianity* is obviously doing the devil's will and work, democracies that guarantee human rights and religious freedom, while still part of the world alienated from God, are in a different category. The world at this historical moment is polarized in two camps, and one of them, in this very moment and in these very conditions, may unwittingly do the will of God by keeping up the rule of law and guaranteeing human rights. Fascism is the declared enemy of freedom, the enemy of the individual human being, the enemy of life (*Kreuzzug*, 42, 71). When the book speaks in commendatory ways of democracy, which it does several times, democracy is used in a supra-political, non-partisan sense: democracy is here the name for all those regimes that respect human dignity and religious freedom, for a political order that is not an open enemy of Christianity (e. g., *Kreuzzug*, 58, 65–66). This view had a tradition. As early as October 1929, years before Hitler came to power and prior to the first major electoral success of the Nazi Party in 1930, the Bible Students' journal *Das goldene Zeitalter* stated:

> National Socialism is one of those extreme phenomena of the German people's collective soul, overwrought by events, of which our age is so rich in. It is without doubt […] a movement which, wittingly or unwittingly, directly serves the enemy of mankind, the devil, and opposes Jehovah, the great creator of heaven and earth. […] National Socialism is a disease which will come to its end in due course. […] After its most extreme escalation, it will meet even more despicable demise.[79]

The widely circulated 1939 booklet *Fascism or Freedom* continued some years later that Hitler, "an unmerciful, cruel, fanatical man who totally despises the freedom of the people", was put into power "by the devil as the devil's deputy".[80] Coherent criticism of National Socialism and the Nazi regime and politics characterized the political-ethical position of the Bible Students and Jehovah's Witnesses in the

---

of "culturally grown and socially eminent celebrations" such as birthday or Christmas in which Jehovah's Witnesses do not participate (9). Not only is a minority blamed for intolerance in German society against minorities, this statement also reveals deep provincialism, Euro- and Germanocentrism. And so it goes on, page after page; space does not allow a discussion of all these insinuations and reproaches against a minority group who were victims of Nazi persecution. It is all about an enemy stereotype, not humans, not individual believers, not the resisters against racism and war. It is a shame that a major German institution has supported as late as 2018 such a defamation of victims of Nazism – an institution that was complicit both in sustaining Nazi dictatorship and in National Socialist crimes; see, e. g., *Robert P. Ericksen and Susannah Heschel*, eds., Betrayal: German Churches and the Holocaust, Minneapolis 1999; *Manfred Gailus*, ed., Täter und Komplizen in Theologie und Kirchen 1933–1945, Göttingen 2015; *idem and Clemens Vollnhals*, eds., "Für ein artgemäßes Christentum der Tat": Völkische Theologen im "Dritten Reich", Göttingen 2016.

[79] Hakenkreuz?, in: Das goldene Zeitalter, 15 October 1929, 316.

[80] *Joseph Franklin Rutherford*, Faschismus oder Freiheit, ed. Watch Tower Bible and Tract Society, Bern 1939, 11. It had a circulation of several millions, was translated in many languages and distributed in 14 countries; Nerdinger/Wilker, eds., Verfolgung der Zeugen Jehovas (note 7), 157. The original by *Rutherford*, Fascism or Freedom, ed. Watch Tower Bible and Tract Society of Pennsylvania, New York 1939, 11 reads: "The Devil has put his representative Hitler in control, a man who is of unsound mind, cruel, malicious and ruthless, and who acts in utter disregard of the liberties of the people."

1920s, 1930s and 1940s. Even inside Nazi Germany, defying the agents of totalitarian surveillance, they clandestinely organized large-scale public protest campaigns with the aim of informing the German people about the criminality of the National Socialist regime.[81]

8. The Christian defense of human rights extended explicitly to other minorities, even to the few persecuted or resisting members of the mainline churches. Jehovah's Witnesses were in fact fighting for what they considered the Jewish-Christian tradition. The persecution of Jews and the anti-Semitism of the Nazi regime were exposed and attacked: "Hitler mobilizes the pagan fire of hatred for Jews and Christians and orders to destroy thousands of Jews and Christians in the Third Reich". Anti-Semitism and the resentment against Jehovah's Witnesses are seen as related and similarly constructed ideologies, based on vicious propaganda that serves the purpose of glorifying violence and justifying terror (*Kreuzzug*, 59, 71). Research by Detlef Garbe has documented that from the very beginning, even before their rise to power, the National Socialists treated the Bible Students as part of an imagined Jewish "world conspiracy" or as a "Jewish-Bolshevist" movement. Many Bible Students' statements from the 1920s and 1930s acknowledged the Jewish roots and foundation of Christianity, defended the Old Testament of the Bible, and occasionally also ascribed to the Jewish people a special role in the present, in a way that was by some read as "pro-Zionist". Right-wingers, anti-Semites, and Nazis attacked the Bible Students' because of their perceived closeness to Jews.[82] In contrast to the Catholic and much more so the Protestant mainline churches, which opened up to advocates of radical anti-Semitism or in fact preached it, even a traditional, theological anti-Judaism was totally foreign to the doctrine of the Bible Students in the 1920s.[83] It is a matter of debate if Jehovah's Witnesses in the 1930s integrated some traditional anti-Judaist theological positions into their doctrine.[84] Still, they never followed the mainline churches' anti-Semitic theology of that time which even started to eliminate all Jewish traces from the Bible and from Christianity.[85] And there is an enormous body of evidence showing that in everyday life Jehovah's Witnesses, even in the face of persecution, were free from anti-Semitism, criticized the persecution of the Jews and anti-Semitism, and, both inside and outside the concentration camps, risked their livelihood, their freedom or their life to support and defend Jews and other victims of Nazi persecution, and their writings reported on the persecution of the Jews.[86] Public statements add to

---

[81] *Garbe*, Widerstand und Martyrium (note 8), 221–237, 245–266; *Nerdinger/Wilker*, eds., Verfolgung der Zeugen Jehovas (note 7), 120–161, with a large number of documents.

[82] Ibid., 63–69, 72–76, 272–277.

[83] Ibid., 66.

[84] Ibid., 103–106.

[85] See, e. g., *Ericksen/Heschel*, eds., Betrayal (note 78); *Gailus*, ed., Täter und Komplizen (note 78).

[86] A brief but succinct summary is given by *Christoph Wilker*, Und wieder war ich gerettet: Wie Alex Ebstein die Konzentrationslager Auschwitz, Sachsenhausen und Flossenbürg überlebte und zu einem erfüllten Leben fand, München 2019, 167–169.

the picture. The early 1929 exposure of National Socialism singled out two features that merited the absolute condemnation of the Nazis by the Bible Students: the neo-pagan, pseudo- or "fetishistic-religious" character of National Socialism and its anti-Semitism and "racial hatred". The Bible Students recognized that the Nazis raged at the name "Jehovah" because for them it was the "Judengott" (Jewish God) and the God of the Old Testament, and they analyzed the Nazi "scapegoating" of the Jews.[87] The 1939 booklet *Fascism or Freedom* condemned the persecution of the Jews in Germany: "In inhuman ways he [Hitler] persecutes the Jews, because they were once Jehovah's covenant people and bore the name of Jehovah, and because Christ Jesus was a Jew."[88] Even the few public articulations that seem to approach traditional anti-Judaist positions allow for ambiguity. A 1937 journal article attempted a theological explanation of the centuries-old hatred for the Jews. In traditional, church-like manner, it is spoken of a curse that haunts the erstwhile covenant people. But the article does not confine itself to abstract theological ruminations. In the same brief text, the historical actors of the persecution of the Jews are named and blamed, including the Christian churches that inflicted "enormous suffering" on the Jews through the ages. And in a pointed interpretation that may have anticipated later understandings of the Holocaust, the Bible Students explained that "the Jew-baiting of the Third Reich is in defiance of all civilization".[89]

The continuous reporting on the politics of exclusion and persecution in Nazi Germany made mention of many groups that were suffering as much from persecution as did Jehovah's Witnesses. A case in point and a historically important document is the 1938 article series by Arthur Winkler, a temporary underground leader of the German Jehovah's Witnesses and a concentration camp prisoner already in the 1930s. Jews, socialists, communists, freemasons, Jehovah's Witnesses, homosexuals and other groups of victims are named. The description of the horrible conditions in Esterwegen concentration camp includes a detailed report of the terror and torture of two leading social-democratic politicians, Reichstag deputy Julius Leber and Prussian parliamentary party leader Eduard Heilmann. Winkler mentioned that he maintained good relations with Leber. Winkler also identified the reason behind this unspeakable and systematic horror: "to instill fear and dread in the prisoners so that even the thought of opposition is stifled, and any thought of insurgency or any freedom of expression becomes unimaginable." Winkler declared that in the face of all dangers, he would "never be silent".[90]

---

[87] Hakenkreuz? (note 79).

[88] *Rutherford*, Faschismus oder Freiheit (note 80), 11. *Rutherford*, Fascism or Freedom (note 80), 11 reads: "He cruelly persecutes the Jews because they were once Jehovah's covenant people and bore the name of Jehovah, and because Christ Jesus was a Jew."

[89] Unter dreifachem Fluche, in: Das goldene Zeitalter, 1 February 1937, 4–5. I want to thank Christoph Wilker for pointing me to this article.

[90] *Artur Winkler*, Im Konzentrationslager Esterwegen, in: Trost, 1 March 1938, 12–13. This is very similar to how *Nikolaus Wachsmann*, KL: A History of the Nazi Concentration Camps, London 2015, characterizes the function of the early concentration camps.

The solidarity of Jehovah's Witnesses extended to members of the mainline churches that resisted the Nazi regime or suffered persecution.[91] In spite of their interpretative pattern of collaboration of mainline churches and the Nazi state, they expected that German dictatorship, now safely holding the reigns of government, might in the future also turn against to two major churches in Germany, Catholicism and Protestantism. This means they recognized, irrespective of a large number of anti-church statements, that the Nazi State was in the driver's seat and that the churches had only ancillary function in the new Germany (*Kreuzzug*, 70). When exposing the Nazi "crusade against the Bible and true Christianity", they added: "Christians (mostly Jehovah's Witnesses)". Thus, some believers from other Christian communities seem also to have qualified as true Christians (*Kreuzzug*, 59). Similarly, when surveying Christian martyrs in Nazi Germany, the book approvingly quotes a representative of the *Bekenntniskirche* (or *Bekennende Kirche*) (*Kreuzzug*, 169). While *Crusade Against Christianity* relentlessly criticized the Nazified, racist and anti-Semitic German Christians, which made up one of the largest and most powerful groups within the Protestant church (*Deutsche Evangelische Kirche*),[92] the book reported the "outcry of the hard-pressed, Bible-believing Confessing Christians in Germany" with genuine acknowledgement and sympathy. Jehovah's Witnesses shared many positions of the Confessing Church, such as that "Christians have the duty to resist, if something is required from them that is opposed to the gospel", or that the "Führer" Hitler should not be given worship "which is owed God only" (*Kreuzzug*, 28–29).

It is striking that Karl Barth was one of the two Protestant theologians whose statements in support of Jehovah's Witnesses were commissioned for and published in *Crusade Against Christianity*. Barth was Dietrich Bonhoeffer's most important theological teacher and friend, and while he may have had a blind spot with regard to East German socialism after the war, he was an astute and determined critic of Nazi totalitarianism. Barth, who is also approvingly quoted in the main text (*Kreuzzug*, 54), explained that Jehovah's Witnesses were especially interested in Biblical prophecy, and while their biblical proclamation touched on political issues, it was far from any political activity, in particular from communism, as right-wing and Nazi as well as church-based enemies of Jehovah's Witnesses, had often insinuated (*Kreuzzug*, plate after 32).[93] So there is, besides the appreciation by his nephew Klaus von Dohnanyi, a second link between Jehovah's Witnesses

---

[91] See also *Garbe*, Widerstand und Martyrium (note 8), 35–36, 120

[92] On mainline Protestant churches in Nazi Germany, see, e.g., *Klaus Scholder*, Die Kirchen und das Dritte Reich, 2 vol.s, Berlin 1977–1985; *Gerhard Besier*, Die Kirchen und das Dritte Reich, vol. 3, Berlin 2001; *Olaf Blaschke*, Die Kirchen und der Nationalsozialismus, Stuttgart 2014.

[93] The most recent biography is *Christiane Tietz*, Karl Barth: Ein Leben im Widerspruch, München 2018. The second theologian was Ernst Staehelin, who had written a critique of the Bible Students in the 1920s that stood out due to its fairness in comparison to the usual anti-Bible Students propaganda of that time; *Garbe*, Widerstand und Martyrium (note 8), 75, 120. Staehelin stated in *Kreuzzug* (plate after 32) that Jehovah's Witnesses had "much of truth" in their doctrine, were part

and Dietrich Bonhoeffer, who may also have encountered this visible community either in Germany or in New York. Correspondingly, some of the few Protestant church leaders who had been part of the resistance against the Nazi regime, such as Martin Niemöller and Hans Lilje, in the immediate post-war period expressed admiration for the religiously motivated conscientious objection and resistance of Jehovah's Witnesses.[94]

9. The view of a Catholic-fascist conspiracy which is repeated several times (*Kreuzzug*, 37–71, 169) seems to represent somewhat of a riddle in contrast to so much lucid analysis. Was the anti-Catholicism of Jehovah's Witnesses so strong that it overlooked the purely instrumental value the Nazis saw in the Catholic Church? Did religious animosity influence their political perceptiveness? To a degree, yes. But again the books gives room for nuance. It openly states that Nazism will ultimately also fight Catholicism when it is no longer useful and that the churches' support of National Socialism equals suicide in the long run. So Nazism is clearly the stronger force, it is politically autonomous, even if the churches facilitated the Nazi take-over of German society and the German State (*Kreuzzug*, 70–71).

However, in the end the concept of a Catholic-fascist conspiracy is not based on Nazi Germany, but on an analysis of much press coverage on Italian Fascism, the Spanish Civil War, and Catholic dictatorship. These parts of the book still provide a valuable depiction and theory of "Mediterranean" fascism (*Kreuzzug*, 37–51). The main thrust of *Crusade Against Christianity* is not at all dependent on the thesis of a Catholic-fascist conspiracy. Rather, it is arguing against the claim that the Catholic Church is opposed to fascism (*Kreuzzug*, 56). The taking of evidence is based mainly on church documents and on reports from international liberal mainstream media, but observers of rather leftist, antifascist, pacifist and anticlerical leanings are also given a hearing. The key piece of evidence, however, is Austria 1938 and the full support that the Austrian episcopate gave to Hitler and the Nazi *Anschluss*. Whatever ambiguities had existed before in Catholic positions towards Nazism now became obsolete (*Kreuzzug*, 56–58). The fight of Catholic laymen and clergymen in many countries, usually with connections to the political right, against Jehovah's Witnesses since the 1920s, documented also in *Crusade Against Christianity*, is the background which lent internal credence

---

of the "history of the Christian churches", were not political and wanted so serve the "message about the kingdom of God".

[94] *Martin Niemöller*, Ach Gott vom Himmel sieh darein: Sechs Predigten, München 1946, 28; *Hans Lilje*, Im finstern Tal, Nürnberg 1947, 59; see *Garbe*, Widerstand und Martyrium (note 8), 11–12, 390; *Marcus Herrberger*, Die Verfolgung der Kriegsdienstverweigerer verschiedener Glaubensrichtungen durch die NS-Justiz im Zweiten Weltkrieg, in: idem, ed., Denn es steht geschrieben (note 7), 19–59, at 20; *idem*, Zeugen Jehovas als Kriegsdienstverweigerer in der NS-Zeit, in: ibid., 61–236, at 63. Lilje remained an ambivalent figure in the Federal Republic. Niemöller, while not overcoming his nationalist and anti-Semitic habits, made the coming-to-terms with the Nazi past one of his commitments; *Benjamin Ziemann*, Martin Niemöller: Ein Leben in Opposition, München 2019.

to the conspiracy interpretation.[95] However, all of this is more of a sideshow in *Crusade Against Christianity*.

10. Finally, *Crusade Against Christianity* is by no means unique in this regard, but it is among the early examples of émigré texts that bear witness to the destruction of the German *Rechtsstaat* and *Kulturstaat* and modern civilization by National Socialism (*Kreuzzug*, 91, 115, 117, 149). Just as with the best minds of the age, the authors of *Crusade Against Christianity* had a keen sense for the fragility and vulnerability of modern democratic civilization. They recognized that religious freedom, human rights, and fundamental freedoms should not to be taken for granted: "What you think you achieved in centuries of cultural development can collapse over night." Modern democratic civilization is no one-way street; the dark forces of history, "barbarism", could be unleashed any time anywhere (*Kreuzzug*, 194).

Therefore, while those who in their lives fought for life, "for the Christian freedom of thought and conscience" were "threatened in Germany by extermination through murder, torture, ostracism and psychological torment of any kind", *Crusade Against Christianity* sounded an "alarm call [...] to the remainders of the world that are not yet enchained but surrounded everywhere by dictatorship: Your human rights, your fundamental freedoms are in danger!" (*Kreuzzug*, 194). *Crusade Against Christianity* was not only one of the most powerful exposés and condemnations of Nazi crimes and terror in the 1930s. It was also a powerful defense of religious freedom, minority rights and human rights, based on a Christian understanding of human dignity that coincided with the views of human rights and human dignity shared among contemporaneous antifascist and democratic voices. Against the restriction of religious freedom supported by mainline churches, Jehovah's Witnesses defended not just their own way of believing and living, but human and minority rights and human dignity. And they did so not only in word, but also in deed.

From today's perspective, political and social contexts have changed decisively. In the political and intellectual force fields of the 1920s and 1930s, Jehovah's Witnesses belonged to the avant-garde of modern human rights and religious freedom rhetoric and activism. In today's world of ubiquitous human rights talk, when even the once (in Germany) anti-pluralist and anti-democratic mainline churches have adopted the language of human rights, it is seldom remembered that this is a debate that was originally shaped by early human rights defenders such as Jehovah's Witnesses who exposed and opposed Nazi and fascist human rights violations and the support of dictatorship by mainline churches.

---

[95] For the German case, in particular the Nazi-Catholic collaboration in Bavaria, see above, section V.

Contexts have changed, and so have the arguments in these contexts. Jehovah's Witnesses are largely viewed as marginal today, even if their human rights record is acknowledged by experts and courts. Only in "distant" places such as Rwanda, where not too long ago a situation similar to that in Europe in the 1930s and 1940s emerged, does it happen that their fight for human dignity and human rights, their Christian commitment to antiracism, pluralism, compassion, decency, and humaneness, become visible again to the international community.[96]

Abstract

While the human rights record of Jehovah's Witnesses is acknowledged by experts and courts, it is hardly known that this Christian community belonged in the 1920s and 1930s to the avant-garde of modern human rights and religious freedom rhetoric and activism. From an intellectual history perspective, this article reconstructs arguments for religious freedom brought forward by Jehovah's Witnesses in Germany and interwar Europe, before and in particular after the Nazi rise to power. The article analyzes the political ethics of a non-political religious community and critically reviews the debate whether the resistance of Jehovah's Witnesses against totalitarian regimes can be considered a role model. The key piece of evidence is the 1938 book *Crusade Against Christianity,* one of the most powerful and widely acknowledged exposés and condemnations of Nazi crimes and terror in the 1930s. The book was also a defense of religious freedom, minority rights and human rights, based on a Christian understanding of human dignity.

---

[96] See the contribution by *Jolene Chu* in this issue.

The Practice and Consequences of Apolitical Christianity by the Rwandan Jehovah's Witness Community Before and During the Genocide

Jolene Chu

During Holy Week leading up to Easter Sunday, Christians worldwide commemorate Maundy Thursday. "Maundy," drawn from the Latin *mandatum novum,* or "new commandment," refers to Jesus' words at John 13:34, 35: "I am giving you a new commandment, that you love one another; just as I have loved you, you also love one another." In 1994, Maundy Thursday fell on the last day of March. Three days later, on Easter Sunday, April 3, Hutu and Tutsi Christians throughout Rwanda – about 90 % of the population – filled the churches, worshipping side by side. They spoke the same language, shared the same culture, and intermarried.[1] The following Wednesday evening, April 6, two missiles brought down the presidential plane as it neared Kigali Airport, killing Juvénal Habyarimana and Cyprien Ntaryamira, the presidents of Rwanda and Burundi.

With that trigger, the highly orchestrated slaughter began. In what was and is one of the most Christian nations in Africa, between 800,000 and one million people perished in a mere 100 days. The genocide targeted the entire Tutsi minority. Political opponents and alleged Tutsi sympathizers also faced violent death, as did those deemed insufficiently committed to the Hutu extremist cause. Among them were Hutu belonging to the apolitical community of Jehovah's Witnesses.

Génocidaires committed more than half the murders with farming tools and other simple implements (Verwimp 2001, 11). It was a gruesome reversal of the Biblical passage in Isaiah foretelling the time when the nations would turn their spears and swords into plows and pruning hooks, and would learn war no more (Isaiah 2:3, 4). In 1994, pruning hooks, hoes, axes, and machetes – wielded skillfully by a largely agrarian people – turned deadly. The methodical murders began in the capital of Kigali and quickly spread to neighboring provinces. Neighbors killed their neighbors. Teachers killed their students. Doctors and nurses killed their patients. Hutu men killed their Tutsi wives. Believers killed fellow believers.

---

[1] In addition to Hutu and Tutsi, the third ethnic group in Rwanda, the Twa, were "a clearly differentiated" minority that was marginalized by both Hutu and Tutsi (Des Forges 1999, "History – The Meaning of "Hutu," "Tutsi," and "Twa"). In 1994, Rwanda's population was composed of about 85 % Hutu, 14 % Tutsi, and 1 % Twa.

Professor of theology and Catholic priest Emannuel Katongole in his anguished reflection, *Mirror to the Church,* recounted the story of Adalbert, a Hutu Catholic who attended church in Kibungo, southeastern Rwanda. On April 10, the Saturday after the plane went down, he went to choir practice. "We sang hymns in good feeling with our Tutsi compatriots," he said, "our voices still blending in chorus." However, the next morning at Mass, there were no Tutsi. They had fled into the bush. Adalbert stated that this angered the Hutu church members. "We left the Lord and our prayers inside to rush home," he recalled. "We changed from our Sunday best into our workaday clothes, we grabbed clubs and machetes, we went straight off to killing" (Katongole and Wilson-Hartgrove 2009, 33).

There were many killing sites in Kibungo; but the most notorious was the Nyarubuye Catholic Church, where the mayor led soldiers and militia in the murder of some 20,000 civilians. During earlier periods of ethnic violence in Rwanda, churches had offered sanctuary to Tutsi refugees. This time houses of worship became death traps. In 1994, Tutsi and moderate Hutu sought sanctuary in vain within the walls of huge church complexes. According to the human rights group African Rights, more Rwandans died in churches than at any other killing site (African Rights 1995, 258, 856). In the opening days of the slaughter, Pope John Paul II decried the violence as "an out-and-out genocide [using a term few world leaders were then willing to speak], for which, unfortunately, even Catholics are responsible" (*L'Osservatore Romano,* May 18, 1994, 1). With genocide raging, the pope dispatched Cardinal Roger Etchegaray to Rwanda. He asked Church leaders: "Are you saying that the blood of tribalism is deeper than the waters of baptism?" (Katongole and Wilson-Hartgrove 2009, 19, 22).

Journalistic and political commentary too initially explained the massacres as yet one more episode of spontaneous combustion in a long history of tribal violence. Closer analysis, though, revealed the complex dimensions of a genocide bearing the unmistakable markers of 20th-century ethno-politics. Scholarly interpreters generally point to polarizing colonial policies or the fraught socio-political relations between Hutu and Tutsi as the main culprit. A smaller body of scholarship has examined the role of Christian churches, specifically religious institutions, as a third contributing factor to genocide. This paper continues that exploration by highlighting politicized religious institutional practices that played a role in overcoming cultural ties, social bonds, and moral resistance to mass violence. This profile will provide a contrast with the apolitical doctrine and practice of the minority Christian group Jehovah's Witnesses.

Scholars have reached a range of conclusions regarding the question of the guilt of institutional religion.[2] Catholic professor of theology J. J. Carney (2014)

---

[2] Except for direct quotations, uppercase "Church" refers to the Catholic Church, which was predominant in Rwanda; lowercase "church(es)" includes other denominations, such as Anglicans, Methodists, and Seventh-day Adventists.

cautions that "one should avoid either exonerating the [Catholic] church from all corporate responsibility or 'blaming the church' for the genocide'" (195). His study of Catholic politics during the colonial era is a nuanced story of Church administrators fixated on institutional survival. The admittedly successful formula they followed for decades drew church and state ever closer until, to many onlookers, no division existed. He concludes: "One of the Rwandan church's greatest sins has been the general failure of church leaders to maintain prophetic distance from state leaders" (203).

Political scientist Timothy Longman (2010), who was an onsite investigator with Human Rights Watch, maintains: "Church personnel, from the bishops to the leaders of small Christian communities, created an environment where good, practicing Christians could kill their neighbors without feeling that they were acting inconsistently with their faith" (191).

Professor Gerard Prunier (1995) from the *Centre national de la recherche scientifique* in Paris writes: "Although ... there were admirable acts of courage among ordinary Christians, the church hierarchies were at best useless and at worst accomplices in the genocide" (250).[3]

Columbia University professor of anthropology, political science, and African studies Mahmood Mamdani (2001) goes further: "But for the army and the Church, the two prime movers, the two organizing and leading forces, one located in the state and the other in society, there would have been no genocide" (223). Mamdani's social history contains one of the most scathing scholarly conclusions, namely: "The church was a direct participant in the genocide" (226).

Accounts of the genocide barely mention Jehovah's Witnesses in Rwanda, a tiny community of 2,500 in 1994. One of the few published sources, the Swiss weekly *Reformierte Nachrichten* (1998),[4] reported that Protestant clergy would soon go on trial for genocide, but that "only Jehovah's Witnesses are accused of nothing." The brief article noted that a 1,200-page study by the human rights group African Rights had proven the involvement of every Christian church in Rwanda except the Witnesses. Peace researcher Christian P. Scherrer (2002) also comments in passing: "All the churches active in Rwanda, with the exception of the Jehovah's Witnesses (of whom only a few survived), were involved at least 'passively' in the genocide" (113). Though no systematic study on this topic has been conducted to date, these assertions are consistent with the available anecdotal evidence based on in-depth interviews with genocide survivors. The reported refusal of Witnesses to engage in genocidal behavior also fits the well-documented fact pattern of the Witnesses' conduct during other periods of war and civil conflict, including

---

[3] Prunier (1995) writes of Hutu rescue of Tutsi in the Rwandan Muslim community (253). See Benda's (2012) thorough analysis of Christian and Muslim behavior during the genocide.

[4] *Reformierte Nachrichten* (Reformed Press) (1998): Harare: Völkermord Ungesühnt, in: Reformierte Nachrichten, December 8, 1998, 1–2. https://archive.li/Xxzmu (accessed: July 10, 2019).

the genocidal Nazi era.[5] As will be shown, prior to the genocide, Rwandan Witnesses had already established a position of apolitical nonviolence, a stance that was subject to stiff opposition from religious and political authorities. It will be argued that the individual, communal, and institutional responses of the Witness community to genocide tie directly to their apolitical ethic and pattern of religious practice in the pre-genocide period.[6]

To set the context, the following is a condensed review of the evolution of the church-state relationship in the colonial and early post-colonial period, and the role of church authorities in the construction of the ethno-political divisions between Hutu and Tutsi.

Ethnic Categories in the Early Colonial Period

According to an ancient myth, Rwanda's three ethnic groups – Hutu, Tutsi, and Twa – are linked to a common ancestor, Kanyarwanda, the son of the god Imana (Benda 2012, 171). Scholars have put forth various theories about the origins of the Rwandan population, whether by gradual migrations or conquests; but most sources agree that the terms Hutu and Tutsi did not refer to strictly biological or tribal divisions but rather to fluid socio-economic categories based partly on occupation (43).

In times past, the magnificent long-horned Inyambo cows were a symbol of wealth. The Human Rights Watch report "Leave None to Tell the Story" (1999) states that the label "Tutsi" initially referred to one who was rich in cows; whereas Hutu meant a subordinate or follower of the superior, referring to the mass of ordinary people who mostly worked the land. Yet, the categories were mutable and porous, and people could change their designation depending on their economic fortunes. Intermarriage at times blurred the boundaries. However, people usually married within their occupational group, which tended to concentrate certain characteristics in the gene pool. This may in part explain the physical features that came to be associated with each ethnic category (31–34). Rwandan society was stratified by a client-patron hierarchy that some historians have called feudal

---

[5] To name a few examples spanning time and space, Witnesses maintained political neutrality under the military junta in Greece; during the Nigerian-Biafran war; amidst the Troubles in Northern Ireland; during the Nicaraguan Revolution; in apartheid South Africa; and for more than 60 years in South Korea, where mandatory military service existed until 2018. Historian Detlef Garbe (2008) has written the definitive work on Jehovah's Witnesses during the Nazi era, in which he asserts that "no other religious denomination opposed the coercion of the National Socialists with comparable determination." He shows that the number of death sentences for Witness conscientious objectors was the highest for any Nazi victim group, political or religious (4, 349–393).

[6] These overlapping distinctions are suggested so as not to conflate the responses of those who acted as individuals adhering to their religious convictions, as a composite social group bound by common religious beliefs and identity, and as the institutional leadership of said religious community.

or caste-like; but the fact remains that for centuries, no incident of intergroup mass violence occurred.

Germany received control of the territory of Ruanda-Urundi during the 1885 Conference of Berlin. They found what Rwandan scholar Richard Benda calls "a united and centralised state, hierarchal in its organisation with heterogeneous populations living in what could be qualified as total harmony" (Benda 2012, 42). At the top of the hierarchy sat the Tutsi monarch Yuhi V Musinga. German colonial authorities, with little interest in maintaining an extensive presence, pursued a divide-and-rule approach, administrating indirectly by cultivating close ties with the Tutsi monarchy. German troops helped Musinga further consolidate his power (Longman 2010, 33).

The Catholic Missionaries of Africa, or White Fathers, founded by Cardinal Charles Lavigerie, were active in Rwanda beginning in the early 1900's (Benda 2012, 54). Ian Linden (1977), scholar of religion in Africa, situates the White Fathers' efforts to create Christian states in Africa in the context of a 19th-century revival of Thomistic philosophy within the Church. Having suffered losses to liberalism in Europe, missionary leaders turned toward Africa with a certain nostalgia for the Christian kingdoms of Constantine and Charlemagne. Linden argues that it was only natural for White Fathers to pursue the strategy of their founder, who had always believed – as the conversion of Constantine had proven – that missions should first focus on the aristocracy (30). Lavigerie asserted: "Once the elites are won to the gospel, their subjects will follow suit" (Longman 2010, 39).

The Tutsi king, however, reacted to the White Fathers' initial overtures with suspicion, literally keeping them at arm's length, for instance, by refusing their request to build a mission near the royal capital at Nyanza. Ironically, Catholic missionaries on the ground found greater response among the peasant population, which hoped that the missionaries offered them a route to an improved social and economic life. Local missionaries found themselves drawn into disputes between peasants and local chiefs, prompting the White Father leadership to actively rein in the field missionaries' sympathies for the peasantry, lest they incur the displeasure of the Tutsi elite and jeopardize their top-down strategy. Missionaries received orders that in local disputes they should always side with the chiefs, right or wrong, a policy that Benda calls "compromising and pragmatic ecclesiology." A White Father diarist wrote: "We want only to raise and affirm the authority of the king. … we want to be always his friends." Vicar Apostolic Jean-Joseph Hirth, considered the founder of the Church in Rwanda, admonished: "Render unto Caesar and Musinga all that can be returned to Caesar and Musinga." The king, in turn, recognized a strategic opportunity and granted permission for missions to be built in areas of contested authority (Benda 2012, 68; Longman 2010, 30–47).

Catholic missionaries were not alone in this "race to the top." Along with the small contingent of German colonial soldiers came Lutheran missionaries, who were introduced by the German colonial residents in 1907. They too made active attempts to win over the Tutsi royal court, providing a counterweight to Catholic influence (Benda 2012, 67–68; Carney 2014, 27–28; Court 2016, 59–60).[7]

After World War I, Catholic Belgium assumed control of Rwanda and continued the strategy of indirect rule. What might have been a ripe field for Lutheran missionizing now became a firmly Catholic field for evangelization (Carney 2014, 16–43). The policy of top-down conversion continued and accelerated under the leadership of Vicar Apostolic Léon Classe, who arrived in 1922. The Tutsi court eventually saw the advantages of rapprochement with the colonial authorities (Benda 2012, 58).

The dominance of the Catholic missions became in some ways self-perpetuating in that many ordinary Rwandans took to Christianity in hopes of bettering their lives and naturally gravitated toward the church that offered the most opportunities and advantages. Lower chiefs as well saw little to gain and much to lose by choosing Protestantism over Catholicism (Benda 2012, 67–68).

Belgian colonial authorities ceded to the churches the important responsibility of education and social services. Catholic control of education gave Church authorities unequalled opportunities to influence the elite, especially the next generation. According to Benda, Catholic education downplayed individual rights and morality, focusing more on baptism to bring the masses into the fold. Protestant missionaries accused the Catholics of being a "religion of the state" (Benda 2012, 69). Protestant and Catholic leaders alike stressed obedience to authority as a Christian value (Gatwa 2005, 77). The White Fathers' efforts began to meet with success in the late 1920's as more and more nobles embraced Catholicism. Increased conversions of nobles and grooming of noble children for leadership meant that the Church could more actively press colonial authorities to elevate Catholic-schooled Tutsi who were baptized and loyal to the Church (Longman 2010, 50–53, 141–143). The Church urged colonial authorities to replace Hutu chiefs with Tutsi, which did take place in the 1920's (Human Rights Watch 1999, Longman 2010, 52).

Despite growing conversion among Tutsi elites in the late 1920's, Musinga remained resistant to Catholic overtures. He signaled openness to newly arrived Adventist and Anglican missionaries, solidifying the White Fathers' view of him as an obstruction. One of Musinga's sons, Rudahigwa, had received a Catholic education, being secretly prepared to succeed his father. In 1931, the Belgian governor, with the Catholic monsignor at his side, announced that Musinga had been deposed in favor of his son Rudahigwa, who assumed the royal name Mutara (Longman 2010, 53–55). The Tutsi elite would now be firmly on the side of the Church.

---

[7] Benda asserts that the White Fathers' political strategies must be seen in the light of Protestant competition for State favor. The Presbyterian, Anglican (Episcopal), and Seventh-day Adventist leadership also pursued the favor of State leaders and held similar views about ethnic divisions and obedience to political authority (Gatwa 2005).

The Hamitic Myth and Hardened Ethnic Identities

In the distorted rationale of ethno-politics, the choice to favor the Tutsi aristocracy received impetus from a curious myth that flourished in the 19th-century ethos of scientific racism and social Darwinism. It was the so-called Hamitic theory, named after Ham, son of the Biblical figure Noah. According to the Genesis account, Noah pronounced a curse on Ham's son Canaan. The account mentions nothing about physiognomic characteristics, but the sixth-century Babylonian Talmud states that the curse on Ham's descendants was blackness (Sanders 1969, 521–522).[8]

Belief in the Negro-Hamite became accepted by about 1600, concurrent with a thriving African slave trade.[9] But a new Hamitic myth arose out of Napoleon's expeditions into Egypt, which encountered a sophisticated civilization even older than those of the Greeks and Romans – and whose descendants were people of color. Here was a paradox: Even while Western powers remained smug in their belief that the Negroid slave population was cursed, or even subhuman, they were confronted with an advanced civilization of non-white origin. The solution: Prove that the Egyptians were not Negroes (Sanders 1969, 525).

In addition to convoluted attempts to rewrite history, the clergy helpfully weighed in, pointing out that though Ham's son Canaan had been cursed, the Egyptians descended from a different son, Mizraim. These Hamites must have been Caucasoid, "uncursed and capable of high civilization." They were seen as "early culture-bearers in Africa owing to the natural superiority of intellect and character of all Caucasoids."[10] The myth animated Western exploration (and exploitation) in Africa. Discoverers on their "civilizing mission" referred to the Hamitic hypothesis to explain any signs of civilization in the "Dark Continent."[11] In the mold of this constructed cultural identity, Hamites discovered south of the Sahara were typecast as pastoralists, in contrast to the typical agrarian African. Hamites had supposedly conquered the inferior Bantu, improved farming implements, and introduced civilization. The myth linked physical features and character traits that allegedly predisposed the Hamites to intelligence, courage, and leadership (Sanders 1969, 530; Longman 2010, 60).

English explorer John Hanning Speke (1864) reached the territory of modern Rwanda in the 1860's and saw the strikingly tall Tutsi ruling class with their fairer skin, thin lips, and aquiline noses. The wealth-holders were pastoralists, of

---

[8] Many Bible commentators name Ham's son Cush, and possibly Put, as the progenitor(s) of various African peoples.

[9] Edith Sanders (1965) observes that "ideas have a way of being accepted when they become useful as a rationalization of an economic fact of life" (522).

[10] Among those deemed Hamite were Berbers, black Ethiopians, Libyans, Watusi, and Masai.

[11] Sanders (1969) states that within the Caucasoid hierarchy that put the Teutons on top and the Slavs on the bottom, the Hamites took up their new position on the bottom rung (526–529).

course, measuring their power by the number of cattle they owned. It is Speke who made the link between the Hamitic hypothesis and this ruling class formerly called Wahuma, but now called Watutsi. They were, he believed, fair-skinned black Caucasians who had conquered the inferior agrarian dark-skinned Bantu. Speke (1864) wrote: "It appears impossible to believe … that they can be of any other race than the semi-Shem-Hamitic of Ethiopia. Both alike are Christians of the greatest antiquity" (99–100). This racist reading of Rwandan society ignored the fact that the vast majority of Tutsi were not nobles but peasants, as impoverished as their Hutu counterparts (Gatwa 2005, 69; Rittner 2004, 148–152).

The existence of the Tutsi elite furnished proof to the Europeans that these impressive nobles possessed inherent leadership qualities, nicely fitting the Hamite mold. With this proof that the complex, centralized structure of Rwandan society had (dark) white fingerprints, the colonists could justify their divide-and-rule approach. Thanks to the Hamitic hypothesis, the Europeans could tell themselves that they were not power-sharing with Negroes but with Caucasians, leading to what Linden (1975) calls "unmitigated racism" in colonial policy (421).

The White Fathers became especially enamored by this theory with its quasi-biblical gloss. In 1907, the White Fathers wrote that Tutsi society "obviously evokes biblical memories, by their customs, often borrowed from Jewish customs" (Linden 1977, 165). One missionary saw the Tutsi as "closer to the White man than the Negro … a European under a black skin" (Eltringham 2006, 8). Protestant missionaries also embraced the myth (Benda 2012, 69, 169; Gatwa 2005, 68–98).

From the divide-and-rule strategy flowed a range of discriminatory practices in civil administration, education, and church hierarchies. The Hamitic hypothesis underpinned Catholic educational practice becoming, in Linden's words, "the great generator and stabiliser of class structure, creating a Christian ruling class, a 'racial aristocracy'" (Linden 1977, 164). From their youth, Tutsi and Hutu students learned the Hamitic hypothesis as a matter of historical fact (Longman 2010, 65–66). A superior education (in French) opened the way for Tutsi to occupy the top echelons of government and the Church, and the inferior education of the Hutu (in Kinyarwanda) virtually guaranteed that they would be unqualified for office (Carney 2014, 32). In the 1930's, Tutsi men and women made up the vast majority of priests, nuns, and religious.

The Church's embrace and institutionalization of the Hamitic theory made it into a self-fulfilling prophecy – Church schools acted unapologetically as what Mamdani calls "a womb of racial ideology," using the Hamitic myth to reinforce the constructed conquering and civilizing profile of the Tutsi "race" (Mamdani 2001, 89; Gatwa 2005, 67).

The exaggeration and hardening of existing social strata eventually "paralysed fluid social dynamics into frozen and polarized ethnic groups." The deliberate policy of converting the elite and cementing its dominance produced profound changes in Rwandan society. Benda (2012) contends that this politicized strategy of top-down proselytizing had a greater impact on subsequent events than any other single colonial-era policy, laying the groundwork for the Hutu social revolution of 1959 (59).

Colonial and church authorities increasingly became intertwined in a mutually supportive relationship that assured maximum stability of and control over the population. The churches stressed obedience to civil authority as a matter of Christian duty, and in return they reaped increasing influence over the social sphere. Both church and state did their part to ensure the Tutsi monopoly on power, which predictably received the Tutsi elite's hearty support. Tutsi overlords were used as colonial proxies to supervise forced labor on public works projects, called *uburetwa,* which utilized only Hutu workers (Mamdani 2001, 113; Longman 2010, 64–65).

However, doling out lavish favors to Tutsi required a clear definition of just who the Tutsi were. The categories of Hutu and Tutsi could no longer be based on fluid economic or occupational lines, nor could intermarriage continue to muddy identities. So in the 1930's, colonial officials created a list of arbitrary criteria, including physical height, shape of the nose, and the number of cattle owned, and an identity-card system locking Rwandans into one of the three artificially bounded racial groups. Ethnic stratification then took hold in earnest in both secular and religious spheres. "Racialization of the Tutsi," writes Mamdani (2001), "was the joint work of the state and the Church." He calls the Church "the original ethnographer of Rwanda." While colonial administrators lived far distant from local communities, Church personnel could reach deep into community life, acting as "the brains and the hands of the colonial state" to enforce ethnic division where it had hardly existed before (98, 232).

With the resistant King Musinga deposed in favor of his Catholic-educated son, Mutara III Rudahigwa, all the pieces were in place to make Rwanda the Catholic jewel of Africa. Léon Classe's top-down strategy reached its apogee in the 1930's. Mass conversions of Tutsi ensued during a period called *la tornade.* This reinforced the Catholic Church's position as a linchpin in the colonial ruling system. As Prunier (1995) maintains, after Mutara, Catholicism became "not only linked with the highest echelons of the state but completely enmeshed in Rwandan society from top to bottom" (34). Mutara had married a non-Christian wife in 1933 but divorced her in 1941, and the next year he married Rosalie Gicanda, a Catholic Tutsi.

In 1943, King Mutara was baptized as a Catholic, and in 1946, he dedicated Rwanda to Christ the King, further solidifying the throne-and-altar alliance (Carney 2014, 39). Mutara proclaimed: "Lord Jesus, it is you who have formed our country. You have given us a long line of kings to govern in your place, even though we did not know you. When the time fixed by your Providence had arrived, You have been

made known. You have sent us your apostles; they have opened to us the light. …
Now that we know you, we recognize publicly that you are our Lord and our King"
(Carney 2014, 40).

Religious Authorities and Hutu Emancipation

In 1950, the Rwandan Catholic Church celebrated 50 years of patient and strategic missionizing that had brought the Church to its apex. However, the golden anniversary celebration belied a less stable picture due to a convergence of factors. Belgian authorities during World War II had imposed forced labor and higher export demands. These measures, along with a series of crop failures that led to 300,000 deaths by famine, prompted widespread social unrest. The postwar rise of nationalist movements coincided with colonial fatigue and talk of autonomy or even independence, raising the question of democratic reform. In the late 1940's and early 1950's, Mutara responded to popular unrest by taking steps to abolish discriminatory practices, such as *uburetwa* (Hutu forced labor) and the patronage system. In the mid-1950's, there was virtually no income gap between the average Hutu and Tutsi families. In 1959, only 4 to 6 % of Rwandan and Burundian Tutsi fell into the category of upper-class elites (Carney 2014, 47–48).

Mutara sought to break the Church's monopoly on education by calling for an independent State school system. Rwandan bishops rejected such calls, arguing that Catholic education was essential to prevent the poor masses from falling prey to Communism and secularism. The hierarchy harbored a deep fear that a swing toward godless ideologies would wipe out a half century of gains in the most missionized country in Africa. Swiss White Father André Perraudin, the powerful archbishop of Kabgayi during this period, presided over an important turn in Church policy toward social justice. In 1956, Perraudin appointed his personal secretary, former seminarian and Hutu intellectual Gregoire Kayibanda, as editor-in-chief of the Kinyarwanda-language Catholic weekly *Kinyamateka*.[12] It became a key channel in sensitizing the masses to social-justice issues.[13] Kayibanda

---

[12] In 1953, the White Fathers had launched the Catholic journal *L'Ami* to cover social and political issues, with Kayibanda as editor. His early writings, directed mainly to lay elites, concerned issues such as land reform and democratization, making no reference to the Hutu-Tutsi question. Kayibanda would go on to become Rwanda's first president.

[13] Scholars often attribute social change in the 1950's to the rise of a Hutu counter-elite, made up of Catholic-educated Hutu intellectuals who were sensitized to social inequity by a new generation of activist European missionaries. But in the early part of the decade, this young intellectual class consisted of several thousand Hutu *and* Tutsi, called *evolués*. They occupied the space between the traditional elite and the common masses. During this period, according to J.J. Carney (2014), social-justice discourse in secular and religious publications focused on metropole-colony or black-white tensions, not ethnic issues (55–57; see also Benda 2012, 70).

quickly learned how to mobilize supporters through the mass media and Catholic Action groups (Carney 2014, 49–52, 55).

In 1957, social-justice rhetoric abruptly shifted toward ethnic division as the single reason for the suffering of the masses – the *Hutu* masses. This charge, which might have been aimed exclusively at the small proportion of Tutsi administrators, instead directed its animosity toward the Tutsi ethnic group as a whole, including the vast proportion of the Tutsi minority that labored alongside the Hutu. The 1957 Bahutu Manifesto, written by Hutu nationalists, including Kayibanda, turned the Hamitic myth on its head by depicting all Tutsi as a foreign race that had long oppressed the Hutu. Instead of the Tutsi being a noble, civilizing elite, they were portrayed as invaders who had oppressed the people of Rwanda for centuries and who harbored further ambitions of domination. The Manifesto called on the Hutu to solve the racial problem once and for all. The document was disseminated through a diocesan printing house and popularized among Hutu through Catholic channels (Gatwa 2005, 152–153). Kayibanda formed the Party of the Hutu Emancipation Movement (Parmehutu). In July 1959, King Mutara died under suspicious circumstances. That October, the Hutu social revolution marked the opening salvo in what would be recurring rounds of ethnic violence. Political theorist Anthony Court (2016) asserts that the revolution "would not have been possible without the allegiance of the Catholic Church" to the Hutu cause (63). With independence on the horizon and the potential enfranchisement of the masses, the Rwandan Catholic hierarchy wholly threw its support behind the Hutu majority (Mamdani 2001, 113–114). Once independence was achieved in 1962, the churches lost no time in building ties with the new Hutu-dominated government. As anti-Tutsi attacks escalated, Carney (2014) asserts that the symbiotic relationship between the hierarchy and the government "cost the church its independence and its prophetic voice, leaving it impotent in the face of the growing violence committed by its state partner" (172).

The succeeding decades followed a similar pattern of church-state collaboration. In 1975, Rwanda's second president, Juvénal Habyarimana, established the Hutu-dominated *Mouvement Révolutionnaire National pour le Développement* (MRND) as Rwanda's only political party (Prunier 1995, 76). Habyarimana appointed his close ally, Catholic archbishop of Kigali Vincent Nsengiyumva, to the MRND central committee, a position he held for nearly 15 years until the Vatican pressured him to resign (Longman 2001, 148).

As for the Protestant and Adventist churches, Longman (2010) has written: "Like the White Fathers Anglican, Seventh Day Adventist, and Presbyterian missionaries all sought to promote their churches by gaining the favor of state leaders, and they held many of the same attitudes as the White Fathers toward ethnicity and civil obedience. The entanglement of church and state and the involvement of churches in ethnic politics in Rwanda are factors that have been consistent across denominational divides as well as across time, and they are at the root of explaining why the churches became so heavily implicated in the Rwandan genocide" (59).

Jehovah's Witnesses and the Practice of Apolitical Christianity

Entering into this landscape of religious power politics, Jehovah's Witnesses had little prospect of gaining a toehold. Their apolitical doctrine would move them to forego any attempt to lobby or cultivate close ties with the government. Moreover, the Witnesses' evangelizing activities would raise the ire of powerful churches that could leverage their government connections to act against potential competitors. In retrospect, the objective of institutional – and even literal – survival apparently did not move the Witnesses to suspend their adherence to strict political neutrality. As will be seen, the Witnesses held to this position despite severe government suppression during the 1980's, throughout the Rwandan Civil War beginning in October 1990, and as genocidal violence erupted in 1994.

To understand the tensile strength of the Witnesses' practice of political neutrality, it is important to place their position vis-à-vis the State within the larger conceptual matrix governing the Witnesses' relationship to the secular world. In brief, the Witnesses' position is grounded in several broad doctrinal categories: (1) secular vs. divine authority, (2) the sanctity of life and Christlike love, and (3) the Kingdom of God.

Secular vs. Divine Authority. Jehovah's Witnesses regard Jehovah, the God of the Bible, as the Supreme Authority (Psalm 36:9; 83:18). All human authority is subordinate to divine law, as defined in the Bible. According to Witness doctrine, Christians are required to render to secular governments ("Caesar") respect and "relative," or conditional, obedience (Mark 12:17; Romans chap. 13). If the requirements of God and human authorities conflict, as when the first-century Jewish Sanhedrin court ordered the apostles to cease evangelizing, the Witnesses believe they must "obey God as ruler rather than men" (Acts 5:29).

Relevant to Witness neutrality is Jesus' statement that his followers are "no part of this world," a position that he warned would incur hostility (John 15:19; 17:16). That same day, Jesus commanded his disciples not to defend him against arrest, saying: "All those who take up the sword will perish by the sword" (Matthew 26:52).[14] The Witnesses apply these principles by abstaining from seeking political office; voting; sharing in patriotic rituals; or participating in war, political disputes, protest movements, and violence in general.

---

[14] The day was Nisan 14, starting at sunset, as reckoned by the Jewish calendar. According to the gospel account, Jesus explicitly taught an object lesson by having the disciples carry swords that evening and then commanding them not to use them in his behalf. Although Jesus took no political position, his accusers charged him with sedition.

Sanctity of Life and Christlike Love. When it comes to Christians and violence, state-sponsored or otherwise, the Witnesses point to basic precepts regarding the sanctity of life and to specific Biblical prohibitions against spilling blood (Genesis 9:6; Exodus 20:13). Two laws, which epitomize humans' obligations toward one another, call on believers to treat and love others as they do themselves (Matthew 7:12; 22:36–40). Within the Christian fold, Jesus' "new commandment" further requires disciples to "love one another just as I have loved you," that is, even to the point of dying for fellow believers, as he did for humankind (John 13:34, 35). Conversely, Scripture equates hatred with murder and calls one "a liar" if he claims to love God but hates his brother (1 John 3:15; 4:20). The Witnesses view nationality and ethnic categories as manmade, irrelevant in determining one's worthiness of life in God's eyes (Acts 10:34, 35; 17:26). The Biblical principles underpinning the borderless Witness community are thus seen as irreconcilable with participation in human war and mass violence.[15]

The Kingdom of God. Central to the Witnesses' political neutrality is their belief in the Kingdom of God as an actual government in heaven to which they owe their primary allegiance, even as they respect and obey the governments under which they live. The apostle Paul compared the Christian's position to that of an ambassador (2 Corinthians 5:20). Addressing the Roman governor Pontius Pilate, Jesus indicated that subjects of the heavenly Kingdom would reject violence, saying: "My Kingdom is no part of this world. If my Kingdom were part of this world, my attendants would have fought that I should not be handed over to the Jews" (John 18:36). The Witnesses believe that they should demonstrate their subjection to God's Kingdom by living according to its laws.[16] The Witnesses evangelize as an expression of loyalty to and advocacy for God's Kingdom. Although political neutrality has at times prompted severe political or social opposition, their apolitical stance enables them to share their faith without raising partisan impediments to the reception of their message.

---

[15] The Witnesses attempt to model their position after the early Christians, who avoided serving in the Roman army (Cadoux 1982). For a general discussion of the development of the Witnesses' doctrine of political neutrality, see Chu (2004) and Knox (2018). During World War I, Witnesses (then called Bible Students) took varying positions toward military conscription but generally refrained from killing. Their publications roundly criticized clergy who publicly supported the war and who agitated for the imprisonment of Bible Students and bans on their literature (Abrams 1933; Herrberger 2016; Knox 2019; Perkins 2016).

[16] According to the Witness reference work *Insight on the Scriptures,* the theme of the Bible is "the vindication of Jehovah's sovereignty and the ultimate fulfillment of his purpose for the earth, by means of his Kingdom under Christ" (Watch Tower 1988, vol. 1, 310).

Jehovah's Witnesses in Rwanda

In some ways, the experience of Jehovah's Witnesses in Rwanda followed a trajectory similar to that in other lands where they have experienced tension with the State, most often for one of two reasons:

1. The leadership of the religious majority contests the Witnesses' right to proselytize or even exist and leverages political ties to have them suppressed. Although essentially a religious dispute, opposers, when calling for government sanctions, commonly use political rationales, such as painting the Witnesses as seditious or otherwise dangerous to society.

2. Political authority rejects the Witnesses' refusal to perform patriotic rituals or military service, as well as their abstention from voting, interpreting their neutrality as a form of disloyalty.

In Rwanda, with church and state so intimately connected, both issues came into play in the persecution of the Witness community, especially during the period of single-party rule.

In 1975, the year of Archbishop Nsengiyumva's appointment to the MRND central committee, Gaspard Rwakabubu, a native Rwandan Witness, left his well-paying job as a mechanic in the copper mines in Congo.[17] Rwakabubu had turned down an offer to further his education in Belgium, instead returning with his family to Rwanda to evangelize. They arrived in June 1975 and moved into a small adobe house with a mud floor, a contrast to their spacious company residence in Congo (Watch Tower 1992, 154). Justin Rwagatore, an ex-soldier, became a baptized Witness the next year. During the late 1970's, the number of Rwandan Witnesses grew by about 50 % each year, surpassing 100 by 1978. Rwakabubu began translating Witness literature into Kinyarwanda, which increased the reach of their message and boosted baptism rates (Watch Tower 1992, 155; Watch Tower 2012, 171). Gaspard Niyongira recounts:

> By the time I got baptized in 1978, the clergy were becoming fearful at seeing so many coming into the truth [becoming Jehovah's Witnesses]. Hundreds attended our assemblies. When we went out preaching, we were like a swarm of locusts! Quite often, about 20 [Witnesses] would leave from the town center of Kigali and go preaching on foot from there to Kanombe, a distance of about six miles [9 km]. After stopping for lunch, they would continue another four miles [7 km] to Masaka before returning to Kigali by bus in the evening. Groups of [Witnesses] did similarly in other parts of the country. Not surprisingly, this intensive preaching gave people the impression that there were thousands of Jehovah's Witnesses. As a result, accusations were leveled against [the Witnesses], influencing the authorities to deny them legal recognition (Watch Tower 2012, 174–175).

---

[17] Starting in 1969, a few Swahili-speaking Witness missionaries had made a start in Rwanda but were denied permission to remain in the country.

In October 1979, the Habyarimana government issued a list of recognized religions. Jehovah's Witnesses were not named. In March 1980, Witnesses submitted documentation with a request for recognition, which went ignored. Despite the displeasure of local clergy, the government did not then mount a systematic campaign against the Witnesses. Their numbers kept growing and material from the Witnesses' *Awake!* magazine was read over the radio. The Kigali congregation even had a simple Kingdom Hall (Watch Tower 1992, 189).[18]

By 1980, Rwakabubu recollects: "Many who had been active Catholics, Protestants, and Adventists sent resignation letters to their former churches. ... The number of those attending the meetings of the Kigali Congregation soon increased to more than 200. In the beginning, the clergy did not take much notice of our presence because we were so few. However, as the numbers increased, some charged that we constituted a danger to the country" (Watch Tower 2012, 175–176).

No statistical breakdown of the Witness community by ethnicity is available; but those who were active during the period recall that the congregations basically reflected the demographics of the general population. While Tutsi Witnesses were subject to the same discrimination and hostile attitudes displayed toward all Tutsi in Rwanda, Hutu Witnesses faced hostility for their refusal to support the Hutu cause and the MRND. For instance, Augustin Murayi, a Witness in the Kigali congregation, belonged to a prominent Hutu family from the same region as President Habyarimana. He had had a traditional Catholic upbringing and used to debate with Witnesses over their rejection of the Trinity doctrine. Eventually, he accepted a Bible study with Witnesses, continuing his studies while in Belgium for secular schooling. Three months after his baptism as a Witness in 1980, Murayi returned to Rwanda. He wrote a letter of resignation to the Catholic Church. His embarrassed mother told him that the priest had read out the letter at Mass and angrily denounced him. Murayi took a teaching job in Butare, Rwanda's intellectual capital. The following year, he met Tutsi professor Tharcisse Seminega on a bus on the way to a seminar. Seminega overheard him quote the gospel of John, chapter 14, verse 28, where Jesus is quoted as saying: "My father is greater than I am." When other riders objected that this statement is not in the Bible, Seminega spoke up to confirm that he had read this verse in his Catholic Bible.

Seminega had spent 15 years training for the priesthood; but having nearly reached the point of taking his vows, he withdrew after facing bald discrimination and efforts by certain White Fathers to force him out of the seminary. He transferred to a secular university and later took up teaching in the Department of Biology at the National University of Rwanda in Butare.

---

[18] A Witness house of worship, so named because God's Kingdom is a central theme of Witness teaching.

Seminega was struck by the Hutu Murayi's willingness to engage with him in regular religious discussions, which they did for about six months. Then Murayi received a presidential appointment to the post of Director General of Primary and Secondary Schools in Kigali. When Murayi left Butare, the former soldier Justin Rwagatore continued to study the Bible with Seminega. His wife, a former nun, did not join in (Seminega 2019).

Suppression on Religious and Political Grounds

In 1982, Gaspard Rwakabubu and two other full-time evangelizers, Joseph Koroti and Ferdinand Mugarura, again sent a letter requesting legal recognition of the Witnesses, this time to the Minister of Justice and the Minister of the Interior. No reply was received. Instead, Rwakabubu underwent interrogation twice by the State Security agency (Watch Tower 1992, 191; Watch Tower 2012, 176–177). The president announced on national radio that he would not tolerate those who "denigrated" the "Rwandan faith." This was a clear reference to Jehovah's Witnesses, a move they saw as an effort to please Archbishop Nsengiyumva, then on the MRND central committee. Not long after, Witness meetings were banned (Watch Tower 2012, 176–177).

Three regional meetings were held discreetly in November 1982, Rwakabubu serving as chairman. In Butare, the assembly took place at the university residence of Tharcisse Seminega, who had continued to study with the Witnesses. He agreed to host the meeting for about 100 people at his home, giving the appearance of a large family reunion. Seminega later learned that the parish priest had hidden in the house next door and listened to the entire program. Rwakabubu went on to chair assemblies in Gisenyi and then Kigali. The day after the Kigali gathering, State Security officers appeared at his home and took him to the presidency. This time he did not return. The two other signees of the registration request were also arrested. Kingdom Halls were closed and the Ministry of Justice formally banned Jehovah's Witnesses (Seminega 2019, 57–58; Watch Tower 2012, 177).

The authorities held the three without charge or trial for 11 months. Finally, prosecutors accused them of "crookery" or "embezzlement of funds of believers." According to Rwakabubu, the prosecutor demanded: 'You have chairs? Where do you get the money for chairs? You must have extorted the money.' Rwakabubu asked: 'Has anyone complained about being tricked into contributing money?' The questioning ceased, and the three received two-year sentences, which they served in full in an overcrowded, vermin-infested prison where they ate one sparse meal a day. Rwakabubu received word that Archbishop Nsengiyumva had paid 500,000 Rwandan francs, roughly equivalent to $ 5,000 (U.S.), for their arrest and imprisonment. During their first week in prison, the archbishop came to conduct Mass. On that occasion and during every subsequent visit, he warned the prisoners to beware of

Jehovah's Witnesses. This aroused the curiosity of many of the 3,500 prisoners, some of whom sought out the three men to ask why the archbishop considered them dangerous. About 40 prisoners attended the Witnesses' Bible study classes (Watch Tower 1992, 191; Rwakabubu 2019).

The number of Witnesses continued to increase. In 1983, Tharcisse Seminega was baptized. He later wrote:

> Despite my years of theological study, I discovered that the simplest and purest Bible teachings had escaped me. For instance, I knew well the 'beatitudes' spoken by our Lord in his Sermon on the Mount. But never before had I truly grasped that the words 'Blessed are the gentle: they shall have the earth as an inheritance' meant just that – that gentleness, love, and peace would one day prevail in Paradise on earth. Racism, hatred, and injustice would not rule forever. So it had been in the beginning, so it would be again. 'Thy will be done on earth, as it is in heaven.' You cannot imagine how much comfort this Bible message brought me.
>
> The Witnesses understood Jesus' words, 'You do not belong to the world,' to mean that they should keep free from all political and military affairs. They showed me historical proof that the first Christians in the Roman Empire had taken this position. Followers of Christ could not allow man-made divisions to hinder their love for one another. Nor would they take up weapons to kill any human.
>
> This beautiful ethic sounded so sweet to me. But how could it be achieved? After all, white, black, Hutu, Tutsi – we had grown up in the same divisive and hateful climate. Many who became Witnesses must have struggled to root out old attitudes and ways. What could make Hutu and Tutsi set aside all the bitterness and prejudice they carried and embrace one another as true brothers and sisters? (Seminega 2019, 56).

Seminega's decision to become a Witness sparked special outrage because he was known in Butare as an educator and a devout Catholic. He too sent a resignation letter to the Church, which the priest read aloud and then nailed to the door of the Catholic cathedral. Shortly thereafter, Seminega left for his doctoral studies in France.

In addition to the irritation of politically influential clergy, tensions arose over political issues. In June 1984, the Minister of Justice wrote to all heads of prefectures denouncing the Witnesses' "damaging ideas" that distracted the population from "development activities." "Such propaganda," he wrote, "is to be energetically combated." For some time, all Rwandans had been automatically considered MRND party members upon reaching age 18. But the party began requiring all members to pay a fee to finance the party. To the Witnesses, this was not a tax but a political contribution.[19] Beginning in October 1985, the government had Witnesses fired from their jobs, expelled their children from school, and confiscated

---

[19] When it became public knowledge that the Witnesses refused to pay the fee, other minority groups, such as the Seventh-day Adventists, also refused. Perhaps they felt that the tax perpetuated the dominance of their religious rival, the Catholic Church. However, for the Witnesses, it was a question of maintaining political neutrality (Rwakabubu 2019).

private property for refusing to pay the party fee. The Witnesses faced arrest, physical abuse, and detention without trial ("Rwanda Persecutes Christians" 1986, 3). In March 1986, authorities rounded up Witnesses in Muvumba, Gisenyi, Mutara, Butare, Gashoba, Nyabisindu, Rwamagana, Ruhengeri, Kibungo, and Byumba. In June, Gaspard Rwakabubu was again arrested. The authorities offered to release him and others if they would sign a document renouncing his faith.

Meanwhile, at the Ministry of Education in Kigali, an official pressed Director General Augustin Murayi to falsify the grades of certain students as a political favor. For three years in a row, Murayi refused.[20] He was also conspicuously absent during patriotic ceremonies. At ministry-level meetings, with Archbishop Nsengiyumva present, officials frequently discussed Murayi's latest offenses. In August 1986, authorities arrested Murayi and his wife, Rachel. The public prosecutor Alphonse Nkubito gave him three days to consider renouncing his faith. If he refused, he would be charged with belonging to an unlawful sect. Government radio and newspapers denounced him as a traitor. Justin Rwagatore, the former soldier, was also arrested for stating that he would refuse to fight for his country. This high-profile case coincided with more mass arrests.

On October 2 to 17, 1986, the State Security Court, Rwanda's highest court, heard arguments against 89 Jehovah's Witnesses and 3 of their infant children. Some had been in prison already for ten months. They were charged with "inciting the populace to rebel against established authority, disobeying obligatory authority, holding prohibited public meetings, and contempt of the emblems of national sovereignty" (Longman 2010, 92; Maryomeza 1987, 3–6; "Rwanda Persecutes Christians" 1986, 1).

Prosecutor Nkubito articulated the mélange of political and religious issues behind the arrests: "These people are a stumbling block to the security of our country. They are not accused because of what they believe, but they are using religion to act against the law knowingly and they are determined to do so. They are disturbing others, making themselves false prophets, misleading the common people" ("Rwanda Persecutes Christians" 1986, 1).

The Witnesses' belief that they owe primary allegiance to the Kingdom of God became a central issue. The government labeled them as outsiders because of their lack of support for the Hutu cause. During the trial, the government newspaper *Imvaho* on October 13, 1986, reprinted a speech by François Muganza, Minister of Health:

> Those individuals feel free to teach that there is no other accepted government except God. And such thinking contributes to their refusing to honor the President of the Republic, to their refusing to respect the national flag and anthem, refusing to do *Umuganda* [community work], opposing the military animation and many other activities

---

[20] On discriminatory educational practices under the MRND, see Gatwa 2005, 117–118.

that support the development of the country. Among those were found even officials in high posts who took an oath before commencing their duties, promising in the name of the almighty God to fulfill their duties and never betray the Republic of Rwanda and the President of the Republic and work to promote Rwandan society. But now they are going against their own promises.

I therefore request that you join the government and fight against those rebels who want to stop our peace, to stop our unity, to stop our development led by President Habyarimana. The Bible also teaches that all authority is from God and that everyone who does not support good leadership refuses God's command and will be judged. Be watchful then, you militias; do not let yourself be confused by these strangers who do not belong to Rwanda. All Rwandans are in a boat, and this boat is our Movement. The government of Rwanda is ready to support religion but will not tolerate religions that constitute threats to security on the basis of God. All local leaders, Prefects, and all in charge of the security of Rwanda, let us stand up as one and fight these rebels who are seeking to disrupt our peace.

After this speech, 70 additional Witnesses were imprisoned and charged as rebels.[21] On October 24, 1986, the court found 49 of the defendants guilty, and most received 10-year sentences. Murayi and his wife, Rachel, and Rwagatore received 12-year sentences. Rwanda Press Agency reported: "The verdict is justified because they were the rare intellectual ones in the group and the government had placed confidence in them by giving them positions of responsibility" (*Dialogue 120* 1987, 102–103; *Dialogue 125* 1987, 3–6; "Rwanda Persecutes Christians" 1986, 3–4).[22] During this period, *The New York Times* of October 26, 1986, reported the arrest of 300 members of four religious minorities (13).[23] One third were Witnesses.

In November 1986, the Witnesses launched a worldwide letter-writing campaign to appeal to Rwandan authorities to honor constitutional guarantees of religious freedom.[24] The foreign minister of each country and the local media were to receive a four-page tract detailing the Witnesses' plight. Three or four individuals were selected in each congregation to write President Habyarimana and six other officials using business or professional letterhead. The instructional letter read: "The letters should not be condemnatory but should appeal to the official's sense of fairness and desire that his country be respected by the rest of the world" (Watchtower 1986). After all, the tract stated, "the President of Rwanda himself is portrayed as a reasonable and fair ruler" ("Rwanda Persecutes Christians" 1986,

---

[21] Information, text, and translation of the Muganza speech provided by Gaspard Niyongira (Rwanda branch office of Jehovah's Witnesses, October 2019).

[22] Belgian constitutional lawyer Filip Reyntjens (1988) later analyzed the Murayi trial and deemed that the charges were invalid and proceedings were based on outdated or misapplied legal principles (2–15).

[23] The four groups were Jehovah's Witnesses, *Abarokore* (the Saved), *Abatempera* (Temperants of Central Africa, broken off from the Seventh-day Adventists), and the *Abantu b'Imana bihana* (the Repentant People of God) (Maryomeza 1987, 4).

[24] Through the years, the Witnesses commonly had mass letter-writing campaigns when their co-believers faced unjust treatment.

4). According to a radio report, on some days the government received 500 protest letters (Watch Tower 1992, 193). It is not known how many letters in total went out; but if even one tenth of the nearly 55,000 congregations responded, over 100,000 pieces of mail would have been sent. In July 1987, all imprisoned Witnesses, about one third of all Witnesses in the country, were released by presidential pardon, likely a result of the letter-writing campaign.

Pressure against the Witnesses persisted both because of their ministry work and their political neutrality. As one example, the October following the prisoner release, a mayor wrote to a militia councilor, thanking him for arresting and handing over the "so-called evangelizers of Jehovah."

THE RWANDAN REPUBLIC	Cyabingo, October 15, 1987
RUHENGERI PREFECTURE	N° 937/04.09.01/4
S/ BUSENGO PREFECTURE	
CYABINGO COMMUNE	
Militia Councilor of Cyabingo Sector	

CYABINGO Commune

Dear Militia Councilor,

I am pleased to write this letter to show appreciation for the zeal and courage you put forth with regard to security of the sector that you govern. This was demonstrated through the arrest of the so-called evangelizers of Jehovah on October 12, 1987, that you handed over to us.

I request your companions to which a copy of this letter will be given to stay alert and keep on the watch regarding the man named HABIMANA Mark, staying in the Sector of Rwaza, Ruhondo Commune, who was the Captain of the Rwandan army and a pilot but now seems to have lost his mind since he teaches about the illegal religion. If you happen to see this man in any of the sectors of which you are in charge, or any other person teaching about this illegal religion, please arrest them and hand them over to us because I warned this man of the sanctions he would receive if ever he comes in our Commune in this way. And please take hold of anything, be it papers, books, or any other publication, that has to do with this particular religion and send them to us.

Mayor of Cyabingo Commune
NKIRANUYE J. Damascène

Witnesses abstained from measures to solidify the MRND party and glorify President Habyarimana, making their stand highly visible. For instance, while the Witnesses participated in the compulsory *Umuganda* on Saturday mornings, they would abstain from the afternoon *animation* sessions, or propaganda meetings (Uwamahoro 2020; Bonnier, Poulsen, Rogall, and Stryjan 2016, 7–8). Witnesses refused to share in armed night patrols. They also would not buy and wear the president's portrait pin, the one that Archbishop Nsengiyumva reportedly wore on his cassock (Rwakabubu 2019; Human Rights Watch 1999a).[25] In 1988, Albert Bahati, a Hutu who had been a Witness since 1979, was beaten and imprisoned. When he refused to put on the president's portrait pin, a soldier pinned it to his skin. Witness schoolchildren received beatings for refusing to sing the national anthem or for not knowing if they were Hutu or Tutsi. (Uwamahoro 2020; Seminega 2019, 172).

But overall, the years 1988 to early 1990 were relatively quiet for the Witnesses. Their situation may have improved in part because Western powers, on which Rwanda relied heavily for aid, were pressuring President Habyarimana to agree to the principle of multi-party rule. For the dominant churches, this meant competition not only from religious minorities but also reduced power-sharing with political parties having little interest in supporting the kind of church-state ties the churches had cultivated with the MRND. Thus, the religious leadership may have had fewer resources to suppress religious minorities. Tharcisse Seminega (2019) reports that amidst all the factional fighting, Rwandans could see more clearly that the neutrality of the Witnesses posed no threat to any side. In Butare, the Witnesses could conduct their ministry and meet discreetly in private homes (69, 76). Gaspard Niyongira (2019) describes how the Witnesses would go door to door carrying vegetables instead of a Bible or literature. Upon being offered the vegetables at an exorbitant price, residents would ask, 'Why so expensive?' and the Witness would reply, 'Because we're in the last days!' and segue to a Bible topic.

The Witnesses' apolitical outlook worked in concert with their universalistic values, which made political divisions and ethnic origins irrelevant to their personal relationships and congregation life. Representatives of the national office and congregation elders modeled inclusive behavior and communicated such in their teaching. The Witnesses conducted their public ministry without respect to ethnic divisions. Charles Rutaganira (2019), a Tutsi, reports that the congregations worked to maintain their unity. Intermarriage was common; and Hutu often helped disadvantaged Tutsi who needed to find work. Eugène Ntabana, supervising minister for all Witness congregations in Kigali, was known for teaching his Bible students that humans are like the red, white, and pink bougainvillea. 'They all belong to the same family. And so it is with humans,' he would say. 'We belong to the family of mankind' (*Watchtower* 1996, 32).

---

[25] Human Rights Watch (1999a) reports: "Once the MRND was firmly established, mobilization took on an added aspect: glorifying the party and its head. In addition to the work days, people were obliged to participate in weekly sessions of *animation*, propaganda meetings leavened with poetry, music, and dance created to honor Habyarimana and the MRND. Propaganda teams of singers and dancers vied for honors in regular competitions, often dressed in fine costumes bought by contributions from the party faithful. Rwandans often proclaimed their loyalty to Habyarimana, wore his image on portrait pins, and posted his picture in their houses or places of business" ("History: The Single-Party State"). According to Bonnier et al. (2016), *Umuganda* played an important role in mobilizing the population during the genocide.

As the numbers attending Witness meetings rose, the supervising office in Kenya thought it would be worth another attempt to apply for registration that would enable them to build houses of worship.[26] In 1991, despite ethnic unrest caused by the unsuccessful October 1990 incursion of the Rwandan Patriotic Front (RPF), the Witnesses arranged an international delegation to visit the new Minister of Justice, Sylvestre Nsanzimana, and other government ministers. The delegation purposely included a representative cross section of the Witness community, including Hutu Gaspard Rwakabubu and Tutsi Tharcisse Seminega, and representatives from Switzerland, France, Germany, and Kenya. The presentation began with each delegate introducing himself and relating his background, and then describing the difficulties faced by Rwandan Witnesses, especially teachers and students. They stressed that they strictly adhere to their political neutrality even if it sometimes results in hardship. The meeting lasted over an hour. Nsanzimana listened sympathetically and expressed appreciation that the Witnesses had not publicized isolated incidents of mistreatment. He suggested that the delegation write a letter referring to the meeting and renewing the request for legal recognition (Moly 2019). The request was finally granted on April 13, 1992 (U.S. Department of State Country Report on Human Rights Practices 1993 – Rwanda, Section 2c).

Religious Hate Speech in the Run-Up to Genocide

In the unstable political climate, virulent ethno-nationalism continued to fester and intensify. Propagandists depicted the extermination of the Tutsi as a matter of self-preservation, and those Tutsi who were now effectively trapped inside the country came under blanket condemnation. The danger increased for Hutu deemed pacifist or politically moderate (Longman 2010, 172).

State and church united in resisting the growing calls for democratic reform. The MRND turned increasingly to polarizing ethnic language to label opponents as traitors to the Hutu cause and accomplices with expatriate Tutsi forces intent on toppling the Habyarimana government. During 1990 to 1992, massacres of Tutsi prepared the population for full-scale genocide. Of this period, Longman (2010) writes: "Because the leaders of the Catholic, Presbyterian, Anglican, Baptist, and Free Methodist churches had all made clear their strong support for the regime ... people at the local level felt that their assertion of Hutu authority was consistent with church doctrines" (185). Archbishop Nsengiyumva "reminded Catholics that love of country was a 'duty incumbent on each one of us. ... We have a duty of protecting the country against all peril and against all menace, from wherever it comes from the interior or the exterior'" (Carney 2014, 197).

---

[26] The population-to-Witness ratio went from 273,357:1 in 1973 to 16,364:1 in 1983 (Watch Tower 1974 and 1984). During the ban (1982–1992), Witnesses ranks increased from 206 to 1,459 (Watch Tower 1983 and 1993). In 2018, there were 30,076 Witnesses (Watch Tower 2018).

As noted by Longman, the Church remained largely silent as eliminationist anti-Tutsi rhetoric and violence escalated, opening the way for political propagandists to co-opt religious language for their own use. This kind of religiously tinged vitriol would have tremendous resonance in a culture steeped in missionary Christianity. The following are among the most blatant and notorious examples of mass-media religious tropes used to mobilize the masses.

The government-supported *Kangura,* published in Kinyarwanda and French, was the most influential and popular newspaper before the genocide.[27] In December 1990, *Kangura* replaced the Mosaic Ten Commandments with the Hutu Ten Commandments. Among them were:

> No. 1: Any Hutu is a traitor who acquires a Tutsi wife.[28]
> No. 4: All Hutu must know that all Tutsi are dishonest in business. Any Hutu is a traitor who forms a business alliance with a Tutsi.
> No. 7: The Rwandan Army must be exclusively Hutu. No soldier may marry a Tutsi woman.
> No. 8: Hutu must stop taking pity on the Tutsi.
> No. 9: Hutu, wherever they be, must stand united, in solidarity. … Hutu must stand firm and vigilant against their common enemy: the Tutsi.

The cover of the January 1991 issue of *Kangura* shows the Christ child conversing with Mary and Joseph. Mary says: 'Son of God, you were just born at Christmas. Do all that you can to save the Hutu of Burundi from death.' Jesus replies: 'I will tell them to love each other as God loves them.' Joseph retorts: 'No, rather, tell the Hutu of the world to unite.' The headline above says: 'God is mobilized for the worldwide battle of the Hutu' (Mitchell n. d.). A poem in the January 1992 issue apologizes to God for rejecting the Trinity, an allusion to the three ethnic groups, in favor of Unity, implying the need for all to rally around the Hutu cause (Ben Dedale 1992, 14).

References to a Biblical adage and the Hamitic myth appear in a speech by Léon Mugesera, vice president of the MRND and a lecturer at the National University of Rwanda (where Seminega also taught). He is considered a prime ideologue of the genocide and was convicted of incitement on the basis of his speech in November 1992, which is considered one of the earliest explicit calls for genocide (Fletcher 2014, 2; Trial International 2016):

"In the gospel it is written: 'If someone slaps you on the cheek, give the other one so he can hit it as well.' I am telling you that this gospel has changed in our movement. If someone slaps you on the cheek, hit him twice on the other so he

---

[27] For a comprehensive discussion of the role of media in the genocide, see *The Media and the Rwanda Genocide,* Allan Thompson (ed.) (2007).
[28] The demonization of Tutsi women is a subject in itself. The horrifying rates of sexual assault and mutilation of Tutsi women can be traced directly to such inflammatory propaganda. See Burnet (2015).

will fall to the ground and will not able to regain consciousness" – that is, a permanent fall, or death.

In an imaginary conversation with a Tutsi, Mugesera invokes the Hamitic myth that church leaders had long implanted in Rwandan culture: '[Y]our home is in Ethiopia, and we will send you back along the Nyabarongo River so you get there quickly.' Here he portrays the Tutsi as invaders. They would return to their home, not by boat on the shallow and unnavigable Nyabarongo River – as listeners well understood – but by floating as dead bodies carried by the current. Radio station RTLM rebroadcast this speech just months before the genocide (Fletcher 2014).

"Hutu Power" radio station RTLM, which began broadcasting in July 1993, played a pivotal role in stoking anti-Tutsi rage. Once the genocide began, RTLM facilitated the work of the killers by coordinating the attackers, even announcing the names, addresses, and license plate numbers of Tutsi. The announcer sings this song about five weeks into the genocide, invoking God as part of their mission:

"Come and rejoice friends,
"Cockroaches are no more;
"Come and rejoice friends,
"God is merciful."[29]

The "Work" Begins

By the end of 1993, Rwanda had imported 581,000 machetes, one for every third Hutu male. (Human Rights Watch 1999b) A common farming implement, the populace knew how to wield this lightweight tool. Killing by hand, though, was hard work, taking several hacks to do the job; often several killers had to work on a single victim. The call to "work" (*gukora*) was coded language that all understood, along with such phrases as "cut down the tall trees," "cut the weeds," and "kill the cockroaches" (Mamdani 2001, 194).

In this fight to the death, there was no neutrality. Katongole (2009) writes: "Every Hutu was required to get involved in the work of killing Tutsis. Whoever would not kill had to be killed" (32). Hutu men with Tutsi wives were forced to kill their wives first as a show of loyalty to Hutu Power.

---

[29] The RTLM audio excerpt (accessed at https://www.youtube.com/watch?v=VNbUeLnxQEI on July 29, 2019) is identified in the on-screen text as a June 19, 1994, broadcast. However, a viewer comment dates the excerpt as July 2, 1994, and identifies the singer as Kantano Hamimana. The Montreal Institute for Genocide and Human Rights Studies of Concordia University maintains an online repository of Rwanda radio transcripts.

After the presidential plane crashed on the evening of April 6, the killing began almost immediately. A few days later, on April 10 at the First African Synod in Rome, the pope denounced the violence without naming the responsible parties. However, indicating that he had some inkling of an orchestrated genocide, the pope said: "I want to appeal to the consciences of those who planned these massacres and those who carry them out" (*Catholic Herald* 1994, 2). Following the pope's plea to "stop the bloodshed," writes J.J. Carney (2014), "Rwanda's bishops remained conspicuously silent." He states that on June 20, "[Rwandan] Catholic bishops and Protestant leaders issued a joint statement blaming both sides for the violence" (198).

Many of the Witnesses killed in the genocide perished because of their ethnicity, but others faced death because they continued to adhere to their apolitical values. A few examples illustrate the typical experiences of Witnesses throughout the country.

The beloved Eugène Ntabana, his wife, Josephat, and their two young children, Shami and Shima, were among the first Tutsi Witnesses murdered in Kigali (*Awake!* 1994, 12). Charles Rutaganira knew his turn had come when a mob of 30, mostly his neighbors, appeared at his house with a soldier who demanded, "What tribe are you?" Rutaganira answered, "Jehovah's Witness." When asked again, he said, "My father was a Tutsi." The mob slashed and stabbed him and dumped him under a tree to die. But a Hutu Witness who lived a few doors away risked his life to rescue Rutaganira and shelter him in his house. The leader of the mob, who was the bishop's driver, came looking for Rutaganira and threatened to kill the entire Hutu family that had rescued him. Before they could do so, a street battle with RPF troops broke out and the killers fled (Rutaganira 2019).

Hutu and Tutsi worked at the Witnesses' translation office in Kigali. The Hutu could have left their colleagues and tried to flee but they decided to stay together. Militiamen came repeatedly to threaten them and loot the office. Translator Emmanuel Ngirente said: "We understood that they would eventually kill us or we would starve to death." But Gaspard Rwakabubu and Lamech Bubegwa, another Hutu Witness, repeatedly brought them food and money to buy off the killers.[30] One day the militia told them the whole team would be killed the following day. Ngirente ran for help and found Rwakabubu on the edge of town. He had just evacuated his family because conditions were growing more dangerous. He agreed to return with Ngirente. They got the team out safely, but two of the Tutsi staff were later killed at a roadblock (*Watchtower* 1994, 26–27).

---

[30] The Kenya office of Jehovah's Witnesses sent relief funds to Goma, Democratic Republic of Congo, for Rwandan Witnesses. Rwakabubu and Bubegwa crossed into the Goma, picked up the money, and returned to distribute it to dozens of Witnesses to supply food and medicine to those in hiding or to buy off the killers (Gaspard Rwakabubu, email communication to author, March 24, 2020).

Albert Bahati hid about 30 people, Witnesses and non-Witnesses, in his house. The *Interahamwe* militiamen came at least three times. At one point they saw Bahati's Tutsi wife, Vestine, and called her outside. Bahati stood between them and said: "If you kill her, you must kill me first." Then they decided to take his wife's brother. Again Bahati pleaded: "For the love of God, leave him be!" They finally left. Among those non-Witnesses that Bahati hid was a Tutsi woman whose Hutu husband had fled, leaving her and their children behind. The husband returned and warned Bahati that the militia would attack him for hiding Tutsi. Bahati replied: "I cannot send them away!" The man then took his family and left (Watch Tower 2012, 208–209). One night, seven widows came to the home of Hutu Witness Joseph Nduwayezu asking for shelter for the night. Joseph agreed, though he did not know them. They said they had come to him because he was a Witness and in that area, his was the only house where they knew they would be safe (Nduwayezu 2020).

Catholic school teacher Consolée Mukanyiligira went with seven children to Hutu Church members, pleading for help. They all turned her away out of fear. An Adventist family that initially sheltered her sent her and the children to a Witness relative to hide. John Munyakazi already had people hiding in his house, but she says: "He did not hesitate one second to take us in." Munyakazi hid and fed more than a dozen Tutsi Witnesses and non-Witnesses in his home. They hid there for 12 days. The teacher Mukanyiligira and her children survived, but militiamen later stopped John and another Witness, Alphonse, on the road. They ordered Alphonse to assault John because they suspected John of hiding Tutsi. When Alphonse refused, both were killed (Mukanyiligira 2019; Uwamahoro 2020).[31]

Tharcisse Seminega and his family were on a death list compiled by his extremist Hutu colleagues at the National University. The day that killing erupted in Butare, his friend and former Bible student, Adolphe Rwamuhizi, arrived at the Seminega home and quickly arranged their escape. Seminega's former Bible teacher, Justin Rwagatore, then coordinated about 20 Hutu Witnesses, who accomplished the unthinkable by sheltering, feeding, and shifting the hunted family of seven from place to place for 75 days. At one point, the burgomaster of Ngoma, commune of Butare City, halted all other killing until the bodies of Seminega and his family were found. In the dead of night, Witness rescuers led the entire family from the goat shack were they had hidden for a month to a Witness home

---

[31] Six of the seven children were Mukanyiligira's and one was her niece. The teacher had seen Munyakazi bring his children to the school but she did not know him personally. She witnessed an earlier incident in which an MRND member slapped Munyakazi for not participating in politics. Munyakazi did not react. Onlookers remarked that his calm reaction must be due to his religious beliefs. Mukanyiligira states: "I was thinking to myself that this man is really courageous to let that man treat him that way. My impression of Jehovah's Witnesses is that they are people that don't like violence and don't get involved in politics and spend their time to teach." The provocateur later joined the militia.

where the house-to-house searches had already been done. Later, the rescuers divided up the family and finally brought them to a tiny underground pit where they hid with three other Tutsi Witnesses until government forces suffered defeat (Seminega 2019).

All told, about 400 Witnesses, Tutsi and Hutu, were murdered. Did the Witnesses as a community adhere to their apolitical, nonviolent stance?[32] In the absence of hard data, the results of in-depth interviews conducted thus far suggest an affirmative answer. Respondents report that: (1) numerous non-Witnesses sought safe haven with Hutu Witnesses, including those they did not previously know; (2) Rwandans in general were aware that Witnesses did not use weapons, man roadblocks, go on armed night patrols, or betray Tutsi in hiding; and (3) soon after the genocide, Witnesses resumed their public evangelizing and met with a marked increase of interest in their message. Within two years, their ranks nearly doubled.[33] Interviewees who accepted the faith after the genocide explicitly state that they did so in large part because it was common knowledge that Witnesses had not taken part in genocide. Further systematic study is needed to determine if these patterns were replicated countrywide during those terrible 100 days in 1994.

Conclusion

It is difficult to envision a greater test of moral and religious values than a genocidal situation in which adherents to a body of teaching must make life-and-death choices – as individual believers, as a collective community, and as the institutional leadership. Well before the genocide, Rwandan Christian communities had varying relationships to the State, ranging from the full embrace of ethno-politics to absolute political neutrality. These preexisting paradigms persisted even as the tragedy unfolded.

Theologian Emmanuel Katongole (2005) ascribes the wholesale failure of the churches to "tribalism" – but not in the sense of a clash of biological or cultural differences. Rather, he writes of "the tribalism of nation-state politics that neatly divides up the world between 'us' and 'them.'" Katongole argues that "the churches' inability to resist the dominant imagination of Rwanda grounded in the Hamitic story" led to an extreme but "predictable conclusion" (78–79). Christians cannot banish tribalism, he posits, "unless they are somehow able to invoke

---

[32] This question refers to the general pattern of response in the Witness community as a whole. It is possible that individual Witnesses compromised their nonviolent principles out of fear or other personal considerations.

[33] Records for September 1996 indicate a peak of 4,223 active Witnesses (participants in the public ministry). From 1994–1996, 1,819 new Witnesses were baptized. Some Witness refugees may also have returned to Rwanda during this period (Watch Tower 1995, 1996, 1997). For a discussion of post-genocide religious membership in Rwanda, see Kubai (2007).

the reality of a church whose social force is located outside or at the margins of the dominant political imagination of Rwanda" (82). And yet, he warns, "such a community may have no choice but to become a church of martyrs" (88).

Jehovah's Witness attempted to practice an apolitical, nonviolent Christian ethic before and during the genocide despite the high cost of their stance. In reflecting on the conduct of Witnesses, Catholic professor of theology J. J. Carney speaks to the ethical framework of their community: "There is a long tradition among the Witnesses of opposing state violence, abstaining from violence, and maintaining a tightknit community. In other words, they are formed in nonviolence long before the 'final test' comes."[34] Genocide scholar Rhoda E. Howard-Hassmann (2019) writes: "Hutu Witnesses were impervious to calls for patriotic Hutu to take part in mass killings. But this does not mean they sat back idly when others suffered because of politics or war; to do nothing was also against their Christian principles" (3). Professor of philosophy John K. Roth observes that "human choices – personal and institutional – are always at play" in genocide. He isolates two aspects of the Witness tradition, "its refusal to put allegiance to a state ahead of allegiance to God" and its defense of "the preciousness of human life." Roth concludes: "Where these priorities prevail, genocide cannot."[35]

References

Abrams, Ray H. (1933): Preachers Present Arms. New York: Round Table Press, Inc.
African Rights (1995): Rwanda – Death, Despair and Defiance. London: African Rights.
Awake! (1994): "Caring for Victims of Rwanda's Tragedy," December 22, 1994, 12–17.
Ben Dedale, François (1992): "Ubumwe Bw'ubutatu Butagatifu Ntibubereye Isi," (The Unity of the Trinity Does Not Work in This World!) in: Kangura, January 1992, 14.
Benda, Richard M. (2012): The Test of Faith: Christians and Muslims in the Rwandan Genocide. PhD thesis: University of Manchester.
Bonnier, E., J. Poulsen, T. Rogall and M. Stryjan (2016): "Preparing for Genocide: Quasi-Experimental Evidence from Rwanda," Working Paper No. 31, Stockholm Institute of Transition Economics (Stockholm School of Economics.)
Burnet, Jennie E. (2015): "Rape as a Weapon on Genocide: Gender, Patriarchy, and Sexual Violence in Rwanda." Georgia State University: Anthropology Faculty Publications, 13. https://doi.org/10.5040/9781474275484.0014.
Cadoux, C. J. (1982): The Early Christian Attitude to War. New York: The Seabury Press.
Carney, J. J. (2014): Rwanda Before the Genocide – Catholic Politics and Ethnic Discourse in the Late Colonial Era. New York: Oxford University Press.
Catholic Herald (1994): "Pope Says Violent Rwandans Will be Judged by History, God," in: Catholic Herald, May 20, 1994.

---

[34] J. J. Carney, E-mail to author, April 4, 2019.
[35] John K. Roth, E-mail to author, April 3, 2019.

Chu, Jolene (2004):"God's Things and Caesar's: Jehovah's Witnesses and Political Neutrality," in: Journal of Genocide Research 6(3), 319–42. https://doi.org/10.1080/1462352 042000265837.

Court, Anthony (2016): "The Christian Churches, the State, and Genocide in Rwanda," in: Missionalia 44 (1), 55–67. https://doi.org/10.7832/44-1-106.

Dialogue 120 (1987): "Halte aux Sectes!" January-February, 102–03.

Eltringham, Nigel (2006): 'Invaders who have stolen the country': The Hamitic Hypothesis, Race and the Rwandan Genocide, in: Social Identities–Journal for the Study of Race, Nation and Culture, 12 (4), 425–446. https://doi.org/10.1080/13504630600823619.

Fletcher, Narelle (2014): Words That Can Kill: The Mugesera Speech and the 1994 Tutsi Genocide in Rwanda, in: PORTAL Journal of Multidisciplinary International Studies, 11 (1), January 2014. https://doi.org/10.5130/portal.v11i1.3293.

Garbe, Detlef (2008): Between Resistance and Martyrdom: Jehovah's Witnesses in the Third Reich. Madison, WI: The University of Wisconsin Press.

Gatwa, Tharcisse (2005): The Churches and Ethnic Ideology in the Rwandan Crisis 1900–1994. Eugene: Wipf and Stock Publishers.

Herrberger, Marcus (2016): "Die deutschen Bibelforscher im Ersten Weltkrieg – zwischen militärischem Ungehorsam und christlichem Gewissen," in: Religion-Staat-Gesellschaft 16 (1–2), 33–73.

Howard-Hassmann, Rhoda E. (2019): "Book Review: No Greater Love: How My Family Survived the Genocide in Rwanda by Tharcisse Seminega," in: Heroism Science: An Interdisciplinary Journal 4 (1), Article 7, 1–4. https://scholarship.richmond.edu/heroism-science/vol4/iss1/7 (accessed October 4, 2019).

Human Rights Watch (1999): "History: The Meaning of 'Hutu,' 'Tutsi,' and 'Twa.'" Leave None to Tell the Story: Genocide in Rwanda. New York: Human Rights Watch. https://www.hrw.org/reports/1999/rwanda/Geno1-3-09.htm#P200_83746 (accessed May 6, 2019).

– (1999a). "History: Single-Party State." Leave None to Tell the Story: Genocide in Rwanda. New York: Human Rights Watch. http://pantheon.hrw.org/legacy/reports/1999/rwanda/Geno1-3-09.htm#P196_82927 (accessed May 6, 2019).

– (1999b). "Choosing War." Leave None to Tell the Story: Genocide in Rwanda. New York: Human Rights Watch. https://www.hrw.org/reports/1999/rwanda/Geno1-3-11.htm (accessed May 6, 2019).

Katongole, Emmanuel (2005): "Christianity, Tribalism, and the Rwandan Genocide: A Catholic Reassessment of Christian 'Social Responsibility,'" in: Logos: A Journal of Catholic Thought and Culture, 8 (3), 67–93. 10.1353/log.2005.0027

Katongole, Emmanuel and Jonathan Wilson-Hartgrove (2009): Mirror to the Church. Grand Rapids: Zondervan.

Knox, Zoe (2018): Jehovah's Witnesses and the Secular World – From the 1870's to the Present. London: Palgrave Macmillan.

– (2019): "'A Greater Danger Than a Division of the German Army': Bible Students and Opposition to War in World War I America," in: Peace & Change 44 (2), 207–243.

Kubai, Anne (2007): "Post-Genocide Rwanda: The Changing Religious Landscape," in: Exchange, 36, 198–214. https://doi.org/10.1163/157254307X176606.

Linden, Ian (1975): "The White Fathers' Mission in Rwanda 1900–1932," Thesis Ph.D., School of Oriental and African Studies (University of London).

– (1977): Church and Revolution in Rwanda. Manchester: Manchester University Press; New York: Africana Pub. Co.

Longman, Timothy (2001): "Christian Churches and Genocide in Rwanda", in: Omer Bartov and Phyllis Mack (eds.), In God's Name: Genocide and Religion in the Twentieth Century. New York, Oxford: Berghahn Books, 139–160.
– (2010): Christianity and Genocide in Rwanda. New York: Cambridge University Press.
Maryomeza, Théophile (1987): "Rwanda, entre la peur et l'anathème," in: Dialogue 125, November-December, 3–7.
Mamdani, Mahmood (2001): When Victims Become Killers: Colonialism, Nativism, and the Genocide in Rwanda. Princeton: Princeton University Press.
Mitchell, J. (n.d.): Remembering the Rwandan Genocide: Reconsidering the Role of Local and Global Media, in: Global Media Journal. http://www.globalmediajournal.com/open-access/remembering-the-rwandan-genocidereconsidering-the-role-of-local-and-global-media.php?aid=35262 (accessed February 10, 2020).
Moly, Pierre (member of the 1991 internatonal delegation) (2019): in discussion with author, August 15, 2019.
Mukanyiligira, Consolée (2019), in discussion with author, March 10, 2019.
Nduwayezu, Joseph (2020), in discussion with Tharcisse Seminega, March 16, 2020.
Niyongira, Gaspard (2019), in discussion with author, October 30, 2019.
Perkins, Gary (2016): Bible Student Conscientious Objectors in World War One – Britain: For the Sake of the Kingdom. Self-published: CreateSpace.
Prunier, Gérard (1995): The Rwanda Crisis: History of a Genocide. New York: Columbia University Press.
Reyntjens, Filip (1988): "Sectes et atteintes à la sûreté de l'Etat," in: Dialogue 127, March-April, 2–15.
Rittner, Carol, J. Roth and W. Whitworth (eds.) (2004): Genocide in Rwanda: Complicity of the Churches? St. Paul: Paragon House.
Rutaganira, Charles (2019), in discussion with author, March 26, 2019.
Rwakabubu, Gaspard (2019), in discussion with author, October 30, 2019.
"Rwanda Persecutes Christians" (1986): Governing Body of Jehovah's Witnesses. Brooklyn, NY.
Sanders, Edith R. (1969): The Hamitic Hypothesis: Its Origin and Functions in Time Perspective, in: The Journal of African History 10 (4), 521–532.
Scherrer, Christian P. (2002): Genocide and Crisis in Central Africa – Conflict Roots, Mass Violence, and Regional War. Westport: Praeger Publishers.
Seminega, Tharcisse (2019): No Greater Love: How My Family Survived the Genocide in Rwanda. Davenport, IA: GM&A Inc.
Speke, John Hanning (1864): Journal of the Discovery of the Source of the Nile. New York: Harper & Brothers.
Thompson, Allan (ed.) (2007): The Media and the Rwanda Genocide. Ann Arbor, MI: Pluto Press.
Trial International (2016): Leon Mugesera. https://trialinternational.org/latest-post/leon-mugesera/ (accessed February 10, 2020).
U.S. Department of State Country Report on Human Rights Practices 1993 – Rwanda (1994). https://www.refworld.org/cgi-bin/texis/vtx/rwmain?page=search&docid=3ae6aa4e6&skip=O&query=jehovah%27s%20witnesses&coi=RWA&searchin (accessed March 13, 2020).

Uwamahoro, Jeanine (daughter of John Munyakazi) (2020), in discussion with author, January 31, 2020.

Verwimp, Philip (2001): A Quantitative Analysis of Genocide in Kibuye Prefecture, Rwanda, in: Discussion Paper Series (DPS) 01.10, May 2001, Center for Economic Studies, Catholic University of Leuven, Belgium. https://ideas.repec.org/p/ete/ceswps/ces0110.html (accessed May 6, 2019).

Watch Tower (1974): 1973 Service Year Report of Jehovah's Witnesses Worldwide, in: 1974 Yearbook of Jehovah's Witnesses. Brooklyn: Watchtower Bible and Tract Society of New York, Inc.

– (1983): 1982 Service Year Report of Jehovah's Witnesses Worldwide, in: 1983 Yearbook of Jehovah's Witnesses. Brooklyn: Watchtower Bible and Tract Society of New York, Inc.

– (1984): 1983 Service Year Report of Jehovah's Witnesses Worldwide, in: 1984 Yearbook of Jehovah's Witnesses. Brooklyn: Watchtower Bible and Tract Society of New York, Inc.

– (1988): "Bible," in: Insight on the Scriptures. Brooklyn: Watchtower Bible and Tract Society of New York, Inc.

– (1992): Kenya and Other Countries, in: 1992 Yearbook of Jehovah' Witnesses. Brooklyn: Watchtower Bible and Tract Society of New York, Inc.

– (1993): 1992 Service Year Report of Jehovah's Witnesses Worldwide, in: 1993 Yearbook of Jehovah's Witnesses. Brooklyn: Watchtower Bible and Tract Society of New York, Inc.

– (1995): 1994 Service Year Report of Jehovah's Witnesses Worldwide, in: 1995 Yearbook of Jehovah's Witnesses. Brooklyn: Watchtower Bible and Tract Society of New York, Inc.

– (1996): 1995 Service Year Report of Jehovah's Witnesses Worldwide, in: 1996 Yearbook of Jehovah's Witnesses. Brooklyn: Watchtower Bible and Tract Society of New York, Inc.

– (1997): 1996 Service Year Report of Jehovah's Witnesses Worldwide, in: 1997 Yearbook of Jehovah's Witnesses. Brooklyn: Watchtower Bible and Tract Society of New York, Inc.

– (2018): 2018 Country and Territory Reports. https://www.jw.org/en/library/books/2018-service-year-report/2018-country-territory/ (accessed March 13, 2020).

Watchtower (1986): To All Branches. Letter dated November 17, 1986.

– (1986a): To All Congregations. Letter dated November 17, 1986.

The Watchtower (1994): "Tragedy in Rwanda – Who is Responsible?" December 15, 1994, 26–29.

– (1996): "We All Belong to the Same Family," November 1, 1996, 32.

– (2012): Rwanda, in: 2012 Yearbook of Jehovah' Witnesses. Brooklyn: Watchtower Bible and Tract Society of New York, Inc.

Abstract

This paper traces the development of religion-state relationships in Rwanda and their influence on the behavior of various Christian groups during the 1994 Genocide against the Tutsi in Rwanda. The colonial-era churches pursued State favor as a survival strategy, embracing the Hamitic myth and using church institutions to enforce and harden ethnic difference. In the lead-up to independence, the churches' abrupt shift in favor from the Tutsi elite to the Hutu majority corresponded to increasing ethnic violence. The trajectory of politicized religion under one-party rule intersects with the inception of the Christian community of Jehovah's Witnesses in Rwanda. Religious and political forces oppressed the Witnesses for their evangelizing and nonviolent and apolitical ethic. In 1994, as genocide survivors testify, the Witnesses refused to participate in killing and risked death to rescue Tutsi inside and outside their community.

Review

19. Jahrgang | 2018 | Heft 1+2

Massimo Introvigne:
Eine Untersuchung der Kirche des Allmächtigen Gottes

1. Einleitung: Der Selbstmord von Frau Liu und andere chinesische Geschichten

2. Chinas Kampf gegen die xie jiao

3. Die Kirche des Allmächtigen Gottes: Ursprünge und Glaubenssätze

4. Der Kirche des Allmächtigen Gottes beitreten

5. Leben in der Kirche des Allmächtigen Gottes

6. Fake News: Der McDonald's Mord von 2014

7. Der Rote Drache und die Pastoren: Entführungsanschuldigungen

8. China entkommen: Die Flüchtlinge

Literatur

Religion – Staat – Gesellschaft
Zeitschrift füür Glaubensformen und Weltanschauungen/
Journal for the Study of Beliefs and Worldviews
hrsg. von /edited by Gerhard Besier

Massimo Introvigne
Eine Untersuchung der *Kirche des Allmächtigen Gottes*
19. Jahrgang (2018), Heft 1+2
Die *Kirche des Allmächtigen Gottes* ist heute die am meisten verfolgte religiöse Bewegung in China. Offiziellen Stellen zufolge gehören dieser Kirche etwa 4 Millionen Mitglieder an. Massimo Introvigne, einem weltweit bekannten Forscher über Neue Religionen, gelang es, sowohl Hunderte von Mitgliedern dieser Kirche zu interviewen als auch die chinesischen Polizeioffiziere, die diese verfolgen. Introvigne erzählt die dramatische Verfolgungsgeschichte dieser Religionsgemeinschaft und rekonstruiert deren eigentümliche Theologie
Bd. 19/1 – 2, 2019, 126 S., 59,90 €, br., ISBN 3-643-99742-5

Religious Freedom
Its Confirmation and Violation During the 20th and 21st Centuries. 18. Jahrgang (2017), Heft 1-2
Restrictions with respect to religious freedom have been in place in authoritarian states for a number of years. We can observe a new period of co-operation between authoritarian states and "state" churches. Some churches have assumed a clearly political position, even in belligerent conflicts, by justifying wars, criminalizing their religious competitors and, thereby, exploiting the Christian Gospel for non-Christian purposes.
In this volume, scholars from Europe and North America discuss the core objective of religious freedom in the West and East seeking measures to encourage religions to act and interact, independent of deliberate political stances – to maintain their distance from territorial governments and to strengthen the principle of religious freedom and, thereby, their own denomination as well.
Bd. 18/1 – 2, , 262 S., 59,90 €, br., ISBN 978-3-643-99745-6

Religiöse Minderheiten in westlichen Gesellschaften. Religious Minorities in Western Societies
17. Jahrgang (2016), Heft 1-2
Vor dem Hintergrund der Tatsache, dass schwere Krisen in vielen Teilen der Welt die Menschen beschäftigen, drohen Probleme religiöser Minderheiten im Westen zunehmend in den Hintergrund zu treten. Dies ist umso mehr dort der Fall, wo in demokratischen Rechtsstaaten die Religionsfreiheit in den Verfassungen garantiert ist. In diesem Heft möchten wir spezifische Probleme kleiner Religionsgemeinschaften in Belgien und Deutschland erörtern.

In view of the fact that people are preoccupied with serious crises across many parts of the world, the problems facing religious minorities in the West are increasingly in danger of being pushed into the background. This is all the more true in places such as democratic constitutional states where religious freedom is guaranteed in the constitution. This issue would like to contribute to the discussion of specific problems for small religious communities in Belgium and Germany.
Bd. 17/1 – 2, 2017, 232 S., 59,90 €, br., ISBN 978-3-643-99780-7

Zum Bibel- und Weltverständnis christlicher Religionen. The Bible and the World. Perspectives among major and minor religions
Bd. 16/1 – 2, 2016, 350 S., 59,90 €, br., ISBN 978-3-643-99792-0

Seit fünfzehn Jahren 21. Jahrhundert. Fifteen Years into the 21st Century
Umbrüche in Gesellschaften und Religionen angesichts neuer politischer und kultureller Herausforderungen. Upheavals in societies and religions in the light of political and cultural challenges
Bd. 15/1 – 2, 2015, 262 S., 59,90 €, br., ISBN 978-3-643-99813-2

Staaten und Kirchen im Norden und Osten Europas. Nations and Churches in Europe's North and East
Bd. 14/2, 2014, 120 S., 29,90 €, br., ISBN 978-3-643-99825-5

LIT Verlag Berlin – Münster – Wien – Zürich – London
Auslieferung Deutschland / Österreich / Schweiz: siehe Impressumsseite

Die Religionsfreiheit und das Staat-Kirche-Verhältnis in Europa und den USA. Religious Freedom and State-Church-Relations in Europe and the USA
Bd. 14/1, 2013, 168 S., 29,90 €, br., ISBN 978-3-643-99850-7

Freedom of Religion or Belief. Anti-Sect Movements and State Neutrality A Case Study: FECRIS
Bd. 13/2, 2012, 224 S., 29,90 €, br., ISBN 978-3-643-99864-4

Inverser Böckenförde – Leben Religionen von politischen Voraussetzungen, die sie selbst nicht garantieren können? Inverted Böckenförde – Do Religions depend upon political Conditions they cannot guarantee?
Bd. 13/1, 2012, 176 S., 29,90 €, br., ISBN 978-3-643-99866-8

Nonkonformismus und europäische Religionsgeschichten. Nonconformism and European Histories of Religions
Bd. 12/2, 2012, 296 S., 29,90 €, br., ISBN 978-3-643-99880-4

Religiöse Intoleranz und Diskriminierung in ausgewählten Ländern Europas – Teil II. Religious Intolerance and Discrimination in selected European Countries – Part II
Bd. 12/1, 2011, 296 S., 29,90 €, br., ISBN 978-3-643-99894-1

Religiöse Intoleranz und Diskriminierung in ausgewählten Ländern Europas – Teil I. Religious Intolerance and Discrimination in selected European Countries – Part I
Bd. 11/2, 2011, 192 S., 29,90 €, br., ISBN 978-3-643-99906-1

Religion und Politik in Afrika – Vereinte Nationen – Bestattungskultur – Gewissensfreiheit. Religion and Politics in Africa – United Nations – Burials – Freedom of Conscience
Bd. 11/1, 2010, 96 S., 29,90 €, br., ISBN 978-3-643-99919-1

On religious liberty in a democratic society: Aspects of law, religion and philosophy in constitutional theory and reality. Über Religionsfreiheit in demokratischen Gesellschaften: Rechtliche, religiöse und philosophische Aspekte in der Verfassungstheorie und in der gelebten Wirklichkeit
Bd. 10/2, 2010, 272 S., 29,90 €, br., ISBN 978-3-643-99928-3, ISSN 1438-955X

Konflikte um nonkonforme Erziehungs- und Bildungsideale. Religious conflicts caused by dissenting views on education and learning
Bd. 10/1, 2009, 144 S., 29,90 €, br., ISBN 978-3-643-99940-5, ISSN 1438-955X

Blut. Blood
Bd. 9/2, 2009, 128 S., 29,90 €, br., ISBN 978-3-643-99942-9, ISSN 1438-955X

Soziale Normen und Skandalisierung. Social Norms and Scandalization
Bd. 9/1, 2008, 128 S., 29,90 €, br., ISBN 978-3-8258-1706-0, ISSN 1438-955X

Politisierung von Religion, religiöser Nonkonformismus und Rationalität
Bd. 8/2, 2008, 160 S., 29,90 €, br., ISBN 978-3-8258-1099-3

Die Zeugen Jehovas in Ostmittel-, Südost- und Südeuropa
Zum Schicksal einer religiösen Minderheit
Bd. 8/1, 2007, 184 S., 29,90 €, br., ISBN 978-3-8258-0683-5, ISSN 1438-955X